GANGLAND:
THE CONTRACT KILLERS

79537/May

GANGLAND: THE CONTRACT KILLERS

James Morton

TIME WARNER
BOOKS

C40922045

TIME WARNER BOOKS

First published in Great Britain in November 2005
by Time Warner Books

A CIP catalogue record for this book
is available from the British Library.

ISBN 0 316 72739 3

Typeset in Berkeley Book by Palimpsest Book Production Ltd
Polmont, Stirlingshire

Printed and bound in Great Britain by Clays Ltd, St Ives plc

Time Warner Books
An imprint of
Time Warner Book Group UK
Brettenham House
Lancaster Place
London WC2E 7EN

To Dock Bateson
with love and thanks

Contents

Introduction

Almost two hundred years ago, in 1806, the Reverend George Parker probably became the first known person in modern England to be the victim of a contract killing. The case has a number of interesting features. The full story did not come out for nearly a quarter of a century, the contractor was a local magistrate and the hired killer became what in modern criminal slang is called a Dixie Cup. That is, he was also killed – as disposable as a paper cup of water.

Parker was not a wholly popular man in his parish of Oddingley, near Worcester. There were suggestions that he was over-zealous in collecting his tithes, and certainly his enemies included the local magistrate Captain Samuel Evans along with Thomas Clewes and John Barnett. At a luncheon held early in 1806 Evans had proposed a left-handed toast to 'The death of the Buonaparte of Oddingley'; he had also been heard to say, 'He is a very bad man and there is no more harm in shooting him than a mad dog.' About 5 p.m. on 24 June 1806 Parker was indeed shot and beaten to death by a carpenter and wheelwright Richard Hemmings. Two men heard the shot and found the vicar with his clothes on fire. One chased after Hemmings, but he turned the gun on him and escaped. Hemmings was to be paid the then enormous sum of £50, and this alone should have put him on his guard.

The next day Hemmings was summoned to see the Captain where he was promptly battered to death by a man named Taylor, again on the orders of Evans. His body was buried under a hayrick and later transferred to a barn on Evans' land, Church Farm. It was a case where almost everyone in the locality knew what had happened but no one was prepared to speak – perhaps they were

too frightened – and the details of the dual killings were not discovered until 1830 when Hemmings' body was found, curiously
enough by his brother-in-law. It was identified because Hemmings
wore distinctive shoes with nails in the heels and because
his carpentry tools had been buried with it. At the inquest Thomas
Clewes was ordered to give evidence and he confessed, implicating
Evans and Taylor – both of whom were dead – along with Barnett
and a popular local man, John Banks. At the trial at Worcester
Assizes, charged with being accessories, they were all acquitted on
the technicality that they could not be tried until after the principal, in this case Evans, had been tried. The acquittals were greeted
with great applause.[1]

It should not be thought that contract killers as such are products
of the twentieth century. They abounded in the American West in its
formative years. In those days they were called hired guns, and one
of the best known was the one-time agent of the Pinkerton Detective
Agency, Tom Horn.

He had been an Indian fighter and army scout before he arrived
in Denver in 1890 with what were described as impeccable refer-
ences. For the next few years he was the Pinkertons' Rocky Mountain
operative, making a number of arrests of train robbers and cattle
rustlers, killing a number as well. Unfortunately he took time out
to commit a robbery for himself in Nevada and was protected by
the Agency. Another agent, Charles Siringo, later wrote:

> . . . on one of his trips to Denver, William A. Pinkerton [one of
> the sons] told me that Tom Horn was guilty of the crime but
> that his people could not afford to let him go to the penitentiary
> while in their employ.[2]

---

[1] Taylor was an old man at the time of the murder, and had the defence been put it
was to be that he was too frail to batter the fit and much younger Hemmings. Early
in his life Taylor had been acquitted, also on a technicality, of stealing communion
plate from a church in Hampton Lovett. For the rest of his life he was known as the
Churchwarden of Hampton Lovett. *The Times*, 30 June 1806, 30 January, 2, 5, 9
February, 11, 20 March 1830. Richard Whittington-Egan, 'A Pellet for the Preacher' in
New Law Journal, 23 November 1991.

[2] Charles Siringo, *Two Evil Isms: Pinkertonism and Anarchism*. For one version of Horn's
career see Tom Horn, *Life of Tom Horn, Government Scout and Interpreter written by
Himself*.

Despite the protection, let alone the salary the Agency offered, Horn felt tied down and resigned in 1894, becoming a freelance detective and hired gun of the Wyoming Cattlemen's Association. He is described as a tidy, patient and skilful murderer. He would wait hours in driving rain, chewing bacon fat, to ensure he had the one necessary clear shot of his target. After each killing he would leave a stone under the head of his victim so there was no doubt as to the killer. Seven years later, however, he made what proved to be his fatal error when he killed 14-year-old Willie Nickell, the son of a sheep farmer, mistaking him in poor light for his father.

For two years, in part because of Horn's powerful protectors, the murder remained unsolved. His eventual undoing was another semi-undercover man, Joe Lefors, a deputy US marshal who became Horn's confidant and when the latter was well in drink obtained a bragging confession from him, something he had taken the precaution of being noted by a hidden shorthand writer and another witness.

Despite his pleas for help from his former employers and a donation of $5,000 to his defence fund from an unknown admirer, Horn was convicted of murder in 1903. He had tried to impugn the confession, suggesting that what he had said was just a tall tale and that the stenographer had added pieces of his own. While awaiting execution he escaped from prison, but was quickly recaptured and was hanged on 20 November 1903. As has often been the case with outlaws, in recent years efforts have been made to rehabilitate Horn. It is said the confession should have been ruled inadmissible and that, indeed, he was not the youth's killer.

In general, criminals' memoirs and confessions must be taken with a very great pinch, perhaps even a handful, of salt. One of the problems with their thoughts and memoirs generally is that as a rule each has a self-serving interest in what he or she tells. They may be getting a kick out of deceiving the worthy probation officer, social worker or sociologist. They may be looking for the better prison conditions and possible parole which come with penitence. On the other hand they may be seeking to preserve their status in their own community by being extra bad; and they may simply be telling the tale for the money – after all, the more lurid the story the better the advance and the sales. Generally speaking there is not much market for the story of the happily married man with 2.4 children and a dog all of whom go to church twice a week, tithe to charity and have never stolen so much as a paper clip or, in the case of the dog, another animal's bone.

Then there are the death-cell confessions. Are these really worth the price of the tape on which they are made? There are of course a number of benefits for those who make them, not least the possibility of a temporary reprieve. Some seem to have genuinely had a desire to clear things up. Charles Peace, the celebrated Victorian burglar and murderer from Sheffield, was one.

Released from prison where he had served a sentence for burglary, in 1872 he moved out of Sheffield to Britannia Road, Darnall, where he lived two doors away from an Arthur Dyson and his wife Katherine. The extremely ugly Peace had a considerable effect on women and he set his mind to seducing Mrs Dyson. Later he maintained they had had an affair, something she denied. Certainly he was able to establish that they had been to a music hall and a fair together; he also produced letters he claimed she had sent him. Whatever is correct, they started off as friends with Peace showing her son the tricks he had trained his parrots and pigeons to perform. There is no doubt either that the relationship, however shallow or deep, did sour. The Dysons moved to Ecclesall Road and found to their horror that Peace had followed them.

He left them alone for a month and then on 29 November 1876 paid a visit to the Vicar of Ecclesall to tell him that the couple were wicked and they had ruined his business. He stalked about the neighbourhood telling one woman that Mrs Dyson was 'a bloody whore' and that before morning he would shoot them both. At 8 p.m. Mrs Dyson saw Peace at the back of their cottage and screamed for her husband. He came running and Peace shot at him twice; the first bullet hit the wall and the second struck Dyson in the temple. He died within three hours. A coroner's jury held that Dyson's death was wilful murder by Peace and £100 reward was offered for his conviction.

Sensibly, Peace left the area and it was now that his career as a burglar really took off. Living with both Hannah Ward – by whom he had a child – and Susan Bailey, he moved to London taking a lease on a large house in the name of Thompson. There the trio maintained an outwardly respectable façade, attending the local church and with Peace playing his violin at musical evenings. He had stained his face with walnut juice and shaved his hair at the front. The burglaries continued.

On 10 October 1878 he was leaving a house in Blackheath through the drawing-room windows when he found the police waiting. He shot at them, hitting one officer, PC Edward Robinson, in the arm; but the constable managed to hold on to Peace and he was arrested. He gave the name John Ward and his age as sixty. On 19 November at the Old Bailey he was sentenced to penal servitude for life for the attempted murder of Robinson.[3]

Unable to keep up with the staining, the walnut colouring on his face now began to fade. But before any serious inquiry was made into his identity he wrote what proved a fatal letter to a former Peckham neighbour, signing it 'John Ward' and asking him to visit him. The man did so and, astounded to find that Ward was in fact his friend John Thompson, he then went to the police. In turn the police went to the Thompson house and discovered a cache of burglar's tools. Of Mrs Thompson, Mrs Ward and the children there was no sign.

Now Susan Bailey, discovering that the £100 reward was still on offer for the murder of Dyson, confirmed Peace's identity. Somewhat unsportingly, she also disclosed that Mrs Ward was back in the north, from where she was retrieved and prosecuted for receiving at the Old Bailey. She was acquitted on the grounds that she had been under Peace's influence.

For Peace things only became worse. Katherine Dyson, who after the death of her husband had emigrated to America, indicated she would return to give evidence against him. He was tried at Leeds Town Hall on 4 February 1879 and was defended by Frank Lockwood, who would later become the Solicitor General. The only witness when the shots were fired had been Mrs Dyson, and Lockwood did what he could to discredit her over the supposed affair. The jury retired a mere ten minutes.

---

[3] For an account of Peace's career see J.P. Bean, *Crime in Sheffield*.

In the condemned cell Peace turned to religion and admitted that he, rather than a young Irishman named Aaron Habron, had shot and killed a PC Nicholas Cook in Manchester in 1876. Habron, who had been heard making threats against the officer, had been sentenced to death but reprieved. Peace had watched the proceedings from the public gallery.

Habron was released to general acclaim. *The Times* noted that his former employer would take him back home, and was pleased that offers to capitalise by way of a figure in the waxworks or press interviews had been turned down. Although details of his train journey north were supposed to be secret, word was soon out and crowds gathered at stations along the route to cheer him. One man gave him £5 and another half a sovereign. After some pressure the government awarded him compensation for his two-and-a-half-year stay in prison. It was thought the money would be sufficient to buy him a small farm.[4]

Peace's confession, if not repentance, was certainly genuine. Some have simply wished to go down in posterity as the man with the greatest number of notches. One of the most dangerous as well as tiresome of false confessors in modern times has been the American Henry Lee Lucas, who undoubtedly did kill his mother in 1960 and was guilty of the 1982 cold-blooded rape and murder of Kate Rich, as well as his longtime girlfriend Becky Powell whom he also dismembered. The problem for investigators was that he also confessed to some 600 murders in nineteen states, a great number of which he could not possibly have committed. He was eventually sentenced to death for one he almost certainly did not commit, the murder of a woman known only as Orange Socks because that was all the unidentified person was wearing when her body was discovered in a culvert in Williamson County in Central Texas.

At his trial he repudiated his confession and called an alibi which showed that he had been some 1,200 miles away working as a roofer. After his conviction he admitted several more murders, but reporters from the *Dallas Times Herald* had been making inquiries and had discovered that a number of his confessions had to be

[4] *The Times*, 24, 26 February 1879.

false.[5] In June 1998 Lucas was eventually reprieved for the Orange Socks murder after a lie detector test was in his favour.

He maintained that he had confessed because: 'I wanted to open up people's eyes to what was going on in law enforcement, how they didn't care if they got the right person or not. I don't think anybody, a human being anyway, could kill 600 people.'[6]

Others more cynically inclined think that he enjoyed being a celebrity. With his increasing number of confessions creating a valuable clear-up rate as far as detectives were concerned, he had reached a point where he wore his own clothes in his cell, was given painting materials and cigarettes, and had Cable TV. He died from a heart condition at the age of 64 in March 2001. He had been making uniforms for prison guards for most of the previous five years. 'He was the best,' said a prison spokesman, presumably referring to his craftsmanship.[7]

Sometimes confessions are simply unreliable as the Court of Appeal found when, after serving twenty years of a life sentence, in 2003 Henry McKenny successfully appealed against his conviction for murder. Mainly on the evidence of John Childs, he had been found guilty of a string of contract killings of characters on the edge of the underworld. Childs had turned Queen's Evidence after first being implicated in a security van hijack and later himself pleading guilty to the murders.

Childs later told the *Mirror* that he had dropped a 25 kg block on a Borstal boy who died, shot a police informer dead, battered a petrol station attendant to death and stabbed a complete stranger in the street. At McKenny's appeal Childs was labelled as having a severe anti-social personality disorder which made him untruthful.[8]

Sadly, some confessions are made too late to be verified. In January 2004 Billy Frank Vickers claimed that he was a hitman involved in more than a dozen other murders. Unfortunately for a number of

---

[5] *Dallas Times Herald*, 14 April 1985. See also Brian Lane and Wilfred Gregg, *The New Encyclopedia of Serial Killers*.
[6] G.H. Gudjonsson, 'The making of a serial false confessor: the confessions of Henry Lee Lucas' in *The Journal of Forensic Psychiatry*, Volume 10, No. 2, September 1999.
[7] *Los Angeles Times*, 14 March 2001.
[8] Jeff Rowlands, 'I Killed Five More People' in *Daily Mirror*, 17 November 1998; *The Guardian*, 16 December 2003.

people, as well as for the record, Vickers made the claim as he lay strapped in the prison death chamber to receive a lethal injection for shooting a grocery shop owner in an apparent robbery in 1993. 'Down through the years there were several more that I had done or had a part of,' he told official witnesses to the execution. 'There must be a dozen or fourteen, I believe, in total.' The career criminal said that he had been hired to kill people, including the man for whose murder he was executed. 'All of these, it was never nothing personal. It was just something I did to make a living. I am sorry for all the grief I have caused,' he said.

He insisted that he would 'like to clear some things up', trying to exonerate two accomplices to his crime as well as an inmate imprisoned for a separate killing and even Cullen Davis, a Texas millionaire who was tried for and acquitted of the murder of his stepdaughter in a notorious 1970s case. Cullen Davis was also later acquitted of hiring a hitman to kill Judge Joe H. Edison in retaliation for fifteen adverse rulings in his divorce case which lasted for four years.[9]

But Vickers, who had been scheduled to die in December 2003 and then granted a last-minute reprieve, was executed thirty minutes after the Supreme Court denied his latest appeal and before he could provide any further details about his claimed role in the other murders.

The case raised questions as to whether the right men were prosecuted and convicted for those crimes. Michelle Lyons, a prison spokesman, said that the authorities did not know if Vickers was telling the truth. He had been on Death Row since being condemned for the 1993 shooting of Phillip Winslow during a robbery outside his home in Arthur City in north-eastern Texas. Two accomplices, Tommy Perkins and Jason Martin, were sentenced to life in prison and twenty-five years respectively. Vickers reversed his previous denials and admitted that he had been involved in the murder, but he tried to clear his two accomplices. In addition, he claimed that an inmate serving a life term for a separate killing was not responsible for the murder. 'I did not do it, but I was with his daddy

[9] *Washington Post*, 6 November 1978, 10 November 1979. For an account of the Cullen Davis case see Gary Cartwright, *Blood Will Tell*.

when it was done,' he said. He concluded with an apology, saying, 'I love you all. That is all I have to say.' He died six minutes later, the fourth Texas prisoner to be executed that year.[10]

In twentieth-century Britain and Ireland, until the abolition of capital punishment very few men and an even smaller number of women – twenty-two in all – were convicted of murder or manslaughter twice. One very sound reason for this is that many first-time killers were executed. Of those who killed twice, only four were executed. However, since abolition the numbers have increased exponentially. From 1966 to November 2004 there have been over 120 second killings. Many have killed a second time in domestic disputes, but a number have killed in the course of theft and several have been gangland figures.

The first execution for a second killing came in 1911 when William Henry Palmer strangled a widow, Ann Harris, at her home in Walcote, Leicestershire. He continued to maintain his innocence and on 19 July 1911, when he was to be hanged at Leicester prison by John Ellis, threw himself at the hangman and the warders yelling, 'Are you going to let these fellows murder me?' Palmer was dragged the forty yards to the gallows struggling and swearing. Apparently Ellis enjoyed the encounter, saying that it had been the most exciting of his career.[11]

In 1900 Palmer had been sentenced to ten years penal servitude in South Africa for killing a native, after the court had rejected his claim of self-defence. At the time of the Walcote killing he was suspected of strangling an elderly woman in Manchester.[12]

James Essex, from South London, a friend of Frankie Fraser, was certainly a gangland figure but his two killings do not seem to have

---

[10] *Los Angeles Times*, 16 December 2003; James Bone, 'Killer admits more murders at execution' in *The Times*, 30 January 2004.
[11] *The Times*, 27 January, 14 June, 18 July 1911; Rocky Stockman, *The Hangman's Diary*, pp. 239–40. Palmer's more famous nineteenth-century namesake Dr William Palmer was thought to have poisoned up to fourteen men along with a number of horses. A degenerate gambler, he murdered his creditors and then his children, legitimate and illegitimate, along with other relatives whom he had insured. His last victim, and the murder for which he was executed, was a fellow gambler John Parsons Cook who was poisoned so that Palmer could go to London and collect the winnings of Cook's horse Polestar. He was hanged at Stafford Gaol by George Smith on 14 June 1856. See Robert Graves, *They Hanged My Saintly Billy*.
[12] *Leicester Chronicle and Leicester Mercury*, 17 June, 22 July 1911.

arisen in the way of business. The first came in May 1942 from a late-night brawl at a coffee stall, and the second in 1944 when he was attacked in the prison workshop at Armley jail. On both occasions he was acquitted of murder and convicted of manslaughter, receiving three and ten years respectively. The same year Thomas Michael Treacey had his conviction for murder quashed; he had previously been sentenced to three years for manslaughter, again in 1942.

On 27 February 1947 Walter Graham Rowland was hanged at Strangeways prison, Manchester. He had already been convicted, sentenced to death and reprieved for killing his two-year-old daughter Mavis Agnes on 2 March 1934. He stood trial for murder a second time when he was charged with killing a Manchester prostitute Olive Balchin on 20 October 1946. There was no doubt as to his guilt in the killing of his daughter, but considerable doubts over the verdict in the Balchin case. He pleaded not guilty but was convicted. While awaiting his own trial a prisoner in Liverpool, David John Ware, confessed to the murder of Olive Balchin, and the confession was a principal ground of appeal. It did not help Rowland. In November 1951 Ware appeared at Bristol Assizes charged with attempted murder. He told the police, 'I have killed a woman. I keep having an urge to hit women on the head.' He was found guilty and sent to a mental hospital.[13]

In 1964 Peter Anthony Dunford became probably the youngest man to have been convicted of murder twice. The first came in 1963 when, at the age of 17, he was given life imprisonment after stabbing Francis Graylin to death in Crawley in what was a power struggle in a right-wing movement. The second followed the next year when, with two others, he was convicted of killing Terence John Buckingham, a fellow inmate at Wakefield prison with whom he had been quarrelling. Because of this second conviction on a different occasion, Dunford was liable to the death penalty under the Homicide Act 1957. Asked whether he admitted the Crawley matter, he denied it and the jury was then sworn to find whether on the evidence he had been so convicted. They did, and he was sentenced

---

[13] Henry Cecil, *The Trial of Walter Rowland*; Leslie Hale, *Hanged in Error*; Bob Woffinden, *Miscarriages of Justice*.

to death before being reprieved thanks largely to the fact that Sidney Silverman's 1964 Abolition Bill had passed its second reading two weeks earlier.[14] He was released after serving twenty years.

Earlier that year in February Christopher Simcox became the only man to have been reprieved twice. In July 1948 he was convicted of killing his wife but was reprieved by the Home Secretary James Chuter-Ede because Parliament was debating the suspension of capital punishment in the Criminal Justice Bill. In February 1964 he was again convicted of murder, this time the shooting of his sister-in-law. Like William Gray – reprieved in 1948 because the noose would slip over his jaw – Simcox had turned the gun on himself and was in such a condition that he would probably have had to be wheeled to the scaffold. The then Home Secretary Henry Brooke granted the reprieve because he could not 'decently' be hanged.

A number who have connections with organised crime have, however, killed after a previous conviction for manslaughter. Joseph Martin had only been released from prison for seven months, where he had served six years for manslaughter after shooting a girlfriend, when shortly before Christmas 1965 he went on an ill-fated raid at the Express Dairy in Wood Green, North London. There a milkman had tried to hold the door against the escaping robbers and was shot through the glass for his pains.

Curiously Norman Parker, who later became a most successful novelist and television writer, also shot his girlfriend in the neck and in 1963 received six years for manslaughter. After his release he was convicted of the gangland killing of the Scottish safebreaker Eddie Coleman. On 26 March 1970 PC Roy Tuck stopped a van in the New Forest and as he went to examine a packing case in it he was clubbed to the ground. A fortnight later Coleman's body was found still in the case, buried near Ringwood. Parker was charged along with David Woods and Stephen Patrick Raymond.

Raymond put up an even more impressive alibi than Billy Hill when he proved he was with the reporters Duncan Webb and Hannen Swaffer at the time of a bullion robbery in 1954. In his turn Raymond

---

[14] *The Times*, 10 October 1964. See Fenton Bresler, *Reprieve*, p. 108.

said he was dining with the Labour luminaries Dingle and Michael Foot and Tom Driberg at the Gay Hussar in Soho at the time of the killing. His alibi was not challenged by the Crown. Raymond was found guilty of impeding the arrest of Parker and Woods and received three years imprisonment.[15] Parker for his part received a sentence of life imprisonment and was released after twenty-four years.

Almost certainly the most recent man convicted of two separate murders is the Glasgow gangster Billy Ferris, brother of the more celebrated Paul. As a young man he left the Blackhills area of Glasgow and went to live in Corby, Northamptonshire. There he served a sentence for armed robbery. On his release he stabbed a man in a quarrel about his former wife. He declined to say anything at the trial and was sentenced for what was seen as an apparently motiveless killing. During his sentence he escaped and stayed on the run for two years. He was finally released, but on 11 December 2003 he was sentenced to another term of life imprisonment for the murder of 15-year-old Jason Hutchinson. Ferris' misfortunes seem to have stemmed from his wives because this killing was over a blow given to Carol Anne by Hutchinson's 18-year-old brother David in a row in the street. David was sent to Tenerife for some months until the affair blew over, but on his return he was warned that he was still at risk. After going out drinking Billy Ferris went to the boy's bedroom and in the dark, by mistake, slashed and stabbed Jason who closely resembled his brother. It was, said Ferris, 'Payback time'.[16]

Early in 2004 the British police came up with the bright idea of interviewing serial killers to try to get a better handle on their thought processes so that they would be able to identify potential murderers. It was not an immediate success, with two of the more celebrated

[15] Raymond later went on to great things, in June 1976 removing £2 million from London Airport for which in 1978 he was sentenced to ten years. While in prison on the impeding charge, he had studied for seven A-levels and was said by one of his counsel to know more about Archbold, the textbook on criminal law, than he did. By 2004 he was living in the South of France. For a survey of his career, see Michael Gillard and Laurie Flynn, *Untouchables*, Chapter 20.

[16] *Daily Record*, 12 December 2003; *Sunday Mail*, 26 September 2004. Most recently, Isabell Coll of Wood Green, North London, stabbed Michael O'Connor to death because she found him a nuisance. She was given a life sentence and her helpmate, Laurine Harrop, nine years for manslaughter. In 1997 she had been convicted of beating a man to death with a rake. *The Times*, 5 August 2004.

declining to take part. They were looking at serial killers in the sense that they had dismembered their victims for sexual *frissons* or murdered prostitutes because they had seen it as God's work. Contract killers, provided they get a good run of luck, are some of the most prolific serial killers of all but have been almost completely overlooked in the scheme of things. In consequence the book concentrates on contract killers, coupled with a look at career criminals who kill in the furtherance of their crimes – to escape from their victims, from the police, from prison, for self-preservation, revenge and so forth: how they begin, how they get their work, what they do with their fees and how, very often, their careers end in death or imprisonment.

In this book, in the main, I have kept with what might be called traditional white, blue-collar killers and criminals. That should not, however, be taken as dismissing the Italian Mafia or denigrating the great advances that the Russians, the American street gangs, the Colombians and the Yardies have made in the field of both contract and random killing, which the last have raised to a new level in Britain. It is something which the Turkish gangs are apparently now doing their best to emulate.

Some criticism may be made that the people with whom I, and others, have spoken are referred to only by initials, first names or pseudonyms. Unfortunately, in this delicate field of operations it is impossible and unsafe from the point of view of a number of people to make any further identification. Readers will simply have to accept my word that, so far as I am concerned, these conversations did take place. As usual some will feel aggrieved that they or their heroes or – to use the new politically correct word – sheroes have been omitted. If they are kind enough to contact me I will be pleased to try to include them in any future edition. All dollars are local currency unless otherwise stated.

My thanks are due in particular to J.P. Bean, who must have asked himself as he was battered with another load of questions, 'Who's writing this book? Him or me?' Thanks are also due to The Apprentice, Tish Armstrong, Tam Bagan, the late Mickey Bailey, Jeremy Beadle, Dave Critchley, Barbara Daniel, Ronnie and Kitty Diamond, the 'stand-up' Nicky Di Pietro, James Dubro, Virginia Donohue, Clifford and Marie Elmer, Paul Ferris, Frank Fraser, Wilf

Gregg, Mike Hallinan, Yves Lavigne, Loretta Lay, Francine Levinov, Barbara Levy, Susanna Lobez, Susan McNeary, Jean Maund, John Rigbey, John Silvester, Matthew Spicer, Joe Swickard, Edda Tasiemka, Tony Thompson, Brian Touhey and Richard Whittington-Egan as well as many others who have preferred not to be named. My thanks are also due in great measure to the staff of the British Library in London and at Colindale as well as those at the Mitchell Library, Glasgow, the New York Public Library, the National Library of Congress in Washington, the Burton Collection at the Detroit Public Library, the Mitchell Library, Sydney, the State Library of Western Australia and the State Library of Victoria.

As always is the case, this book could not even have been begun without the tireless help and support of Dock Bateson.

PART ONE: THE JOB

1

Am I Suitable for the Job?

Just what makes a good hitman? The make-up of a professional contract killer – the body count of whose victims may well exceed that of a serial killer – has never really attracted the interest and study of the psychologist or criminologist. This is possibly because few are caught and, unsurprisingly, the men themselves have never been over keen on giving interviews. There is not therefore any great body of literature on their make-up and lifestyles. Over the years, however, there have been twitches on the curtain.

In a recent Australian study[1] the trade has been divided into three categories. At the bottom end of the scale are the amateurs. Seen as often having a history of psychopathology, instability and marginal adjustment, they are likely to have had some prior involvement in criminality. They are able partly to rationalise their behaviour and the killing 'serves as a vent for built-up aggression and hostility'.[2] They are used for low-level work such as the removal of an unwanted spouse or partner. And it is because of the low level of their intelligence, and the fact that most people are killed by or on behalf of those they know well, that these killers are the

---

[1] Jenny Mouzos and John Venditto, *Contract Killings in Australia*, 2003.
[2] L.B. Schlesinger, 'The contract murderer: Patterns, characteristics and dynamics' in *Journal of Forensic Science*, vol. 46, no. 5, p.1120.

most likely to be caught. In turn they can often be persuaded to talk.

Sometimes the behaviour of the amateur killer is beyond belief. When Angus Young stood trial in Wales in 1993 for the killing of R. Sheehan, part of the evidence against him was that he had sent a bill to the widow:

Ref. Mr B. Sheehan (deceased) For professional services rendered to kill, extract, remove and dispose of said body, £10,000.

There was also an additional £250 to cover 'petrol, sheets, ropes etc.' He apparently had some assistance from Mrs Sheehan because there was an allowance of £5,000. His total bill came to £5,355. He received life imprisonment and so did she.[3]

Even those who should be able to arrange their affairs have found hiring a suitable hitman beyond them. Indeed the story could also appear in the section dealing with innocent bystanders, for on this occasion the victim was a wholly blameless Great Dane, Rinka. His death occurred after Jeremy Thorpe, the then leader of the Liberal party, had entered into an unwise relationship with a younger man Norman Scott who alleged that Thorpe had buggered him and in turn he was given money and sent to live on Dartmoor. This did not stop the unstable Scott from telling his story to anyone who was prepared to listen. In 1975, so the prosecution alleged, the sum of £5,000 was given by several senior members of the party to another unstable man, an airline pilot, to shoot Scott. A further £5,000 was to be payable on completion of the contract. The whole thing was mishandled. The pilot shot the dog and then said to Scott, 'It's your turn next.' Either the gun jammed or the man panicked because he then drove off. At the subsequent trial the accused were acquitted. They had claimed that Scott was merely to be frightened.[4]

The semi-professionals are likely to adopt a more sophisticated *modus operandi* and are seen as individuals who believe the only way they can achieve success in their lives is through criminal

[3] Frank Jones, *Paid to Kill*, p8
[4] For a fuller account see James Morton, *Sex, Crimes and Misdemeanours*.

behaviour. With admittedly limited data available, they are also seen to have less overall personality disturbance than their rank amateur colleagues.

It is of course the third category, the professional contract killers, which is the most interesting. To them killing is conceptualised as 'just a job' or 'business'.[5] They will, when necessary, take great care to make the death appear accidental. 'They go about their business unobtrusively, indistinguishable from their fellow citizens, and frequently maintain strong family and community ties.'[6]

In 1995 the lawyer-writer Fenton Bresler profiled the typical killer as white, 25–35, often with a military background, physically fit and able to ride a motorbike. DI Frank Perriam, quoted in the piece, thought very reasonably that the man must know how to kill skilfully and 'then – perhaps even more important – be able to walk away from it as if nothing had happened'. Perriam thought £2,000 was then a fair price for a South London hit: 'These are his movements, it's safe. There's no way it's going to come back to you because the man's a slag anyway. No one cares about him.' However, the price for the removal of a top villain could be in the region of £100,000.[7]

However, it is almost impossible to put together a detailed profile of the professional contract killer; they come in so many different shapes and sizes. For example Verne Miller, involved in the Kansas City Massacre of 1933 and later killed by Detroit's Purple Gang, was a former law officer who disliked hearing profane or foul language and apparently would have nothing whatsoever to do with the Barker-Karpis Gang after they took up kidnapping. Described as a handsome man of 5'7", weighing around 145 lbs, with medium-blond hair and melancholy grey eyes, he was born in 1896 and served with distinction in the 164th Infantry in France during the First World War. He became a police officer in 1920 and was made Beadle County Sheriff in South Dakota the following year. Unfortunately he was soon found to have embezzled $2,600 and

---

[5] K. Levi, 'Becoming a hitman: Neutralization in a very deviant career' in *Urban Life*, vol.10, no.1, pp. 47–83.
[6] B.J. Hurwood, *Society and the Assassin: A Background Book on Political Murder*, p.129.
[7] Fenton Bresler, 'Contract Killers . . . it's murder 90's style' in *Daily Express*, 27 March 1995.

in 1926 was sent to South Dakota State prison. From then on his career hurtled downwards and he worked for Al Capone and the Purple Gang as well as being a hitman for Louis Lepke, (known also as Louis Buchalter) of the New York-based Murder Inc. As a former soldier, his funeral in White Lake, South Dakota, on 6 December 1933 was with full military honours.

Others such as the Canadian Cecil Kirby have come from outlaw biker gangs. Again, in contrast, some of the worst hitmen have come from respectable families and have not undertaken their first contracts until relatively late in life. Roy DeMeo, who worked extensively for New York's Gambino Family until his own demise in the boot of a car, had an uncle who was a top prosecutor at the Brooklyn District Attorney's office before becoming a professor at the Brooklyn Law School. Another uncle had a Buick dealership, and his father's cousin was the Medical Examiner for New York City. His mother did not work and his father, who had no convictions, was a laundry delivery man. DeMeo's mother hoped her son would become a doctor. Instead he began a career as a loan shark, financed by his earnings as a delivery boy before graduating to extortion and blackmail. He committed his first murder at the age of 32 and from then on never looked back. His victim, Paul Rothenberg, was a porn film maker who had been paying him protection money and whom he now, quite rightly, believed was talking to the authorities. As a test for DeMeo, Nino Gaggi had him shoot Rothenberg twice in the head. Afterwards DeMeo was quoted as saying, 'Ya know somethin'? After you kill someone, anything is possible.'[8]

One day the New York prosecutor Burton Turkus asked the 1940s turncoat Abe 'Kid Twist' Reles how he brought himself to kill so casually:

> 'Did your conscience ever bother you?' I inquired. 'Didn't you feel anything?'
> His agate eyes showed no expression. 'How did you feel when you tried your first law case?' he countered coldly.
> 'I was rather nervous,' I admitted.
> 'And how about your second case?'

[8] Gene Mustina and Jerry Capeci, *Murder Machine*, p. 39.

'It wasn't so bad, but I was still a little nervous.'

'And after that?'

'Oh, after that, I was all right; I was used to it.'

'You've answered your own question,' the Kid rasped. 'It's the same with murder. I got used to it.'[9]

None of which really explained how he came to kill his first man.

Rich Cohen in *Tough Jews* thinks that Reles became a killer because of his treatment at the hands of the Shapiro brothers:

> Before he got mixed up with Meyer (Shapiro) I don't even think he was that violent. He probably could have gone on and lived a life like other people – got a job, raised a family, *not* killed handfuls of men. But the way he was treated by the Shapiros – abused, humiliated, threatened, shot, girlfriend raped – turned him into a killer.[10]

On the other hand Cohen thought Harry 'Pittsburgh Phil' Strauss of Murder Inc. lived in a deeply moral world:

> His views – on punishment, responsibility, covenant – were, in many ways, Jewish views. For Strauss, God was present in every move, gesture, act. If you associated with him, you would, sooner or later, cross a line, defy his code. And when you did, he was there, beyond hearing but within view. He sometimes couldn't tell where his authority ended and that of the world began. He was like the God of the Old Testament, seeing, judging, punishing. Punishing was more fun.[11]

Others who have offered some often self-justifying words on their profession include the Mafia hitman Jimmy 'The Weasel' Fratianno who, following the 'we only kill our own' line of thought, commented:

> I didn't have much feeling because I never killed nobody that was innocent. They were all gangsters, they were killers themselves. It might bother me if I killed an innocent person, somebody that

[9] Burton Turkus and Sid Feder, *Murder Inc.*, p. 55.
[10] Rich Cohen, *Tough Jews*, p. 73.
[11] Rich Cohen, *Tough Jews*. p. 74.

didn't deserve it. Guys that I fooled with, they were out to kill us. I couldn't kill a woman, innocent people, kids. I couldn't do that.[12]

Chicago Boss Sam Giancana acknowledged there could be mistakes: 'Seven out of ten times when we hit a guy, we're wrong. But the other three times we hit, we make up for it.'[13]

The Russian hitman Simon Evseich, sentenced in 1992 to six years for the killing of Moscow drug baron Alexis Praskoya and his bodyguard, also had some thoughts to offer on his professional conduct. He had been a sergeant in the Russian Army who had been on hard times after his discharge. He was paid £2,350 up front before the killing. He had a fine line in self-justification and would decline to exercise a contract on children but he would take out a woman: 'Once you're an adult you can make a choice between good and evil. Just because the evil is being done by a woman doesn't mean she should be spared.'

He had begun to question whether he was taking the work for the money or because he enjoyed it: 'However, I've reconciled myself with the reality that I am sending bad men to their fate. In this way I am doing God's will and have made my peace with Him.'[14]

A glimpse of the working life if not thoughts of a possible contract killer is provided by David Bieber, sentenced on 2 December 2004 to life imprisonment for the cold-blooded killing of PC Ian Broadhurst. Bieber had been found in a stolen BMW and when the police officers tried to handcuff him he shot PC Broadhurst and wounded two others. He then deliberately executed the injured officer who was pleading for his life.

Bieber had assumed the name of Nathan Wayne Coleman which he appears to have taken from a headstone in Georgia. He then used a copy of the birth certificate of the boy, who had died at the age of six, to obtain a passport. In America he was wanted for contracting the killing of a former business rival Markus Mueller with whom he had dealt in steroids. They had both fallen in love with the same woman, Danielle Labelle, who married Bieber but

---

[12] Quoted by J.P. Bean in *Verbals*.
[13] *Ibid*.
[14] 'The Contract Killer' in *FHM*, March 2000.

two days later decided to return to Mueller. Through a bodybuilder friend, John Saladino, Bieber acquired a hitman for $1,000. Mueller was shot on his doorstep and died instantly. Another hit was attempted on a former girlfriend and following a tip-off Saladino and the hitman, David Snipes, were arrested. Bieber fled to Europe where it is thought he took up the profession himself.

He bigamously married an English woman in 1997, but had all the negatives of the wedding photographs destroyed. When in lodgings he would have the curtains closed during the daytime, and he regularly changed his appearance. When arrested he was carrying a gun, 220 bullets, a substantial sum in cash, a blank driving licence and four different birth certificates.[15]

Peter Wyden in *The Hired Killers* suggests there are only two rather than three categories of hitman; the professional hired killer, and the amateur hired killer who flits in and out of jobs. It is the latter who gets caught. However, it is sometimes difficult to place a man in one specific category. Take Donald 'Tony the Greek' Frankos as an example. He seems to have been a thoroughly professional hitman whose killings were exemplary, but he was unable to eschew other criminal activities such as drug dealing. His arrests, and there were many, came through his extra-killing activities.

Frankos himself gives some insight into his early career as a hitman. Assuming his recollections are accurate, he was on the run as a naval deserter and was selling drugs when he became involved with Mary, a West Side madam, for whom he provided protection. He was caught AWOL and sentenced to a term in the brig, but escaped and on his return to the brothel was told that a black pimp was stealing from the girls and trying to coerce them into working for him. '"You have to kill this pimp," Mary told me.' Frankos found the man on Broadway and stabbed him in the heart:

Society says I should have remorse for the murders I committed but I'm not sure that I do. Even if I ignored the dubious qualities of those I hit, there is the fact that I viewed myself as a soldier

---

[15] *The Times*, 3 December 2004; *Daily Mail*, 3 December 2004.

and my victim as an enemy, and in that warrior context there can be no regret; rather, I felt a sense of mission accomplished.

I can't say either that my first killing committed at the age of twenty was harder than the others or that it sticks out in my memory. I went out and did it and that was that. I enjoyed the praise and recognition it brought. Clearly I had become that most envied criminal, a cold-blooded hitman, and daily I saw my new-found status reflected in the deterrent, fearful eyes of others. *Respect*.[16]

A little later in the book he returns to the theme after he has killed three rival drug dealers on behalf of his employer:

The killings didn't arouse any remorse. Maybe all the heroin I had again begun to snort deadened my conscience, or perhaps I'd just grown accustomed to murder. But I don't think so. I found a rationalisation, something I referred to before, which I call the Soldier's Syndrome. A soldier isn't usually haunted when he kills in the service of his country – he has murdered an enemy, and that's how I viewed my victims. Additionally, the soldier gets honoured for what he did, is lavished with respect, praise, and medals, which are not dissimilar to rewards I received. Soldiers are told the enemy is evil, often a questionable assertion, but I know the guys I killed fit the description.[17]

His self-justifying thoughts are very much along the same lines as those of the Asian killer Charles Sobraj:

If some will ask me whether I feel remorse – and many will – I answer: Does a professional soldier feel any remorse after having killed a hundred men with a machine gun? Did the American pilots feel remorse after dropping napalm on my homeland? No, Society condoned the soldiers, telling them: You have the right to kill; it is your duty to kill – the more you kill the bigger the promotion. Don't I have the same right? In the interests of my own minority?[18]

---

[16] Donald Frankos as told to William Hoffman and Lake Headley, *Contract Killer*, p. 77.
[17] *Ibid*, pp. 141–2.
[18] Quoted in J.P. Bean, *Verbals*.

'Jake', interviewed by Wensley Clarkson, adopted a very matter-of-fact attitude claiming his basic price was £20,000, 'unless I'm being asked to take out a big-time face who's got a lot of protection'. He would always, he said, 'get paid in full, in advance, in cash', which seems eminently sensible. Nor did the expense stop with the £20,000 either. Jake also explained that if by misfortune he was arrested the contractor had to take care of his legal expenses, put up the money for bail and provide creature comforts while Jake was inside, as well as providing for 'his missus'. After his release there would be more cash waiting for him: 'This is done to guarantee silence. As long as all obligations are taken care of, I'm not going to say a word to no one. I'm certainly not going to land anyone in the shit. They'd finish me off'.[19]

Seemingly not all employers have been as generous and reliable as Jake's. It is sometimes surprising that Glasgow boss Arthur Thompson held on as long as he did and commanded such support. When he instructed Tam Bagan to shoot two men on his behalf, Bagan was told that he would be provided for while on the run and matters died down. In the event he was not and they did not and Bagan, after living almost rough, eventually gave himself up. Thompson never communicated with him while he served his sentence, but Bagan never betrayed him.

Jake was contemptuous of some of his contemporaries:

> There are other so-called pros out there popping people for five grand. But you get what you pay for and these cut-price operators all get caught in the end and then they start singing. Let's face it, a gran in Blackpool who wants shot of her old man after thirty years of abuse is goin' to end up hiring a fuckin' amateur or an undercover cozzer.[20]

A good example of what Jake means is the case of Angela Bristow whose husband Mario Commateo was killed with a sawn-off shotgun

---

[19] Wensley Clarkson, *Gangsters*, pp. 224–5.
[20] Wensley Clarkson, *Gangsters*, pp. 224–5. There may be problems with Jake's story. Either that or he has a Spanish half-brother. In Clarkson's recent book *Costa Del Crime* the half-Spanish half-English hitman Luis offers the same comments, in some cases word for word. Benidorm, however, is substituted for Blackpool.

at the couple's home in Whyteleafe, Surrey, in March 2000. The pair ran a group of bakeries and sandwich shops in Surrey. At first Bristow played the grieving widow but things unravelled when the hitman Raymond Ryan told his girlfriend about the killing, for which the fee was apparently £10,000. Nor had Bristow exactly helped herself; customers in the sandwich shop told police that before his death she had been asking them to help kill Mario. Bristow, Ryan and a middleman were each jailed for life at the Central Criminal Court in July 2001. She is not the only person to have made indiscreet approaches. In Adelaide one woman hawked the contract on her husband at the gate of her children's primary school.[21]

It is surprising how some would-be contractors survive at all. One Glaswegian intermediary commented:

> Guy I knew wanted a hit. He wanted a swap. He would do mine and I would do his. He must have been watching the fillums. I said no. It was all over a quarrel over drugs in a club in Glasgow. It took him four years to find someone. The man was given a lethal overdose of drugs up in Dundee.[22]

Another example of the tangles in which amateurs and low-level hitmen can find themselves showed up in the case of Matthew Lee. In fact he falls absolutely into the profile of the first category of hitman. Sentenced in 1981, Lee served a sentence for murder. After his release seventeen years later he moved to Uttoxeter to begin a new life. There he was recruited by Sandra Jones to dispose of her husband, Clifford, at a price of £5,500. Mrs Jones, who had taken out a £6,000 loan to cover the cost of the contract, had already made earlier approaches to find someone to 'do over' her husband. Lee was given a key and attacked Jones while he was in bed after his overnight factory shift, hitting him with a crowbar. He failed to kill him and the pair struggled into the garden, after which Lee fled. Earlier Mrs Jones had taken her children to school, and she expected to find her husband dead on her return. To her surprise he was giving a statement to the police. Although she stood to

---

[21] *Sunday Age* (Melbourne), 8 August 2004.
[22] McS. Conversation with author, August 2004.

benefit to the tune of £96,000, the police thought her unhappy marriage was the prime motive. In January 2000 she received a merciful three years; a friend who had plotted with her was sentenced to eighteen months and the unfortunate Lee received another life sentence.[23]

'A closed mouth is a prerequisite', says Glasgow's The Apprentice. Even years after the event hitmen sometimes have an unhealthy compulsion to discuss their work which may lead to all sorts of problems. Simply because the killer talked, one of the more mysterious of the contract killings of recent years was finally solved to the satisfaction of the police – if not the relatives of the deceased – twenty-six years after newsagent Geoffrey Small was killed on 6 September 1976. At about 5.30 in the morning Small was shot seven times in the head with a 7.65 automatic pistol as he stepped into his shop in Westmead Road, Sutton, Surrey. He had been married for twenty years, during the latter part of which he had had a mistress, but by all accounts that affair had dwindled and was effectively ended by the summer of that year. He and his wife had then bought a house away from the shop and were in the process of renovating it.

The gunman entered the shop through a ground-floor window and sat and waited for Small. After the murder he said, 'Good morning' to an early customer who had come to collect a morning paper and walked away. He was described as 55 years old, 5'6" , slim with brown hair and was wearing a checked sports jacket and brown trousers. The gun was never found and only two of the seven cartridges were retrieved.

The killer took Small's wallet containing £150, but no one thought it was a robbery gone wrong; he had adopted the double-tap method of firing two shots and then changing position. It was suggested that Small might have been killed by mistake for the supergrass Bertie Smalls, on whom there was said to be a contract at the time. The difficulty with this theory was that Small looked nothing like Smalls. In November 1976 a former mercenary in Angola was arrested and questioned before being released without charge.

[23] *The Guardian*, 28 January 2000.

In February 2003 Alan Savage, now aged 72 – which made the age estimate of the gunman fairly accurate – and suffering from bladder cancer, was jailed for life. He had been paid £750 or £2,000 – reports vary – for the hit, by a man believed to be jealous of Small's serial womanising. It was said that Savage would give evidence against his employer but in the event, to the fury of Small's relatives, he declined. He was given an eighteen-month sentence for contempt and told that his refusal to give evidence would affect his release from his life sentence. The man said to have paid for the contract was discharged and afterwards commented that Savage was a 'very sad, delusional man'.[24]

Savage's arrest came about through opening his mouth. He was sitting in his flat in Hastings watching the BBC TV programme *Crimewatch* one night in 2001 when it featured Small's murder. He couldn't resist making a remark to his wife which seemed to imply that the job was his handiwork. Police had bugged the flat after getting a tip-off that he had done the killing. They hoped the programme would make him say something untoward.

A far better example from the employer's point of view is James Frederick Bazley who shot both the drug reformer Donald Mackay in July 1977, and Douglas and Isabel Wilson who were cheating on the Mr Asia Syndicate, in 1979. Almost certainly he took the Mackay contract for $10,000 from Robert Trimbole, the Mafia boss whom many believe was himself killed. Then aged 74 and Australia's oldest known contract killer, Bazley was released in early 2001 after serving fifteen years. When asked where the Mackay body might be found he declined to comment.[25]

One essential for a contract killer is to get clear of the scene of death as soon as is reasonably possible. One who failed was Edward 'Snakes' Ryan, shot in New York on 28 August 1953 by Patrolman Langan shortly after he had killed the supposedly squeaky-clean labour leader Tom Lewis in the block of flats where he lived. Ryan was known to shoot on sight, but on this occasion the last word was with the officer. Of course, it turned out that Lewis was

[24] *Evening Standard*, 28 February 2003; *The Times*, 18 September 2003.
[25] *Northern Territory News*, 2 February 2001.

by no means as clean as all that; the killing had been over a power struggle for the control of harness racing.[26]

Some hitmen are clearly temperamentally unsuited for the life. Aimé Simard came from Quebec City and criminologists would no doubt attribute his subsequent career in part to his alcoholic father whom, when he was ten, Simard found dead on the living-room sofa. Later he studied management, accounting and police administration. At one time he wished to be a policeman, but weighing 25 stones told against him. In addition to his studies, or perhaps to finance them, he committed a series of relatively petty crimes totalling over eighty offences, mostly theft from shops and passing false cheques.

On his release from prison he went to Montreal. He was now 29 years old and, the eternal student, thinking he might study forensic science. He took out an advertisement in *Rencontres Selectes*, a gay dating magazine run by Dany Kane and funded by the Royal Canadian Mounted Police as part of a sting operation to enable them to infiltrate the Hells Angels. Kane himself answered Simard's advert and apparently it was love, or lust, at first sight. Simard took Kane to his mother's house while she was away in Florida. Kane saw the whirlpool in the basement. Both stripped off and jumped in. Simard saw a Hells Angels tattoo on Kane's arm and was told that he was an Angel prospect; something of an exaggeration since he was still only a Rocker, an Angels subsidiary. Kane asked Simard whether he would like to go to bed and the union was consummated there and then.

It must have been an attraction of opposites. Simard, the archetypal biker, was so gross that he had to have his stomach stapled. Kane, much more the new, controlled face of bikerdom, was an immaculate dresser with polished boots, black designer jeans and leather jackets. Now Kane began to use him as a part-time chauffeur and general gofer, even having Simard drive him to his meetings with his RCMP contacts.

In February 1997 a man and a woman were shot on a street in Quebec City. Within a fortnight Kane was questioned by his RCMP handlers and told them that the shooter was Simard, who had been

---

[26] *New York Times*, 29 August 1953.

fired on by people connected with the Rock Machine, one side of the biker war which had been running for a number of years. Simard had returned the fire with his .44 Magnum and later he threw the gun away. More accurately, Simard had gone to Quebec City with a friend who owed money to a drug dealer and had shot the man and his girlfriend.

It was then that a contract came on offer. The victim was to be a thoroughly unpleasant biker in Halifax, Bob McFarlane. On 27 February he was shot dead by Kane and Simard. After that Simard was offered a position on what the Rockers called their football team. This was the killing arm of the biker group; the baseball team merely hurt people. However, Simard's career as a hitman was short. He was next invited to kill a drug dealer Jean-Marc Caissy, something he did on 28 March. Unfortunately after the killing he left the gun, a .357 revolver, in a gym locker and was filmed in the process of hiding the weapon by a security camera. Simard was arrested on 11 April. In exchange for a deal he pleaded guilty and received a life sentence with eligibility for parole after twelve years. Now he gave evidence against Kane.

The trial was not a success. On 10 November 1988 the judge declared a mistrial and Kane was released. Then in March 2000 he signed a contract with the police to assist their anti-biker squad, the Wolverines. It was a contract worthy of a Premier League footballer and was worth $1.75 million. The agreement provided $580,000 on the arrest of gang members, a further $580,000 when he gave evidence at preliminary hearings and the same again when he testified at the trial proper. In the meantime he received $2,000 weekly support payments.

As part of the arrangement the police paid for his house, two vans, suits, money for his lawyer and $1,000 as a gift for the wedding of René Charlebois, a fellow Hells Angel. Now Kane embarked on a thoroughly dangerous life. He allowed himself to carry a wire and became a bodyguard and driver for David 'Wolf' Carroll and Normand Robitaille, two members of the Nomads, the elite arm of the Angels, recording conversations by the men about their drug deals with the Montreal Mafia.

On 6 August 2000 he gassed himself at his five-room home in

St Luc, south of Montreal near St Jean, the headquarters of the Rockers. One letter he left indicated the turmoil he was in: 'Am I good or evil? Am I straight or gay? Am I rich or poor? Am I honest or dishonest?'[27] Before his death he had, however, told the police that his cocaine supply came from another Rocker, Jean-Richard Larivière. On 18 and 19 May the police had already taken the precaution of making a lengthy videotape in case Kane should not be able to give evidence in court. It led to the arrest of over 130 Hells Angels and their associates. The trials of nine defendants including Larivière ended in September 2003 with pleas of guilty to charges of trafficking, conspiracy to murder and being a member of a criminal gang.[28]

Aimé Simard, like many another informant, found life particularly difficult behind bars and tried to commit suicide by slashing his wrists and taking pills. Later he told the Montreal newspaper *La Presse*, 'I feel hunted.' As Julian Sher and William Marsden comment, 'The hunt ended' when Simard was found at 10 p.m. on 18 July 2003 unconscious in his cell at the Saskatchewan Penitentiary in Prince Albert. He had been stabbed 106 times.[29] 'It's worrisome,' said Guy Ouellette, a retired Quebec police biker expert, under-statedly. 'He's the first informant to die in gaol.'[30] It is certain he would not be the last.

The penalty for hitting the wrong person can be high. In 1987 lawyer George M. Aronwald was shot dead when he was hit by five bullets near his Queens home in New York. It was thought at the time that perhaps he had been killed because of his son's career as a prosecution lawyer. It was also suggested that he might have been killed by mistake. The latter seems more likely because in 1997 an informer told the FBI that he heard it had been a Mob hit by two brothers, Enrico and Vincent Carini. In turn they had been killed for murdering the wrong man.[31]

Another similar case occurred in Chicago in May 1999 when

---

[27] *Globe and Mail*, 15 May 2002.
[28] A biker who failed to burn a getaway car in which Larivière's fingerprints were found was later killed along with his wife. *Globe and Mail*, 12 September 2003.
[29] Julian Sher and William Marsden, *The Road to Hell*, p. 375.
[30] *Globe and Mail*, 22 July 2003.
[31] *New York Times*, 29 July 2001.

Leroy Williams and Lavonne Carter were found dead in the Leydown Motel, Melrose Park. Carter shot Williams and then turned the gun on himself. Earlier in the day they had shot two men in Roosevelt Road but the victims had survived. Carter had made seventeen calls from the motel room before he shot Williams. He feared there would be blame and severe reprisals for their botched job.[32]

On the more positive side, during his research for his best-selling book *Britain's Gangland*, Tony Thompson met a man named Max who claimed to be a contract killer and who spoke about some of his work. A man with a legitimate building business in the north of England, he travels south to work where his services are on offer. On one occasion in the 1990s he was invited to undertake a contract on a nightclub owner in Tenerife, that home-from-home of the Timeshare and its attendant problems. He obtained a yearly passport in a false name and went for a week, taking the view that this could not be an in-and-out job. He thought the airports would be sealed if the body was discovered, and going in and out within twenty-four hours might have drawn attention to him. Instead, he decided to leave the killing until shortly before his return flight and, blending in the community during the week, took to drinking in the victim's club:

> So by the time the last day came, we were quite pally and I'd stay behind with him each night after the bar shift, drinking and chatting. On the last night, I stayed late and gradually the staff filtered off and it was just the two of us left. We were both pretty tanked up so I suggested we took the jeep I'd hired for the week and went off for a tear round the island.

They drove along the TF7 and when they stopped to urinate the victim went first. Max followed behind him and shot him in the head, dragged the body into the bushes and returned to the hotel. He was on the plane home before the body was discovered. Thompson asked Max what emotions, if any, he had over the killing of a man whom he knew:

[32] *Chicago Tribune*, 5 May 1999.

It's not like he was a friend and then someone asked me to do it. Someone asked me to do it first. It's just a job. It's just like you coming here to do this interview. There ain't no bad dreams, no remorse, no guilt, nothing.

But there was some self-justification creeping into Max's account:

I like to know I'm doing things for the right reason. If someone was a really nice guy, I probably wouldn't . . . well, I'd think about it a bit more. I've just done this job in Birmingham and that was a real arsehole drug dealer. People like that just piss me off. I wanna put 'em down anyway.

I always ask, I always want to know. A lot of people wouldn't but that's just me – I like to know why I'm putting a bullet in someone. If I feel justified in doing it then I'm justified. I wouldn't go and work for an arsehole and shoot a nice guy, but I'd do it the other way around.[33]

The Glaswegian who goes by the name of The Apprentice says:

I would expect to be given all the necessary information and I would expect the contractor to supply that information – 'he leaves the house in a morning at 9.30 and comes back between six and seven'. That sort of thing. And he'd have to supply a photograph. Then the hitman has to decide on the quality of the information. If he needed more that's where expenses would come in. He'd get someone to do the reccie for him. Of course he might want to do reconnaissance himself and that dry run might turn out to be the real thing. A hitman has to be fully prepared to be an opportunist.

I would want a clean – unused – gun and that might cost £200. It would be destroyed after use. What the hitman must avoid is leaving calling cards such as using the same gun more than once or using a motor bike every time.[34]

It is the same the whole world over. This is Mafia enforcer Cecil Kirby writing about his 1979 contract to kill Irving Kott

---

[33] Tony Thompson, *Britain's Gangland*, pp. 13–14. I am very grateful indeed to Tony Thompson for allowing me to quote 'Max' so extensively. Conversation with the author.
[34] Thomas C. Renner and Cecil Kirby, *Mafia Enforcer*, pp. 127–9.

who had offended members of Montreal's powerful Commisso
Family:

> Before I was ready to handle the job, I travelled back and forth
> to Montreal a couple of times, staying a different place each time
> as I stalked Kott's every move. I wanted this guy down pat before
> I blew him away.
>
>   I took other precautions, I changed the type of clothes I'd
> wear and my appearance each day. Sometimes I'd comb my hair
> down, wear a baseball cap or a winter hat with a tassel. Sometimes
> I'd wear sunglasses and dark clothes. It always was different,
> and I'd always look for the quickest way to exit an area before
> parking or walking around.[35]

Another Canadian hitman, Réal Simard – no relation to Aimé and
known as The Nephew – knew his disguise had been successful
when a man sitting at the table with his first victim warned him,
a few days later, not to go in the restaurant because a killing had
recently taken place there. Simard, who had undergone commando
training as a young man, was groomed for his position as hitman
by the Montreal boss Frank Cotroni. This is Simard's account of
Cotroni's advice before the first hit:

> You weave a spider web around a man. And you wait. If he goes
> to a certain restaurant? You go there too. You plot one route for
> going there, and another for your escape. Check out the land-
> mark; get to know his habits. He goes home afterwards? Plot a
> route for going to his place. He always goes to the same bar?
> Plot a route for the bar too. Every day you go to these places
> one by one. And if one day you go by and he's there, alone,
> with no police around, he's yours because you've done your
> homework.

And as for the killing itself, he added: 'Never walk away from a
body until you have put one more bullet in the head.'[36]
   His thoughts are remarkably like those of The Apprentice, and

---

[35] ibid.
[36] Réal Simard, *The Nephew*, pp. 129–31.

indeed Roy DeMeo who gave this helpful advice to his son: 'Never use a gun unless you absolutely have to; but if you must, use it efficiently for you may not get a second chance. Two in the head, make sure they're dead.'[37]

Phil Leonetti, a senior member of the Philadelphia Mafia, provided some insight into how a murder was carried out when he gave evidence to the New Jersey Organised Crime Commission and, as with Max and the nightclub owner, it involved cosying up to the victim. It is an interesting example of some of the precautions taken in a Mob hit and why they are so rarely solved. In 1962 Nicky Scarfo, Sal Merlino (the father of Skinny Joe), Santo Idone, Anthony Casella and Santo Romero were ordered by the then boss Angelo Bruno to strangle Dominick 'Reds' Caruso who had shown disrespect towards the *consiglieri*, Joe Rugnetta, by slapping him. Scarfo was known to be close to Caruso and for several weeks sought his company. Then on the day of the murder Caruso was invited to go to Anthony 'King Kong' Perella's bar in Vineland, New Jersey. Sal Merlino was ordered to take Caruso to Scarfo's car. The plan was that Idone should strangle Caruso. In fact Idone was late and instead Scarfo shot the unfortunate Caruso five times without killing him. Scarfo then took an ice-pick to the man and succeeded in burying it so deeply in Caruso's back that it had to be broken off. At the end of it all Idone appeared with a rope which was then wrapped round Caruso's neck. The body was taken to Bruno to inspect before burial and a grave was dug in rural Vineland. Bruno ordered that the corpse was to be left next to the grave so that those detailed to bury it would be able to do so. Finally the body was dug up and removed, thus ensuring that if in the future an informer told the authorities where it was buried he would be proved wrong and so his whole story would be doubted.[38]

And the payment? In general, half up front as well as expenses for the independent contractor. And the fee? As little as two ounces of heroin for a modern-day prison hit. This either keeps the killer going or, if he is not addicted, he can deal and parlay this into two

[37] Albert DeMeo, *Sins of the Father*, p. 114.
[38] Evidence of Philip Leonetti to the State of New Jersey Commission of Investigation, *Organised Crime in Bars, Part II*, June 1995.

years of earnings. Not all contract killers have been good business-men, nor employers good paymasters. 'Do it for a cenny,' was Arthur Thompson's demand back in the 1980s, says his former right-hand man Tam Bagan. Probably in a mob killing in America a minimum of $20,000 is now the going rate, with higher profile or more difficult targets commanding up to and over $100,000.

According to his account of matters Cecil Kirby was always being stiffed for his payments by his masters, the Commisso Family. He was to receive $10,000 for bombing a debtor's business but was paid a mere $1,000. When he complained, 'We don't get every-thing we're supposed to get. When we get it, you get it,' said Cosimo Commisso. He never did.[39]

When Nicky 'The Crow' Caramandi, the former contract killer, gave evidence against the Philadelphia Mob in 2001 he admitted to some twenty-five hits, which might be an underestimate. He thought that the greed of the victim was the most usual reason for a hit: 'Greed is the ultimate thing that will get anyone into trouble.' Asked on television what went through his mind on a hit he replied:

> We don't think anything – we just want to do what we got to do. Just forget about it and go on. That's the best answer I can give. Kill them and forget about it. I don't want to sound too harsh, but that's the truth.[40]

Only one hit had apparently troubled him. This had been on Sal Testa, who was killed not because of greed but because he had fallen in love with the wrong girl. Testa was engaged to the daughter of the underboss of the Philadelphia Mob and when he broke it off the man ordered Testa's death.[41] Caramandi, who claimed to have admired Testa, appears to have had a modicum of remorse:

[39] Thomas C. Renner and Cecil Kirby, *Mafia Enforcer*, p. 118.
[40] *ABC News*, 19 January 2000.
[41] At the 1988 trial of Nicky Scarfo the prosecution was not so sure the killing was for love. Assistant District Attorney Barbara Christie suggested that 'he was getting too powerful and possibly had treason on his mind'. Scarfo was acquitted. For an account of the long-running troubles in the Philadelphia Mob and the killing of Testa see James Morton, *Gangland International* and *Gangland Today*.

> When we bounced him (killed him) I knew he shouldn't have died. He was only twenty-six but all man. He died for just principles that he believed in. He tried to defy the Mob, the politics of the Mob, and that's why he was killed. I had nightmares about that. When we had to kill him, it really affected me a lot. I don't know, I can't explain why, but it affected me.

Shortly after that Caramandi, believing that Nicky Scarfo had ordered him to be hit, went into the Witness Protection Program. His thoughts are echoed by another East Coast hitman: 'Killing is easy. It's not hard but your mind has to be strong, 'cause it haunts some guys.'[42]

And how does the wannabe contract killer learn his or her trade? Some, such as The Apprentice, attach themselves to a more experienced man and learn by osmosis. For those not in that fortunate position, for a time the publication by Paladin Press in Boulder, Colorado, of the clearly pseudonymous Rex Feral's 130-page *Hit Man* effectively provided a bible for the aspirant killer. Regularly advertised in *Soldier of Fortune*, it helpfully pointed out on the first page that it was 'For Informational Purposes Only!' But this did not stop it becoming a steady if not spectacular seller. Red-blooded Americans were keen to learn the techniques of surveillance of a victim, choosing a weapon, killing in silence and eliminating blood-splatters. Recommendations included the AR-7 rifle as being both accurate and inexpensive.

Fortunately wannabe Detroit hitman James Perry, or 'Dr J. Perry, spiritual adviser and case buster' as his calling card stated, did not study the text sufficiently. He was hired by Lawrence Horn to eliminate his former wife, their disabled son Trevor and the boy's nurse, Janice Saunders. The motive was simply money. Horn was $16,000 in arrears with maintenance and owed more than $60,000 in legal fees. Killing his eight-year-old son would also ensure that he inherited much of the $2 million settlement made after the boy suffered brain damage when a hospital respirator failed.

In 1992 Horn was introduced by a cousin to the ex-felon turned store-front preacher, Perry, who carried out the contract following the manual. He shot the nurse in the face, smothered the boy and then,

---

[42] Letter to the author.

disturbed by Millie Horn, shot her also in the face. The book had recommended that the killer should aim for the head – preferably the eye sockets.

Naturally in a case of this nature the ex-husband was the first suspect. Unsurprisingly, he had a cast-iron alibi: he was at home in California with his girlfriend, and they had taken the trouble to record themselves with a television news broadcast in the background confirming the date and time. However, the search of his apartment produced a videotape showing the route to his ex-wife's home as well as a hand-drawn map of the layout of her street. Shortly after the murder he had received a telephone call from a payphone near the Horn home. Motels in the area were checked and Perry was identified as staying at Days Inn in Rockville from midnight to 6 a.m. on the night of the murders. When, in turn, his home was searched there was a mail order catalogue from Paladin, and a check with the company showed he had ordered *Hit Man*.

Mildred Horn's family subsequently brought a civil action against Paladin. In September 1996 the case was initially dismissed with a Maryland judge ruling that books do not kill – people do. The action had been brought on the basis of product liability – the too-hot apple-pie syndrome. After all, Perry had followed the manual almost one hundred per cent. Unfortunately, he had not read the helpful section on obtaining a false identity. That and the making of the telephone calls led to his conviction and stay on Death Row. Horn was sentenced to life imprisonment. Both continue to maintain their innocence.

After the judge's ruling, claims were made that the publishers were sheltering behind the First Amendment and the right to free speech. Three years later the action was settled out of court. *Hit Man* was withdrawn and damages and a donation to charity were paid. Before the killing of Millie Horn, sales had hovered around the 13,000 mark, but they were said to have rocketed after it was discovered that Perry had taken stock of the manual.[43]

Few contract killers have relied solely on their profession for an income. To his regret and downfall Frankos dealt in drugs; the

---

[43] Rex Feral, *Hit Man; Observer*, 8 September 1996; 'Murder He Wrote' in *GQ*, August 1997; *The Guardian*, 24 May 1999.

Londoner Alfie Gerard ran a successful fish restaurant The Blue Plaice where his pie and mash was said to be 'blinding'; and many North American hitmen have doubled as chauffeurs for the bosses. One Glaswegian hitman of the 1980s worked hard at genuine occupations. At one time he had an interest in three public houses in which he himself worked, some ice-cream vans and a double-glazing company. He was another who believed that the ability to lure the victim was an essential part of his other occupation.[44]

Robert Carey had a less attractive sideline, working a version of the badger game with his girlfriend Rose. Born in 1884 and raised in St Louis where he was a member of Jack Egan's Rats in their continuing struggle with the Hogan Gang, he fled to Detroit after the murder of Harry 'Cherries' Dunn in September 1916. An associate of the Detroit killers Fred Burke and Gus Winkler, he was suspected of involvement in the St Valentine's Day Massacre as well as a double murder in Detroit in 1927, the murder of a Toledo police officer George Zientara and a Cincinnati officer the next year, as well as a Los Angeles gangster in 1929.[45] He and his girlfriend then fled to New York. The pair were found shot dead in their apartment at 220 W 104th on 31 July 1932; they were thought to have died some forty-eight hours earlier. The official verdict was that Carey had shot Rose and then killed himself. He had no family to claim his body, which may well have ended up in a medical school.

Of course, contract killers have many qualities hidden from the general public, some of which are made known only after their deaths or imprisonment. For example, on the death of Alphonse Gangitano, the leader of Melbourne's New Boys, his solicitors thought so well of him that they inserted a death notice in the *Herald-Sun* which read:

> In loving memory of a loyal friend that we now entrust to God. Together now with your dear parents. Partners and Staff, Pryles & Defteros.

---

[44] Conversation with the author.
[45] Winkler's body was discovered on a Chicago street in October 1934. He had attempted to alter his fingerprints by acid, not realising they would grow back. At the time of his death he was wanted for murder and robbery.

Gangitano was well regarded by others, not least the bail justice Rowena Allsop. She knew both him and his great friend Mick Gatto, regarding the fallen leader as a man of parts unknown to those not close to him. In turn Ms Allsop came under some criticism for being quite as close to Gangitano as she had been. Only a few hours before his death they had been drinking together shortly before his curfew came into effect for the night. Now prevailed upon to speak at his funeral, held at the underworld's favourite church St Mary's Star of the Sea, West Melbourne, dressed in turquoise and with her voice trembling with emotion, she spoke of his wit, his love of Oscar Wilde and his passion for Dolce e Gabbano aftershave lotion.

Roy DeMeo, one of the most ruthless of all the 1980s New York killers, cried when he realised he had shot an innocent vacuum cleaner salesman. Earlier, rather more creditably, he had pulled a man from a burning car. The ruthless contract and multiple killer Sandy Macrae once tried to help his then boss Geoffrey Lamb to break his heroin habit by chaining him up, à la Popeye Doyle in *The French Connection 2*. The fact that he was unsuccessful and the multi-millionaire brothel-keeper blew his fortune in drugs should not in any way be allowed to detract from his efforts. Similarly Joe 'Little Joey' Bernstein of Detroit's Purple Gang was nearly killed in May 1930 when Harry Kirschbaum, whom he was trying to wean off opium, shot him in the spleen.

The killer Lewis Caine, also known amongst other names as Sean Vincent – shot and killed in a cul-de-sac in Brunswick, Melbourne, on 8 May 2004 – must also have had good qualities. At the time it was thought he had accepted a contract to take out Carlton Crew member Maurice Condello as a reprisal for the death of Benji Veniamin. After his release following the killing of David Templeton in a nightclub fight on 18 September 1988, he took up with a woman solicitor from a leading Melbourne firm, and when he was killed she applied to have his sperm taken and frozen. Of him, killer Keith Faure spoke appreciatively, 'I thought he was trying to go lead a normal life, I don't think he was a gangster or a big timer.'[46] And there are doubtless countless other unrecorded examples.

---

[46] Two weeks later Faure was arrested over Caine's death.

2

##

Contractors, Great and Small

Contractors come in all shapes and sizes, from the Mafia and the millionaires such as Patrizia Reggiani Martinelli and John Gaul, to the ordinary housewife who wants to be rid of an importunate husband or boyfriend. And it is particularly at the lower end of the scale that the troubles begin for contractor and contracted.

So how does Joe and more usually Josephine Public obtain the services of a contract killer? Some killers have advertised on the Internet, which has meant they have been arrested before they could assist. Agents of the Moscow police posing as potential clients approached a man, appropriately enough in Samara, offering him several thousand dollars to carry out a killing. The moment he accepted the money and gave a date when he would carry out the contract he was arrested.

That Moscow Internet advertiser was by no means the first to use the media. In July 1996 Dimitri Kashnisky advertised in the St Petersburg paper *Reklama Shans*, 'Seeking any kind of one-off dangerous work', and provided a telephone number. He was duly contacted by Leonid Andronov who had personal problems. He had married a woman Irina Rukavishnikova in order to obtain a residency permit. She was schizophrenic, but her mother Raisa realised her daughter had been duped and filed on her behalf for a divorce. Andronov offered Kashnisky £3,600 to kill both women, something he did by battering them to death outside their flat. Andronov received fifteen years in a penal colony and Kashnisky was sent to a mental hospital which may have been worse. In a city in which advertisements for soap powder and contract killers run side by side, it was the thirteenth recorded such case.[1] Internet advertising can be a two-way exchange. Paul Clark advertised on the Internet for someone to murder American Brandy Arnett. He had become her pen pal but when she revealed that, far from wishing to marry him, she was indeed already married, he offered a contract of £25,000 on her and her husband.[2]

Nor with relaxed discipline and the use of the telephone is the impediment of imprisonment any real bar to arranging a contract. In 1997, after he had ordered killings from his cell, Luis Felipe of the New York Chapter of the Latin Kings agreed to a plea bargain in which he would be denied contact with all but his lawyers and immediate family in return for being spared the electric chair.

People simply do not learn. In November 2000 the leading member of the Bronx-based Sex, Money and Murder Gang, Peter Rollack, agreed to similar terms. While in prison in North Carolina he ordered the killing of two people during the annual Thanksgiving football game between residents of the Soundview Houses and the Castle Hill Houses in the Bronx.

Nor is the use of the prison telephone confined to the United States. In England in November 2002 Stuart Spring pleaded guilty to soliciting a murder. The paedophile wanted a fellow prisoner to murder the nine-year-old girl who had given evidence against him at his earlier trial which had resulted in a four-year sentence. Spring was offering between £7,000 and £10,000 for the girl's body to be discovered in 'woodlands somewhere'. The fellow prisoner was, in fact, an undercover police officer.[3] On 31 January 2003 Spring received life imprisonment.[4]

[1] *The Times*, 26 August 1998.
[2] *Daily Mirror*, 1, 2 December 2000.
[3] *Daily Mirror*, 18 November 2002.
[4] *Daily Express*, 1 February 2003.

One of the richest women accused in recent years of contracting a killer is Patrizia Reggiani Martinelli, one of many women known as The Black Widow because of the loss of their nearest and dearest. Her former husband Maurizio Gucci, to whom she was married for twelve years before he took up with interior designer Paola Franchi, was shot dead near his office in Milan on 27 March 1995.

After the divorce Signora Reggiani, who underwent an operation for a brain tumour in 1992, continually spoke of wanting her husband dead, and she maintained that her confidante Pina Auriemma – who fortunately was also her personal clairvoyant – took matters into her own hands. Through an underworld contact, Ivano Savioni, the killing was set in motion with Benedetto Ceraulo as the hitman and Orazio Cicala as the getaway driver. Set against this fortuitous piece of star-gazing were two entries in the Reggiani diary. The first, a week before the killing, read, 'There is no crime that cannot be bought.' On the day of her ex-husband's death she wrote 'Paradiso' and decorated the word with a tasteful black border. She was sentenced to twenty-nine years imprisonment, reduced on appeal to twenty-six. In May 2004 in a further appeal, heard in Venice to ensure 'complete objectivity', a retrial was ordered so that the court could decide whether she was in full possession of her mental faculties at the time of the killing.

In modern times one of the first women to be found employing a hitman was Elizabeth Duncan, on the face of it a respectable citizen living in Santa Barbara, California, in the 1950s. Mrs Duncan doted on Frank, her 29-year-old lawyer son, and the intended victim was her daughter-in-law, a nurse Olga Kupczyk. Mrs Duncan was not, however, all she seemed. She had already run up about nine bigamous marriages. However, she did not take kindly to the fiancée whom she deemed not to be good enough for her boy and, apart from accusing her of promiscuity and fraud, threatened to kill her should she marry Frank. The pair defied Mrs Duncan, who next plotted to kidnap Olga and mark her with acid. Frank intervened, but failed to move his mother who now upped the stakes and set off to find a contract killer.

It is yet another good example of the dangers which face an amateur who goes looking for a hitman. She first approached a Mexican woman who ran a café and through her recruited two unemployed Mexican youths, Luis Moya and Augustine Baldonado. On 17 November 1958 they went to Olga's flat and took the now seven-months-pregnant woman to the mountains where they battered her into unconsciousness. She was then buried, possibly still alive, in a sandy grave. The plan fell apart through Mrs Duncan's meanness. She refused to pay the men, saying she had no funds, and instead of the promised $6,000 she handed over a grand total of $35.

Frank Duncan had reported his wife missing and told the police of his mother's antipathy to her. Questioned, she claimed that she was being blackmailed by two unnamed Mexicans who had threatened to kill her daughter-in-law. In turn Moya and Baldonado were arrested and Baldonado confessed. All three were sent to the gas chamber in August 1962.[5]

Another example of the botched contract, and poor choice of hitman, came in what was one of the more sensational cases of the late 1950s. It is also a good example of the belief that where a wife is killed, look first at the husband, and if the husband is a doctor look nowhere else.

This time the killing took place a few hours' drive from Santa Barbara in Los Angeles where Bernard Finch ran a medical centre. There was some sort of agreed separation between Finch and his wife Barbara in 1957, and he rented a flat where he could meet his new girlfriend Carole Tregoff. So far so good, but the problem arose over the question of money. He wanted a divorce and Barbara refused, knowing that in a contested case she would be awarded a good share of the property. Coupled with alimony, he might be wiped out financially. And so he and his ex-model lover decided to hire a contract killer.

Their choice, ex-marine John Patrick Cody, was a poor one. At the time he was on the run from the Minneapolis Workhouse where he was serving time for bouncing cheques, and was introduced to Carole Tregoff through a mutual friend, a law student. When he later gave evidence Cody explained his financial thinking. He wanted $2,000, but was told it was too much and agreed on a

---

[5] For a comprehensive account of the case see Peter Wyden, _Hired Killers_.

rather smaller fee; a $350 down payment on a $1,400 contract which included $100 for a gun and a similar sum for a car. He was also provided with a plane ticket. Patriotically, or better still a day when one would remember an alibi, the date was to be 4 July 1959.

The whole episode was one of Greek meeting Greek. Cody was a con man and Tregoff was not going to pay the full fee if she could help it. He had no intention of killing Barbara Finch. He cashed in the plane ticket, spent three days in Hollywood without going near the intended target and then returned to tell Carole Tregoff of his success. She was wary and asked whether he hadn't received a better offer from Mrs Finch, before giving him six or seven hundred dollars. It was later that Finch spoke to his wife and, finding her alive and well, thought Cody had killed the wrong woman. When offered a further $100 to go back and complete the contract, Cody took the money and welshed a second time.

This left the pair to do the work themselves and Mrs Finch was shot dead in her driveway a fortnight later. They would claim that she had drawn a gun and threatened them. Barbara Finch was shot in the back and the maid, hearing the gunfire, called the police. On the lawn was an attaché case containing what was described as a 'do-it-yourself' murder kit including a gun, a butcher's knife and two hypodermic needles.

Two juries, treated to the distressing spectacle of Finch giving evidence as to how his dying wife took the blame, saying she had loved him too much, disagreed but the pair were finally convicted of murder and conspiracy and received sentences of life imprisonment. Carole Tregoff was released in 1971.[6]

It is difficult to say for certain which was the first contract killing in twentieth-century Britain, but probably it is that of Leslie Hutchinson, the co-owner of Fulkstryde Boarding Kennels near Hessle, Hull, on 19 October 1962. His partner Roy Bigby reported his death to the police, saying he had found Hutchinson's body and motorcycle in a lane near the kennels. His head injuries were consistent with having been in a motorcycle accident. However, the police found he had been strangled with a belt wrapped twice

[6] Leonard Gribble, *Such Women are Deadly.*

around his neck. A trip-wire had been placed across the lane which knocked him off his bike; ironically, he would have died from the injuries received without the strangling. From then the details of the killing quickly unravelled. Hutchinson's wife Marge had begun an affair with the married Bigby and had paid an alcoholic Charles Green £37 for the murder. This included £12 to buy an Alsatian puppy so that he had an excuse to visit the kennels. After the killing she gave him another £30 or so to replace his ruined blood-splattered clothing. She had already asked around the neighbourhood if anyone was interested in killing her philandering and wife-beating husband by whom she was again pregnant. She had said, 'If they want to earn any money they can do him in for me,' Green told the police. He soon confessed, implicating both Bigby – described by prosecuting counsel as having 'not only the morals of a rabbit but the spirit of one too' – and Marge Hutchinson. Things moved fast in those days. The trio went on trial in early 1963 and Green and Marge Hutchinson received life sentences on 6 February. Bigby, cleared of murder, received three years for conspiracy to assault. Marge had already written her story for a Sunday newspaper: 'I have gambled and lost. My husband is dead. My lover is dead to me. But the bitterest thought of all is: what is to become of my unborn child?' Green, who had pleaded guilty, was released after nine years. She served two years longer before being released in 1974.[7]

One of the more tangled contracts, and one which shows the risks of the hirer, is the Australian case of the 30-year-old woman and the 42-year-old married man who had been conducting a lengthy affair. He promised to leave his wife, but to facilitate matters they decided that a hitman should be acquired. This was done by the woman, who was sleeping with the hitman as well. The offer was $50,000 for both the wife and the woman's own estranged husband. On the night of the killing the husband took his three children to a video store while the woman and the hitman battered and stabbed the wife. It was a joint enterprise in the truest sense of the word because the woman then rang the husband at the store. In turn he sent the children into

[7] Nat Arch. Assi 45 567; *Master Detective*, April 2000; *Hull Daily Mail*, 30, 31 January 1, 5, 6 February 1973. Marge Hutchinson, 'I stood and watched my husband fight to live' in *Sunday Pictorial*, 17 February 1963.

the house to make the discovery of his wife's body. The hitman sensibly turned prosecution witness and received twenty years, while the pair were sentenced to mandatory life imprisonment.[8]

Former police officer Gary Johnson, who worked with the Houston police as a decoy killer, believed that one reason for the failure of low-level contracts was that people approached petty criminals who, startled out of their *modus vivendi*, went to the police instead of accepting the offer. He found that most contracts were domestic, but occasionally neighbours became the target as did those of 72-year-old Tom Moon and his 48-year-old son Steven. In 1999 they were in dispute over the use of a dirt road. The intermediary contacted the police and the Moons were arrested after handing over a pistol, a picture of the intended victims and $2,500. However, not all slights to the Moons required death. There was also to be a bonus payment if the agent beat up a teenager who had been annoying the elder Moon.[9]

One complaint by domestic contractors when they end up in court is that they have been led on by police officers masquerading as hitmen and so effectively have been entrapped. Until the Police and Criminal Evidence Act 1984 there was no such defence in English law, but the Act provided that evidence which had been improperly obtained could be excluded. One of the problems is that the would-be contractor confides his or her hopes to part- or full-time police informers, and the test in future would be whether the evidence of the undercover officer was unfairly obtained. In the late 1980s and early 1990s seven men and women were, so they said, entrapped. They included Alan Bainbridge, jailed in 1989 for seven years at Chelmsford Crown Court, who claimed that a work colleague, knowing his marriage was unhappy, encouraged him to kill his wife. The friend then arranged for him to meet a 'hitman' and he was intimidated into making compromising statements. Then there was Keith Smurthwaite, a part-time builder. He was one who confided in an informer and three years after Bainbridge he received six years at Teesside Crown Court. That same year Harbel Mann

[8] R. v Mathews and Burgess SASC 2003 [unreported]; Jenny Mouzos and John Venditto, *Contract Killings in Australia*, p. 28.
[9] 'The Hit Man is shooting for arrests' in *The National Law Journal*, 18 October 1993.

went down for a similar term at Oxford Crown Court. As the daughter of a policeman, Susan Gill should have known better. She claimed that she was encouraged by a local thief who was also an informer to dispose of her husband. In time the informer provided her with a hitman who, naturally, was an undercover officer.[10]

The attitude of the police is typified by 'John': 'What I will never do is talk them into it. But I don't talk them out of it either, because I worry that if I talk them out of it, a week later they'll go and ask someone else'.[11]

The thoughts of those acting for the defendants ran along the lines that as the third person – that is the one who had contacted the police – was an informer and had not given evidence at the trial, the evidence was unfair. An informer might have ulterior motives of his own (and most of them do), and by the time the undercover officer had been introduced the husband or wife had been incited to commit a crime which but for the informer they would never have done.

The Court of Appeal (Criminal Division) with the Lord Chief Justice presiding was having one of its more robust days – not that they often have anything else:

> One of the main reasons for using undercover police officers in such cases was to avoid having to rely on informants of bad character, who might be regarded by the jury as unreliable witnesses. In many cases, moreover, there were other good reasons of public policy for not calling informants. They, or their families, might be put at risk of reprisal and their value as informants in ongoing or future cases might be destroyed.[12]

Philip Etienne, the *nom-de-livre* of another undercover officer, writes about his discussions with a woman he names as Jean. It is almost a textbook description of how not to go about finding a contract killer. It seems Jean had used a regular minicab driver for her weekly girls' night out, and in what was described as a mildly flirtatious

[10] *The Guardian*, 18 July 1994; *Reg v Dixon (Paul)*, *Mann (Harbel)*; *The Times*, 31 December 1994.
[11] R. Fleming and H. Miller, *Scotland Yard*, p. 122.
[12] *The Times*, 31 December 1994.

conversation he asked her how things were at home. She replied that things were bad, adding, 'Honestly, if I knew I could get away with it, I'd kill him myself.' The sort of remark any dissatisfied wife might make after a few too many glasses of Babycham. However, the minicab driver's ears pricked up and he arrived at her home uninvited two days later to take matters a stage further. She apparently was in poor humour with her husband and said that if he got what was coming to him it would be better than winning the lottery. The minicab driver was a police informer and Etienne was called in and wired up.

Etienne behaved in very much the way 'John' described. He did not encourage her but he wanted to know, '. . . whether I was wasting my time or not, whether her husband was genuinely in danger'. In the end she never kept a second appointment.[13]

Commonplace has been the contract for money. The higher the insurance, the more the potential victim is at risk. On the morning of 8 February 1995 the corpse of Barry Trigwell, a private investigator, was found in his three-bedroomed rented house in Fowey Close, Walmley, Sutton Coldfield, a well-to-do Birmingham suburb. His severely beaten body wearing only trousers was in a half-filled bath; he had been attacked with a blunt object and had sustained severe fractures to his skull and face. It appeared that he had been killed after returning home from an Indian restaurant sometime after 7 p.m. on the previous evening. His body was found by a colleague who came the next morning to drive him to work – Trigwell was disqualified from driving.

Trigwell had bought a Nationwide Investigations franchise and, based in Birmingham, worked with two other detectives. Unusually, he was not listed in the professional directories and was thought to have carried out much of his work in Hong Kong and the Middle East. Known as Barry the Bastard by his colleagues, who regarded the short stocky man as fearless, he particularly enjoyed snatching children back from abroad. As a result he had made many enemies. One of his former colleagues believed that at the time of his death he might have been investigating money laundering.

---

[13] Philip Etienne and Martin Maynard, *The Infiltrators*, Chapter 6.

On 26 February 1995, when an article in the *Sunday Times* reported that a gang of South African mercenaries was operating in the contract killing market at a price of £20,000 a hit, it was suggested that Trigwell's killing might have been one of their efforts.[14]

In fact the contractor, something she denied throughout her trial, was Trigwell's wife, Ethel Anne. In July 1996 the Birmingham Crown Court was told how she had stood to gain in the region of £380,000 in the event of her husband's death. According to the prosecution, she had discussed the possibility of the death of her husband with a Johannesburg nightclub owner, offering him £15,000 to set up the contract when she visited the country in January 1995. Two men were subsequently recruited and flew to England. The prosecution claimed that she supplied them with a key to her husband's house and £300 in expenses which she left at the Clover Hotel in Sutton Coldfield where they were staying. The receptionist was suspicious that the package might contain drugs and had it opened, found it to be innocent and resealed it. It was only when the news of Trigwell's death became known that she recalled the woman, whom she identified as Mrs Trigwell, as having left the packet. Mrs Trigwell had an alibi for the killing; she was back in South Africa, where she dined with her lover on the night of her husband's death. She was arrested when she returned to England to attend the inquest. On 25 July 1996 she was sentenced to life imprisonment for what the trial judge called a 'cold, calculated and chilling' murder. Earlier, Mrs Trigwell's son by a previous marriage had died with gunshot wounds to the head. He had inherited a substantial sum of money shortly before his death; he and his father died within a short time of each other.

The article in the *Sunday Times* had been substantially correct and the chapter was closed when on 25 July 2003 Paul Ras and Loren Sundkvist, both South African criminals, were jailed for life after being convicted of being the hitmen. They were the first men to be extradited from South Africa to England to face murder charges. The book, however, remains open. The nightclub owner has not been arrested and former model Linda Smith, a principal

[14] *Sunday Times*, 26 February 1995.

witness against Mrs Trigwell, died in a mysterious car crash in Durban in 1999. A detective who went to arrest Ras and Sundkvist also died in another car accident in South Africa.[15]

Some of the potential benefits seem paltry compared with the risk involved. In 1997 in Texas, Bruce and Michelle Gilmore took out a $12,000 contract on their friend Jeanette Williams whom they had insured for $25,000. They both received life imprisonment and the killer Richard Williams, who was no relation of the victim, was executed at Huntsville on 25 February 2003.

Often the killers themselves have little time for such clients. One East Coast hitman believes:

> We've had square people come to us with plots to kill family members for insurance or to sell the family owned business. People are sick. I would say twenty dimes (twenty thousand dollars) to fifty dimes is the going rate. Up to one hundred dimes, nowadays with drugs. People's morals are low.[16]

Nor should the contractor shop around to find the best price. In one case cited by Jenny Mouzos and John Venditto in their study *Contract Killings in Australia*, the hitman contacted the potential victims because he learned that the contractor was asking around, trying to find a cheaper killer. In turn the victims contacted the police.[17]

Insulation is the keyword in a Mob or any other professional killing, and it should be a rule for domestic contracts as well. The contractor will go to a gangster who will find an intermediary who in turn will find the actual killer – the whole exercise providing a series of cut-outs. A classic example is the killing of Mob leader Albert Anastasia – shot in a barber's chair in 1957 in the Sheraton Regis – which followed the rules he had designed twenty-five years earlier for his Murder Inc. The contract, which was executed on 25 October, was ordered by Vito Genovese who gave instructions to Carlo Gambino. In turn he passed it to Joe Profaci who gave it to the three Gallo brothers. It is thought the actual killing was carried

---

[15] *Sunday Mercury* (Birmingham), 27 July 2003.
[16] Letter to author.
[17] Case no. 1065/99.

out by the Squillante brothers who told Anastasia's bodyguard, 'Tough' Tony Coppola, of the oncoming local difficulties. Coppola took a short stroll. As for the killing itself, the story has it that after the first volley of bullets Anastasia jumped from his chair and tried to reach his killers with his bare hands. In fact he was attacking their reflections in the mirror. Although there were no charges the killing may also be an example of a case where, for security purposes, far too many people were involved.

Charles Kray is a good example of a man who provided insulation. After his release from prison following the trials in 1969, he lived an interesting existence until his conviction for drug dealing. He is represented by the underworld as someone who was not really of their world, but this is far from the case. Because of his name he was used as a greeter in a Bishopsgate restaurant, and there were also plans to use him in a similar position on the Costa Blanca. Like so many other top men, he had the ability to live a life of some ease without the need for bank accounts, social security numbers and the like. Nipper Read thought, 'In fact, he didn't need to use violence. The mere use of his name coupled with his brothers' reputations was sufficient to enforce his demands.'[18] He was also regarded as a fixer and, from time to time, a go-between for a beating or on occasion a contract killing. Again it was unlikely that an arrested hitman would readily give up a man with such powerful connections.

One hit which he was said to have brokered was the killing of Barbara Gaul, the estranged wife of the Maltese-born sinister property dealer John Gaul, a man whose career shows how close what is called polite society may become to the underworld. Gaul had two wartime convictions – for falsifying his age in relation to call-up papers, and for obtaining petrol without surrendering coupons. On 11 October 1962 he was fined £25,000 for living off prostitution, and he was also named in both the Profumo and Lambton scandals as a top person's procurer. For much of his career he was represented by the highly influential if dubious solicitor Arnold Goodman, who was a mortgagee of a Gaul-owned property in Soho.[19]

---

[18] Leonard Read, *Nipper Read, The Man Who Nicked The Krays*, p. 297.
[19] *Private Eye*, 2 February 1978.

Barbara Gaul was shot outside the Black Lion public house in Patcham near Brighton on 12 January 1977, when she had been visiting her daughter Samantha; she died eleven weeks later. Gaul was taken in for questioning and explained his position. His wife had agreed to an undefended divorce claiming neither maintenance nor costs. She had already relinquished her claim to her daughter. What reason was there for him to have her killed? He was almost immediately released and promptly flew to Rio de Janeiro.

It was not really a difficult matter to trace the actual killers because the shotgun used was dropped from the car during the getaway. The contract had been arranged through Kray with two East End brothers, Keith and Roy Edgeler. At his trial, very sensibly Roy Edgeler had little to say on the handling of the matter except that from his limited knowledge he did not think Gaul was the contractor.

On 24 April 1978 a blast destroyed a minicab office and flats in Hackney Road owned by Printing House Properties, a £100 Gaul company. A Maltese, John Borg, who had been involved in West End properties, died. In 1953 Borg had been gaoled for ten years after gunning down another Maltese outside a Stepney café that year. Suggestions made in a statement by a Carlos Amazonas indicated that Borg had been approached to kill Barbara Gaul. He was thought to have been in the block at the time of the fire, and his body was found in the wreckage on 3 May, but tellingly there was no smoke in his lungs.

By 1981 Gaul was safe in Malta. The official explanation is that insufficient evidence against him had been supplied. Now he built and leased out a 240-room hotel. In March that year he was reported to have had a serious heart attack, and on 17 July a magistrate said the prosecution case was weak and refused to order extradition.

In April 1984 it was reported that the police had given up. Even if Gaul came back, the passage of time had made witnesses' memories unreliable. He was also said to be seriously ill. The warrant was dropped and Gaul at once flew to Switzerland before returning to England for his son's wedding in the September. He died in September 1989 in Italy; he had been posted missing, and it was three days before it was realised he had died in a Milan hospital.

Shortly after Gaul's death, Keith Edgeler gave an interview from Ford open prison. The contract had indeed been on Gaul's behalf; the millionaire had feared Barbara was going to blow the whistle on his dealings. Nor had Edgeler received his promised payment; he had not spoken before because of fears for his family.[20]

In early 2001 Kray was linked to the murder of the businessman Donald Urquhart, shot in Marylebone High Street on 2 January 1993 allegedly on the instructions of a solicitor. The hitman, Graeme West, received life imprisonment but the contractor has never been charged. When two men were arrested in London and released after questioning, the police said that Kray might have been an adviser after the murder. At one time it was thought that Urquhart had been killed over an international gun-running and drug-smuggling operation, but it is much more likely that it was over a business deal which had soured. After his death, a will was found which left his property to his lawyer and business associate Jonathan Levene, the solicitor son of a prominent barrister. Levene then went to Switzerland.[21]

On his deathbed Kray is said to have asked for the killing of the drug dealer and probable informer Peter Beaumont Gowling, shot in the afternoon of St Valentine's Day 2001 at his home in Osborne Road, Jesmond, Tyneside. His body was discovered later that evening when his girlfriend returned home.

Until that day Gowling was rightly described as a larger-than-life character. Undoubtedly a talented businessman with prodigious appetites, he was reputed to have enjoyed the services of thirteen prostitutes in one evening and to have drunk a London hotel out of champagne. Gowling had been caught taking money to Ireland and was convicted of laundering. Kray in turn was convicted in 1997 in what he regarded as a sting and, dying in prison, asked for contracts to be taken out on both Gowling – whom he regarded as responsible for his misfortune – and the undercover police officers involved. No one has been charged with the Gowling murder.[22]

---

[20] *The Sun*, 19 June 1978, 31 October 1989.
[21] For an account of the case see James Morton, *Gangland Today*.
[22] *Express on Sunday*, 25 February 2001.

At a professional level perhaps the most dangerous situation of all is when the contract killer operates with the licence, and sometimes encouragement, of the authorities. This was a widespread practice amongst FBI officers from the late 1950s to the 1990s. Eleven informants were known to have killed a total of over fifty people. One of them, Gregory Scarpa senior, while working as an FBI informant, was engaged in an all-out war for control of the Colombo crime Family. He may have killed up to thirteen rivals before his own death after he contracted AIDS from a blood transfusion.

Joseph O'Brien, a former FBI informant co-ordinator in New York City, commented: 'The Bureau has to encourage these guys to be themselves and do what they do. If they stop just because they are working with the FBI, somebody's going to question them.'

Another former agent had a pragmatic attitude. Speaking of the killing by an FBI informant of a small-time Chicago gangster, M. Wesley Swearigen thought, 'The information that the FBI was getting was more important. Somebody in the Mob is going to kill that person anyway.'[23]

Apart from Scarpa, the best known of the FBI killer-informers have been Stephen 'The Rifleman' Flemmi and James 'Whitey' Bulger in South Boston, working under the direction of FBI agent John Connolly. After the destruction of Howie Winter's Winter Hill Mob with indictments in February 1979, their interests were taken over by Flemmi and Bulger. Flemmi, an Italian-born former paratrooper in Korea, who had preferred the relative independence of the Winter Hill Gang rather than the more structured format of the Mafia, had nevertheless worked closely with the Family's Larry Zannino. What was not realised was that he had been a fully paid-up FBI informant for years. Flemmi, who operated out of the Marconi Club described as 'a combination bookie joint, massage parlour and brothel', had been recruited in the mid-1960s and had worked under FBI agent Paul Rico.

James Bulger, known as Whitey from his yellow hair, had grown up in the Irish immigrant quarter of South Boston ('Southie'), where

---

[23] 'Uncovering FBI informant underworld' in *Washington Post*, 16 March 2003; Dick Lehy and Gerard O'Neill, *Black Mass*.

he had been friendly with John Connolly who went on to carve out a career in the FBI. Bulger's brother, William, ran for public office in 1960 when Connolly was one of his campaign workers. Qualified as a lawyer, Bill Bulger maintained a small practice and moved up from the House of Representatives to the Senate in 1970.

As with many a good *film noir*, his brother took an opposite path. At the age of 27 in 1956, he was doing nine years for bank robbery in a chain of Federal prisons from Alcatraz to Leavenworth and then home via Lewisburg.

After the compulsory retirement of Howard Winter, from then it was onwards and upwards for Flemmi and Whitey Bulger along with their friends and helpers. And all the time, it turned out, as they robbed and murdered they were protected by Connolly and another FBI agent John Morris.

In the late 1990s the whole situation unravelled with Flemmi charged with a series of murders including that of a long-time girl-friend, and Whitey Bulger, also charged with murders, on the run. Flemmi finally arranged a plea bargain under which he was spared the death penalty. Former agent John Connolly, indicted on charges of obstructing the course of justice, bribery and associating with Bulger's Winter Hill Gang, was sentenced to ten years.

Meanwhile, definitely at the bottom end of the scale of potential hirers is the 17-year-old computer whizz-kid 'with the social skills of a twelve-year-old' who offered Gary Johnson, the under-cover agent working with the Houston police, $5.30 plus two Atari tapes to kill a school rival. The boy counted out a number of nickels and dimes to pay for the killing and advised Johnson that now he would not need change for the road tolls.[24] Also at the lower end of hitmen comes a 16-year-old hired by Canadian housewife Isabelle Berthiaume for $1,000 to kill her ex-husband. The boy, seeing a potential target, began to blackmail her for more money. She confessed, blaming her aberrant behaviour on the drug Paxil, and received a suspended sentence. The husband was unharmed.[25]

[24] 'The Hit Man is shooting for arrests' in *The National Law Journal*, 18 October 1993.
[25] *Montreal Mirror Archives*, 23 December 2003–7 January 2004.

3

Weapons of Choice

In the good old days when forensic techniques were much less sophisticated and those who carried out autopsies were less careful, the ice-pick was a long-time favourite weapon in Mob killings. For example, the victim would be taken to a lavatory and, while two or three men held him still, the killer would pierce the brain through the eardrum. The pick produced only a tiny hole in the ear and little bleeding at the point of entry, which would be wiped clean. There would, however, be massive bleeding in the brain. A doctor would generally attribute the death to a cerebral haemorrhage. Perhaps the greatest exponent of the technique was Harry 'Pittsburgh Phil' Strauss of Brooklyn's Murder Inc., whom some suggest may have killed up to five hundred people – not all, of course, with the pick.

At the beginning of the film *The Godfather*, and again at the end, characters are killed by use of the garrotte, another one-time weapon of choice which has to an extent gone out of fashion. It was, however, used in the 1999 contract killing of a young Colombian boy foolish enough to snatch a £500 gold chain from the neck of Juan Carlos Fernandez. The killing arose out of a quarrel in El Barco Latino, a bar near Temple underground station in London. Fernandez had been there with his girlfriend, Luisa Bolivar, a one-time cleaner who, in a staggeringly short five years, had worked her way to being effectively the London head of a Colombian cartel. With a lifestyle which required £75,000 to run her flat, now she was known as La Padrona.

In the bar was a young boy, 16-year-old George Castillo known as 'Little Egg'. There were suggestions that Fernandez had behaved improperly towards a friend of Castillo, and in the ensuing macho-fuelled quarrel the boy snatched the gold chain from the neck of Fernandez and made off.

Bolivar then hired Hector Cedano and Hernando Guevara-Jarmailo – known as The Skunk because of a blonde streak in the middle of his otherwise shaven head – both of them at the time asylum seekers, to abduct and kill Castillo. The boy was lured in the front of a car and Cedano, wearing white gloves, tightened a ligature around his neck. As the boy was dying Cedano rang Bolivar on a mobile telephone to ask whether she wanted to hear him die. Castillo's body was then dumped in a waste bin in a children's playground in South London. Her half-brother, Diego Bolivar, was sent to pay off the killers and in turn went to the police. On 16 February 2000 all three received life imprisonment. Hernando had fled to Spain.

Induced drug overdoses are now a common method of contract killing. One celebrated death in Glasgow, believed by the underworld to be drug-induced – despite an inquest verdict of suicide – is that in 1999 of Gerald Rae, a drug dealer and housebreaker who was the main witness in a police perjury trial. He was found in his L registration white Vauxhall in Drysdale Street, Yoker, on 15 October when the seven accused officers were still on trial in Edinburgh. It was thought he had died of a self-induced overdose even though he was not a known injector. When his body was found he was clutching 'tenner deals' of heroin. Three rocks of diamorphine were also found. All the officers were acquitted.[1]

Quite how the word buckwheats came to mean a spite killing, and a gratuitously nasty and painful death, is unclear but in both fact and fiction buckwheating is particularly feared by offending villains. One of the earlier victims of buckwheats was Steve Franse

---

[1] For an account of Rae's civil claim against the Strathclyde police and the subsequent criminal trial see James Morton, *Gangland Today*.

who fell foul of the fearsome New York don, Vito Genovese. At one time Franse had been a trusted Genovese lieutenant, but when the Mob leader had to flee to Italy to avoid a murder charge Franse was left to look after both Genovese's money and his wife. He did not do a sufficiently good job in his latter role, for she strayed and Genovese ordered Franse to be killed 'buckwheats'. According to the Mafia turncoat Joe Valachi, two hitmen attacked him in a kitchen restaurant. One held him while the other punched him in the stomach and face. When Franse collapsed a chain was wrapped around his throat and he was strangled, but not before one of the men had stamped on his throat to stop him struggling.

The Chicago-based 300 lb Willie 'Action' Jackson was another to suffer buckwheats. For many years he had led a treble and charmed life as loan shark, knock-down artist and, most dangerously, informer. Then his luck ran out. He was taken by Fiore 'Fifi' Buccieri and Jacky 'The Lackey' Cerone to a meat-rendering plant where he was tied up and hung from a meat-hook. He was shot and stabbed as well as being worked over with baseball bats, and an electric cattle prod was inserted in his rectum. The details of his killing emerged on a wiretap run by the FBI which later recorded his killers laughing and reminiscing about his death. One complaint they had against him was that he had not lived longer.[2]

Another mobster who suffered a singularly painful death was Albert Agueci, a one-time soldier in the Magaddino Family in Buffalo. His crime was to complain when he and his brother, Vito, were arrested in a drugs case, and he let it be known that if money for bail was unforthcoming he would turn informer. It was an unwise move. No money was produced and their release came only when the family house was sold. Agueci then began making threats against Stephen Magaddino. As a result he was kidnapped and taken to a farm near Rochester, New York. On 23 November 1961 his corpse was found in a field. His arms had been tied behind his back and he had been strangled with a clothesline before his body

[2] Buccieri died of cancer in 1973. Cerone later took over the Chicago Mob. On 28 May 1986 he was sentenced to twenty-eight-and-a-half years after being found guilty on an eight-count conspiracy indictment. See Joseph Valachi, *The Valachi Papers*; Carl Sifakis, *The Mafia File*.

was set alight. His teeth had been kicked out and identification was possible only through a single unburned finger. While alive some thirty pounds of flesh had been stripped from his body.

Failure to carry out a mission cleanly could also result in buck-wheats as Sal Moretti, one-time driver for Chicago boss Sam Giancana, discovered on 4 October 1951. Moretti had successfully killed businessman Leon Marcus on Giancana's behalf, but unfortunately he had left behind a document which linked Giancana to Marcus in a secret hotel deal. Moretti died hard. He was tortured before being shot and left in a dry-cleaning bag in the boot of an abandoned car.

One man who specialised in the buckwheat killing was Sam De Stefano, who built a soundproof torture chamber in his basement. Known as Mad Sam, he was perhaps the most violent of all Chicago loan sharks over the years. De Stefano grew up in Little Italy and served three years for rape and another eleven in Wisconsin for bank robbery before becoming a loyal servant of Sam Giancana, graduating from the West Side 42 Gang. Ordered to kill his own drug-dealing brother Michael in 1955, he did so without hesitation and indeed with a great deal of enthusiasm. During the torture killing of a Mob associate Leo Foreman, he ordered the underlings to shoot him in non-vital parts first. After Foreman's death chunks of flesh were torn from his arms. It was this killing which brought about De Stefano's downfall. Charles Grimaldi, who had been one of the soldiers working on Foreman, turned informant and on 22 February 1972 De Stefano attacked him in the court building. For this he received three and a half years.

On 14 April 1973 he was shot to death in his garage. Already on bail pending an appeal against his conviction, he had been due to stand trial along with Tony Spilotro, one of his earlier apprentices, for the murder of a client who had defaulted on his loan.[3]

It is not all that often that women are singled out for killing by the Mob, and when they are it is rare for a contract to include buckwheats. However, an exception was made in the case of the

---

[3] Another De Stefano brother, Mario Anthony, was also a party to the killing of Mike De Stefano. Mario De Stefano was found guilty of his part in the Foreman killing and received forty years. His conviction was quashed on appeal, but on 12 August 1975 following a heart attack he died before a second trial.

girlfriend of Nick Circella whom it was feared might turn informer in a deal to secure his early release from an eight-year sentence. To show him the folly of such behaviour his girlfriend, croupier Estelle Carey, was murdered in 1941.

Estelle Carey was what was known as a twenty-six girl. Twenty-six was a game in which punters threw dice on a board three feet square. If they showed twenty-six then the house paid three to one. In theory the prize was a voucher for drinks, but in reality there was serious betting. Carey, used to attract players to the game, was also expected to work as a prostitute for favoured customers. The chronicler of the Chicago Mob, William Roemer, says her fees would run between $50 and $500 depending on how busy the establishment was that night.

She was tied to a chair in her flat near the lake on Chicago's North Side, tortured, her nose broken, stabbed and her throat cut before being set alight after having petrol poured over her; the fire destroyed her legs to her knees. The only witness was her poodle, later found cowering in a corner. The killers were allegedly led by the feared Marshall Caifano acting on the orders of the then Chicago boss Tony Accardo. It had also been hoped that Carey would reveal where Circella had hidden his share of extortion money extracted from Hollywood union officials.[4]

Another woman who possibly died at the hands of a *mafioso* was the first wife of 'Trigger Mike' Coppola. She died in hospital after giving birth to a baby daughter, but Coppola would later brag that he had killed her. The first Mrs Coppola had been due to give evidence against her husband regarding the murder of a political worker Joseph Scottoriggio.[5]

Ann, the second Mrs Coppola, did not fare too well either. She was shot at by her husband during a party. When she petitioned for divorce he had her beaten up and dumped on a beach, but she was still prepared to give evidence against him. She managed to

---

[4] For a full account of Circella and Carey's murder see William Roemer, *Accardo*, pp. 94–7. For an account of the extortion of Hollywood union officials by Willie Bioff as well as an account of the career of the feared killer Marshall Caifano, see James Morton, *Gangland International*, Chapter 5.

[5] Hank Messick, *Syndicate Wife*.

steal some $250,000 of Mafia money from him and skipped to Europe where in 1962 she committed suicide in Rome. Coppola, now in disgrace with the Mob, died four years later.

Yet another unfortunate wife was that of Philip 'Rusty' Rastelli, the temporary boss of the Bonanno Family while Carmine Galante was in prison. He ordered her death when he feared she was talking to the Feds about his drug dealing. In fairness theirs had been a stormy relationship. While Connie Rastelli had in most ways been a great help, keeping his books and driving getaway cars, she objected to his playing away from home. Finding out about a new love, she shot him twice on a Brooklyn street. After that they separated, but she continued to talk with the authorities. In turn she was shot before she could give evidence against him. He is reputed to have said of her death, 'Hey, you play you gotta pay.'[6]

The one-way ride was not exactly a weapon but the term was coined in Chicago during the Prohibition wars. The credit goes to Dion O'Banion's second in command, the fearsome Earl Wajciechowski, known for convenience as Earl Weiss. The first recipient, in July 1921, was Steve Wisniewski who had hijacked an O'Banion beer truck. He was lured into a car and his body was found near Libertyville, some twenty-five miles out of central Chicago.[7]

So what does the modern up-to-date hitman carry? Long gone are the days when for much of his career Pittsburgh Phil Strauss more or less contented himself with a single ice-pick and made do with a handy jukebox with which to try to weigh down his victim. When one man was arrested in 2003 at his riverside flat in Woolwich, South-East London, he was found to have a 9mm Browning pistol with a laser sight which he called 'my special thing', a silencer, a stun-gun, two holsters and twenty-four rounds of ammunition. He was said to wear body armour even in bed. He was something of a fanatic. Some years earlier when he had been arrested for another offence the police found thirty pairs of training shoes lined up with the same distance between each pair.

---

[6] Donald Frankos, *Contract Killer*, p. 188.
[7] Robert Schoenberg, *Mr Capone*, p. 70, credits Terry Druggan and Frankie Lake for the killing of Wisniewski and the coining of the phrase, but Weiss, along with helpmates George 'Bugsy' Moran and Sam 'Nails' Morton, is more usually cited.

Max, the contract killer interviewed by Tony Thompson, was quite snobbish about some of his colleagues whom he saw as amateurs:

> I know a lot of people go for these automatics nowadays, but the trouble is they leave shell cases all over the place. Too much forensic.
>
> You get a nice thirty-eight revolver, snub-nosed, it's very small, very compact, very powerful. It'll rip through people. You get some nice nickel- and lead-tipped bullets, white plastic-nosed ones or hollow-point . . . you don't want full metal jacket – they leave nice clean holes – you want to do as much damage as possible.[8]

And where does the hitman obtain his equipment? Increasingly from gangland armourers. Over a period of years during which they worked without hindrance from the authorities, father and son William and Mitchell Greenwood flooded Britain with thousands of deactivated weapons together with kits and instructions on how they could be reactivated. Working from their converted farm building in Little Eaton, they sold supposedly safe AK-47 rifles, Uzi sub-machine guns and pistols along with Browning pistols and the Mac-10s favoured by drug gangs. They had operated quite openly – advertising in trade journals as Regional Instauration Firearms, Little Eaton (RIFLE) – for the better part of ten years. As long ago as 1995 a reporter from the television programme the Cook Report posed as a customer and was filmed being given advice by them. Then in 1998 and 1999 an undercover detective was offered a variety of machine guns and pistols and told how to reactivate them. The shop was raided in 1999 after a police officer paid over £2,000 cash for twenty-two French MAB handguns, tools and ammunition. Altogether 700 weapons were seized. Another 3,000 are thought to be in circulation.

Some of the Greenwood weapons were passed on and used in murders and woundings in Dublin, Manchester and Glasgow as well as London. The Greenwoods had been ordered to dispose of their stock when they received suspended sentences for possessing illegal weapons in 1994. This time they each received seven years.[9]

---

[8] Tony Thompson, *Britain's Gangland*, p. 15.
[9] *The Times*, 27 January 2004; *The Guardian*, 9 March 2004; *Sunday Mail* (Glasgow), 14 March 2004.

One client Anthony Mitchell, a former special constable from Brighton who in April 1999 was jailed for eight years, bought 400 guns including Ingram Mac-10 sub-machine guns capable of firing 1,100 rounds a minute. He then converted them and others he bought, and in 1999 the going rate for an illegal Mac-10 with silencer was £1,100.

Mitchell came to police notice long before he was finally arrested. In 1993 he was stopped at Gatwick by Customs officers and found to have more than his permitted allocation of ammunition. As a result he was required to resign from the special constabulary. However, this did not stop him entering military and police shooting contests abroad as part of a team, Black Shod.

His undoing came about when a Glasgow gangster Joe McAuley became drunk in the buffet car of the London-to-Glasgow train. By the time Preston was reached he was frightening the other passengers and the police boarded the train. He was found to have a Czech-made Ceska pistol, silencer and ammunition. One of his associates was the Glasgow gangster, Paul Ferris, and it was learned that he was travelling to London to buy guns from John Ackerman whom Mitchell used as part of his distribution chain. In May 1997 Ackerman was arrested and he gave up Mitchell. In October 1997 after being released on bail he was rearrested as he was loading up his car with clothing and passports. Ackerman received six years, McAuley four, and Ferris ten which on appeal was reduced to seven. One of his weapons was used when Devon Dawson, a Jamaican on a six-month visa, was shot ten times in April 1997 outside the Green Man in Coldharbour Lane, Brixton.[10]

More recently, Londoners Stephen Herbert and Gary Beard admitted selling 574 guns. They had been bulk buying £40 replica Walther PPK handguns and converting them at Beard's flat, selling them on at a rate of one a day for around £600 each. At the time of their trial some 500 guns had still to be recovered. The pair were jailed for six years and seemed pleased with the result: 'That's lovely. Six years. Thanks very much – we got away with it,' said Herbert to Judge David Paget QC.[11]

---

[10] Peter Walsh, 'Lock, stock and barrel' in *The Guardian*, 9 September 1999.
[11] *Daily Mail*, 11 September 2004. On 27 April 2005 each had his sentence increased to nine years.

A more unusual form of killing was putting broken glass in a victim's drink. Some believe that the old Glaswegian hardman, Danny Cronin, died this way at the end of the 1940s. However, it is by no means a guaranteed way of disposing of a victim. Frank Fraser recalled, 'Once when I was in Manchester when I was doing it as a contract, the man must have had a cast-iron stomach; never so much as a murmur.'[12]

Obviously, some form of transport is essential for the contract killer. Mostly the cars used are stolen, and in recent years at least there has been a tendency for them to be dumped and set alight in an endeavour to destroy any forensic evidence. For a time 'Milwaukee Phil' Alderisio, who operated as a contract killer in the 1960s, had a car of which James Bond would have approved. On 2 May 1960 a Ford sedan was discovered in front of 1750 Superior Street, Chicago. In it were Alderisio and his fellow hitman Charles Nicolletti. When the car was searched the police found that under the dashboard were three switches; two of these enabled the driver to disconnect the tail-lights, and the third switch opened a hidden compartment in the back rest of the front seat fitted with brackets to hold shotguns, rifles and a machine gun. It was also possible to revolve the number plates. Alderisio and Nicolletti were released without charge, but the car was confiscated by the police.

There are many who claim to have invented the motorcycle hit team. It is suggested that a North London family are its progenitors, and they may have been so far as Britain is concerned, but it is the Colombians and the Mexican Griselda Trujillo-Blanco who can really claim the dubious honour. Since the first of these contracts in England there has been a steady stream beginning with Donald Urquhart, shot in Marylebone in 1993. In June that year came the killing of Tommy Roche, a one-time loose associate of the Krays, who was shot while he worked on the M4 at West Drayton. The legendary 'Mad' Frank Fraser was questioned about both killings but claimed he was far too old to ride on the back of a motorcycle – something of a prerequisite, as Fenton Bresler suggested. Killing with the shootist riding on the pillion seat is not common in

[12] Frank Fraser, *Mad Frank's Britain*, pp. 211–12.

Scotland, where motorcycles are rather the exception and so attract unwanted attention.

There were a variety of reasons why the Thompson Machine Gun – or Chicago Piano or typewriter or chopper, as it was variously known – was the weapon of choice in Chicago in the 1920s and 30s. First, Brigadier General John T. Thompson's weapon could fire 1,500 rounds a minute; second, it weighed less than nine pounds and was easy to handle and, almost as importantly, early in its career it was not a prohibited weapon. The 1911 Sullivan Act in New York State prohibited the carrying of easily concealed weapons and many other states enacted similar legislation. At first, the 'Tommy Gun' was an unrestricted weapon and could be obtained by mail order. The earliest recorded case of its use is by the bespectacled Frank McErlane on 25 September 1925 to spray a storefront at 63rd and Western Avenue where he correctly suspected his rival Edward 'Spike' O'Donnell might be found.[13] O'Donnell wasn't hit, but he was so terrified that he moved out of the bootlegging industry forthwith. Its effectiveness proved, the machine gun was adopted enthusiastically by the other combatants.

The drive-by shootings now favoured by gangs such as the Crips and Bloods and their affiliates have their origins in the heyday of the Mob. Genuinely innocent bystanders were far safer before the arrival of the motor car and machine gun. Now being in the wrong place at the wrong time has become something of a daily hazard. Again it is unclear exactly who originated what were described then as motor-cade murders. It is possible that the credit should go to the Chicago gangsters Earl Weiss or Bugs Moran, perhaps the latter. Certainly he made good use of them; he and his colleagues, armed with their Thompson machine guns, would drive past the potential victims' homes and spray a thousand or more bullets. Al Capone survived one such attack at the Hawthorne Inn in Cicero which had been specifically converted with bulletproof steel shutters at the windows as a counter measure. On 26 September 1926 Capone and Frank Rio, his bodyguard, were dining at the inn when, as a car drove past, the occupants opened fire. When the shooting stopped, Capone and

---

[13] *Chicago Tribune*, 26 September 1925.

Rio went to see what had happened. The attack had been a diversion with the shooters using blanks. Almost immediately a convoy of up to ten cars drove by, the gunmen in them tearing the restaurant and its lobby apart. One Capone man, Louis Barko, was shot in the shoulder but only he and one diner, a Mrs Clyde Freeman, were seriously hurt. She was sitting with her husband in a car which was riddled in the attack and was hit by a shard of glass which caused partial blindness. Another bullet grazed the knee of her son sitting in her lap. Mr Freeman's hat and their car were ruined. Legend, if not fact, has it that Capone paid her medical bills.[14]

Popular though they may be on the West Coast of America, drive-by shootings have generally not been favoured by contract killers in Russia. For a start, *mafiya* members and legitimate businessmen alike have tended to be heavily protected. By the middle of the 1990s over 800,000 people were employed in the private security industry. Over the years these people have had legal access to automatic and light support weapons, grenade launchers and armoured personnel carriers. As a result more precise methods, such as the use of a professional sniper, have been employed. Il'ya Mitkov, a merchant banker, was the target of one such operation; he was shot through the shoulder, so avoiding the banker's body armour. There have also been more unusual deaths. In 1995 Ivan Kivelidi, the chairman of Rosbiznesbank, died after a deadly nerve powder was sprinkled in his office.

During the Kray trial in 1969 there was an allegation that the London club owner George Caruana was marked for a most curious death. He had fallen out with the Mifsud-Silver syndicate who approached the Twins to help with his disposal. The planned method of execution was bizarre. A Paul Elvey was to inject him with cyanide by means of a poisoned syringe sewn into a suitcase: by pulling a small ring near the handle the contents of the syringe could be discharged. The case had been made by ex-speedway rider Francis 'Split' Waterman, and both he and the investigating officer Nipper Read thought it was a 'beautiful piece of craftsmanship'. The venue was to be the waiting area at the Old Bailey in the days when

---

[14] F.D. Pasley, *Al Capone*. The editions of the papers of the time which I have read do not record Capone's act of generosity.

security was non-existent. Elvey also told Read of a crossbow he had been given for practice, but nothing had ever come of that. Elvey produced both the bow and the suitcase which he had been keeping in his garage. At the committal proceedings the charge was dismissed by the stipendiary magistrate who found the whole idea too fanciful.[15]

Not all that fanciful. At about 6 pm. on 7 September 1979, the Bulgarian refugee journalist Georgi Markov was stabbed in the right thigh with the point of an umbrella as he walked along the Strand. The man with the umbrella, who seemed to have merely been passing, apologised and then hailed a cab. By the evening Markov's leg had stiffened and he felt feverish. He was taken to hospital and died there four days later. The post-mortem showed that a minuscule hollowed-out pellet containing ricin was lodged in his thigh. A year earlier there had been a similar attack in Paris when on 24 August Vladimir Kostov was shot with a poisonous pellet, but this time there was not sufficient poison to do more than cause a stinging sensation. These were undoubtedly political attacks, but it is an example of how far ahead of the real world the underworld may sometimes be.

A definite crossbow killing was that of Camden Town sauna owner Patricia Parsons. On 23 June 1990 the strikingly attractive 42-year-old was due to go to help at the restaurant owned by her Turkish boyfriend in Harlow. She never arrived and the next day her body was found in her Volkswagen Cabriolet in Epping Forest. At first it was thought she had been shot with a speargun, but it turned out that the weapon was a crossbow. Her black book, believed to contain over two hundred names including at least one judge as well as barristers and television personalities, was never found. She was thought to have been made to drive from her home to Epping where she was shot. The reason for her death is said to have been that she was about to tell her story to a Sunday paper. The name of former Richardson associate James Moody has often been mentioned as her killer, but there is no hard evidence to support that theory.[16]

---

[15] For an account of the investigation see Leonard Read, *Nipper Read, The Man Who Nicked The Krays*, p. 176.
[16] For an account of this and other killings attributed rightly or wrongly to Moody, who was himself killed in the East End, see James Morton, *Gangland*.

4

Where Have all the Bodies Gone?

One problem for the contract killer is the disposal of the body, and that process itself divides into several categories. In the case of the gang feud it may be thoroughly desirable to leave the body in a place where it will be found to serve as a warning. A good example is that of the San Diego hitman, Frank 'The Bomp' Bompensiero, one-time claimant for the mantle of Nick Licata as head of the Californian Mafia. Bompensiero was shot and killed with a .22 calibre weapon outside a telephone kiosk in his hometown on 10 February 1977. As well as extorting money from gamblers, bookmakers and pornographers – including $7,500 from undercover FBI agents posing as pornographers who had set up a sting operation in Van Nuys – Bompensiero had passed the word around and paid for his double life. He had been turned by the FBI some ten years earlier and by his body were three dime coins, a traditional sign that it was known the man had been grassing his colleagues.

Five years later a body left on public view was that of Robert Calvi, the so-called God's banker who fell foul of the Italian Mafia. On 17 June 1982 he was found hanging from Blackfriars Bridge in London, a death said to symbolise the retribution of a masonic lodge. Along with Licio Gelli, another member of the closed masonic lodge P2, he had been embezzling from the Mafia to keep his bank afloat. According to a *pentito*, Mannino Mannoia, he was killed on the orders of one of the Mafia's bankers, Pippo 'The Cashier' Calo, after Calvi had been forced into repaying a substantial amount of lost Mafia money from his own pocket.

As for Calvi, he was ruled to have committed suicide. Later, investigators found witnesses who said that he had been taken from his London flat by two large men on the night of his death. The investigations were paid for by his widow who, apart from the interest in finding out exactly how her husband died, stood to benefit from a $10 million insurance policy if it could be proved that he had been killed. Mannoia's version is that Calvi was strangled by Francesco Di Carlo. It was something a 'Man of Honour' would have to do personally. In June 1996 it was announced that Di Carlo, who had been sentenced to twenty-five years for his part in a drugs conspiracy in Southampton, had returned to Italy to become a *pentito*. He accepted that he had been approached for the killing, but said he had been out of the country at the time. Another man, Vicenzo Casillo, was named as Calvi's murderer. In turn he had been killed.[1]

Gangland executions often have to take place very publicly simply to demonstrate just who is the boss. Contracts such as these include that of Charles Binaggio who was shot along with his bodyguard, Charles Gargetta, on 6 April 1950 in the First District Democratic Club in Kansas City; 'Uncle' Frank Costello, who was waylaid by Vincent 'The Chin' Gigante at the Majestic Apartments, 115 Central Park West, but survived; and Albert Anastasia, shot in the barber's shop of the Park Sheraton on 7th Avenue and 55th on 25 October 1957, who did not. More recently, on 16 December 1985 Paul Castellano was killed on the pavement as he left the one-time Mafia hangout Spark's Restaurant at 210 E. 34th Street. In September 2000 the Marseilles gangster François Vanverberghe was shot dead in Paris as he gambled in the Artois Club off the Champs Elysées.

Sometimes life in the underworld does imitate art. Just as the American Mafia of the 1970s is said to have watched *The Godfather*,

---

[1] *The Independent*, 28 July 2003; *Daily Telegraph*, 4 October 2003.

and those of today *The Sopranos* for tips on how to conduct themselves, so Robert Pike's *Mute Witness* (filmed as *Bullitt*) and William
Roemer's *The War of the Godfathers* served as blueprints for the 2002
murder in a Tokyo hospital of Takashi Ishizuka, the head of the
Sumiyoshi-kai. At the time he was recuperating from a failed hit.[2]

As for independent killings, it is of course necessary for the body to
be found in insurance cases or when the contracting spouse wishes to
remarry. After the trouble and expense to which they have gone, they
do not wish to wait a further seven years to obtain a declaration of
death from the courts. A separate problem then arises. Given that
statistically people are the victims of family or close friends, the
discovery of bodies will quickly focus attention on the husband or
wife. Alibis are essential, but with time and a little trouble they can
often be broken. Indeed a fortunate absence at the time of death may
trigger off – if that is an apposite phrase – an inquiry.

The corollary of this is that a careful killer does not want to leave
a body, because once there's a body, a murder inquiry follows. If the
victim is a known criminal it may not – although the police would
deny this – be an especially rigorous murder hunt. But there will be
a hunt nonetheless, and, said 'Barry' – a contract killer offering his
thoughts on the matter – 'for a respectable (murdered) Englishman
living with his wife and children there is going to be a very intensive
murder hunt indeed'. 'The one thing the police are really good at,'
agreed a second hitman 'Dennis', 'is legwork. Once there is a body
on the floor to investigate, they will investigate. They will interview
everybody. If there is something in the closet, somebody with a griev-
ance, they will find out. So, for five or ten grand, you are taking a
big risk. You've really got to have the person took away.'[3]

That euphemism means that the victim is killed and bundled into
the boot of a car or, more likely, kidnapped or lured to a place where
the body is disposed of and never seen again. For those prepared to
wait, however, the object is for there to be no 'victim' at all officially
– rather, a 'missing person'. 'The body must therefore be destroyed,
not hidden,' said a third hitman 'Stuart'.

[2] *Sydney Morning Herald*, 27 February 2002.
[3] 'Shooting somebody is the easiest thing in the world' in *The Times*, 17 January 1998.

In the past, the successful disposal of the body has been very much a matter of chance. The so-called barrel murders were fashionable in the late 1880s, the body of the victim being put in a barrel and dropped in the sea. The fact that bodies tend to float to the surface unless care is taken to let the air out is probably something beyond the knowledge of the average contract killer. Indeed in November 1937, after the body of Walter Sage had surfaced despite being tied to a pinball machine, his killer Harry 'Pittsburgh Phil' Strauss was said to have remarked, 'With this bum, you gotta be a doctor or he floats.'

Nevertheless the technique has had its adherents. In America one of the most notable of the barrel jobs was the killing of 71-year-old Johnny Roselli who was involved in the Mafia plot to assassinate Fidel Castro. In 1975 five days after the killing of Chicago boss Sam Giancana, also said to be involved, Roselli gave evidence to a Senate Intelligence Committee generally fudging the issues put to him. He did, however, admit that both he and Giancana were close to Judith Campbell Exner who at the time of their relationship was also close to J.F.Kennedy. Roselli was warned by his lawyer to obtain a bodyguard but dismissed the suggestion, asking rhetorically, 'Who would want to kill an old man like me?' Somebody would, was the answer, for on 28 July 1976 Roselli disappeared. His body was put into a 55-gallon oil drum and on 7 August it duly floated to the surface in Dumfoundling Bay off the Miami coastline. No one was ever charged with his murder and there is some speculation that it was a CIA killing made to look like a Mafia failure. Another suggestion is that he was killed on the orders of the new Chicago boss, Tony 'Batters' Arcado, over a failure to account properly for the takings at the Frontier Hotel in Las Vegas. The best view is that the killing was ordered by Florida don Santo Trafficante, whom he had named in the anti-Castro plot.[4]

Alternatively, in the early years the barrels were sent by rail across country to a non-existent address or simply, and more cheaply, left on a vacant lot or street corner. On 14 April 1903 Carmelina Zillo, emptying trash into the street, saw a barrel which she thought might

---

[4] 'Deep Six for Johnny' in *Time*, 23 August 1976; Charles Rappleye and Ed Becker, *All American Mafioso*.

be of use. Unfortunately, on closer inspection it was found to be full of sawdust and a man's head with his genitalia poking out of his mouth. The body was just one of the hundred or so victims attributed to the almost tautologous Lupo the Wolf, also known as Ignazio Saietta or Ignazio Lupo, a Black Hand chief in Italian Harlem, who had arrived in New York in 1899. Saietta owned what became known as the Murder Stable at 323 East 10th St. Some reports have it that eventually the bodies of over sixty victims were found. Many of the victims were thought to be those who had disobeyed Black Hand letters, but there is little doubt that he was also operating an early contract killing agency. Although Saietta survived for some thirty years, by the 1920s the barrel murder had become un-fashionable. It carried too many marks of a Mob hit. It is always useful to shift the blame on to gangland, and freelance contractors had taken up the technique as a diversionary tactic.[5]

In England the long-time associate of the Krays and independent worker, Freddie Foreman, gave a somewhat surprising television inter-view in which he revealed some of the secrets of the trade, saying he favoured a boat taken out into the fishing lanes of the Channel. But sleeping with the fishes is by no means always restful. Although there is no suggestion that Foreman had anything to do with that drop, one gangster whose body surfaced there was Jack Buggy. Scotch Jack, as he was known, was shot in May 1965 in the Mayfair Bridge Club in Mount Street, London. His body was first wrapped in the club carpet and then taken out to sea bound in baling wire. Two men were later charged with the murder and acquitted.[6]

In April 2003 the body of businessman Amarjit Chohan was found floating near Bournemouth pier. In July that year the body of his wife Nancy was caught in a net off Dorset, and in the November that of his mother-in-law washed up on the Isle of Wight. At a trial in November 2004 the prosecution alleged that all three, together with their two children, had been killed when a decision was made to take over Chohan's fruit import-export business to use as a front for drug dealing.[7]

[5] Andrew Roth, *Infamous Manhattan*.
[6] For an account of the case see Leonard Read, *Nipper Read, The Man Who Nicked the Krays*, pp. 121–4.
[7] *The Times*, 9 November 2004.

Recently it has been claimed that the concrete overcoat or boots are passé and the motorway flyover of Mafia legend is a burial place of the past. This is not guaranteed. Given that the Mobs have become more and more involved in the construction industry, foundations and cement roads are still Happy Hunting Grounds for victims. There is apparently something comforting about burying a victim under a high-rise block of flats. 'Sort of like a real tombstone,' one gangster told the police.[8] The final resting places of disappeared mobsters have provided many happy hours of speculation. James Hoffa, the Teamsters leader who disappeared after a visit to the Red Fox Inn near Detroit, is variously said to have been processed in a meat grinding plant, cut in pieces and thrown in a swamp in Florida, dumped in the Gulf of Mexico in a 55-gallon drum filled with wet cement, or dismembered and kept in a freezer before burial in the end-zone of the New York Giants' stadium in New Jersey.

The propounder of the theory that concrete is passé has it that, nowadays, a killer is more likely to have access to a furnace, or to a corrupt undertaker who, for a fee, will provide a two-tier coffin. This is by no means new and is a method long used to dispose of many of London gangland's disappeared. It is Joseph Bonanno, himself an undertaker, who is generally credited by the New York police with the so-called Mafia Coffin. Frank Fraser has often claimed that Billy Hill in the 1950s would have his victims cremated and that he, Fraser, would then scatter their ashes outside Wandsworth prison.[9]

Similarly, in the days when there were bathhouses used for public bathing the janitor could often be persuaded to take a little extra fuel for the boilers. Nipper Read thought that the body of Jack 'The Hat' McVitie might have been disposed of in that way:

Just opposite their home on Vallence Road was the Cheshire Street Baths which were run by a man named Harry Granshaw. He had known the Twins since they were boys and consequently he was very friendly with them. He had allowed the baths to be used by them as an unofficial *poste restante* and I wondered whether he might have allowed them to be used for a more

[8] Quoted in Carl Sifakis, *The Mafia File*, p. 55.
[9] Conversation with author.

sinister purpose. First, I checked to find that the boilers serving the baths would be large enough to consume a human body and then I had Mr Granshaw brought in. He was patently loyal to the Krays and defended them vigorously. He agreed it would be possible for a body to be consumed in the furnace but denied that it had ever been used for this purpose. It was not a matter I could pursue much further. There would be no possibility of remains being found in the ash cans after all this time and I bade Mr Granshaw good day. It was something that had teased my mind for some time. I always thought how convenient it would be to have a disposal unit so handy.[10]

Recently Frank 'The Irishman' Sheeran has claimed that the stories of Hoffa's death and disposal are incorrect, and that he was the killer on instructions from Russell Bufalino. Sheeran, having done his work shooting Hoffa twice behind the right ear, went on his way leaving the disposal to a 'cleaner'. He later heard that the body had been sent to a funeral home in Detroit for subsequent cremation. Sheeran says that he later attended a meeting with Bufalino who commented, 'There won't be a body . . . Dust to dust.'[11]

Sometimes someone else's grave will do nicely. On 19 February 1998 a gravedigger at Forest Lawn cemetery, Victoria, found the body of Rocky Iaria in that of an elderly lady. Iaria had disappeared in September 1991 after being charged with others over a $1 million burglary in Bendigo. He had been killed with a shotgun blast to the head, and the best idea was that his death had been to prevent him turning on his colleagues and giving evidence for the Crown.[12]

Mafia burial grounds have long been sought, often unavailingly, by the Federal Bureau of Investigation. In the 1930s Murder Inc. had its own burial ground in a chicken yard near the house of a brother-in-law of one of the outfit's top killers. It was there that, amongst others, the union leader Peter Panto was buried. In the 1940s and early 1950s Charles and Joe Dippolito, father and son, soldiers in the Dragna Los Angeles crime Family, planted their

---

[10] Leonard Read, *Nipper Read, The Man Who Nicked The Krays*, p. 303.
[11] Charles Brandt, '*I Heard You Paint Houses*'; Letter in *The New York Times Book Review*, 15 August 2004.
[12] *Sunday Herald Sun* (Melbourne), 22 June 2003.

victims' bodies in a sack of lime in their vineyard at Cucamonga. Given the story that the body of a horse improves a vine, their grapes must have greatly benefited.

In August 1985 a Mobil garage in Bensonhurst, Brooklyn at 86th and Bay 7th Street was excavated following a tip-off that three bodies would be found. Some three weeks later, with no positive results, the garage was restored to working order.

There has been more success in Lovers' Lane on the Brooklyn-Queens border. In 1981 Alphonse 'Sonny Red' Indelicato's tattooed arm was found poking out of the soil. More recently, following the conviction of the Bonanno crime boss Joseph Massino, the earth-movers moved in. Amongst the bodies sought were those of Philip 'Lucky Phil' Giaccone and Dominick 'Big Trin' Trinchera, killed along with Indelicato. It was also hoped that the body of Thomas DeSimone, missing since 1979, might be turned up. More interestingly, it was thought that the body of an innocent bystander would be recovered. John Favara, a salesman who lived near John Gotti's family, had the misfortune to run down and kill Gotti's 12-year-old son who emerged from behind a parked car. Despite being warned to move away, Favara hoped his apologies would be sufficient. They were not.

After a week of digging, a muddy Piaget watch and a 23-year-old Citibank card were found with the skeletal remains of two men buried together. The Citibank card carried the name of Trinchera, and the Piaget watch was described by Giaccone's widow, who said it was similar to the one he wore.[13]

One Bonanno Family figure, Thomas Pitera – known to his peers as Tommy Karate for his fondness for the martial arts – dismembered at least six bodies, packed them in garbage bags and suitcases and buried them on the edge of the William T. Davis Wildlife Refuge on Staten Island. According to David Shapiro, who prosecuted the Federal case in 1992, Pitera had learned from previous Mob mistakes. He sometimes pierced the lungs and stomachs of his victims so that gases would not build up and push the bodies to the surface. He received a life sentence with no possibility of parole.

[13] *New York Times*, 6, 12, 13 October 2004. DeSimone was played by Joe Pesci in the film *Goodfellas*. The killing of Indelicato and his comrades is featured in the film *Donnie Brasco*.

Another crew, headed by a Gambino Family soldier Roy DeMeo, used to saw the bodies of victims on a pool liner in an apartment in the Flatlands section of Brooklyn behind the Gemini Lounge, a bar that was his base of operations. Mobsters would carve the bodies into nine pieces, pack them in cardboard boxes and leave them in commercial trash bins, which were picked up by a Mob-connected carting company and hauled to the Fountain Avenue dump in Brooklyn. DeMeo, who headed a car theft ring, oversaw the systematic elimination of scores of victims, mostly car thieves and petty criminals with whom he or members of his crew had had disputes. He ended his life in the boot of his Cadillac, himself the victim of 'Trunk Music', so called because of the noise made by the body's escaping gases.

In England, Epping Forest, just outside London, has proved a long-time and very successful burial ground. Bodies rarely surface if properly buried in its depths. One who rested in the forest was the so-called tattooed man Jerry Hawley who had starred in a number of blue movies made for the appropriately-named Climax Films in a flat in Bedford Hill, Balham. It was a quarrel over money which led to his death, with Hawley wanting a bigger share of the profits from the films. In May 1969 he was stabbed a total of eighty-nine times and then driven out to the forest. His employer Mick Muldoon received a life sentence.

Other alternative methods of disposal of the unwanted corpse include a tree shredder, the sort of machine that can turn a log into sawdust and spray it across a field. And being fed to pigs is the fate which possibly befell the unpopular Melbourne contract killer Donald Flannery on 9 May 1985, and almost certainly Mrs McKay, kidnapped at her home in Wimbledon and murdered in December 1969 by the Hossein brothers after a failed extortion demand.

One disastrous effort in disposing of the victim happened in Japan in February 2002. The killer left the mutilated corpse on a river bank and the forearms, which had been cut off, were floated downstream. It all came to nothing because the man was identified through the extensive tattoos on the top half of his body.[14]

[14] *Sydney Morning Herald*, 27 February 2002.

Not all victims find a burial ground immediately. It would be fair to say that even in gangland terms the Westies from New York's Hell's Kitchen followed the description of Lord Byron and were 'mad, bad, and dangerous to know'. The gang functioned on and off for the better part of the twentieth century, but the incumbents of the 1980s were quite exceptional. Quite apart from their evening entertainment of playing Russian Roulette at $1,000 a pull, they were torturers and regularly dismembered the bodies of their victims. After the 1991 killing of Paddy Dugan, who despite warnings had continued independently to shake down loan sharks, his fingers were put in a bag of other severed digits and used, very successfully, to frighten potential victims. Not that the Westies were without a certain amount of old-fashioned Irish sentimentality in their make-up. Dugan's head was also cut off and, placed on the bar of a local tavern, members drank to it throughout one evening, offering it Paddy's favourite cigarettes the while. His severed penis had been put in a bottle which also toured the bars that night with its former owner's head.[15]

'The professionalism in a murder comes in the disposing of the body, not in pulling the trigger,' explained hitman Dennis. 'Shooting someone is the easiest thing in the world. It's easier to shoot someone than beat them up or nick their car.'[16]

One who failed to come up to the required standard was the Melbourne killer Dennis Allen. After he had killed the prostitute Helga Wagnegg it was left to his half-brother Victor Peirce to dispose of the body. When he killed Anton Kenny, again it was Peirce who cut the biker's legs off with a chainsaw and, when that became stuck full of skin and blood, with a chopper so that the man could be put in a barrel of cement. 'Dennis was good as a killer but not as a disposalist,' said his nephew Jason Ryan, so adding a new word to the English language.[17]

---

[15] T.J. English, *The Westies*. See also Joseph Coffey and Jerry Schmetterer, *The Coffey Files*, Chapter II, for an account by the eponymous New York detective of his arrests of the Westies.
[16] 'Shooting somebody is the easiest thing in the world' in *The Times*, 17 January 1998.
[17] Quoted by Paul Anderson, *Shotgun City*, p. 167.

PART TWO:
THE PLAYERS AND THE
PLAYED OUT

5

Killing Machines

Although from the end of the nineteenth century there have been gangs of contract killers such as the Mafia in New Orleans, Saietta in New York and Jack Egan's Rats in St Louis, it was Prohibition which really turned organised crime into a business. And to protect their interests the leaders employed two killing machines to eliminate their enemies and protect their interests nationwide. First came the Purple Gang from Detroit, and a little later Murder Inc. The former are perhaps now best recalled as the 'whole rhythm section' in Elvis Presley's *Jailhouse Rock*, but they and their activities should in no way be underestimated.

Jazz clarinettist Mezz Mezzrow, who played in Detroit during Prohibition, recalled them:

> The Purple Gang was a lot of hard guys, so tough they made Capone's playmates look like a kindergarten class, and Detroit's snooty set used to feel it was really living to talk to them hoodlums without getting their ounce-brains blown out.[1]

There is considerable dispute as to how the Purples acquired their nickname. A Detroit Divisional Detective Inspector Henry Garvin

---

[1] Mezz Mezzrow, *Really the Blues*, p. 92.

claimed that honour for himself, saying it came from the nickname of an early leader named Sammy Purple. Other suggestions included the fact that the members wore purple swimsuits, that when the gang was deciding on a name they chanced on the fact that one of those present was wearing a purple sweater and, the most popular, that someone described them as not being quite straight: 'They're a bit purple.'

Whatever the origin of their name, they were the amalgamation of two sets of second-generation Jewish immigrants from Detroit's East Side. The first was the Oakland Sugar House Gang whose leaders shortly after the First World War were Harry Fleischer, Henry (Harry) Shorr who was the financial man, Irving Milberg, Harry Altman and Morris and Phil Raider.

The other was based on the talents of Sammy Cohen, known as Sammy Purple, until the Bernstein brothers Abe, Isidore and Ray took over control. By 1923 they had been joined by a number of dissatisfied members of Dinty Colbeck's Egan's Rats – the St Louis-based operation which was, at the time, in disarray[2] – as well as Abe Axler and Eddie Fletcher, a run-of-the-mill featherweight from New York. When he arrived in Detroit Fletcher boxed wearing a purple vest at the Fairview Athletic Club, and this is yet another suggestion as to how the Purples acquired their name.

There is disagreement as to who was their actual leader. Some say it was the short, slightly built Ray Bernstein, but more likely it was his brother Abe, described as 'small and dapper with the soft hands of a woman and a quiet way of speaking'.[3]

As the years passed the activities of the gang expanded from shoplifting and extortion through bootlegging to include kidnapping, fraud, drug dealing and contract killing. They were by no means the most scrupulous of the contracted killers, however. Regularly their employers found themselves out of their money but, because of the power of the gang, were unable to do anything about it.

---

[2] Egan's Rats were founded in about 1900 by Jack 'Jellyroll' Egan, principally as strike-breakers. By the 1920s with unions more firmly established, the members turned to safe-breaking and, once Prohibition was announced, entered the game with enthusiasm under the leadership of Dinty Colbeck. It is sometimes suggested that Fred Burke was a Rat rather than a member of the Purple Gang. Certainly they hired out as contract killers. The Rats did not really survive the end of the era; Colbeck was shot and the gang split up in the late 1930s.
[3] *New York Times*, 9 March 1968.

The first of their major contract killings occurred in 1927 when local gamblers employed them to dispose of members of the re-formed Egan's Rats. That year the Purples were thought to be between forty and fifty strong and were in almost sole control of the 25,000 drinking clubs known as blind pigs – 150 of them in one block – throughout the city. On 15 June, Axler completed a contract on the St Louis gunman Milford Jones, who imprudently sat with his back to the door of the Stork Club at 47 Rowena Street. There were no witnesses. On 13 August, Axler and Irving Milberg, together with their girlfriends, came into a black and tan cabaret – a non-segregated bar – at 1708 St Antoine, quarrelled with two black players, Geoffrey Quales and Hobart Harris, and shot them dead. They claimed self-defence and again, in the absence of witnesses to say otherwise, were released without charge.

The Purples were also involved in what was known as the Cleaners and Dyers War which lasted for two years in the mid-1920s. Even without the intervention of the Purples the almost wholly Jewish-owned garment-cleaning industry was in turmoil and Capone apparently sent an envoy, Harry Abrams, from Chicago to try to sort out the warring parties. He negotiated a settlement between Charles Jacoby of Jacoby's Cleaners and Dyers and Frank X. Martel, the president of the Detroit Federation of Labor.

It did not last long, and Jacoby turned to his brother-in-law Abe Bernstein for a more permanent solution. The two-year war resulted in the deaths of Sam Polakoff, the President of Union Cleaners and Dyers, and of another cleaner, Sam Sigman, whose premises were bombed. The Purples' interest in the affair ended with the arrest of a number of members including the Bernsteins, Irving Milberg, Harry Keywell and Eddie Fletcher along with Jacoby, and charges of conspiracy to extort $12,000 at $1,000 a week over a three-month period. The defence was that it was all the fault of Martel, described in a closing speech as 'ruler of stench bombers, window breakers and perjurers who has duped the prosecutor's office'. There may have been something in this. One of his men was Louis Green who had sadly been killed when he ran into the path of a car as he was fleeing after the stench-bombing of a barber's shop. There may also have been some help from members of the Purples not under arrest, because the ten were triumphantly acquitted. Jacoby announced he was going to sue for $1 million for pain and suffering and damage to his business. The Purples must have thought enough was enough. There is no further record of their close interest in that industry.

There is little doubt that the Purples were actively concerned in the St Valentine's Day Massacre of the Moran Mob in Chicago in 1929. Apart from Fred Burke, three other members, George Lewis and Phil and Harry Keywell, were identified from photographs but never charged. Quite apart from the fact that they were contract killers, their willingness to assist arose from the hijacking by Moran's men of a shipment of the Purples' 'Old Log Cabin Whiskey'.

But there were signs that efforts were being made to deal with the Purples and that they were not inviolate. On 24 July 1929 Abe Axler, Irving Milberg, Harry Sutton and Eddie Fletcher each received twenty-two months and $5,000 fines for liquor offences. In that same month Irving Shapiro was shot dead and dumped from a car on Taylor Avenue. One reason advanced for his killing was that it was feared the police were leaning on him to become an informer. Another is that he wanted an unacceptable increase in his share of the profits. The first may have been correct. There is no doubt that the Purples were highly sensitive to outside interest in their activities.

By now the gang was quite clearly under siege, both internally and externally. The great Collingwood Massacre would soon take out three key players, and the Italian element in the Detroit underworld was growing progressively stronger. The years from 1929 to 1937 show the terminal decline of the Purples.

In October 1929 Zigie Selbin was shot to death in a blind pig on 12th St; Harry Millman and his brother Abe were killed together; Joe 'Little Joey' Bernstein was nearly killed in May 1930 when Harry Kirschbaum shot him. Little Joey retired from the rackets and went into the oil business at which he was a notable success, becoming treasurer of the Garfield Oil Company. He and his brother Abe, along with Moe Dalitz, give the lie to the story that the Purples were simply strong-arm men, all brawn and no brains. It was clear that the Bernsteins as a family, if not the Purples as a whole, had extensive and nationwide interests. Joey Bernstein had been in New Orleans in 1927 when his partner in a roadhouse operation, Ted

Werner, was shot dead, unfortunately in the apartment they shared. Bernstein was held for several months before being released.

In July 1930 Phil Keywell killed a black youth Arthur Mixon, whom he thought was spying on the warehouse and liquor-cutting business he ran at the rear of Jaslove's butcher's shop. The boy turned out to be 17, and may have been backward. His story to Keywell was that he had been playing with a ball which had run under a door, but his responses were not deemed satisfactory and he was shot. The police charged Keywell and Morris Raider, who was said to have a perfect alibi which he did not call. The first jury disagreed, but the second convicted Keywell inside ninety minutes. Raider received twelve to fifteen years and Keywell life imprisonment. All the defence witnesses were charged with perjury, but only one was tried and he was discharged on the direction of the judge. The first Purple to be convicted of a murder charge, Keywell served thirty-two years, becoming a prison trusty before his release.

But it was their ruthless and ill-thought-out behaviour in the so-called Collingwood Massacre of 1931, in which they sank the remainder of the Little Jewish Navy and after which a number of their key men were sentenced to long terms of imprisonment, that most seriously depleted the Purples.[4]

In November 1933 Eddie Fletcher and the fearsome Abe Axler were found dead holding hands in the back seat of Axler's car in Oakland County. Both had been shot a dozen times in the face. Fletcher was wearing his Purple shirt and there were no signs of a struggle. The theory was that Fletcher was shot by the driver who turned around to fire, and Axler was killed by the man sitting next to him in the back seat. Their hands had been linked as a gesture of contempt for the pair, referred to as 'the Siamese Twins'. They had probably known they were marked men for some time before their execution. One suggestion was that Axler had defaulted on a $30,000 contract. Another was that Axler and Fletcher had been trying to take over the gang and had double-crossed the Bernstein brothers, Harry Millman and Harry Fleischer.

In 1936 Harry Fleischer, who had started life as a driver for the

---

[4] See Chapter 9.

Oakland Old Sugar House, eventually went down along with his brother Sam. He received eight years for liquor violations, and a year after his release in 1944 he was convicted of armed robbery of an Oakland County gambling joint. This time he received twenty-five to fifty and was paroled in 1965 at the age of 62.

Along the way Fleischer was suspected of a number of crimes including the murder of the financier of the Purples, Harry Shorr, who simply disappeared one day in December 1935. His body was never found, but his bloodstains were discovered in the back of Fleischer's car and they had been seen together in a delicatessen earlier in the evening. Fleischer had an unbreakable alibi.

The last serious player of the Purples to be killed was Harry Millman, who in November 1937 was gunned down in Boesky's Deli on Hazelwood and 12th. From a respectable family, the good-looking ladies' man Millman, a first-class swimmer, had been to high school at a Kentucky military academy from which he graduated in 1928. By the next year he was regarded as a rather uncontrollable Purple hijacker and gunman, reliable until he had a drink. In November 1933 it was he who organised the killing of senior Purples Abe Axler and Eddie Fletcher. Despite twenty-eight arrests for murder, extortion, armed robbery and assault, he never spent a night in jail. Over the years he became more and more of a loose cannon targeting Mafia-protected brothels and blind pigs. He was regularly called to account by the Purple leader Abe Bernstein, but no amount of lecturing could quieten him down.[5]

He had earlier survived a bomb attack when ten pounds of dynamite were placed in his car, triggered to explode when the accelerator was pressed. Unfortunately Willie Holmes, a parking attendant at the 1040 Club, started the car that day. Millman's killers were said to be Pittsburgh Phil Strauss and Harry 'Happy' Maione of Anastasia's Murder Inc., but they were never charged. A colleague describing his death put it poignantly:

It was very simple. He was a big handsome Jewish guy. God, he was a good-looking bastard, big and handsome and well dressed

[5] Paul. R. Kavieff, *The Purple Gang*, pp. 181–4.

and he was knocking off whorehouses and he didn't know that the whorehouses at that period were protected by the Dago Mob . . . I forget the name but there was a very fancy blind pig on 12th Street and he was at the bar having a good time with some people and in walked the Dagos and shot the shit out of him.[6]

This time there was no question of a delicate use of Strauss's trademark ice-pick. They also 'shot the shit out of' five innocent bystanders. On 24 November 1937, Thanksgiving Eve, Millman along with Hymie Cooper and Harry Gross went to Boesky's cocktail lounge. About 1 a.m. as Millman went to the bar, two men walked up and fired from point-blank range. Gross and Cooper tried to hide under a table but in turn they were shot at, as was a customer who simply was in the way. Gross died in hospital without naming his killers, if indeed he knew them. Cooper, who survived, sensibly had nothing to say.[7]

Finally, Sidney Markman was electrocuted in New York for the murder-robbery of a Brooklyn merchant, Isidore Frank, in 1938. Along with David Goldberg he had shot Frank dead in front of his home at 733 Alabama Avenue. Markman was later arrested in Detroit for possession of a machine gun and was linked to Goldberg. He was executed on 18 January 1940.[8]

Despite their loss of power to the Italians who would rule Detroit's underworld for the next seventy years, the Purples had one last outrage to commit. As bold as anything they had previously managed, this was the killing of the State senator Warren Hooper on 11 January 1945. Hooper, due to testify before a Grand Jury into horserace gambling, had been collected from his hotel. His body was found on a road three miles north of Springpoint shot in the head, almost certainly by the unknown driver, who it was said had been released from prison that morning to undertake the contract. He had not been signed out or reported missing and consequently had an unimpeachable alibi. Not so Harry Fleischer who was jailed again, this time for conspiracy.

[6] *Detroit Free Press*, 26 June 1963.
[7] *Ibid.*
[8] See *New York Times*, 14, 15 January, 28 November 1938, 19 January 1940; *True Detective*, June 1939.

The story finally came out that, in January a month before the senator's death, several of the inmates of Jackson including Ray Bernstein and Harry Keywell were offered $15,000 to kill Hooper. The deal was struck in the office of the Deputy Warden D.C. Petit and the men were provided with $10,000 as an advance, guns, street clothes and false licence plates. They left the prison in Petit's car and when Hooper drove past they forced his car to the side of the road and Ray Bernstein shot him. Later, said Louis Brown, the inmate who finally told the story, they had bragged about the killing.[9]

Just how many men were killed by members of Murder Inc. is open to considerable speculation. According to a memorandum in the New York Municipal Archives, a conservative estimate was eighty-five murders which could be definitely laid at the doors of its members. The crime historian Carl Sifakis suggests a figure of between four and five hundred, and that Pittsburgh Phil Strauss may have killed between fifty and a hundred himself. J. Robert Nash suggests that Frank Abbandando, known as 'The Dasher' – either because of the speed he showed when he played in a reformatory baseball team at Elmira or because of the speed with which he chased one of his early victims – executed half that number.[10] There are even suggestions that Strauss, a particularly dedicated killer, murdered up to 500 people nationwide.

At the beginning of the 1930s, with Prohibition still in force, a group from Brooklyn at first known as the Brownsville Mob was formed and led by Abe 'Kid Twist' Reles, the dapper Louis Capone (who was no relation of the more famous Al), Pittsburgh Phil Strauss (who came from Brooklyn and merely liked the name and was also known as Pep) and Marty 'Bugsy' Goldstein. Underlings included Walter Sage (who would later be killed for skimming from his superiors), Abraham 'Pretty' Levine, 'Dukey' Maffetore, Seymour Magoon, Jacob Drucker, Mikey Sycoff, Sholem Bernstein and Irving 'Gangy' Cohen.

About a year later the Brownsville Mob formed an alliance with the Ocean Hill Mob then led by Happy Maione, Frank Abbandando, Angelo Julie Catalano (sometimes Catalino) and Vito 'Socko' Gurino,

[9] Paul R. Kavieff, *The Purple Gang*.
[10] Carl Sifakis, *The Encyclopedia of American Crime*; J. Robert Nash, *World Encyclopedia of Organized Crime*.

also known as 'Chicken Head' because of his habit of shooting chickens as target practice.

The combined gangs now became the notorious Murder Inc., a specific arm of the new-generation crime syndicate led by Salvatore Luciana (better known as Lucky Luciano), Albert Anastasia, Frank Costello, Meyer Lansky and the lesser known but perhaps most influential of all, Moe Dalitz, formerly a member of the Purple Gang and later of the Cleveland Road Syndicate. The aim of the crime syndicate was to bring order to the disorganisation of Al Capone and the wars in Chicago. The rackets were to divide profits in an orderly manner. The founders, quite correctly, foresaw opposition to their well-intentioned plans and Murder Inc. was to be, and indeed was, the enforcement arm.

The gang introduced a whole new language into the underworld and in turn the newspapers. A 'contract' was a murder assignment; a 'bum' – possibly signifying his low station in life – was the victim; a 'hit' or a 'pop', the actual killing. Fees paid ranged from $1,000 to $5,000 and the members were on retainers of between $125 and $150 a week. Additionally they would be given percentages of rackets such as the numbers game in a particular area. This was a time when men were machine-gunned, stabbed, ice-picked and strangled. Their bodies were burned, buried, tied to jukeboxes and sunk in lakes or left on street corners as examples. The name Murder Inc. was invented for them by Harry Feeney of the *World-Telegram*, but in fact they liked to refer to themselves as The Combination.

The rules drawn up by Lansky and Dalitz were that the members of Murder Inc. were only to be used for the most pressing of business reasons, and – correctly, seeing that the murder of public figures would only bring down the wrath of the authorities on their heads – lawyers, judges and reporters were to be inviolate. Except, of course, if those lawyers, judges and reporters mixed business with pleasure so to speak.

By 1937 the racketeers Louis Lepke and Jacob Shapiro (known as Gurrah because of his pronunciation of 'Get out of here') had formed an alliance with Murder Inc. In turn their underlings included Charlie 'The Bug' Workman, Samuel 'Tootsie' Feinstein and Albert 'Tick Tock' Tannenbaum.

As always, there are conflicting versions as to how the gang came to be chosen as executioners. One is that Reles was at war with the Shapiro brothers (no relation of Jacob), who by some accounts had raped his girlfriend and generally treated him badly. It was something of a test to see how he would deal with the problem, and when the brothers were killed in the so-called Battle of Brooklyn in June 1931 his worth was realised. Irving Shapiro was killed in his flat. Meyer was killed a few days later, and Joey Silver shortly after that. Willie Shapiro was garrotted by Reles some years later in a bar in East New York. He was then tied up, put in a laundry bag and buried in Canarsie. When he was later the subject of an autopsy it was found that he had dirt in his lungs. Reles had not killed him with the garrotte; Shapiro had been buried alive.

In direct charge of Murder Inc. was Albert Anastasia, often referred to as the Lord High Executioner. He had changed the last letter of his name from an 'o' to avoid causing embarrassment to his mother when she read the newspapers. Anastasia's personal principal enforcers included Jack Parisi and his then superiors were Louis Buchalter, known as Louis Lepke, and from time to time Joe Dio known as Joe Adonis. However, these in turn reported to the informal board of a combination of Bugsy Siegel, Lansky, Luciano, Dalitz and Costello. It was they who gave the go-ahead for the contracts which took place nationwide. Arthur Flegenheimer (far better known as Dutch Schultz), regarded as becoming increasingly unstable and whose interests were under threat from Luciano, was not invited to join.[11]

Members of Murder Inc. received their instructions and undertook their planning in a candy store at the corner of Saratoga and Livonia Avenues in Brownsville. Run by Rose Gold, then in her sixties and who could neither read nor write English, it was open twenty-four hours a day and was consequently known as Midnight Rose's. One reason for its importance was that in the days when telephones were almost unheard of luxuries for

---

[11] Journalist Martin Mooney may be credited with the first information on the organisation when he wrote of a meeting of 'the executives of Crime, Incorporated' in a New York hotel. Although he named no names he said the meeting was graced by at least three important local and national politicians. W. Balsamo, W. and G. Carpozi jnr, *Crime Incorporated*, p. 38.

the immigrant communities, Rose Gold had one and would take messages. When she was later arrested and refused to become a prosecution witness she was asked, 'Why do you let so many criminals frequent your store?' Her reply was, 'Why don't the police keep them out?'[12]

Perhaps, however, the most important piece of work undertaken by members of Murder Inc. was the killing of the less than charismatic Dutch Schultz. Regarded as a much less appealing man than Al Capone, he was the son of a German Jew who deserted the family, leaving young Arthur to a life of juvenile crime. Born on 6 August 1902, he grew up in the Bronx where he was a member of the Bergen gang of pickpockets and shoplifters and by the age of twenty had interests in beer, slot machines, restaurants, taxi companies and professional boxing as well as the numbers racket. In his entire career he acquired only one conviction when in 1917 he was sentenced to fifteen months for burglary.

By 1930 Schultz held New York in the same way that Capone did Chicago. His rivals were simply eliminated. He was also regarded as a pathological miser. It was said that: 'You can insult Arthur's girl, even steal her from him; spit in his face and push him around and he'd laugh it off. But don't steal even a dollar that belongs to him. You're dead if you do.'[13]

Schultz's death followed his announcement that he would kill the special prosecutor of organised crime, Thomas Dewey, who was in the process of breaking up his slot-machine empires. When Schultz put the proposition to Johnny Torrio and Luciano, the syndicate refused to sanction it, however inconvenient the talented Michigan lawyer was becoming. Schultz, not Dewey, had to go.

Schultz was killed on 23 October 1935 in the Palace Chop House, Newark. With him went his wizard accountant Otto 'Abbadabba' Berman – who had devised an improved way of tampering with policy numbers pay-outs and who was opposed to the killing of Dewey – and gunmen Abe Landau and the broken-nosed Lulu Rosenkrantz, who were not. Their killers were Emmanuel 'Mendy'

[12] Rich Cohen, *Tough Jews*, p. 75.
[13] Quoted by Christopher Hibberd, *The Roots of Evil*, p. 338.

Weiss, Charles 'The Bug' Workman, and a man named Piggy who has never been identified. The three walked into the tavern and shot Rosenkrantz, Landau and Berman. It is, however, Workman who takes most of the credit for the incident. He then went to the washroom where he shot Schultz while he was urinating, took his money and rejoined the others.

In fact the murder of Schultz was mishandled. Charlie Workman came out of the restaurant to find Mendy Weiss and Piggy gone, along with the getaway car, and he began to run back to his New York flat. He later complained to his superiors about their desertion. Weiss said that Piggy had simply panicked and driven off. He was cleared of blame as it was felt that Workman had, to an extent, been the author of his own misfortunes by going back to rob the dying Schultz. Piggy was not so fortunate. He was found some weeks later and taken to Brownsville where he was tortured and shot; his body was then set alight. Later the turncoat Abe Reles accepted his part in Piggy's murder and named Strauss and Happy Maione as being involved.

All the men died in the hours following the attack. Schultz survived the longest, dying at 8.40 p.m. after making a series of incoherent rambling statements in front of a police stenographer who was hoping he would name his killers. He is reputed to have said, 'Please crack down on the Chinaman's friends and Hitler's commander . . . Mother is the best and don't let Satan draw you too fast.' The remarks have been variously interpreted as the ramblings of a dying man or to have had some reason behind them. The gangland chronicler Hank Messick believed that 'Hitler's Commander' was the one who ordered Schultz's death, but the reference to the Chinaman caused more problems. His answer is that it was Louis Dalitz, known as Louis the Chinaman, and brother of Moe Dalitz of the Cleveland Syndicate who were, at the time, trying to take over the Coney Island race track.[14] Others suggest it is Charles 'Chink' Sherman to whom he was referring in his delirium. The pair had quarrelled in the Broadway speakeasy Club Abbey

---

[14] Despite its name the track was in Cincinatti. After Schultz's death when it reopened it was renamed River Downs and was indeed owned by the Cleveland Syndicate.

and Sherman had shot him in the shoulder. In turn Sherman was stabbed and clubbed with a chair. However, by the time Schultz was killed Sherman was already dead and dumped.[15]

Killings by Murder Inc. were done not only for money, but as favours and importantly to prevent witnesses giving evidence. John 'The Polack' Bagdonowitz was killed in 1932 as a favour to Longy Zwillman, the New Jersey boss. He had double-crossed Zwillman in a deal and was hiding out on Long Island. His killers were Vito Gurino and Joe Mercaldo from the Happy Maione end of the gang. Abraham Meer and Irving Myron were killed in 1935 as a favour to Jimmy 'Blue Eyes' Alo, an associate of Meyer Lansky, because they had kidnapped his associate, Bot Salvio. The gunmen on this occasion were Harry Strauss, Bugsy Goldstein and Walter Sage.

Amongst the many other executions by Murder Inc., in 1935 John 'Spider' Murtha was killed in Brooklyn by Frank Abbandando and Max Golob. Golob received five years in 1942 for what was then bargained down to a felonious assault on Murtha. Hymie Yuran and Solomon Goldstein were killed in Sullivan County in 1939 and Morris Diamond in Brooklyn the same year. Goldstein was killed as a favour to Socks Lanza, the racket boss of the Fulton Fish Market in the 1930s; Goldstein was giving evidence against him.

On 13 September 1936 came a seminal moment for Murder Inc. when Joseph Rosen was killed at 725 Sutter Avenue, Brooklyn, where he had a candy store. He was found at 6.50 a.m. lying in a pool of blood. He had once owned the New York and New Jersey Clothing Transportation Company with three others, including a Louis Cooper who in turn had been associated with Lepke and Jacob Augen. The company had dissolved and parts had been hived off to Garfield Express Co. in which Lepke was a silent partner. Lepke then employed Rosen as a manager for $150 a week. They had quarrelled and for a time Rosen had been promised that he could have work of his own. Eventually he opened a candy store, but then refused to pay protection.[16] Before the killing Lepke had warned Rosen to leave town and when he ignored this, the instructions were

---

[15] Ed Reid, *The Shame of New York*, pp. 59–66; Hank Messick, *The Silent Syndicate*, pp. 149–50.
[16] *New York Post*, 21 September 1936.

given by Louis Capone. Strauss and Weiss were the gunmen who actually went into the store. It had been feared Rosen might talk to the prosecutor Thomas Dewey.

Murder Inc. was broken in a curious way. A small-time thief Harry Rudolph, then serving a short sentence on Rikers Island, wrote to the Brooklyn District Attorney saying that he knew about a murder in East New York and wished to speak to someone. Rudolph was not considered the most reliable of witnesses but the information he gave was about the killing of his friend, Alex 'Red' Alpert, a member of Murder Inc., on 25 November 1933. He named Abe Reles, Bugsy Goldstein and Dukey Maffetore as the three men involved.

Maffetore was little more than the bag boy, a man who read comic strips and was used as a driver. He rolled over into the District Attorney's arms, but appears genuinely to have known little. Nor did the next convert, Pretty Levine, but in a domino effect members were falling. It was yet another turncoat, Albert Tannenbaum, who told Assistant District Attorney Burton Turkus where to find the body of the labour leader Peter Panto, who had disappeared on 14 July 1939, and from then Murder Inc. started to unravel. Strauss had wanted to help in the killing of Panto but Anastasia had already dealt with the matter.

As for Abe 'Kid' Reles, as the years passed he had declined in stature in the organisation. During his career he had been arrested for murder on six occasions, assault seven times, assault and robbery twice and robbery or burglary a further six. He had only once been convicted – of assault. In 1940 he was charged with robbery, possession of narcotics and six charges linked to murder. In custody and now charged with murder itself, unexpectedly he sent a message by his wife that he wanted to talk. He feared, probably correctly, that some of those arrested with him might endeavour to arrange a deal by informing on him and, so to speak, he had the first drop on them. Reles became the canary for whom the prosecutors were looking; as a result of his information the police were able to clear up some forty-nine killings in Brooklyn alone. He named Frank Abbandando and Charlie Workman in the killing of Dutch Schultz, and his information was in a large part responsible for the conviction of his former superiors Louis Lepke and Mendy Weiss. When questioned, Reles said he believed that Panto's body would be found at 'The Farm' where Anastasia was said to dispose of bodies in general. It was, he thought, about 30 miles out on Sunrise Highway and was owned by an Italian he knew as Jimmy. On 28 January 1941, Panto's body was found near the home of Jimmy Ferraro, an Anastasia man.

For a year Reles, like so many subsequent informers, was held in protective custody. It was thought that he might have had tuberculosis and he was hidden out in Harbour Hospital under the name of Albert Smith from 1 to 9 November 1941. Then his safe home became the sixth floor of the Half Moon Hotel on Coney Island, New York, where he was kept under constant surveillance by six uniformed police officers. From time to time he, Mickie Syckoff, Sholem Bernstein and Allie Tannenbaum, all now turned State's witnesses, were taken to Heckster State Park on Long Island for recreation. It was from there that Reles travelled to the New York courts to give his evidence. One of the problems for the prosecution was the question of providing corroboration of his evidence and that of the others in what was called a material particular. In the case of Charlie Workman it was Reles who provided the solution. As a result of a shooting Workman had a pinched nerve in his hand and would not be able to hold a glass for any length of time. Reles suggested that as corroboration he be asked to hold a glass of water. It was a success and Workman received a sentence of life imprisonment for the killing of Schultz. He served twenty-four years and was released in 1956. Nothing further was heard of him.[17]

Now Reles and Tannenbaum were to be flown to California to give evidence against Bugsy Siegel and Frankie Carbo, then under indictment for the 1939 murder of Harry 'Big Greenie' Greenberg who was killed to eliminate a potential witness against Lepke. There appears to have been a conspiracy between the police, the District Attorney and surviving members of The Combination to ensure that he did not testify.

---

[17] According to a statement made on 5 June 1941 by Albert Tannenbaum, his associates included Hymie Segal (Bugsy Siegel's trigger man), Phil Farvel, 'Doc' Rosen, and Abe Zwillman who was Workman's boss. Workman had killed numerous bootleggers because they would carry up to $10,000 in cash and the killer kept the findings.

Apparently guarded by police, on 12 November 1941 he fell to his death from his room in the Half Moon Hotel, landing on the pavement. One of the more ingenious theories about his death is that he was playing a practical joke, climbing out of the window on knotted bedsheets and then running back upstairs to frighten the guards outside his room. Another is that he committed suicide. To do so he must have lowered himself to the third floor and then jumped; as his body was found twenty feet out into the street this seems unlikely. The Grand Jury, however, was perfectly happy. It found that:

> [Reles] met his death whilst trying to escape by means of a knotted sheet attached to a radiator in his room. We find that Reles did not meet with foul play and that he did not die by suicide. It would be sheer speculation to attempt to disarm [sic] his motive for wanting to escape.

The only really acceptable argument is that it was a gangland hit. At the time Reles was also due to testify against Anastasia who was on trial for the Panto killing. After Reles' death the case against Anastasia was dropped and although it was reopened in 1951 no progress was made. The case against Bugsy Siegel in California was also dropped. Luciano was later to say that the killing had been done by police officers who had thrown Reles from his room, and that the contract price had been $50,000. Meyer Lansky said the fee paid was $100,000.

Before Reles' death Lepke sensibly went into hiding, one of the places being the Oriental Palace (curiously enough also on Coney Island) owned by Zaccarino Cavitola, related to Louis Capone through marriage. A massive hunt was launched with rewards totalling $50,000, and some one million flyers were circulated advertising the offer. In contrast only 20,000 were printed seeking help over the kidnap of Charles Lindbergh's baby.[18] It was Anastasia himself who persuaded Lepke to give himself up to Turkus. As for Lepke's surrender there are, as usual, conflicting stories. The one

---

[18] *New York Times*, 25 August 1939.

favourable to Anastasia is that he arranged this in the unfounded belief that Lepke would only receive a prison sentence and not the electric chair. The less favourable version is that a body was needed to take away unnecessary heat from the Brooklyn Mob and that from his prison cell Luciano, on trial for running prostitutes, ordered Lepke's surrender. Anastasia was used as the persuader. It was said of Lepke that he was the director of at least 250 criminal enterprises and that, at the time, he was 'possibly the greatest criminal of the nation'.[19]

Who actually did the negotiating with the FBI and its Director J. Edgar Hoover is again open to question. It may have been Frank Costello, but more probably it was done at one stage removed through Lewis Solon Rosentiel.[20] Lepke was led to believe by Anastasia and his lieutenant, Moey 'Dimples' Wolensky, that he would not be turned over to the State courts, and that in a plea bargain he would receive between ten and twelve years. The celebrated journalist and broadcaster Walter Winchell was also involved; on 5 August 1939 he received an anonymous message to the effect that Lepke wanted to surrender but was afraid he would be shot if he did so.

Winchell knew Hoover well through their meetings at the Stork Club, 'the place to be seen if you wish to feel important', where he was often joined by Hoover at his favourite Table 50. It was a relationship which turned into a mutual admiration society. Quite improperly, Hoover would supply Winchell with gossip from the FBI files. In return Winchell was the Director's unofficial press agent and, had there been a fan club of the man rather than the Bureau, he would have been president. He obtained assurances from Hoover that if Lepke surrendered he would not be harmed and broadcast this over the radio.

[19] For more information on Lepke, see Andrew Tully, *Treasury Agent*.
[20] Rosentiel had long had ties with the Mafia. He made his fortune through building massive whiskey stocks during Prohibition, and it was then, like so many other liquor barons, that he made friends in crime. He had long-standing ties with both Meyer Lansky and Frank Costello. A philanthropist, he gave over $100 million to a variety of American universities. According to Anthony Summers he also enjoyed a corrupt relationship with Hoover based on homosexual orgies. Anthony Summers, *Official and Confidential*, pp. 312 *et seq*.

On 24 August 1939 around 10 p.m. Lepke emerged from his hide-out on Foster Avenue in Brooklyn and was driven by Anastasia over the bridge into Manhattan. Lepke got out and walked to a prearranged spot where there was a parked car with Winchell in the driving seat and J. Edgar Hoover in the back. Together they 'captured' Lepke who got in beside Hoover. The car was immediately surrounded by FBI agents.

It was only a short time before Lepke discovered the depth of his betrayal. The electric chair was to be the end of the road for him, but there were still some miles to be travelled before that appointment. First, in January 1940 Lepke received a total of 192 years, something which, since most were concurrent, boiled down to fourteen years for drug trafficking. Then Thomas Dewey prosecuted him for his bakery operations and in the April he received thirty years to life to begin after the fourteen. As he boarded the train to take him to Sing Sing he told reporters, 'I may have done a hundred things wrong but my conscience is clear. I never did one-millionth of the things they said I did.'

There was worse to come. On 28 May the King's County Grand Jury presented a true bill of murder in the first degree over the killing of Joseph Rosen. On 1 December he was found guilty and sentenced to death along with Louis Capone and Mendy Weiss for the murder. There were still years of legal wrangling before the appeals were dismissed and they were all executed at Sing Sing on 4 March 1944. Scheduled to die two days previously, they had ordered steak, french-fried potatoes, salad and pie for lunch and roast chicken for dinner, but were temporarily reprieved. They were electrocuted, with Capone (who had a weak heart) going first. He was followed by Weiss and Lepke, now described as 'a beaten, frightened little man'.[21]

In the weeks before he died Lepke asked to see Frank Hogan, the District Attorney of Manhattan. There was considerable speculation that, in return for a pardon, he might name names in high places, particularly in relation to the murder of Guido Ferrari, who was a casualty of the power struggle in the Amalgamated Clothing Workers. He did not. Wolensky had already paid for the betrayal

[21] *New York Times*, 4, 5 March 1944.

of his employer; even before Lepke died he had been shot on a Manhattan street corner. Without a doubt, Lepke was the most senior gangster to die in the electric chair. In all probability the reason he kept his silence was for fear of repercussions for his family.

The stone-cold killer Pittsburgh Phil Strauss, along with Marty Goldstein, had already been executed on 12 June 1941 for the killing of Puggy Feinstein who had tried to muscle into loan sharking. The unfortunate Feinstein had been trussed so that his struggle would tighten the noose around his neck, then doused with petrol and set on fire. During his trial the normally dapper Strauss feigned insanity, appearing unshaven and unclean, chewing on a leather strap and remaining mute.[22]

The last member of Murder Inc. to appear before the courts on murder charges was Jack Parisi. Accused of the murder of Morris Diamond in 1935, he managed to avoid capture until 1949 by hiding out in the Pennsylvania coalfields. Now Tannenbaum was the principal witness along with Angelo Catalano, the getaway driver. The only eyewitness had at first said he did not recognise Parisi, and to compound matters had over the years undergone a series of operations on his eyes.

The Hon. Louis Goldstein, dismissing the charge, said:

> The Court is convinced beyond any shadow of doubt that the defendant is the one who shot and killed the deceased Morris Diamond. It is indeed fortunate for this defendant that he is being tried in a State court for this case.
>
> It is my understanding that you have an engagement with the District Attorney of Bronx County on a charge of murder in the first degree. I earnestly hope for the good of the public that his office will find itself in a better position than we were to give you your just deserts.

The District Attorney also chipped in:

> I agree with you that this defendant is a most fortunate person. He is a murderer, a triggerman and deserved to go to the electric

[22] *New York Times*, 13 June 1941.

chair, but unfortunately due to the length of time or lack of evidence we were not able to accomplish that here. I wish Bronx County better luck.

Depending on one's point of view, they didn't have it. Now called Jack 'The Dandy', Parisi was acquitted on 14 June that year when Chief Assistant District Attorney Edward F. Breslin threw in his hand saying:

> I know in my mind and conscience that the killer in this case is Parisi. I had an accomplice's testimony, the finest you could assemble, but I have that and nothing more. Frankly, I am not in a position legally to proceed against Parisi.[23]

Tannenbaum survived the wrath of the Mob and became a lampshade salesman in Georgia. Reles' wife was given permission to change her name.[24]

There were, of course, other hired killers working in New York outside Murder Inc.'s umbrella. Two such were Alex Carrion and Frank Negron who, on 24 August 1933, were electrocuted for the killing of a produce seller Thomas deBellis who had refused to pay protection money at his store. He was shot by three hitmen using handguns with silencers who calmly walked in and out of his store at 672 Tinton Avenue in the Bronx.[25]

Two more were Carlo Barone and Dominic Grippio, convicted of the murder of Barone's former partner Pietro Marsellino in Brooklyn on 10 February 1941. They were regarded by the trial judge Sam Liebowitz as:

> Two of the worst killers that Brooklyn ever had. They are to be classed with the worst killers of the Brooklyn murder ring. I have information that Barone was responsible for eighteen murders and Grippio is an even worse murderer than he, which rates them highly indeed.

[23] *New York Times*, 15 June 1949.
[24] Ibid., 5 June 1942.
[25] Ibid., 6 March 1932, 25 August 1933; *Master Detective*, June 1938.

During the trial Barone was another who feigned insanity, ripping off his shirt and shouting abuse at Liebowitz, the lawyers and the jury. He then played an imaginary game of cards. Liebowitz would have none of this and the next day had Barone put in a straitjacket and gagged with a tape and towel. This was believed to be the first time such a thing had happened in New York and Liebowitz, covering his back, asked Dr Gladys McDermott if it constituted cruel and inhumane treatment. 'Absolutely not', replied the doughty doctor. Barone had been examined after his arrest and was thought to be a malingerer. Now if he wished to communicate with his lawyers he was to tap his foot three times. He promptly did so and the gag was removed. Did he wish to say anything? Barone smiled and said, 'No'. The gag was reapplied and when, at the end of the session, it was removed again he apologised for his bad behaviour.

Both Barone and Grippio were convicted and sentenced to death. They were linked to the Esposito brothers and had supplied them with the guns used in a thwarted robbery which resulted in the murder of a policeman. Grippio was given a retrial but on 10 September 1942 Barone was executed at Sing Sing, visited by neither family nor friends during his time on Death Row.[26]

[26] *New York Times*, 11 February, 10, 11, 19 December 1941, 11 September 1942; *Startling Detective*, August 1941; *True Detective*, June 1944. Anthony and William Esposito, also known respectively as Anhelo and Joseph DiStefano, were electrocuted following the killing in a robbery of Alfred Klausman on 14 January 1941. A policeman was also shot. Anthony was captured by the crowd and almost beaten to death. These Espositos should not be confused with their contemporaries Joseph 'Diamond Joe' and Rafael Esposito who at one time were aligned to Al Capone. 'Diamond Joe' Esposito was killed, probably by the hitmen Scalise and Anselmi, after a fall out with the great man. See *New York Times*, 15 January 1941, 13 March 1942; J. Robert Nash, *World Encyclopedia of Organized Crime*; Laurence Bergreen, *Capone*.

6

More Deadly than the Male

It is curious how women attach themselves to terrorist and political organisations for which they will kill enthusiastically but have rarely taken up financial contract killing as a profession. Statistically they are the ones to employ contract killers, but women who pull the trigger for money are a definite rarity. Overall, women contract killers are creatures of the screen, novels and video games.

Nevertheless, over the years there have been a few female contract killers around the world. With the exception of the Italian Mafia, the first in modern times seems to have been the black 21-year-old Blanche Wright who, with her boyfriend Robert Young, killed a series of drug dealers in the Bronx in January and February 1980. They were an ill-assorted couple. She was born in 1959 to an alcoholic mother and was repeatedly sexually abused by a series of foster-fathers from the age of seven; one man died following a heart attack while trying to rape her. In 1974 Young was interrupted during the burglary of the home of a nurse; he shot her dead and sodomised her corpse before leaving the flat. Arrested some weeks later for an attack on an 11-year-old girl, police searching Young's home found the gun used to kill the nurse. He received an eighteen-year sentence and went to the Matteawan State Hospital for the Criminally Insane. He escaped in a mass break-out in May 1977 and after that met Wright.

On 21 January 1980 she knocked on the door of Felipe Rodriguez in Bedford Park in the Bronx and asked to buy dope. When the door was opened she and Young pushed their way in. Rodriguez was forced to the floor, handcuffed and shot once in the head. His common-law wife Martha Navas was also shot three times in the head. The pair were ransacking the house when a neighbour Luis Martin came to find out what was happening, and he too was shot dead. Rodriguez survived. The pair escaped with $8,000.

A fortnight later another dealer, Marshall Howells, and his body-guard Sam Nevins were leaving a flat in Mount Kisko when Young shot him at point-blank range. The bodyguard returned the fire and shot Young in the chest. Wright then shot at Nevins who fled. Before leaving the scene she calmly shot the dying Howells once more.

Wright was traced when a woman calling herself Lupe Ocasio, and saying she was the boy's aunt, tried to claim Young's body. Officers called at her flat and there was Wright along with the gun used to murder Howells. She admitted it had been a contract killing because Howells had defaulted on a drug debt. She also admitted her part in the Rodriguez shooting and in the killing of another dealer Carlos Medina in 1979. Her trial was postponed because of her pregnancy and she then ran a defence of duress, claiming Young had forced her to help. She was convicted of murder and received a sentence of eighteen years to life in the Howells murder and another of fifteen years to life for the Navas-Martin killings.[1]

In a matter of months she was followed by the 28-year-old Cynthia Marler who on 10 August 1980 flew from Oakland, California, to Sea-Tac airport to kill the divorced Wanda Touchstone in Seattle for cash and – reports vary – either the title to a pick-up truck or to four acres of land. When she undertook the contract, the 5' blonde Marler was already a career criminal with arrests for burglary, kidnapping, receiving stolen property, forgery and conspiracy, and with a husband serving a sentence for armed robbery. The day after her arrival she shot Touchstone in broad daylight in a car park and was seen trying to climb a fence to escape. The number of her rented

[1] See Michael Newton, *Bad Girls Do It*, pp. 184–5.

car was also noted and Marler was arrested as she sat on the 9 p.m. flight back to Oakland awaiting take-off.

Questioned by the police, she claimed that the contract had been arranged by an intermediary, Milos Panich, the son-in-law of Wanda Touchstone's former husband, Lew. Initially Marler was offered a plea bargain: she would be able to plead to second-degree murder if her evidence led to charges being brought against Panich and Lew Touchstone. She told the police she had been offered the contract because her husband had worked for Panich before his arrest for robbery. In the event she proved unreliable and the deal was revoked; it was thought that she had somehow warned Panich that she would be telephoning him from prison, with the conversation to be overheard and recorded by the police. She was found guilty of first-degree murder and sentenced to life imprisonment with a minimum of 312 months. The murder was believed to have been over a $17,000 diamond engagement ring which Wanda Touchstone refused to hand back on her divorce.[2]

Women contract killers may not have been exactly thick on the ground in America, but one who undoubtedly qualifies is the former pickpocket and prostitute Griselda Blanco de Trujillo, known as Muneca because of her doll-like looks and Blanco because of her stutter. She was also one of the Black Widows whose husbands and boyfriends died at increasingly regular intervals. It was alleged that she boasted she had shot her second husband, Alberto Bravo, in the mouth. Blanco was 5'2" in height, very pretty and totally un-principled. She ran her own gang, Los Pistoleros, full membership of which required that the aspirant had cut off the ear or finger of an enemy, and by the mid-1970s she was said to have several hundred people on her payroll. The Pistoleros, along with several other claimants including the Columbian gangs, are named as having invented the art of killing from the back of a high-speed motorcycle. One member's speciality was to tape shut the eyes and mouths of victims, drain their blood in the bath and pack the bodies into TV packing cartons. In 1974 Blanco was indicted over 150

---

[2] *State v Marler* 32 Wn App 503,648 P2d 903 (1982); Ann Rule, 'The Hit Person' in *A Rose For Her Grave*; *Master Detective*, Summer Special, 1990.

kilos of cocaine, and by 1979 she was the best known cocaine smuggler in the United States.

On 11 July that year came the Dade County massacre in the Dadeland Mall, Miami, something which would prove to be a turning point for Blanco. The machine-gunning by her men of two victims, and the subsequent shooting up of the car park as the killers fled, was the culmination of a war which had been running since the previous November and which resulted in the deaths of twenty-four Latin drug smugglers. The Dadeland massacre happened, it would appear, over the theft of four kilos of cocaine.

Finally sentenced to a Federal prison on drug charges, in 1994 it was announced that the police were about to charge Blanco with three murders in the Miami area in 1992. These included the shooting of three-year-old Johnny Castro while sitting next to his father, the target, who had offended Blanco by kicking one of her sons in the buttocks during an argument. The other two murders were of drug dealers Alfred and Grizel Lorenzo, who were killed in their bedroom while their children watched television in another room. The Lorenzos had been late with a drug payment.

Towards the end of 1997 it was decided that she would finally stand trial for murder. Her former gunman and lover, Jorge Ayala, had been arrested on a relatively minor robbery charge and was turned by the authorities. He would give evidence against her in exchange for no death penalty and a sentence of twenty-five years without parole being imposed for his part in the murders he had undertaken for Blanco. This was when the troubles began. Unfortunately the authorities had not bargained for his undoubted charm, particularly over the telephone. He met his wife Marisol by telephone in 1994 and, although this cannot have been down the line, had impregnated her during a jailhouse visit. Now he turned his attentions to women in the Major Crimes Unit at the State Attorney's Office.

Ayala had been moved to a state/county jail facility in Florida where things were much freer and easier, and he became a frequent caller to the Unit. The calls, which were on an almost daily basis and often lasted for hours at a time, were made collect and recorded in the SAO telephone bills. When questioned, several secretaries/witness co-ordinators, who had been lacking guidance and supervision, accepted they had received personal calls from Ayala. However, these had developed into personal relationships and, with Ayala happy to spread his telephonic favours, quarrelling broke out amongst them over who should take the calls. By February 1998 the women were no longer speaking to each other. The reasons they gave for the dispute varied – telephone sex, jealousy, a long-standing dislike. Allegations that they personally had taken part in telephone sex were denied, each suggesting one or more of the others had enjoyed this.

Ayala, who defined phone sex as conversations that involved masturbation, sometimes accepted he had telephone sex, denying it on other occasions. He agreed that he had discussed opening an escort agency with one of the girls, Raquel Navarro, and sent a number of $50 money orders to be used for lunches. He also discussed obtaining a firearm for another of the girls, who then spoke of blowing away a third witness co-ordinator.

With these revelations, the possibility of using Ayala as a witness against Blanco was over and in October 1998 it was announced that she had been allowed to plead 'no contest' to three counts of second-degree murder for which she was sentenced to concurrent terms of twenty years.[3]

Another undoubted contract killer was Eliana Escobar who worked for Medellin cartel boss Pablo Escobar. In July 1993 she was arrested in the New Orleans suburb of Metairie. It was alleged she had run an operation killing dealers in Queens, New York who had refused to pay their debts to Escobar. She had been under observation but had spotted a van outside her Queens apartment and fled.

The first recorded woman contract killer in Britain was a 27-year-old Maori woman Rangimara Ngarimu employed in May 1992. And there does not seem to have been another who has since been arrested.[4] Certainly Ngarimu would fall into the category of amateur.

The contract was taken out by Paul Tubbs and New Zealander

[3] See Paul Eddy and Sara Walden, 'Natural Born Killers' in *Sunday Times Magazine*, 23 November 1997, for an account of the career of Griselda Blanco and Jorge Ayala; for an account of the troubles in the SAO see *Palm Beach Daily Business Review*, 19 June 1998 and Tristram Korten, 'The strange saga of a smooth-talking hit man, jealous secretaries, and a ruined prosecutor' in *Miami New Times*, 26 November 1998.
[4] James Morton, *Supergrasses and Informers*, pp. 4–5.

Deith Bridges on their former business associate, 38-year-old George Woodhatch, and Ngarimu was recruited in the fairly desultory way which seems to characterise so many amateurs in this field. The prosecution's case was that Woodhatch had swindled his business partners in a roofing business out of some £50,000. Despite, or perhaps because of, a lifestyle which included a Porsche and a Japanese-style home in Hertfordshire, Woodhatch was in serious financial difficulties which included a tax bill of £400,000. He was also becoming increasingly irrational, and at the time of his death was on bail for threatening to kill his secretary.

Now Tubbs and Bridges decided to hire a contract killer and Bridges latched on to Ngarimu at a fee of £7,000. She was working as a barmaid when first approached, and initially thought Bridges was joking but was soon persuaded otherwise. The money would go to pay for a mobile home.

The plan was that she would shoot Woodhatch, who was at the time undergoing an operation for piles in the Royal Free Hospital. She would then leave her clothes and the gun with Bridges and fly to New Zealand. Things began to fall apart when on her first visit on 23 May, although she found the ward on which Woodhatch was being treated, she panicked and fled. She returned the next day wearing a baseball cap, tracksuit and gloves, with instructions to shoot him twice in the head and twice in the body to make sure. This time she shot Woodhatch while he was making a telephone call, left the gun and her clothes at Bridges' flat as instructed and caught the 4.30 flight from Gatwick.

At first it was thought that Woodhatch had died following a heart attack, and it was not until a post-mortem examination was being conducted five hours later that the bullet wounds were discovered. By this time Ngarimu was long gone, but things almost immediately began to unravel further. After the killing Tubbs telephoned a friend and asked him to meet Bridges to help get rid of the holdall with the clothes and gun. The friend looked inside before throwing it in a pond. Later he helped the police to retrieve it.

Bridges and Tubbs were arrested and charged with murder, but the committing magistrate held there was insufficient evidence of their involvement in the murder itself and later they pleaded guilty to conspiracy to pervert the course of justice. Meanwhile the police in New Zealand were pressing Ngarimu, and her extradition to England was sought. At first she contested the proceedings, telling the police she was a vegetarian and could not bring herself to kill even a chicken, but over the years at some point she saw The Light. Apparently one day walking past a church she 'felt herself drawn inside'. Following her conversion she voluntarily returned to England to clear her conscience and, in so doing, better her position as far as the courts were concerned.

In 1994 Tubbs and Bridges were convicted, largely on her evidence. They were sentenced to life imprisonment, with recommendations they serve sixteen and fifteen years respectively. The trial judge also suggested the Home Secretary might wish to add a third on to each sentence.

As for Ngarimu, her counsel made a grand-standing speech, telling the Recorder of London that she now attended Bible class three times a week and her conversion to Christianity was total. 'She knows that beyond my Lord's sentence, she faces the judgement of her Lord,' he said in something of a throwback to the Marshall Hall style of advocacy nearly a century earlier. She also received life imprisonment, but was rewarded when the Recorder told her that he did not consider her a professional killer and accepted that she had expressed a deep remorse. The £7,000 had indeed been spent on realising her dream of purchasing a mobile home. Ngarimu's reward was that no tariff was imposed on her life sentence. The case is also curious in that while on bail in May 1994 Bridges was shot in the leg and chest while walking in Ruislip.

Nor have hitwomen been that much more plentiful in Canada. Christine Lepage was only arrested nearly twenty years after her alleged foray. In 1981 she was allegedly employed by Benôit Baillargeon to kill a funeral director, Germain Derome. Accordingly she went to his house posing as a reporter conducting a survey of funeral homes. Invited in, she was offered a glass of water and then shot Derome twice as well as the German Shepherd belonging to Derome's housemate, the television actor Julien Bessette. She ran away after Bessette threw a chair at her, so deflecting another shot.

There were fingerprints on both the glass and the notepad she left behind, but there was no match with the criminal records trawled. A year later she was fingerprinted in a fraud case, but again the prints were not matched and it was not until the murder case was re-examined in 2000 that the link was established.

Now Ms Lepage was wooed by an RCMP woman undercover officer who first offered her cosmetic samples and entered her into a draw for the prize of a weekend at a Château Montebello hotel which unsurprisingly, since she was the only contestant, she won. She apparently admitted that she would do anything for money and that she moonlighted as a prostitute. She was then introduced to other agents, into a fake criminal gang and sent on spurious jobs. At a party in her honour she met a bogus crime boss with whom she discussed the killing, believing he could arrange the destruction of the evidence. Unfortunately she was videotaped. In turn she claimed she had been entrapped.

On 10 March 2005 Ms Lepage was convicted of the murder of Derome and the attempted murder of Bessette. She accepted she had been at their home but claimed she was there as a call girl. Her lawyer had argued that the killer was the jealous Bessette who had walked in on the pair. Lepage was sentenced to life imprisonment, with twenty-five years to be served before she is eligible for parole. Her lawyer indicated he was lodging an appeal: 'I'm surprised that with everything we presented not even a piece of doubt entered the minds of the jury.'

The reason for her fingerprints not matching years earlier was that they had been run through a database containing only men's prints.[5]

One of the more unusual hitwomen was Larisa Roshina, aged 21, with a small child and an apparent passion for art. Until 2001 she worked as a secretary in a Russian court and led a seemingly blameless life. Then to repay a £2,000 debt she was hired as a contract killer. Now she was known as 'Russia's Nikita', after the hitwoman of the French film and the later television series. An

---

[5] *Globe and Mail*, 8 January 2003; *Journal de Montréal*, 23, 26, February 2005; *Montreal Gazette*, 10 March 2005; *Globe and Mail*, 11 March 2005.

orphan brought up on the outskirts of Moscow by her police investigator aunt, Roshina was deserted by her husband Vladimir and left
to care for their son on a monthly salary of less than £100. She
borrowed to set herself up in business, buying and selling mobile
phones and television sets. But her business partner went bust,
she lost the money she had invested and found herself unable to
pay her creditors.

'By September last year one man to whom I owed nearly £2,000
put pressure on me,' wrote Roshina in her confession. 'He said he
urgently needed the money and if I was not able to pay him back
I would have to "work off" the debt:'

> He warned me that his friends were keeping an eye on my baby
> and that if I refused to do what he told me to, they would slit
> the child's throat. He took out a handgun wrapped in plastic and
> put it in my hands. I told him that I didn't know how to use a
> gun. He said that all I needed to do was pull the trigger. I was
> very scared.

Until the moment when she accepted the gun, Roshina's story was
typical of post-communist Russia. Many women marry young and
have children early, only to end up divorced and struggling to
survive by their mid-twenties. Pimps lure the most vulnerable and
desperate into prostitution. The more enterprising, like Roshina,
are attracted to loan sharks, as banks rarely give business loans or
mortgages to single mothers.

Roshina's life took its unparalleled turn on 21 September when
she and her creditor lured two small-time businessmen to a meeting
at an apartment block in eastern Moscow with the promise of a
lucrative deal. According to Roshina, her creditor never explained
why he wanted Yuri Vassiliev and Alexander Kuzovlev dead. The
pair arrived in a dark BMW; Roshina walked into the building with
Vassiliev while his colleague waited in the car. Inside her handbag
was the Soviet-made TT handgun.

'Vassiliev and I took the lift up to the 12th floor. As he walked
onto the landing I pulled out the gun from my handbag and shot
him in the back,' said Roshina. She ran downstairs past a cleaner

– who later identified her in court – to find the creditor, who was hiding in the next-door entrance:

> He asked how many times I had shot Vassiliev and when I said once he told me to go back upstairs and shoot him again to make sure he was dead. I went back but when I got there a woman and a man had come to help him. I shot in their direction. Then the woman jumped at me and we got into a fight and fell on the floor. She begged me to let her go. I told her to leave. Then I realised that I had no more bullets and I ran downstairs again.

Roshina's creditor reloaded her gun and sent her to kill Kuzovlev, who was dozing in the BMW, and obediently she shot him in the back of the head. She maintained the creditor then ran away and she never saw him again. About £20,000 soaked in blood was found at the scene, but investigators were unable to establish a motive for the murders. An artist's impression of Roshina was shown on television and she gave herself up.

The police hauled in her creditor, but he denied any involvement and when officers confronted him with Roshina she changed her story. Perhaps because she was afraid, she claimed he had had nothing to do with the killings after all, and he left a free man.

'When I first saw her I had serious doubts that she had been the one to commit these murders,' said Vladimir Medvedev, the judge who imprisoned her for twelve years, taking into account her youth, child and willingness to confess if not co-operate. 'I saw this small, fragile-looking single mother and wondered if she was capable of shooting two men in cold blood at point-blank range,' he added. 'But then I read her confession: no emotions, no remorse. I have been sentencing criminals for twenty years but I've never come across anyone like Roshina.'[6]

More often than pulling the trigger, women are used as lures. When in 1914 the English-born Owen 'Owney The Killer' Madden, now plying his trade in New York, quarrelled with Patsy Doyle over the favours of Freda Horner, she, along with her friend Margaret Everdeane, was part of a trap set for Doyle. Everdeane,

[6] 'Debts turn mother into gun for hire' in *Sunday Times*, 14 July 2002.

apparently from a respectable family but who hung around with Madden's gang, told Doyle that Freda wanted to make things up and to meet him at a saloon on 8th Avenue. Doyle went there but found Everdeane and no Horner. She told him Freda would be along in a moment. A telephone call was made and Everdeane conveniently left with a friend William Mott. As they were going into the Brighton Club she heard shots. Rather callously after that she, Mott, Madden and Horner all went to a dance at the Moose Inn.

In later rose-tinted accounts it is Madden who enters the saloon, calls out 'You rat' and shoots Doyle once and accurately in the lung. In fact five shots were fired by Arthur Bledler and Thomas McArdle while Madden prudently waited outside. The killing may not have been over Horner at all. Earlier Doyle had been arrested over the shooting of Tee Romanello who had declined to give evidence. One version of events is that Doyle was to be punished for this; another theory is that he had been trying to take advantage of Madden's wounds from an earlier fight and was endeavouring to assume control of the Gophers. He had also been bad-mouthing the Madden Gang.

The two girls were duly questioned by the police and gave evidence against Bledler, who received eighteen years, and McArdle who collected five years less. In late May 1915 they were paraded again to give evidence against Madden himself. Despite running an alibi defence and complaining that the girls had been made to give false evidence, Madden was convicted. He was nevertheless well pleased with the resulting manslaughter conviction and wanted to be sentenced there and then. In the event, sentencing was delayed until the following week when he received a term of from ten to twenty years. This did not please him, and there followed efforts to have the conviction overturned on the basis that the girls had been made to perjure themselves. It did Madden no good and he was eventually released in 1922.[7]

Perhaps the best-known use by the FBI of a woman lure was Anna Sage, the so-called 'Woman in Red' who fingered John

---

[7] *New York Times*, 17 December 1914, 25, 27, 28 May 1915.

Dillinger. Sage, a Romanian-born brothel-keeper whose real name was Ana Cumpanas, had convictions for running houses in both Chicago and Gary, Indiana, and – facing a third conviction, and with it inevitable deportation – she contacted the FBI to say that her room-mate Polly Hamilton had Dillinger as a boyfriend. She had heard the stories that Dillinger, then living as Jimmy Lawrence, was telling Hamilton and, putting two and two together, she went to agent Melvin Purvis to try to negotiate not only the reward but also a relaxation of the deportation proceedings.

On 22 July 1934 Dillinger, together with Sage and Hamilton, went to the Biograph Theatre to see Clark Gable in *Manhattan Melodrama*. As arranged, Sage was wearing red to indicate that Dillinger was with her. According to some versions, Purvis called on Dillinger to stop and then the FBI opened fire. Dillinger was hit along with two women passers-by. Hamilton and Sage simply disappeared from the scene and were taken to Detroit to ensure their silence. Sage later received $5,000, half the amount she anticipated. On 29 April 1936 she was deported to Romania where she died in Timisoara in 1947.[8]

A strange case is that of the Russian woman known only as Madame Popova, arrested in Samara in 1909 and thought to have killed up to three hundred men on behalf of their wives and girlfriends. Accounts have it that she was executed by a firing squad.[9]

Two similar English women killers worthy of note are Catherine Flanagan and her sister Margaret Higgins who were hanged on 5 March 1884 by executioners Bartholomew Binns and Samuel Heath respectively. Flanagan had insured her husband Thomas with five different companies, while she gave him small doses of arsenic in an effort to make it seem he was terminally ill. He died in September 1883. The body of Mary Jennings, a lodger who had died earlier in the year, was exhumed and found also to contain traces of arsenic. Margaret Higgins was charged with her

[8] There is a probably untenable theory that the FBI were duped and it was a small-time gangster Jimmy Lawrence who was actually killed. If it is correct Dillinger lived on, founding a colony to be later populated by JFK, Lord Lucan and Elvis Presley. See J. Robert Nash, *Dillinger: Dead or Alive?*
[9] *New York Times*, 9 March 1909. This appears to be the only contemporary account of her story in the English language press.

elder sister and the pair were believed responsible for a number of other insurance-based killings on behalf of other women.[10]

That pair seem to have been a cottage industry in their own right, but in America women were recruited by the Petrillo cousins in what was a wholesale slaughter of the insured. Herman and Paul Petrillo, along with their cousin Dr Morris Bolber, were members of a long-running killing ring in Philadelphia which flourished from 1932 until the early 1940s. It began when Bolber and Paul Petrillo conspired for the latter to seduce the wife of one of the doctor's patients. She was then prevailed upon to take out an insurance policy for £10,000 on her husband, Anthony Giscobbi. One winter night when the unfortunate man arrived home the worse for drink, Petrillo and the wife undressed him and left him in front of an open window. No one thought that his resulting death from pneumonia was anything but his own fault. Herman was now recruited into the business of seduction, insurance and subsequent murder, as was Carino Favato, a faith-healer known as The Witch who was thought to have killed three of her husbands and helped other women in the disposing of theirs. She charged a fee, but until then had not cottoned on to the additional benefits of insurance.

Over a period of five years the ring disposed of at least thirty and probably fifty unwanted husbands. One man was pushed off an eight-storey building. Before he was pushed Petrillo gave him some dirty postcards, and it was easy for the police to think he had been distracted by these saucy delights and so lost his footing. Others were disposed of with a blow from a canvas bag filled with sand which produced a cerebral haemorrhage, and death appeared to be from natural causes.

The end came when a newly released convict approached Herman Petrillo with a proposal. Petrillo turned him down, saying, 'Go dig somebody up we can murder for insurance and you can make some dough with us.' Murder was apparently beyond the scope of the man and he went to the police. Bolber and Favato were perhaps fortunate to be sentenced to life imprisonment. The Petrillo cousins

[10] See Steve Fielding, *The Hangman's Record*, Volume One.

went to the electric chair.[11]

Florence Lassandro had the dubious distinction of being the first woman to be hanged for twenty-four years and the last woman hanged in Alberta. In 1922 she was involved in the shooting of Constable Steve Lawson, but whether she pulled the trigger is open to question. Lassandro was probably the mistress of the Blairmore rum-running king Emilio 'Emperor Pic' Picariello. Certainly she kept close company with him, being used as a shield in his smuggling activities. With her in the car, the police were reluctant to shoot when he failed to stop at their checkpoints.

She was with him in September 1922 when he heard that his son, Steve, had been shot and killed by Lawson. The information was wrong; Steve was only slightly wounded. Nevertheless Picariello sought out Lawson and either he or Lassandro shot him. It was thought by their lawyers that the judge would not authorise the hanging of a woman and so she took the blame. The lawyers were wrong. The pair were refused a reprieve and were hanged at Fort Saskatchewan prison on 2 May 1923. He went first at 5.10 a.m. and she followed half an hour later. 'You are hanging an innocent man, God help me,' said Picariello. 'Why are you doing this to me, have you no pity?' she is said to have asked.[12]

It is difficult to say whether Jean Lee was the lure or the leader of the trio which included Robert Clayton and Norman Andrews. On 7 November 1949 they tortured and then strangled and stabbed the elderly William 'Old Bill' Kent, a 73-year-old bookmaker in Carlton, a Melbourne suburb. At the time Lee – known also as Smith, White, Brown, Duncan, Marjorie Brees and Marie Williams – was an attractive red-headed 32-year-old girl from a respectable working-class home in Dubbo, New South Wales. After leaving school she worked for a milliner, then as a waitress, then as a clerk and finally in a factory. At the age of 18 she married a man from Sydney and had a daughter. When, at the beginning of the war, her marriage broke up she became a prostitute working in the King's Cross area of Sydney. After acquiring a number of convictions she

[11] *Thomson's Weekly News*, 3 June 1939; *New York Times*, 25 March 1941; Brian Lane and Wilfred Gregg, *The New Encyclopedia of Serial Killers*.
[12] *The Calgary Herald*, 1, 2 May 1923.

realised she needed a minder and took up with Robert David Clayton, a known bludger or ponce. It was only a matter of time before they latched on to the badger game as being an easier and more profitable form of work.

Lee would go with men to hotel rooms or the backs of cars only to be 'discovered' by Clayton who, as the aggrieved husband, naturally demanded financial recompense. When Clayton discovered that some of the victims were prepared to fight it out with him, it was necessary to recruit another member of the team. In 1949 Norman Andrews, whom he met in a bar, joined the team as 'husband's friend' and he supplied the strong-arm stuff when the victims showed any reluctance to pay.

Unfortunately one of the men went to the police and reported the beating and robbery he had sustained. Doubly unfortunately, although the police were able to identify the trio from the descriptions – Andrews had a number of convictions for robbery – they did not arrest them immediately.

On 7 November 1949 they went to a bar in Lygon Street and latched on to the small and fat Kent. It was only a matter of drink and time before he was persuaded to go with Jean Lee to his flea and lice-infested rooming house in Dorritt Street. She told him her stage name was Valez and wrote it down for him. She then got him more drunk and while performing oral sex, tried to pick his pocket. When he would not let go of his wallet she hit him on the head with a bottle and then a piece of wood and, joined by the others, tortured him. Kent was placed on a chair with his thumbs tied together with a bootlace while for over an hour he was repeatedly kicked and beaten. Finally he was strangled and left tied to the chair.

With the stolen money, Clayton bought tickets for a flight to Sydney and the trio went to a club to celebrate. After their night out they returned to their hotel room at 4 a.m. to find the police waiting for them. Lee had been traced by an astute officer who linked her to the name Valez. It was Clayton who broke first, blaming the others. When the jury announced its verdict Lee threw her arms around Clayton screaming, 'I didn't do it.' When the convictions were quashed by the State Court which excluded some of the police

evidence, she began kissing Clayton and had to be physically separated from him before being led from the dock laughing. The High
Court reversed the State Court's ruling and restored the death
penalty sentence. Lee could not believe that the government would
hang a woman, but she was wrong. The Sydney standover man
Chow Hayes wrote of them: 'I'd been in jail with Norm Andrews,
who wasn't a bad bloke . . . It was never revealed in the newspapers,
but the whisper was that they'd cut off their victim's penis and
stuffed it in his mouth.'

Which would account, at least in part, for the government's
reluctance to grant a reprieve. That was partly confirmed by the
veteran reporter Alan Dower who wrote that Kent's penis had
been bound with a bootlace and repeatedly stabbed. At 8.01 a.m.
on 19 February 1951 Lee was hanged at Pentridge prison. Heavily
sedated, she was carried to the gallows wearing what were described
as khaki pedal pushers, a white shirt and sandals, and hanged sitting
in a chair in which she had to be supported by the hangman's assistant. Clayton and Andrews were hanged in a double execution two
hours later. Outside the jail a section of the crowd sang, 'Nearer my
God to Thee'. She was the last woman to be hanged in Australia.[13]

More recently Mary Ryan of Kings Park, Glasgow, was convicted
of the murder of the con-man and drug dealer Manus 'Manny'
O'Donnell who was found shot and wrapped in a tarpaulin in a
lover's lane in November 1998. He had made a number of enemies
and one of his problems seems to have been over the Shamrock
Club in Dublin which he owned in partnership. It was said he had
tried to take out a £50,000 contract on his former partner. After
O'Donnell's death the partner was reported to have said that it was
regrettable in the sense that he had not been there to see it.

Mary Ryan, who worked for O'Donnell fronting his Pretty Woman
escort agency in Clydebank, was said to have been the lure to take
her employer to his death. They had been drinking at the Tinto
Firs hotel in Glasgow's South Side; she maintained that when they
left two men forced their way into the car – a hired yellow Renault

---

[13] *R v Lee and ors.* (1950) 82 CLR 32; *Sydney Morning Herald*, 20 February 1951; *The Age* (Melbourne), 20 February 1951; David Hickie, *Chow Hayes, Gunman*; Vince Kelly, *The Charge is Murder*.

Megane – put something she believed to be a gun to her head and forced her to drive away. She was told to stop in Bellahouston, pulled from the car, given the keys and told to report the vehicle stolen in the morning. Having made her way to the flat of a Patrick Devine, she spent the night with him. At first she maintained she had been with Devine from 8 p.m. on the night of the murder, but changed her story which was discredited when she was found to have the only set of keys to the now burned-out Renault which could not be hot-wired. There was also a call on her mobile phone made around 10 p.m. in the area where the car was found. Convicted and sentenced to life imprisonment with a recommendation she serve at least fifteen years, her appeal was rejected on 23 June 2003.[14]

In passing, O'Donnell's lawyer Jack Quar had been found hanging from the banisters in his office some days before the discovery of O'Donnell's body. The verdict was that he had committed suicide, but there were suggestions in the underworld that he had been murdered after O'Donnell gave him £100,000 from £250,000 he had stolen from a drug baron. Certainly Quar had had financial difficulties. He had sold a substantial house, and at the time of his death was living in a £40,000 ground-floor former council flat. The police dismissed the claim that he had been murdered as 'arrant nonsense', but the rumours still persist.[15]

[14] *The Herald and Sunday Herald*, 4 September 1999; *The Scotsman*, 4 September, 4 December 1999, 24 June 2003.
[15] *The Sun*, 19 November 1998; *The Scotsman*, 5 January 1999.

7

Dead Bosses

Overall, the risks involved in being a traditional blue-collar gang-land boss in England have not been that great – at least, not until drugs and the Yardies came along. Certainly not as great as in say France, Italy, America and Australia where the death toll has been consistently high. In England Darby Sabini, his rival Fred Kimber of the Brummagen Boys, Billy Hill and Jack Spot all died in their beds. Apart from one minor skirmish with some rivals whom they immediately saw off, the Messina brothers, the Kings of Vice in Soho and Mayfair for over twenty years, were never really at risk from anyone but the police. No one ever seriously tried to assas-sinate the Krays – or Charlie Richardson in the days when he was working. Arthur Thompson in Glasgow seems to have been the kingpin most at risk. Over the years he survived some gang wars – although his mother-in-law did not – and being shot in the testicles by a disgruntled employee, only to succumb years later to a heart attack. Admittedly Newcastle's Viv Graham was killed on the pavement in the city but, when it is all added together, until recently there has been a low mortality rate at the top. The reason for the survival of these early bosses is twofold. First, unfashionable as it may be to say it, the death penalty was in force. Spot's maxim was, 'You must never cut below the line here, 'cause, if you do, you cut the jugular – and the hangman is waiting for you.'[1] Second, the stakes were tiny compared with the profits generated by today's drug trade.

One exception in London was one of the bosses of pre-war prostitution Emil Allard, known as Max Kessel or Red Max, whose bullet-ridden body was found on 24 January 1936 under a hedge near St Albans in Hertfordshire. This scar-faced, well-built man had been shot five times. All means of identification had been removed.

A Latvian by birth, Allard lived in James Street off Oxford Street and had the occupation of 'diamond merchant', that cover beloved of the procurer. In and out of London since 1913, he was a prime mover in the pre-First World War white slave traffic, selling girls to Latin-American brothels. They may have travelled to Buenos Aires in style, but that was the last luxury the girls saw in their lives. As the police investigated deeper into Allard's background they traced back his connection to the murder of a number of Soho prostitutes including Josephine Martin, known as French Fifi, strangled with her own silk stockings in her Archer Street flat. She had been a police informer as well as one of Allard's aides looking after the foreign prostitutes smuggled into this country.

Allard's murder was investigated by Chief Inspector 'Nutty' Sharpe who found the flat at 36 Little Newport Street where he had been killed. The occupier had been George Edward Lacroix alias Marcel Vernon. He had lived with Suzanne Bertrand who had gone through a form of marriage to an Englishman, Naylor, and now was working the Soho streets. By the time Sharpe caught up with them they had fled to France from where the authorities refused to extradite them. They did, however, agree to put them on trial there for Allard's murder.

The killing was thought to have occurred because Suzanne Bertrand was working for both Vernon and Allard and they had quarrelled over her earnings. Marcelle Aubin, Suzanne's maid, gave evidence at an inquest held in London that Allard had called on her mistress and she had taken him in to Vernon. Later she heard the sound of an argument followed by several shots. Called by Vernon, she and Suzanne rushed in and found Allard shot in the

[1] James Morton and Gerry Parker, *Gangland Bosses*, p. 92.

stomach and back. As he was dying he broke two panes of glass in the window with his forearm in an effort to attract attention. It was one of the matching pieces of glass on the pavement that had led Sharpe to No. 36. Marcelle Aubin had been told to order a car from a garage in Soho Square owned by another Frenchman, Pierre Alexandre, and the body of Allard had been bundled in the back to be dumped near St Albans.

At the trial at the Seine Assizes in April 1937 the garage proprietor gave evidence against Vernon, who was sentenced to ten years' penal servitude and twenty years' exclusion. Suzanne Bertrand was acquitted after she had laid bare the details of Vernon's partnership with Allard, as well as Alexandre's agency for marrying off foreign women to threadbare Englishmen. Allard and Vernon, who had first met in Montreal, had worked the white slave trade together for years. The breakdown of their relationship does seem to have been over Bertrand, for whom Vernon had left his wife in Paris in 1933.

In March 1992 Arthur Thompson, a man who had a genuine claim to be the 'King of Glasgow's Gangland', possibly even that of Britain, died following a heart attack. The weekend before his death he had been out dancing with his wife and friends. Perhaps of all Glasgow hardmen he could be said to have been a genuine gangland boss in the old traditional style. According to his lawyer Joe Beltrami:

> [Thompson] was an impressive looking figure – about five feet ten inches tall and weighing about 12 stones. He was well-built, in a not-so-obvious way – his suits were well cut and sober, his ties and shirts conservative. Distinguished looking and slightly older than I, his face displayed small marks of bygone conflicts. He had more acquittals to his name than most.

Beltrami added that Thompson had 'gun-metal eyes'.[2]

Thompson was born in 1931, the year of the introduction of the Means Test. His parents lived in a tenement in Springburn on Glasgow's North side and were eventually rehoused in Blackhill. His brothers became barmen-cum-bouncers in the Provanmill Inn

[2] Joe Beltrami, *A Deadly Innocence*, pp. 58–9.

near the family home, but Thompson himself had greater ambition. He wished to be a landlord and not merely a bouncer.

By the 1950s and 1960s Thompson had built up a reputation as a hardman dealing with villains such as Gorbals' street baron, Teddy Martin – described as having the Italian looks which drove women wild, and a ferocious temper – who was shot by him on 25 March 1961. From the 1950s he maintained links with English criminals. He was a friend of Billy Hill and also organised a system under which Glasgow hardmen could be contracted for attacks in London. 'They were cheaper, they weren't known and they did the job better,' said a Strathclyde policeman. Thompson could also be relied on to provide a safe home for wanted London criminals.

But he really made his mark over his twenty-five-year-long war for control of the North side with the powerful Welsh family, also from Blackhill. First, Patrick Welsh and his friend James Goldie died when their van hit a wall and then a lamp-post. Thompson was charged with causing their deaths by running them off the road, but was acquitted after the jury had retired for rather less than an hour. The original charge of murder had been reduced to one of unjustifiable homicide. Three months later Thompson and his mother-in-law, Maggie Johnstone, climbed into his MG parked outside his house in Provanmill Road. When he started the car there was an explosion. She was killed; he was injured. Three of the Welshes were later acquitted. In July 1967 Thompson's wife Rita went to prison after admitting to leading a raid on the Welsh family's home. The police, if not actually frightened, were certainly wary of Thompson. One senior officer evacuated his family from his home during the prosecution for the deaths of Welsh and Goldie, fearing it would be bombed. Another officer emigrated after the case.[3]

It was through his son Arthur junior – known as Fat Boy because of a predilection for Mars Bars – and some of his London contacts that Thompson moved into drugs, operating from a base in

---

[3] It is said that it was because of the Welsh-Thompson war that the Criminal Injuries Compensation Act 1964 was changed so that criminals could not benefit from injuries suffered in the course of duty.

Blackpool. But by the end of the 1980s attempts to overthrow him were coming thick and fast. In November 1989 he was shot by his own henchman Tam Bagan, while washing his car in front of a lock-up garage. 'It was a warning, I never intended to kill him then. It was just to show him what I could do.'[4] Thompson booked himself into the private Nuffield Alpine Clinic and told the police and the doctor who removed the bullet that he had injured himself with a drill bit which had sheared off during use. Three years later he was run down again by disgruntled employees outside his council house home, which by now he had converted into something like a luxury fortress – two houses, overlooking the local cemetery, knocked into one and heavily barricaded with steel doors. Again he survived.

His son Arthur junior did not survive for long, and it was drugs that proved to be his downfall. In 1985 he went to prison for eleven years on heroin-dealing charges. During the early part of his sentence Arthur junior was able to demand a cut from his team, the Barlanark Gang, but he was by no means a popular leader and a rival organisation was in place within the year. Although he may have assisted his son, rather as The Godfather, Don Corleone, was never keen to join Sollazzo in the drug trade, nor was Arthur Thompson senior. Nevertheless he loyally protected his son against drug-dealing allegations, maintaining that the Fat Boy had been framed by the police.

It is not wholly clear whether the killing of the Fat Boy was intentional. Apart from the theory of a contract hit by rivals, one story is that his attacker had intended simply to capture him and, after glue and feathering him, to deposit him in full view of a waiting journalist. A third version of events is that the Fat Boy was only intended to have been shot in his ample buttocks, but that the shooter missed the designated target when Thompson moved at the crucial moment.

The circumstances of his death were indeed curious. Released on weekend home leave after serving some seven years of his sentence, he arranged to have a meal with his sister in an Italian

[4] Interview with author.

restaurant. Although the house in which he lived was part of Thompson's fortress, the Fat Boy apparently took no great protective measures for his safety. Almost at the last minute the venue was changed and he went to Café India, a smart Indian restaurant in the centre of the city, with his mother and his common-law wife Catherine. Shortly before he arrived at the restaurant, a man later said to be the Glasgow hardman Paul Ferris approached the manager and insisted on searching the dining area with its two hundred-plus customers before he was satisfied there was no Thompson about. After his meal Thompson returned to the fortress, had a word with his father, then walked to the end house to check whether his brother Billy was recording a film on the video. He rang the bell and a woman in the house who went to the door sensed that something was wrong; she saw the Fat Boy staggering away, shot. One bullet had grazed his cheek, one fractured two ribs and the third hit his heart. His last words were, 'I've been shot, hen. I'm going to collapse.' The family did not wait for an ambulance but drove him to hospital where he was found to be dead on arrival.

Now, say underworld acquaintances, it was the moment for Thompson to show who really was the master. As his son's cortege went to the graveyard it passed a car in which the bodies of the two men Joe 'Bananas' Hanlon[5] and Robert Glover, suspected of Arthur junior's killing, had been left. They had each been shot in the head with a .22 pistol. Overall Hanlon had not led a lucky life. A car he owned had been blown up, his ice-cream van from which he sold heroin had been torched and he had been shot on two occasions, once in the penis.

In 1992 after a trial lasting fifty-four days Paul Ferris, suspected of being the third of Thompson junior's murderers, was acquitted.

Ferris – 'clever, articulate and passionate,' according to one trial observer – was also cleared of charges of supplying drugs, kneecapping a former member of the Barlanark team, Willie Gillen, and attempting to murder Arthur Thompson himself. He later wrote a

---

[5] He was called Bananas not because of any mental instability but because he had once taken part in a school fundraiser by dressing as a banana.

book about his experiences in this and other cases.[6] So far as the attempt on Arthur senior's life was concerned, this could not possibly have been done by Ferris because Arthur, himself a great performer, went into the witness box to say he regarded Ferris almost as a son.

After Ferris's acquittal the *Daily Record* reported that there was a £30,000 contract on his life. Indeed, in the ensuing troubles Ferris' family has not escaped unscathed. Willie Ferris, his father, needed over 100 stitches following an attack. He was beaten with a hammer and baseball bat and his car, bought with a disability pension, had its tyres slashed and was later set on fire. Ferris' brother Billy, then serving a life sentence for murder, asked to be moved to a prison nearer to his father.

Back in 1988, a second son Billy Thompson had been the object of a kidnap exercise as he was drinking with friends in the Open Arms in Riddrie. He owed money and two men posing as policemen held and handcuffed him. Thompson called out that they were bogus, and he was rescued when the handcuffs broke. One of the men, Gordon Ross senior, was stabbed to death in September 2002. With his father dead Billy fared even worse. In 2000, almost outside his home, he was attacked and stamped on by Robert Morrison and Christopher Irvine, leaving him brain-damaged. They received eight and five years respectively. The next year, when showing his friends how effective was his new bulletproof vest, he stabbed himself in the stomach. Then in June 2003 he was attacked again and stabbed in a dispute allegedly over money, near his home at Provanmill.[7]

Arthur Thompson may have been an old and fearful man when he died but, within a few years of his death, stability in Glasgow's gangland was in freefall. By the end of the twentieth century the gang scene in Glasgow was thoroughly destabilised, with yet another protection war raging. In the past protection had generally been of clubs and pubs, and who should have whose bouncers in place, but recently the fighting has been over contracts for the security of building sites and schools.

[6] Paul Ferris, *The Ferris Conspiracy*.
[7] *News of the World*, 22 June 2003.

With the growth in the drug trade, the life expectancy of top Glasgow criminals has shortened dramatically. On 10 May 2000 another old-timer, Frank McPhie, was shot dead. One explanation on offer was that he had fallen foul of former Northern Ireland terrorists who had moved into the drug trade. Apart from negotiating between dealers in the North and the rest of England, he was thought to have been one of the powers behind a big dog-fighting ring. In 1991 he was fined £1,000 after being found at a fight. Another suggested reason for his death was that he had beaten up the son of another gangland figure. A third theory was that he had stabbed a member of another Glasgow gang whom he believed to be an informer. It was thought a contract had been out on him for a year.

Since 1978 McPhie had served a total of eighteen years. First, a five-year sentence, followed by eight years and then another five. In 1992 he was acquitted of involvement in an armed robbery at the Dundee branch of the Royal Bank of Scotland. The next year came his eight-year sentence for dealing in drugs. He was alleged to have been the go-between for a London-based dealer and a Glasgow baron. It was while he was serving this sentence that he was accused and acquitted of killing the murderer William 'Worm' Toye in Perth prison.

Three months after finishing his sentence McPhie was once again charged with murder. This time the victim was the milkman by trade, Christopher McGrory. Despite being unemployed, McGrory owned three houses in Ireland and was thought to be smuggling cocaine and heroin. McPhie had been an usher at McGrory's Dublin wedding only a fortnight previously. Now the groom was found strangled on a golf course near Milngavie. McPhie and another man were acquitted following non-proven verdicts.

On the day of his death, after a quarrel at his allotment McPhie drove back to the sanctuary of his home in a tenement block – itself only 400 yards from the police station – on the drug-riddled Maryhill estate which he ruled by terror. He failed to make his ground. On the 8th floor of a block opposite was a trained marksman who shot him on his doorstep. The man escaped through the flats while paramedics tried to save McPhie as he died on the pavement.

John McCabe, a man close to the important Daniels family, was arrested for McPhie's killing but released when no evidence was forthcoming. McPhie was known to have badly cut a member of the family for not showing him sufficient respect, but it was remarked that it was easier to find people whom he had upset than those he had not.

A police officer offered as an epitaph: 'He had been a dead man walking for years. For McPhie the end was always going to come like this.'[8]

In late 2001 there were suggestions that efforts were being made to set up an Appalachian-style peace conference, with senior Glasgow figures invited to attend. The idea of a meeting was prompted by various shootings including the attempt on the life of Duncan McIntyre who was shot as he left a barber's shop in Springburn in June 2001. He was taken to hospital while the gunman caught a No. 45 bus. McIntyre survived, just as he had survived a previous effort outside his home in the Gallowgate some years previously. Shortly before the attack on McIntyre, Tommy McGovern was taken to the car park of the Talisman bar in Springburn and shot. He survived. Another McGovern brother, Tony, had been shot in September 2000 outside the New Morven public house in Balornock. Despite wearing a £400 bullet-proof vest he had not survived and, it was said, the secret of where he kept his money died with him.

How had it all come on top? The McGoverns and the McIntyres, at one time rival enterprises in the Springburn area, were more recently thought to have been working in partnership but had again fallen out. The catalyst was the relationship which Tony McGovern had formed in 1997 with James Stevenson, the so-called Iceman also known as The Bull. It was not a relationship which appealed to Tommy McGovern and the pair suggested that he had stolen £60,000 from them. They went looking for it and shortly afterwards Tommy McGovern was shot and run over by one of his own ice-cream vans. After that Tony McGovern and the Iceman began to establish an empire based on drugs and moneylending. Meanwhile Tommy McGovern went to prison to serve a four-year sentence for firearms and other offences.

[8] See Tony Thompson in *The Observer*, 13 August 2000.

While there his elder brother, Joe, tried to broker a settlement between the brothers. Unfortunately the price demanded was that Tony dispose of the Iceman. He was taken out to the country near Fintry but Tony botched the killing, merely grazing his neck, and The Iceman survived, running into woodlands. The next week Tony McGovern was shot in the shower of his home in Kenmure Crescent, Bishopriggs. Amazingly, only a single bullet lodged and he also survived.

Attack and counter-attack followed. A garage in Springburn owned by the Iceman was continually robbed. In turn the Café Cini, a nightclub in Greenock owned by former Celtic player Charlie Nicholas, was set alight. There is no suggestion that Nicholas knew anything of the feud which had engulfed him; it was simply a place which the McGoverns used.

By the summer of 2001, it was alleged that the Protestant Ulster Volunteer Force, along with some members of the Carbin, Madden and McIntyre families, was backing James Stevenson. Ranged with the McGoverns were the Catholic sympathisers, Frank Boyle, a schoolfriend of theirs and Tam McGraw, known as The Licensee. There was also Frank Carberry, who had been convicted in 1995 after throwing a horse's ear at a woman. James Milligan, who had an interest in Café Cini, had disappeared in January 2001.

Jamie McGovern had previously been in the wars when he was shot in the face. His other brother, Paul McGovern, ran the thriving security firm M.&M. which had contracts with the Scottish Executive. The Carbins were friends of both the Stevensons and the McGoverns. Indeed Caroline Stevenson had once been married to Gerry Carbin senior, known as 'Cyclops' after a cataract left him blind in one eye, and Tony McGovern was the best man at the James Stevenson-Caroline Carbin wedding. Carbin senior received a nine-year sentence in Spain for drug smuggling. Gerry Carbin junior, in his early twenties, was given a bad beating by Tony McGovern shortly before the latter's death.

As for the McIntyres, they had also been friends of the McGoverns. The one-time head of that family, the now deceased Joe 'Fat Boy' McIntyre, had been a career criminal. An ex-lawyer relative, James, went to prison in 1997 after the police found pistols and ammunition at his home in West Lothian.

In 1985 Charles Madden had been stabbed to death outside a club in Saracen, North Glasgow, allegedly by a man from the McGovern camp. He was acquitted, but from then on the Maddens aligned themselves with the Stevensons.[9] On 24 August 2001 James Stevenson was charged with the murder of Tony McGovern; he had been found the previous week in Blackpool and was remanded in custody. It was expected that the committal for trial would be something of a formality, but then came a sensational development. Stevenson was released on the authority of the Procurator Fiscal who then legally had a year to bring him to court again but did not do so. In practice this has generally meant that, in the absence of further evidence, it was the end of the matter.

No one has ever been wholly clear about the reasons for the death of Newcastle's Viv Graham. Back in the 1980s it was thought that a reputation was easier to make in that city rather than say Manchester or Liverpool. Graham had certainly made a reputation in a bouncers' war in 1988. In April the next year he survived a drive-by shooting outside the Manhattan nightclub. Four years later on New Year's Eve 1993, after drinking with friends in the Anchor and Queen's Head public houses, he was killed by three shots from a .357 Magnum handgun as he walked to his car in the Wallsend district of the city.

As is always the case there have been a number of suggestions on offer as to why he was killed: he was negotiating with black drug dealers in Leeds – apparently he had been seen in the Hilton Hotel there; the killers came from Liverpool; or from London; Italians had been brought up on contract; it was a team from Yorkshire wanting to muscle in on the North East; he had crossed up far too many families including a powerful one from South Shields. It may be that he was killed as a result of the death of an arch rival Andy Winter. Graham and Winter had fought in a bar in Tenerife and as a result Winter took out a £30,000 contract on Graham to be executed after his own death. That came in late September 1993. Another suggestion was that Graham had not been involved in the rackets at all. In September 2002 Lee Shaun Watson,

[9] For a full account of the feud and how the parties line up see Russell Findlay, 'Revenge of the Iceman' in *Sunday Mail*, 24 September 2000 and David Leslie, 'Gang Wars' in *News of the World*, 8 July 2001.

convicted of the murder of another North-Easterner Freddie Knights who was shot dead on his mother's doorstep, indicated he knew the identity of Graham's killer. No charges have yet been brought.[10]

In recent years with the increase in the drugs trade more small-time bosses, who have perhaps controlled distribution in one town or even only part of it, have become vulnerable. One was Billy Webb, shot in a flat in Whitelegg Road, Wigan, while awaiting trial. He had led a team which controlled drug dealing in Bolton operating from Debbie's Diner, a café beneath a railway arch which they effectively used as a boardroom. Webb was the man who, while on remand in Strangeways awaiting trial for attempted murder, had organised a hit on John Bates in Bolton on 7 August 1997. Instead of Bates, his five-year-old stepson Dillon Hull was killed. Paul Seddon, who was given £5,000 for the hit, was jailed for life.[11]

Another small-time boss was the formidable Chris Little, who ran the drug scene in Stockport for a time. Regarded as having heart but little ability in the ring, he had been a short-term professional boxer for the well-known Jack Trickett stable before turning his talent to organising club doormen in the area. Men who crossed him could expect a beating or, worse, have Little's fighting dogs turned on them. One man was crucified and another, mistaken for a rival, was thrown off Brinnington Bridge onto the M63 motorway. As a show of strength in 1994 Little organised a team to fire-bomb premises in the area, and in the space of an hour eight schools, three shops and a number of cars were bombed. His downfall began when he tangled with a Manchester firm who wanted to take over the Stockport club doors.

On 22 July 1994 a small party he was giving ran out of drink, and he was driving to an off-licence in his open-topped Mercedes when he was ambushed at traffic lights near the Jolly Sailor public house in Marple, Cheshire. Several men in a white Ford Granada fitted with false number plates drew up beside him and he was shot twice in the head. Over the months he had joked that since he always wore a bulletproof vest it would have to be a head shot

[10] For an account of Graham's career see Stephen Richards, *Viv (Graham) Simply the Best.*

[11] *Manchester Evening News*, 26 May 2001; *Sunday Mirror*, 27 May 2001.

which did for him. By the next day tributes and flowers were being laid outside his house. A sour note came from someone who wrote on a yellow Post-it sticker, 'Good-bye and good riddance. May Stockport now rest in peace.' It was immediately destroyed. A police spokesman said, 'Mr Little had a reputation for intimidation and being involved in the supply of drugs. There is no evidence to that effect.' A week later the local paper set out the facts of life along with a suggestion that the hitman might have been brought down from Glasgow.[12] In January 1996, to great acclaim from the public gallery, three men were acquitted at Manchester Crown Court. Peter Birkett QC told the court: 'Men like this make enemies and Christopher Little no doubt made enemies. No doubt there were many people who might have wished him dead.'[13]

Another local boss to go down was Paul Reilly, who controlled drug dealing in the Lancashire Hill area of Stockport and clashed with Andrew and Michael Synott, known respectively as 'Red' and 'Menace', from the Adswood district. Following a fight at a nightclub Reilly decided to take control of their business and ban them from their former territory. His methods included ordering their local licensee not to serve them and distributing fake 'wanted' posters around the area. In turn the Synotts looked for outside help and recruited Kasam Essa from Manchester's Cheetham Hill who put together what the prosecution called a professional team.

With Reilly at home with his girlfriend and her two young boys, three men burst in and shot him in the pelvis and chest. One of the boys ran outside into the back garden; the other was upstairs. The Synotts and their half-brother Paul Arden, along with Kasam Essa, were all sentenced to life imprisonment.[14]

More recently, extreme precautions to protect a witness were taken in the trial of members of the Burger Bar Gang convicted of shooting two young women on 1 January 2003. Another gang

---

[12] *Stockport Express Advertiser*, 27 July 1994; 'Little's 1,001 Damnations' in *Stockport Express Advertiser*, 3 August 1994. One of the men acquitted was also acquitted of the killing of a small-time dealer David Barnshaw who had been doused with petrol and set on fire. Mr Justice Penry-Davey stopped the case, ruling that the police had withheld potentially exculpatory evidence.
[13] For a full account of Little's life and death see Peter Walsh, *Gang War*.
[14] *Manchester Evening News*, February 2003.

member, the pseudonymous Mark Brown, not only gave evidence from behind a screen but his identity was hidden from the defendants and their lawyers. His voice was electronically distorted and a fifteen-second time delay was set up in case he inadvertently disclosed anything which could lead to his identification.[15]

Since the death of art thief, robber and all-round pain in the side of the authorities Martin Cahill ('The General') on 18 August 1994, the life expectancy of the bosses of Irish organised crime has shortened dramatically. Cahill was shot and killed in an ambush in the Ranelagh area of Dublin.[16] The shooting took place about half a mile from his home. Two men – one on a black motorcycle, posing as a council worker checking registration numbers – lay in wait for him. When Cahill stopped his Renault 5, the man ran to him and fired a single shot. The car went out of control and hit a pole. The gunman then fired four more shots and escaped on the motorcycle. Within a matter of hours the IRA telephoned a Dublin radio station to say that a member had carried out the execution.

The new leaders in the struggle for power, and often a share of the drug trade, also seem either to have adopted or been given exotic soubriquets. There has been a Warehouseman, a Boxer, a Psycho, a Viper, a Scam Man, a Builder, and a Penguin. Not all have lived.

Within a year there was an escalating battle for control of the Dublin drugs trade. In the evening of 5 December 1995 Martin Foley, known as The Viper, and former right-hand man to The General, was shot as he left a block of flats on McCarthy's Terrace on Dublin's North Side. He was hit twice in the side but survived, staggering to another block of flats.

In February 1996 a hit list with thirty-nine names of alleged drug dealers and criminals was sent to a Dublin newspaper. The first on the list to go was Gerry Lee, said to be a close friend of a major robber and to have taken part in the £3 million robbery the previous year. He was shot at 7 a.m. on 9 March when a hitman came to a party Lee was holding for his birthday.[17]

---

[15] *The Guardian*, 19 March 2005.
[16] For his career see Paul Williams, *The General*.
[17] Another alleged member of the gang on the robbery, Patrick McDonald, was shot dead in 1992.

Even with the glare of the world media on their city following the death of journalist Veronica Guerin, the Dublin hardmen continued with their lives and deaths. Down on 8 December 1996 went one of the four Mr Bigs: The Psycho, Peter Joseph Judge, shot as he sat in his car outside the Royal Oak public house in Finglas near his home. His was the fourteenth gang-related death since The General was shot.

Judge himself was responsible for three of those deaths – Michael Godfrey, a money launderer, in 1991; William Corbally, who disappeared in February 1996 and whose body was never found; and Michael Brady, shot by the pillion passenger of a motorcyclist on the Quays in the September of 1996. Brady had previously been convicted of killing his wife, Julie, and his daughters said they were by no means sorry he had been shot.

Judge, once an armed robber, had stepped into the vacuum which followed the dismantling of a gang by the Gardai and a killing spree in November 1995 when four people died in a nine-day period. At his death he held a large share of the drug business in Finglas and Ballymum, north Dublin. He was buried at St Canice's Church, Finglas, to the strains of 'I will always love you' sung by Whitney Houston and 'The Rose' by Bette Midler.

Within days of Judge's death, on the night of 13 December his lieutenant, Mark Dwyer, was abducted from his girlfriend's flat at gunpoint by three masked men. He and another man were taken to Scribblestown Lane near Finglas, where both were beaten and Dwyer killed. It was thought that Dwyer may have been involved in the murder of Corbally and, now that Judge was dead, reprisals could be taken.

Over the years the drug wars continued. In February 2000 two men were found dead in a Dublin canal and, at the end of April 2000, Thomas Byrne went down outside O'Beill's pub in Summerhill. A man walked up to him, shot him in the head and quickly retired. He had been a relatively small-time drug dealer and his killing may have been part of the series which included the thwarting by the Gardai of an attempt to kill Seamus Hogan. In July, Dundalk publican Stephen Connolly was shot dead. It was thought he had been killed on the orders of another boss Nick O'Hare, who was himself later murdered.

One of the relatively more fortunate Limerick players has been 27-year-old John Creamer who, on 11 October 2001, survived a machine-gun attack. Relatively is probably the correct word because a hail of the bullets left him with part of his mouth shot out. After recovering consciousness he wished to keep one of the bullets as a souvenir. He took over the dubious record of surviving the most bullets from Martin Foley, The Viper, who has lived through three gun attacks. Foley had fallen out with Brian Meehan who, the court was told at Meehan's trial for the killing of Veronica Guerin, first shot him in a bar and then opened fire with a sub-machine gun when he found him in January 1996 in the Liberties.

Creamer's attacker is alleged to be a 19-year-old contract killer suspected of at least two more shootings. No stranger to violence in his career, in 2000 a murder charge was dropped against Creamer when a witness to the 1996 incident died. Two years ago he survived another serious attack, declining to name his attacker. It was thought he later dealt with the matter himself.

Things took another turn for the worse with the death in his flat in the Singerstraat suburb of Amsterdam in early June 2000 of The Penguin's protégé and son-in-law, Derek Dunne. The 27-year-old had left Dublin in 1996 after a public quarrel with the nephew of Gerry 'The Monk' Hutch – a man not involved in the drug trade – to whom he had given a beating. Now, three men burst into the apartment and opened fire. Dunne died outside the flat and his children fled to a neighbour.

An attempt had been made to kill Dunne after the battering he gave to the teenager, and he left for Liverpool with a contract on his head. Then, following an unsuccessful prosecution for heroin dealing, he had gone to the Continent. Once in Amsterdam he had established himself as one of the biggest heroin suppliers to Dublin where there were an estimated 14,000 addicts. It was thought that he supplied fifty kilos a week, and a further 1,000 kilos of cannabis. Not all the batches made it safely to Dublin. The result of the losses was that two couriers, Darren Carey and Patrick Murray, were killed at the end of December 2000 and their bodies dumped in the Grand Canal. Their killer was believed to be a man from the Westies, and the son of a former associate of Martin Cahill. It was also thought that back in 1995 the Westie had killed Gerard Connolly, a courier for a Ballyfermot gang who was suspected of passing information to the Gardai.

Two associates of Dunne were believed to have been at his home when he was shot. One managed his business, testing the purity of the heroin for which Dunne was highly regarded. The other was alleged to be a member of the gang which had shot Veronica Guerin. Neither was immediately visible, but they surfaced within a matter of hours to be treated for their injuries. Dunne had been on the hit list of a rival gang once more and was thought to have paid another ransom of £20,000 shortly before his death to have his name removed. There were suggestions that he had been trading with Yugoslav gangs and the hit squad included one of their members.[18]

Earlier in June 2001 in Cork, Kieran O'Flynn was not as fortunate as Creamer. The 39-year-old O'Flynn had long been regarded as one of the leaders of the city's best established gangs. There had been some erosion in its membership over the years due to a number of the gang being sent to prison and, seeing its weakened state, other gangs had thought to make inroads into its territory. There was also a suggestion that O'Flynn had behaved unsportingly by disclosing information about his rivals to the Gardai. It was not the first gangland death in the family. On 9 April 1995 his brother-in-law Michael Crinnon, who had failed to pay a debt to the Gilligan organisation, was shot and killed.

The killing in August 2003 in the Brookwood Inn, Blanchardstown, of Bernard Sugg, a leader of the Westies, was the eleventh in Dublin that year and the forty-fourth since the beginning of 1998. It is likely to go unprosecuted, as only two gangland killings have led to charges, both in the South Central 'A' Garda Division.

No firm suspect emerged for the killing of the 23-year-old Sugg, a violent young man who had many enemies in the Corduff area where he lived. No witnesses came forward with a description of the gunman and none is now likely to appear. Sugg was despised locally, and a big cheer went up in the pub where he had been

[18] *Irish Times*; *Mirror*, 5 May 2000

drinking after the gunman walked out to escape on a motorcycle. He had previously been shot in the stomach.[19]

It is possible Sugg was killed by the IRA rather than by a rival criminal. Towards the end of the twentieth century the IRA killed at least five criminals in Dublin, and was active in the Finglas area where Sugg supplied heroin. One of the victims, Joe Foran, was another member of the same gang, the Westies, dubbed by newspapers because its base is in the western suburbs of Blanchardstown-Finglas. Its main income has come from buying heroin from bigger criminals and selling it to middlemen, who then sell it to street dealers.

The Viper survived the three attempted hits to bring an action against the *Sunday World* which had described him as a 'Dead Man Walking', a grossly irresponsible statement, said his lawyer.[20]

One interesting feud between two families in the area has been running on and off for the better part of twenty years. It resurfaced in September 2000 after a fight in a disco between two girls. A straightener was arranged for the following day in which, it is alleged, part of an ear went missing. The biter's mother was then captured and the letter 'S' carved on her face. Within a matter of days the younger children of each family were being taken to school in convoys. Very much like the Tibbs-Nicholls war in London's East End in the 1970s, violence escalated and a bomb was placed under a car. Throughout 2001 there were at least ten gun-related incidents, and Gardai investigations under the name *Operation Oileann* resulted in arrests and the confiscation of guns. The result may yet determine who controls the drugs trade in the Limerick-Shannon area.[21]

The murder of crime boss Kieran Keane in January 2003 was seen as setting a new standard for crime in the city. It took place against the background of a city feud that has been running for three years and has now claimed the lives of four men. Since it blew up in late 2000, there have been over 150 incidents including petrol

[19] *Irish Times*, 23 August 2003.
[20] Ibid., 17 December 2004.
[21] Jim Cusack, 'New ferocity to gang "wars" outside Dublin' in *Irish Times*, 11 June 2001.

bombings, drive-by shootings, stabbings, beatings and alleged abductions.

At the time of his death Keane was the chief suspect for the cold-blooded killing of his gang's one-time hitman, Eddie Ryan, in a packed city pub on 12 November 2000. Two men, of whom Keane was thought to be one, walked into the Moose Bar on Cathedral Place and shot at Ryan eleven times. The killing effectively signed his own death warrant.

On 29 January a previously uninvolved third gang, friends of Eddie Ryan, entered the fray. The intention was that Anthony 'Noddy' McCarthy and Dessie Dundon from the third gang, but one with criminal ties with the Keane outfit, would merely deliver Keane for killing to another team. That night the unsuspecting Keane collected his nephew, Owen Treacy, to travel to a house at The Fairgreen, Limerick, but when they arrived they were confronted by McCarthy, holding a revolver. Keane and Treacy were taken to another house and placed in the hands of David 'Frog Eyes' Stanners, Christopher 'Smokey' Costello and James McCarthy – all close friends of the family of the late Eddie Ryan.

By 9.30 p.m. Keane, with his hands tied behind his back, was dead in a narrow country lane at Drombanna, Ballyneety, some four miles from Limerick city centre. However, his killers had made a serious error. Owen Treacy, although stabbed seventeen times, somehow lived to tell the tale. Just as many years earlier Gaetan Zampa's failure to kill Jackie Imbert cost him dearly, so did failing to kill Treacy off cost the quintet. This time, however, it was in the form of long prison sentences.[22]

All this must seem very parochial compared with their European counterparts, of whom at least one of the families had links to the very highest echelons of society. First in time, the kings of the Paris milieu in the 1960s and 1970s were undoubtedly the Zemour brothers who were a living – which should certainly be dying – example of the dangers of being a gang boss. Sephardic Jews from Sétif in Algeria, the family began criminal life by passing off Algerian

---

[22] Jim Cusack, 'New ferocity to gang "wars" outside Dublin' in *Irish Times*, 11 June 2001.

wine as Bordeaux and cotton as silk. They also provided girls for sex shops in Germany. The father, Raymond Zemour, came to Paris with his sons William, Gilbert and Edward in the early 1950s. Another brother, Roland, had already been shot and killed on 17 November 1947 on rue Blondel near the Champs-Elysées in an argument over a prostitute.

Within a decade of arriving in France, the Zemour gang had taken a large slice of the Paris underworld. At first they allied themselves with the then current boulevard kings of pimping, the six Atlan brothers, originally from Batna, who included Armand, ostensibly a café owner in Lyon; Jacob, in theory a Paris butcher; Charles (Chaloum) a wholesaler; Sion and Maurice. At the time the Atlans were engaged in a war for control of prostitution in the Pigalle and Grands Boulevards areas with the Perret brothers, Marius, Clément and Gilbert, in theory wine and spirit providers and known as 'half Jews'. For their part the Perrets operated out of the Bar des Cornouailles in the avenue des Martyrs and owned or controlled La Romance in the rue Pigalle where their mother worked as a cashier. They were also prominent in the fixing of horse-racing and in particular of trotting at the tracks around Paris. In 1962 Marius Perret was bold enough to sue the PMU (the French equivalent of the Tote) after it refused to pay him on the result of the Prix de Bordeaux at Vincennes. In 1963, during a raid on their mother's home a quantity of machine guns as well as burglary tools were found. The brothers claimed their money came from winnings on the PMU.

On 2 October 1965 Sion Atlan was killed while playing cards in the Poussin Bleu near the Folies-Bergères. The year after, when René Atlan was killed in the Bon Coin at 4 rue de Choron on 21 December, the stark choice was for the Zemours to be absorbed into the Perret organisation or strike out on their own. They chose the latter course.

Perret men were shot. Notably, Lucian Sans known as Bouboule survived a point-blank attack in the Don Camillo nightclub in the rue des Saintes Pères. Vehicles belonging to the Perrets themselves were machine-gunned; two other men, Ben Loulou and Flershinger, were gunned down. In December 1965 Clément Perret was arrested for possession of firearms, and Gilbert followed him the next June. The brothers took off, first for Brest, then the South and finally Spain. Even there they were not safe. Clément was killed on 16 August 1985 in the pizzeria he owned in Castellon de la Plana.

The Zemours, particularly Gilbert, invested heavily in property and the garment trade with contacts in Canada, Germany and Hong Kong. There were prostitution links from Germany to Africa, and the family also had a fix in horse-racing at various tracks. Dapper 'Eddie' Zemour always carried at least £1,500 with him, had a large flat near the Arc de Triomphe and changed his car twice a year. At the time this was thought to be the height of gangster-style. He was also regarded as a prodigious womaniser. Gilbert, married and the father of two children, dreamed of the big time and approached the grand old man of French crime, the now politically well-connected Marcel Francisci, to go into partnership in some high-class gaming clubs. He was turned down. William and Eddie also wanted to expand their interests into Israel and open clubs in Tel Aviv with the powerful Abitbol brothers. This also came to nothing. Gilbert now had La Gipola Properties, a building company in Canada, and spent his weekends in Miami.

Throughout the early 1970s there had, however, been problems. Roger Bacry, known as Petit Roger, led a split of members from the southern suburbs. He wished to go into drugs, and in true Godfather tradition the Zemours did not want to go down that route. Bacry took with him Jean-Claude 'Petites-Pattes' Vella and Marcel Gauthier. Initially their dealing was successful and they bought from André Condemine, but then the business soured and Bacry wanted to return to the fold. His overtures were rejected and battle commenced as the Sicilians, as they were known, battled the Zemours for control of the girls and the clubs. The first to go was Raphaël Dadoun in March 1973, a year in which there were ten deaths. In 1974 Bacry committed suicide, and the following year came the pivotal meeting in the decline and fall of the Zemours.

On 28 October 1975 a meeting was arranged for peace talks at the Café Thélème at the corner of rue Cardinal Lemoine and Boulevard Saint-Germain, barely a hundred yards from the celebrated restaurant Le Tour d'Argent. Waiting in Le Bon Tabac, another café opposite, was the newly formed anti-gang squad. At a sign the police raided the café, allegedly to intervene in a quarrel. There is little doubt that a Zemour man, Joseph Elbaz, fired the first shot. In the ensuing mêlée William was killed and Gilbert was shot in the back. Elbaz and Roland Attali were also killed. The whole affair was watched by two barristers who were taking coffee.[23]

William's funeral at Bagneux cemetery at Chateau Montrouge was in the great traditions of gangland obsequies. His young widow, Fabienne, and the other women wailed as the hearse, groaning with a mountain of wreaths, arrived at the cemetery. The coffin was solid mahogany with gilt handles. The mourners wore anything from mink and astrakhan collars to jeans and polo-neck sweaters. Photographers were threatened and ordered to hand over their film.[24]

Eddie went to Miami and Gilbert to prison for several months, but there were naturally reprisals. After the café shoot-out, on 13 September 1975 the first of the Sicilians' four remaining leaders, Jean-Claude Vella, was found dead in the boot of a car outside his flat. The Sicilians then lost two more chiefs and, as a safety measure, the Zemours imported Israeli bodyguards after one of their most dependable killers was found in a side street with thirty-nine bullets in him. On 17 September 1976 the surviving Sicilian chief Marcel Gauthier was shot dead in Nice as he stepped ashore after a holiday in Corsica. In all, the deaths in the feud totalled nearly seventy.

From then on, however, it was downhill for the family. Gilbert, released from prison but barred from Canada, then reputedly turned quasi-respectable and went into the restaurant business in Brussels, but he was still in close contact with members of the underworld.

While Eddie had managed to get into America where he opened a restaurant, La Bonne Maison, in Miami he was unable to obtain a liquor licence for it. Reputedly from the start he had trouble, with the local Mafia complaining that they controlled all aspects of the restaurant from providing the parking to laundering the linen.[25]

[23] *Le Figaro*, 1, 3, 4 March 1975.
[24] For those who wish to visit his and his brothers' handsome tomb, it is in Division 66, Ligne 14.
[25] *Miami Herald*, 20 February 1977. The Mafia had always had control of the provision of restaurant services. See *Life*, February 1959.

Then came an incident which spelled, one way or another, the final end of the Zemours. On 15 January 1982 Marcel Francisci was shot dead with a Colt 11.43, the classic French gangland weapon, while sitting in his white Jaguar in the underground car park of his flat in the rue de la Faisenderie in Paris's fashionable 16th arrondissement. In his pocket was a tape-recording of a conversation between two prominent lawyers with connections to the top of the Mitterand administration.

Francisci received one shot in the stomach and one in the forehead, the traditional gangland coup. Then aged 62, he was described as the owner of several Paris gambling houses. Back in 1952 he had been a financier of the *Combinatie* expedition and in 1971 was one of the five big fish who ran the French Connection from Marseilles. On the plus side, Francisci had been decorated in the Free French Forces in the war. Small, round and balding, he believed that in recent years he had escaped from the gangland wars. He had certainly had some luck; when two Corsican gunmen went to bomb his home in Bougival outside Paris, they blew themselves up.

At one time Francisci had tried to set up gambling in London at the Victoria Sporting Club then run by a former London solicitor, the legendary entrepreneur Judah Binstock.[26] He failed in this, but his feud with fellow-Corsican Jean-Baptiste Andreani left a trail of bodies in Paris and Nice. Francisci had built up a political career as a local government leader of the Gaullist RPR in Corsica, where he was the mayor of his home town of Ciamacce. All went well until the pride of his gaming empire, the Cercle Haussman, was shut down. It was thought Francisci had fallen foul of the new administration. In turn the police believed it was the closure of this club that unleashed another battle for control of the remaining clubs in Paris.

Francisci was sumptuously buried in his native village where he was regarded as a great benefactor. An airbus was chartered at a cost

---

[26] There is a scene in the film *The Krays* in which they are confronted by a team of Maltese gunmen as they try to take over a gambling club. This is based on their attempted take-over of the Victoria Sporting Club when they were met by Francisci's Corsicans. The Corsicans also had a considerable interest in gambling on the South Coast of England, centred on Brighton, during that period.

of £20,000 to fly 150 mourners to Corsica. On 12 March 1982 Andreani, then aged 76 and the leading figure in the gaming-club world, was arrested and charged with illegally changing foreign currency for gamblers. Police raided his home the day after Francisci's death and found a stock of gold worth around £2 million. Gilbert Zemour was strongly fancied for the killing and was questioned at length by the police who believed that, having been rejected as a partner, he was trying to take over the Francisci empire. He was in Paris at the time of the great man's death, although apparently he had an alibi.

At around 10.30 in the evening of 8 April 1983, with his American wife Betty and their sons out at the cinema and his daughter from a previous marriage in another room of the apartment, Eddie Zemour was shot by a hired professional killer at his home in Keystone Bay, Miami. Usually he took care to keep curtains and shutters closed, but this night his guard was down. He was hit in the chest with five bullets from a Colt automatic as he relaxed in pink silk pyjamas. It was claimed he had been trying to gain a foothold into the lucrative Caribbean gambling market said to be controlled by the Mafia.[27] There are also suggestions that it may have been something of a domestic matter, but it is much more likely to have been a reprisal for the death of Francisci.

It was after his brother's death that Gilbert Zemour gave an interview to *Paris Match*. In free translation he said in his last reply, so possibly sealing his own fate, 'If justice does not punish his murderer, I'll do what I have to do and if that makes me a *voyou* then unfortunately so be it.'[28]

Three months later, on 28 July 1983, he was shot down near his home on the avenue de Segur as he walked his four miniature poodles. As always there were a number of eye witnesses who gave contradictory evidence about the killer. Likewise there were contradictory suggestions offered; the most likely is that he was killed as a final reprisal for the death of Francisci, and to eliminate any

[27] In 1982 a film *Le Grand Pardon* was made of the rise of the Zemours. Eddie was played by Roger Hanin, President Mitterand's brother-in-law.
[28] Jean-Michel Caradec'h, 'Interview with Gilbert Zemour' in *Paris Match*, 29 April 1983.

possibility of a revenge attack for the death of Eddie Zemour. The last surviving member of the clan, Dédé Zemour, first went into hiding in Palma, Majorca, before returning to Martinique where he had business interests.[29]

Now the Tunisian-born Claude Genova 'Le Gros', from Villemobile, and his friends took over and, known as the Clan Genova, for a time held a stranglehold on the milieu of the Faubourgs. Genova was noted for the tattoo of a butterfly on what the papers described as a 'sensitive part of his anatomy'; apparently at moments of passion it flapped its wings. Unfortunately, in 1994 they were effectively eliminated in a brief but bloody battle with a family from Belleville led by the Frères Hornec, of whom the youngest – Marc Le Forain – is said to be the most formidable. The brothers, described as sedentary gypsies, have run Champs-Elysées night bars along with their associates Ihmed Mohieddine, known as La Gelée because of the supposed state of his brains, and Nordine Mansouri. Their henchmen are said to have been involved in bank robberies, smuggling and drug dealing as well as the *machines à sous*. Other friends include the gypsies Michel and Serge Lepage, a father and son who are alleged to run the south *banlieu*.

The serious trouble started in February 1994 when Eric Pasquet, known as Petit Riquet, the right-hand man of Genova, foolishly kidnapped Ihmed Mohieddine and tortured him to reveal the whereabouts of his savings. The Clan Genova paid heavily. Petit Riquet and Christophe Tizzo were trapped when Riquet carelessly left his revolver in the boot of his car, and were killed in the rue de Charonne. After this bodies fell on both sides until the war ended when Claude Genova, on a temporary release from prison, was shot

[29] The Zemours were not the only family systematically wiped out. In the 1970s the Violi Family in Montreal was similarly destroyed. They had been at war with the Rizzuto clan who had the ear of the New York Gambino Family. First, Francesco, the enforcer of the Family, was killed on 11 February 1977 backed against a wall and shot at a Violi importation company premises. Then on 22 January 1978 Paolo, the head of the Family, was shot as he played cards in his Jean Talon Street Bar; it is thought he knew he was to be killed but decided to stay rather than run. Finally Rocco was killed on 17 October 1980 by a single shot from a sniper as he sat at his kitchen table. He had previously survived being shot at traffic lights in the July. For an account of the Violi power struggles see Peter Edwards and Antonio Nicaso, *Deadly Silence*; James Morton, *Gangland International*. For the rise and fall of the Zemours see Roger le Taillenter, *Les Derniers Seigneurs de la pègre*.

at 8 p.m. on 22 August 1994 as he left a bar at the Concorde-Lafayette near Porte Maillot. He was said to be carrying Ff800,000 as a payment to end the war which had broken out. He was shot three times; the third, the traditional bullet behind the right ear. In January 2003 one of his killers, known as Kadda H. or Karim, was sentenced to thirty years in his absence. Shortly after the killing he was believed to have fled to Algeria.[30] Another, said to be Roger Poletti, was killed by Nordine Benali and his brother Djamiel. In turn Nordine lasted until his death on 4 October 2001, while Djamiel failed to survive the millennium. He was killed in Seville on 17 December 2000.

The streets in the eighth arrondissement are only yards from the tourist-dominated Champs-Elysées, but they are miles away in character. Here another dominant member of the milieu passed over at 3.20 in the afternoon of 27 September 2000, shortly before the 'off' for the Prix d'Amiens at Saint Cloud. He was Francis Vanverberghe, 'François le Belge', said to have been the mastermind of the French Connection, and known as the Last Godfather. Outside the Club d'Artois in the street of the same name was a group of straying Japanese tourists who watched as a motorcyclist with a pillion rider drew up. Inside, Vanverberghe was watching the televised racing in the basement when he was shot nine times – seven bullets in the body followed by two in the head. He had on him at the time approximately £20,000 in francs, and was probably following one of the traditional ways of laundering money made, in his case, from slot machines, prostitution and drugs. He would buy a winning PMU ticket from a gambler and, being able to show he had been paid out, so clean the money. The 54-year-old Vanverberghe, half Belgian and half Spanish, born on 3 March 1946 in the Belle-de-Mai quarter of Marseilles, had been a top and ruthless player on the Cote d'Azur and in Paris for nearly a quarter of a century.

He began his documented criminal career at the age of 16 with

---

[30] Some of Genova's men continued operations in one way or another. Two, the son and ex-chauffeur of one of the fallen clan, were found dead in December 2000. They had been masterminding twelve prostitutes who had been serving lorry drivers in the forest of Armainvilliers. The scheme had been run with some give and take. In return for their earnings the girls were provided with social security when ill and a five-week annual holiday.

an arrest for the theft of a caravan and then, three years later, he was into prostitution. At the age of 22 it was into the big time. This was the age of Gaetan 'Tony' Zampa and his rival Jacky 'Le Mat' or 'The Fool' Imbert – one-time champion trotting driver and friend of actor Alain Delon – warring from their Pigalle hangout, the Equipe des Trois Canards, with the then all-powerful brothers Guerini. Vanverberghe joined in enthusiastically.

Zampa took out six Belle-de-Mai men in a six-month period and on 31 March 1973 reprisals came at the Tanagra, a bar in the old port, when four of his men were shot at cocktail time. Zampa escaped but Vanverberghe was caught by the police the next month when in bed with a starlet in Paris. Brought before a judge and questioned about the social qualities of her lover, she commented, 'When I have a fine boy like the Belgian in my bed I don't ask for his police file.'

But in Vanverberghe's hideaway, the flat of his official girlfriend and one of the women he had on the street, the police found false papers and three guns hidden behind the bath. He received thirty months, during which time Zampa reinforced his position in Marseilles. Vanverberghe was out for only a few days in 1975 before he went back to prison. This time he was betrayed by an American over his part in the French Connection drug-smuggling ring. Fourteen years. Now, Vanverberghe blamed his former ally Zampa for his misfortunes and sided with Imbert.

On 1 February 1977 Imbert was ambushed as he drove his Alpha Romeo to his home at Cassis. Years later a Parisian gunman who had been present told the newspaper *Libération:*

> The Chief gave an order to the men 'Don't finish him off. Leave him whimpering like a dog.' He then lifted his hood and said to The Fool, 'Cunt, look at who has killed you.' It was Gaetan Zampa. Only The Fool survived.[31]

He did survive, but with eight bullets in him and a paralysed right arm. From then on, along with Vanverberghe and the Lebanese

---

[31] Patricia Tourancheau, 'Neuf Balles au bout de la route du Belge' in *Libération*, 30 September–1 October 2000. See also Patricia Tourancheau, 'François le Belge, un mort bien nettoyé' in *Libération*, 14–15 October 2000.

Hoareau brothers, he waged an all-out war against Zampa in which an estimated twenty-eight men were killed. In fact Imbert survived the longest of all. In December 2004 he appeared in court in Marseilles accused of planning to open an underground cigarette factory. By then all his previous convictions had been wiped from his record because of the length of time since the last one.[32]

In 1984 Vanverberghe was again betrayed, this time by François Scapula, another informer from the days of the French Connection who was at the time serving a thirty-year sentence over the exportation of some twenty kilos of heroin from Asia to the United States. That year he and Zampa were in the same prison after his arch rival and his wife had been arrested on tax-evasion charges. Zampa took the responsibility, and he and Vanverberghe found themselves in Les Baumettes prison. Both were clients of the same lawyer, Jean-Louis Pelletier, who maintained the splendid balancing act of visiting each of them every Saturday. A month after Vanverberghe's release Zampa hanged himself in his cell, and the war between the remainder of his men and the Hoareaus intensified.

Vanverberghe served four years before his conviction was quashed. Later he was awarded £11,000 for wrongful imprisonment. He promptly announced that he was donating all the winnings to the 81-year-old Abbé Pierre's Emmaus movement of self-supporting communities for outcasts and dropouts. Despite the Abbé saying the gangster had a good heart, he rejected this kindly act. But by this gesture Vanverberghe took another step up the ladder towards folk hero. His death followed the increasingly popular pattern, with two helmeted men on a motorcycle. One kept the engine revving and the other pulled the trigger. There were thoughts that Vanverberghe was slipping. He had been arrested for running prostitutes from a bar in the rue François Ier in March 2000 and sentenced to two months imprisonment. This was regarded as a downward step in his career.

Worse, perhaps, the killing of his godson François Boglietto on 28 February the previous year in Aix en Provence had passed without reaction. When Vanverberghe's brother, José, had been shot

[32] *France Soir*, 23 November 2004; *Daily Telegraph*, 24 November 2004.

ten years earlier his killers had not lasted four days. Although he had consistently said that after his brother's death he expected to be killed, over the years Vanverberghe took no great precautions. He generally went without bodyguards, and for that reason no one was particularly keen to sit next to him in public.

Why was he shot? The reason almost certainly lay in the continuing war over the highly lucrative gaming machines. He was thought to have owned about 150 of these *machines à sous* which provided him with an income of some 3 to 4.5 million francs a month.[33] Additionally he had interests in girly bars and nightclubs. He declared an income of around £500,000, claiming it was due to his success at gambling on horse-racing. If he was indeed killed over slot machines, then he would not have been the first to go down in recent times. On 9 January 2000 Roger Spanu, once a lieutenant to Imbert, and known as Roger Specs or Petit Roger, was shot in the neck after leaving a pizzeria in Marseilles. The previous day Marc Monge, the so-called Godfather of the Vaucluse, and another with known interests in machines, had strayed into the Paris *banlieu* and was killed also near the Champs-Elysées.

Monge, who had a long criminal career, was also politically connected. In May 1983 he was arrested and released after Daniel Scotti and Jean Chicin had been killed in a car bombing the previous March near the main synagogue in Marseilles. In fact the bombing seems to have had no anti-Semitic connections; the inept pair had been intending to blow up a bar on the rue du Dragon. Monge's criminal career nearly came to an end when he fell through a window and was partially paralysed during a 1986 robbery. He made his way to Belgium where in September 1989 he was shot while working with Fréderic Godfroid, an ex-policeman, in a series of hold-ups After his release it was back to drugs in Marseilles and hashish in Spain where he was imprisoned in 1993. He was shot again in the summer of 1997. One of the men questioned and released, Paul Faruggia 'Petit Paul', was himself killed in an 'account settling' on 1 October 1999.

In 1999, although said to be in semi-retirement, Vanverberghe

---

[33] *Le Figaro*, 26 July 2001.

– along with his two heavies, Joel the Turk and Phillipe the SS –
attended a meeting with the Hornec brothers. One report suggested
that the meeting had been called to arrange for the division of spoils
between former rivals and that an agreement had been reached.
Another scenario is that the brothers reneged on the agreement and
sent youths from the *banlieu* to kill Vanverberghe.[34]

It is also possible that Vanverberghe was killed by or on the
orders of Djilali Zitouni who, along with Boualem Talata, also sought
to control part of the milieu. If so, it did neither of them any good.
Talata was killed and his brother injured in an attack on them on
19 November 2000 at Dreux, while Zitouni was killed in broad
daylight when he stopped at a red light at Gennevilliers in July
2001. Forty shots were fired in the attack.

Until the early 1980s the drug trade in Holland had been run
on what might be called gentlemanly lines. Klass Bruinsma from a
wealthy middle-class background – his father was a director of a
Dutch drink company – with an inner circle of about ten men
changed all that. Born on 6 October 1953 Bruinsma, socialite and an
expert ocean-going sailor, made a fortune from trafficking and was
one of the main sources of the cannabis that reached Ireland in the
1980s. He took yachts down to Morocco and sailed them home
crammed with hash. In the early 1980s he moved up to commercial shipping and hired gangs of men to do his work, much of his
dope being landed off the south-west coast of Ireland.

In 1975 he was given six months, three of which were served on
probation, over a 100 kilos deal of cannabis. After that he changed
his name to Frans van Arker and took up with his dealer Thea Moear
when she left her husband. In 1978 they started to expand their
empire, taking on the Surinam-born Etienne Urka and the kick-
boxer André Brilleman. They began buying properties, turning them
into fortresses and opening coffee bars. One floor of their main
building was converted into a gymnasium for their minders. Now

---

[34] For an account of the state of play amongst the Paris *milieu* see Eric Furrier, 'Les
nouveaux caïd' in *L'Exprés*, 16 October 2004 and James Morton, *Gangland Today*. For
further accounts of the careers of Le Belge and some of the others see Jérôme Pierrat,
Une histoire du Milieu and Alain Léauthier, *Mort d'un voyou*. In this case the death in
question is that of Michel Regnier, son of the legendary Louis 'Loulou' Regnier.

a construction business was set up to launder the profits. In England the purchaser was Roy Adkins, who subsequently became a close associate and was himself later killed in Holland. In 1979 Bruinsma was sentenced to eighteen months, reduced to twelve, over the importation of 1,500 kilos of cannabis from Pakistan.

Discipline in his outfit was strictly enforced. When one former employee, Pietje Pieterse, disgruntled at the level of his wages, stole 600 kilos of cannabis, Bruinsma went to his house. It was a meeting which ended with one man dead and Bruinsma and Pieterse both badly injured. Bruinsma was not without a sense of humour. When the police arrived he was heard to say, 'Jesus Christ, Piet, how come you always have such a mess in your home.' This apparent badinage did Pieterse no good whatsoever. A contract was put out on him and although he fled to Switzerland he later spent some time in a wheelchair. On 19 December 1984 Bruinsma was sentenced to a term of three years for his part in the affair.

On his release he spent a good deal of time in the Okura Hotel where, surrounded by bodyguards, he would parade barefooted in the lobby in a towelling robe. He was finally asked to leave and then took up residence in the Amstel Hotel. Now changes were made in the hierarchy of the operation. Moear was demoted and Urka took her place. The drugs division went to Adkins. Gambling was controlled by Sam Klepper and John Mieremet became his right-hand man.

Bruinsma was thought to have killed three rivals, or had them murdered, and had attempted to kill three others. André Brilleman, the kick-boxer, was one of the victims. Like Pieterse he had been stealing, and he was lured to a warehouse where he was beaten unconscious. When he recovered his penis was cut off and a saw was taken to his legs. Scientific evidence showed that this had been done before he was killed. His body was found in concrete in a steel drum; he had been shot in the face at close range. After that Bruinsma was able to command total loyalty at street level.

By the late 1980s, and with a staff of some two hundred, he had managed to distance himself from the dirty work. Bruinsma was then able to devote more time to his pleasures: ski resorts in winter, sailing in summer, and he was one of the few gang leaders who genuinely was an accepted part of European society. It says something for the egalitarian nature of the Dutch as well as their relaxed attitude to soft drugs that he was able to do so.

As always, there was to be one last deal prior to retirement and Bruinsma stashed away 45,000 kilos of drugs, worth around $250 million. Unfortunately his warehouse was raided and, although no one was arrested, his stock was burned. Now, with a cocaine addiction, he became increasingly unstable. 'I'm going to eat you,' he would tell his men and rivals. Adkins was fired and there followed a shoot-out between the men in the fashionable Yab Yum brothel in Amsterdam. Day-to-day control passed to Urka as Bruinsma moved into prostitution and tried to force his slot machines into all the Amsterdam coffee houses. In 1990 Adkins was shot and killed. Bruinsma lasted a further year. After a quarrel in the Amsterdam Hilton in a long drinking session on 27 June 1991, he was shot at close range on the pavement outside the hotel by a former police officer Martin Hoogland. The third bullet was placed behind his right ear.

Bruinsma's former lieutenant Sam Klepper lasted until October 2000 when, now the so-called Godfather of Dutch crime, he was shot at 5 p.m. in the middle of a crowded shopping precinct. The death of Bruinsma had caused him great problems and under threat from Yugoslavian criminals he more or less gave himself up to the police, pleased to serve an eighteen-month sentence for possessing firearms. On his release he was suspected of dealing in cocaine and arms trafficking. At the time of his death he had been inducted into the Hells Angels, but without the tiresome duties usually undertaken by a probationary member. Of his thirty-six death notices, he received five in Serbo-Croat. One from an Angels' chapter read, 'We don't die. We just go to hell and regroup.'

In 2003 Bruinsma reached out from his grave to grab the attention of both the Dutch public and Parliament when it was announced that Prince Johan Friso, third in line to the throne, was to marry the human rights activist Mabel Wisse Smit. Unfortunately a bodyguard then claimed that she had been Bruinsma's lover, something she denied. The press campaign on behalf of the royal household and Ms Smit was perhaps not as well handled as it might have been.

Initially she told the Dutch prime minister that she had known Bruinsma vaguely through a mutual interest in sailing, but when she learned how he had made his money she had broken off the friendship. It then emerged that Ms Smit had spent a number of nights on Bruinsma's boat. Wholly platonic, maintained Ms Smit, and the Prince appeared on television to say that suggestions that she had been Bruinsma's lover were unbelievable nonsense. Despite this the prime minister claimed that she had given 'false and incomplete information', saying that, 'Trust has been violated . . . there is no remedy for untruths.' The upshot was that the Dutch Parliament refused to approve the marriage and Prince Johan Friso renounced his right to succession. When the couple married in Delft on 24 April 2004, there were some notable royal absentees.[35]

[35] *The Times*, 24 April 2004.

8

More Dead Bosses

In America the situation has always been difficult for the gang boss. The death on 3 April 1882 of poor Jesse James – shot in the back by Bob Ford while he was re-hanging a sampler – provided a dangerous precedent.[1] And ever since, while being a gang boss may have been lucrative it has been a dangerous way to make money. First, there is the rise to the top which itself is full of pitfalls and second, there is the problem of staying there. The number of bosses who have been killed by rivals and potential upstarts is legion. One made guy remembers: 'His capo wanted to be boss so he paid some outside guys to kill him and make it look like a robbery but he then killed them to act out the power play. Then took control of the Family.'[2]

And not only in America. In August 2002 the killers of Danny

---

[1] Robert Newton Ford, described on James's gravestone as 'a coward whose name is not worthy to appear here', was convicted of James's murder but was immediately pardoned and received his promised reward money. In September 1882, amidst great and unfavourable hype, he and his brother Charles appeared at Bunnell's Museum, New York. The museum was said to be in a state of defence against the Jesse James avengers: 'Manager Starr will wear an armour-lined shirt and will be seated on a Gatling gun while taking tickets.' *Police Gazette*, September 1882. Ford was killed on 8 June 1892 in Creede, Colorado, shot by Edward O'Kelly, related by marriage to James's cousins, the Youngers. O'Kelly was sentenced to twenty years and, to public acclaim, was released after two.

[2] Letter to author.

Karam, the leader of Sydney's DK's Boys, were sentenced. He had dominated the King's Cross cocaine trade until his underlings, tired of doing the work while he took the profits, shot at him sixteen times from two high-powered pistols. There had already been one unsuccessful attempt on Karam when on 23 February 1993 Leslie Betcher was killed at his Lugano home. He had been mistaken for Karam.[3]

In America over the years the roll call of fallen gangleaders has reached heroic proportions and the body count is still rising. Amongst the more famous – beginning at the beginning – was Don Nicholas Morello who, decades before Lucky Luciano thought of a national crime syndicate, had that same idea. His family had arrived in New York at the end of the nineteenth century after emigrating from Corleone. The founder of the clan was Antonio, believed to have personally committed between thirty and forty murders, and succession passed to his brother Joe – brother-in-law of the killer Ignazio Saietta – and then to Nicholas.

Unfortunately Nicholas Morello lacked the muscle to impose his wishes. While his Sicilian gang controlled the rackets in East Harlem and Greenwich Village he was unable to explain the wisdom of his vision to Don Pellegrino Morano, the leader of the Camorristas, who ran Brooklyn. Instead of co-operating to make one happy family, Morano continually cut into the interests of Morello until in 1916 he sued for peace. A meeting was arranged at the Navy Café and as Morello stepped from his car he and his bodyguards were ambushed and killed. Morano, somewhat to his surprise since he thought the killings had been authorised by the police, was sentenced to life imprisonment. When his sentence was announced his supporters showered kisses on his face and forehead. On the way to prison Italians again broke through the guard to kiss him. The succession passed to the so-called artichoke king, Ciro Terranova.[4]

Another member of the Family, Peter Morello, known as The Clutching Hand, was a leading adviser to Joe 'The Boss' Masseria, the undisputed boss of the New York Mafia in the 1920s. The

[3] *Sydney Morning Herald*, 24 February 1993, 18 December 1998, 16 April, 30 August 2002.
[4] G. Selvaggi, *The Rise of the Mafia in New York*, pp. 22–42.

Castellamarese War of August 1930 saw the end of him, killed possibly by Frank Scalise and Albert Anastasia. According to Lucky Luciano they took $30,000 which he and Guiseppe Pariano had been counting. Pariano, being in the wrong place at the wrong time, was also shot. According to commentators, with Morello's death – since he was the brains behind Masseria – any hope of victory died with him. Another version, that of the Mafia turncoat Joe Valachi, has it that a gunman 'Buster of Chicago' imported by Salvatore Maranzano, the principal opponent of Masseria, did the killing. This has been doubted, but new research may establish the existence of this previously mythical gunman.[5] Masseria died on 15 April 1931, killed by Bugsy Siegel, Joe Adonis, Vito Genovese and Anastasia as he lunched with Lucky Luciano. When Luciano disappeared to the lavatory, the four men burst in and opened fire. According to police records the actual shootist was John Giustra; his coat was found in the restaurant and some weeks later he himself was found shot dead in Manhattan. The file on Masseria's death was closed on 27 November 1940. The story that he died with the Ace of Diamonds in his hand, thus making it a card of ill-fortune, is apocryphal. Irving Lieberman of the *New York Post* believes it was put there after the killing by an inventive reporter from another paper to add spice to the story.[6]

Maranzano did not last long. After the funeral of his rival, he called peace talks. According to Gay Talese, this man who was said to speak twelve languages, and was a serious student of the campaigns of Julius Caesar, presided over a meeting of 500 men in Brooklyn and outlined his plans for the future with a reorganisation of the gangs into a structure loosely based on Caesar's military command.[7]

According to his biographer Leonard Katz, the future 'Prime Minister of the Underworld', Frank Costello, had so far managed to avoid taking any active part in the struggle. Now, together with Luciano and Genovese, he recognised a dictatorship in the making and, after ensuring there was adequate support including the Jewish gangs, they set out to overthrow him. In turn Maranzano drew up

[5] Dave Critchley, conversation with the author.
[6] New York Municipal Archives, 3049/22; Leonard Katz, *Uncle Frank*, p. 82.
[7] Gay Talese, *Honour Thy Father*.

a list of those whom he sought to eliminate.

Accounts of the next months vary depending on the role and alignment of the person recounting them but according to Joe Valachi, the first of the modern Mafia informers, Maranzano's death list included Luciano, Genovese, Dutch Schultz, Joe Adonis, Costello and Vincent Mangano. In turn Costello and Luciano were plotting the removal of not only Maranzano but all the old Moustachio Petes whom they believed stood in the way of progress.

On 10 September 1931 a meeting was arranged for 2 p.m. to be held, as protocol dictated, at Maranzano's offices. He was to meet Luciano and Genovese, but he had arranged for the services of Vincent 'Mad Dog' Coll to deal with the pair. In turn they had arranged for Lansky and Bugsy Siegel to provide gunmen. Lansky's men arrived at half-past one. Maranzano was shot and, like Caesar, stabbed. According to legend, as they left, one of the killers Sam 'Red' Levine, as a matter of professional courtesy told Coll, who was just coming into the building, to leave as the police would soon be there.

That night is said to have been a modern Sicilian Vespers when Moustachio Petes across America were eliminated on the orders of the clearly very talented Luciano.[8] He became the most powerful man in the Mafia, with Frank Costello modestly standing by as adviser.

Costello survived one assassination attempt by Vince 'The Chin' Gigante to die peacefully as a retired Don in 1973. Luciano may or may not have survived to die naturally. Convicted of running prostitutes, in 1936 he was eventually deported to Italy from where he illegally commuted to supervise Mafia interests in Havana. On 26 January 1962 he died following a heart attack at Naples' Capodichino airport. One account of his death is that he was poisoned. Apparently he had been negotiating to sell the story of his life to an American film producer, something which was not regarded as good form.

The life expectancy of a gangleader in Chicago during Prohibition was little more than that of a young officer in France during the

---

[8] There are some who doubt that the American Night of the Sicilian Vespers did take place. See Alan A. Block in *East Side, West Side, Organising Crime in New York 1930–50.*

First World War. Al Capone survived but most of his rivals did not. Capone's predecessor, Big Jim Colosimo, was one.

From 1910 to 1920 the nominal boss of the Chicago underworld was Big – sometimes 'Diamond' as a tribute to his penchant for the gems which he wore on every finger and which he carried in his pocket to distribute to police and politicians alike – Jim Colosimo. But the brains behind the throne were those of Johnny Torrio. Colosimo was content to leave things in the hands of his wife's cousin while he toyed with his own merchandise and generally displayed himself about town, finally leaving the elderly and increasingly fat Mrs Colosimo for a young singer named Dale Winters. She and Colosimo dreamed of Grand Opera for her. Caruso was invited to hear her sing and, with a favourable report from both him and the conductor Campanini, she enrolled in the Chicago Musical College.

By 1919 Torrio, adopting the Marxist principle that it is necessary to change in order to maintain the status quo, was keen to take advantage of the forthcoming Volstead Act which introduced Prohibition. Curiously, he had difficulty in explaining the benefits to the besotted Colosimo. It appears he eventually persuaded him to take an interest, but now the great man's heart belonged not in business but to Dale. He would allow Torrio only to acquire sufficient liquor to stock their own brothels and speakeasies rather than deal on the open market. He was becoming an encumbrance.

On 11 May 1920, four months after Prohibition came into force, Torrio arranged for Colosimo to be at his café to receive a shipment of whiskey. An unknown man leaped from the checkroom and shot Colosimo twice in the back of the head.

On hearing the news, Torrio, who had a cast-iron alibi, was suitably upset. 'Big Jim and me were like brothers,' he is reported to have said. He arranged the funeral with a silver and mahogany casket costing $7,500, while those who were to act as honorary or active pall-bearers included two congressmen, three judges, one Federal judge-designate, and ten aldermen including the notorious 'Bathhouse' John Coughlin who led the prayers. Mr Coughlin paid tribute to Colosimo's charity: 'You know what he did? He fixed up an old farmhouse for broken-down prostitutes.

They rested up and got back into shape and he never charged them a cent.'[9]

Police inquiries into the murder latched on to Capone's mentor Frankie Yale, brought by Torrio from New York for the purpose. Indeed a waiter who was an eyewitness was taken to New York, to which Yale had promptly returned, to identify him. On the journey the waiter sensibly changed his mind and went back to the Midwest, leaving Colosimo's death unsolved.[10]

Torrio survived the Prohibition wars, but only just. He had organised the killing of his rival, the flower-shop-owning Dion O'Banion. Now on 24 January 1925, as he and his wife Anna climbed out of their chauffeur-driven limousine in front of their South Shore apartment building, Torrio was shot by Bugs Moran and Earl Weiss. His chauffeur, Robert Barton, fired on the men and in turn was hit in the leg. Moran stood over Torrio and, saying, 'This is for Deanie O'Banion, you dago bastard', pulled the trigger. Amazingly, he had miscounted and the gun was empty. Torrio managed to drag himself into the apartment building and, shot in the neck and believing the story that bullets steeped in garlic were fatal, yelled for his wounds to be cauterized.

On 9 February 1925, with his wounds healed, Torrio had his appeal dismissed against a short prison sentence for possession of a firearm and was sent to Waukegan County jail, where there was also a friendly sheriff who allowed Capone to protect his prisoner for him. Torrio served his sentence in some comfort and towards the end he called in Capone to say he would retire to Italy if he could get out of Chicago alive. Capone promised that he would, and he kept his promise. Torrio was escorted to the railroad in Capone's armour-plated car and put on a train east. Gangsters patrolled the Gary, Indiana depot and Capone personally saw Torrio into his compartment. He is reported to have said, 'I'll never be back,' and he never was.

Frankie Yale was not so fortunate. He took to siphoning off the liquor which Capone had been buying from New York. In practice

---

[9] Quoted in Richard Hammer, *Playboy's Illustrated History of Organized Crime*, p. 38.
[10] Laurence Bergreen, *Capone*, p. 84, takes the view that Yale was acting independently of Torrio.

his convoys should have had a safe passage guaranteed by Yale; there was always going to be some wastage en route, but it became clear that quantities were not even leaving New York. Capone contacted his old schoolfriend Jimmy Filesy DeAmato, who reported back that what Capone feared was correct: Yale's men were hijacking the Chicago shipments. It seems that the 41-year-old DeAmato spoke too loudly on the telephone extension. At 9.30 p.m. on 7 July 1927 he was shot with dum-dum bullets as he walked along 20th to a speakeasy.

Yale lasted another year. Capone was still unhappy, with even less of his shipments reaching Chicago. Scalise, Anselmi and two others, probably including Fred Burke from the Purple Gang, were sent by the vacationing Capone from Florida to Brooklyn. On 1 July, while Yale was trying out his new Lincoln coupé before sending it back to have bulletproof glass put in the windows, he was shot. In a bar when he received a message that something was wrong at home, once outside he was killed when a black Buick came alongside him and its occupants opened fire with a sub-machine gun. His funeral was to set the standard by which other gangster funerals would be measured: the silver casket cost $15,000 and it was borne from St Rosalie's Church to Holy Cross Cemetery on an open hearse. Two hundred and fifty cars followed, watched by an estimated 10,000 people who lined the roadside.

It is recorded that the watching Capone said to 'Machine Gun' Jack McGurn, 'I feel so sorry for this poor fellow . . . my heart is all broke up. Come, we go. I can't stand no more . . . this too much for me.'[11]

Yale's death was also a first – the first by sub-machine gun in New York. Before that they had been used exclusively in Chicago.

Sam 'Nails' Morton was a First World War hero who received the Croix de Guerre. While being a member of the Dion O'Banion Gang, he was also quite independently the protector of Jewish interests. He died quite by accident. Generally a fine horseman, on 13 May 1923 he was unseated and then kicked in the head by a hack he had rented from a livery stable in Lincoln Park. His death

---

[11] William Balsamo and George Carpozi jnr, *Crime Incorporated*, p. 215.

was avenged in true gangland style by Bugs Moran and Hymie Weiss who shot the horse, telling the stable owner that if he wished he could go and collect the tack. Five thousand attended his funeral and the *Chicago Daily News* noted approvingly that he had 'made the West Side safe for his race'.[12]

Nor was Chicago always a healthy place for the gangleader after Capone. When his successor Frank 'The Enforcer' Nitti, who suffered from claustrophobia and could not face another prison sentence, shot himself at 2 a.m. on 19 March 1943 on the tracks of the Illinois Central Railroad, Paul Ricca assumed control before he himself went to prison. This really left only Tony 'Batters' Accardo and 'Dago' Lawrence Mangano as serious contenders for top honours. The matter was soon resolved. On 3 August 1944 the *Chicago Herald American*, ignoring Allied war successes, carried the banner headline 'Mangano, Pal slain by Gang'. It told how he had been followed from Cicero and shot with at least 200 shotgun pellets and five .45 calibre bullets rubbed in garlic. He had begged the doctors who treated him to 'Put me to sleep'. His bodyguard, 'Big' Mike Pantillo, also died in the attack. Accardo became either the acknowledged head of Chicago, or the titular one running things for Paul Ricca until he was released from prison after serving three years.[13]

Whether it was Accardo on his own, acting as a front for Ricca, or in a joint ownership, for the next seventeen years there was a tight, efficient mob in Chicago. Orders ensured that street taxes were paid by prostitutes, shylocks, visiting burglars or Chicago burglars who worked out of town. On a wider front, Accardo had the foresight to extend Chicago's interests west to California, Colorado and Arizona. In return for sharing with New York and East Coast interests, Chicago was granted points in hotels and gambling in Cuba, the Bahamas and Florida. There were few crises.

It was in the late 1950s that Accardo lost interest or heart and wanted to quit. It was pointed out to him that he could not simply

[12] The scene was re-enacted by James Cagney in the film *Public Enemy No. 1*.
[13] Mangano had without doubt been a high-ranking member of the Chicago outfit. He was arrested over 200 times but never served a prison sentence. He attributed this to 'bum raps' and 'good lawyers'.

walk away from his combine, but he wished to hand over the day-to-day running of affairs. Now the question of his successor was broached. Paul Ricca was too old to take sole control, and at 43 his one-time chauffeur Jacky 'The Lackey' Cerone was regarded as too young.

In 1957 the choice of leadership fell on the shoulders of Sam 'Momo' Giancana, who later had the dubious distinction of going down while cooking sausages. Born in 1908, in the 1920s Giancana had been a member of the 42 Gang which hung out on The Patch, the intersection of Taylor and Halsted. Like the Circus Café Gang which was based on the corner of Grand and Ogdon Avenues, it was a spawning ground for talent, used for routine chores like car theft. Giancana was said to be an excellent getaway driver. He had been nurtured by Ricca and Accardo and had the additional attraction of having brought into the outfit former 42 Gang members such as Phil Alderisio and Marshall Caifano. During the war Giancana, regarded as a constitutional psychopath, had not been required for service.

Again it was a period of expansion for the Mob but, unlike the more careful Accardo, Giancana adopted a high profile and openly cultivated politicians. His son-in-law, Anthony Tisci, was installed at a salary of $10,800 as secretary to Roland Libonati, a congressman and member of the House Judicial Committee who 'seemed to go out of his way to sponsor bills that helped Giancana and his friends avoid government surveillance'.[14]

To the singer's subsequent detriment, Giancana became involved with Frank Sinatra. In the 1960s Sinatra acquired a controlling interest in the Cal-Neva Lodge, a hotel-casino complex overlooking Lake Tahoe which was run by Paul D'Amato, a long-standing crime figure from New Jersey. It was suggested that the real purpose of D'Amato's appointment was to secure the interests of Giancana, at the time banned from even entering a Nevada casino let alone owning an interest in one. To make things worse he was a long-time lover of Phyllis McGuire of the singing McGuire sisters, and he took her to the Lodge. Sinatra was there and in a subsequent

[14] Richard Hammer, *Playboy's Illustrated History of Organized Crime*, p. 311.

investigation by the Nevada gaming board, held to strip the premises of the licence, he explained that the meeting had been accidental. Unfortunately he then said he saw no reason why he should not continue to meet with his friend Giancana over the State line. The Governor was lobbied to aid Sinatra but, when this failed, the entertainer sold his interest.

Giancana's relationships with the Kennedy family have been described as complex and, for a time, he and John F. Kennedy shared a mistress, Judy Campbell Exner. It would seem that he now became heavily involved in politics and was part of the supposed attempts to eliminate Castro. Under his nine-year rule the number of organised crime killings in Chicago ran at a staggering total of seventy-nine. In the eight years after his reign there were a mere twenty-four.

By the middle 1960s Giancana's star was beginning to wane. His high-profile career had attracted far too much attention. In 1965 he refused to testify before a Federal jury inquiry into organised crime and served a year in prison. On his release he went to Mexico. Again it is not clear exactly what he did there or on his tours – with former Chicago policeman Richard Cain acting as his adviser, companion and bodyguard – to Peru, Beirut and Puerto Rico.

Cain, whose real name was Scalzitti, had by some accounts been a CIA operative. After the Bay of Pigs fiasco he became chief investigator to the Cook County Sheriff's office and so, for Giancana, was a useful spy in the midst. In 1967 when back in Illinois, Cain was arrested over an earlier robbery and served a four-year sentence. It was shortly after his release that he fell out with his employer and apparently became an FBI informant. He was killed on 20 December 1973 outside Rose's Sandwich Shop, then at the top of Grand and Ogdon Avenues, near the old home of Patsy Spilotro's restaurant.[15]

Giancana was forcibly deported from Mexico in 1974 and literally deposited across the border in San Antonio for questioning in front of a Grand Jury over the death of Cain and syndicated gambling. He began to demand that his former colleagues act to

---

[15] Antoinette Giancana and Thomas C. Renner, *Mafia Princess*, p. 340; Sam and Chuck Giancana, *Double Cross*, p. 350.

call in IOUs from friendly congressmen and to take the Justice Department off his back. Clearly they were unwilling or unable to do so.

In the spring of 1975 Giancana went into hospital for gall-bladder surgery and on 19 June, just two days out, he was shot in the back of the head with a .22 automatic with a silencer while frying sausages in his kitchen. There is no doubt that Giancana knew his killer, who shot him six more times in the face and head. In her memoir of her father, Antoinette Giancana suggests their deaths may have been because of a refusal by Cain and her father to share the profits of cruise-ship gambling with the Mob. On the other hand, Sam junior and Chuck Giancana in their memoir suggest that Cain had completely fallen out with his employer by this time. According to Alva Johnson Rogers, who gave evidence in the 1985 trial of Joey 'The Clown' Lombardo and Roy Williams for bribing a United States senator, Cain was killed by Lombardo for fear he would reveal the interests of the Chicago organisation. Both the outfit and the CIA denied any involvement and it will not be for several more years, if ever, that blame can be accurately attached. There was a conspicuously low Mob presence at Giancana's funeral. Curiously he left no money whatsoever, and Antoinette supplemented her income by posing topless in the bath for *Playboy*. She would later say in an interview that if her father had been alive the photographer would have been killed.[16]

In New York the list of dead bosses reads like a role of dishonour. Albert Anastasia, who ran Murder Inc. in the 1930s, was shot to death on 26 October 1957 while having a haircut in the barbershop at the Park Sheraton, at the corner of Seventh Avenue and 55th Street. He was in disgrace over both the shooting of Arnold Schuster (who had given up the bank robber Willie Sutton) and that of Frank Scalise on 17 June while he was buying peaches and a lettuce, as well as the disappearance of Scalise's brother Joe who had been selling membership of the Family at a reputed $50,000 a time. Joe Scalise is said to have been killed in the home of Jimmy Squillante

---

[16] W. Brashler, *The Don: The Life and Death of Sam Giancana*; Antoinette Giancana, *Mafia Princess*; *Master Detective*, November 2004.

and his body wrapped in plastic bags before being put in a garbage truck. Appropriately enough, Squillante controlled the garbage industry in New York. The hit on Anastasia was by no means an efficient one; of ten bullets fired, only five hit the sitting target.

Tony Bender, nominal head of the Genovese Family, simply disappeared on 8 April 1962. When his wife told him to put on a coat before he went for a walk, he replied that he would not be long and that in any event he was wearing his thermal underwear. He is still missing. The hit, which it undoubtedly was, had been organised by Vito Genovese, the real head of the Family but then serving a fifteen-year sentence over a drug deal. Genovese rightly suspected Bender of having had him set up.

Ten years later Tommy Eboli, the next titular head, was shot as he left his mistress's apartment in Crown Heights, Brooklyn, on 1 July 1972. He had made the mistake of treating with Carlo Gambino and then failing to pay him properly. Gambino survived to die of natural causes, but on 16 December 1985 his successor Paul Castellano was killed by John Gotti in a palace coup as he left Sparks' Steak House on E 46th street, a few steps from Third Avenue. Castellano had not wanted the Family to deal in drugs, and he paid the price along with his chauffeur Tommy Bilotti.

On 12 July 1979, Carmine 'Cigar' Galante who took over the Gambino Family was shot and killed as he lunched with his cousin Giuseppe Turano at Joe and Mary's Restaurant in Bushwick, Brooklyn. He was sitting on the patio with his bodyguards when several men appeared with machine guns and opened fire. Appropriately Galante died with a cigar in his mouth. His death was followed by that of the so-called 'Gentle Don' Angelo Bruno Annaloro, shot outside Cous' Little Italy restaurant in Philadelphia on 21 April 1980. There have been many theories over the death of Bruno including a contract put out after Galante's death; the fear that Bruno was about to talk to the authorities; and a simple power struggle. If the latter, it was an unresolved one. The killings of gangleaders in South Philadelphia have continued for the next twenty-five years.[17]

---

[17] For those interested in this power struggle see James Morton, *Gangland International* and *Gangland Today*; Joe Salerno, *The Plumber*.

One who has survived the North American battlefields over the years has been Vito Rizzuto, the reputed head of Montreal's Mafia in the absence of the repeatedly imprisoned Frank Cotroni. In many ways Rizzuto's has been a charmed life altogether. In July 2001 the police foiled a plot by Christian Deschênes and Denis-Rolland Girouard to kill him and two of his associates, Francesco Arcadi and Frank Martorana.[18] The police had arrested them when the pair were allegedly making a reconnaissance of a Mafia café in the St-Leonard district.

Naturally, there was some speculation as to why there should be an attack on Rizzuto, and one line of thought was that it harked back to the killing in 2000 of Salvatore Gervasi, the son of bar owner Paulo who had run the Castel Tina strip bar. Salvatore's body was found wrapped in a carpet in the boot of his Porsche in front of the family home; he had been shot in the head. Four months later his father survived a shooting as he came out of a bank on Jean Talon Street. At one time Paulo Gervasi and Rizzuto were thought to have been friendly, but Salvatore Gervasi had been a Rock Machine supporter in the bikers' seemingly endless struggle with the Hells Angels, with whom Rizzuto was in an uneasy alliance.

A blip in Rizzuto's career came on 8 December 2004 when he was ordered to be extradited to New York to face charges of being involved in the 1981 killing of three Bonanno foot soldiers, Alphonse 'Sonny Red' Indelicato, Philip 'Lucky Phil' Giaccone and Dominic 'Big Trin' Trinchera. It is alleged that he was brought in from Canada to carry out the killings, and from then on his career was onwards and upwards.[19]

Not so fortunate as Rizzuto was Johnny 'Pops' Papalia, extortioner, loan-shark, gambler; a man who 'never let a deal slip by without making it a swindle', former head of the Hamilton, Ontario Mafia. At a time in life when gangleaders should be thinking of their carpet slippers and Floridian sunshine, he was shot dead on 31 May 1997.

His death was quickly followed by the killing of his lieutenant,

---

[18] *The Globe and Mail*, 16 July 2001.
[19] For the exhumation of their bodies see Chapter 4.

Carmen Barillaro, at his home in Niagara Falls where he was a crime boss in his own right. Barillaro had been a made man in the Magaddino crime Family in Buffalo and had steadily worked his way up the Papalia hierarchy.

In his seventies, the immaculately dressed Johnny Pops gave an interview to the crime writer Peter Moon in which he expressed his great disappointment in life as never having graduated from high school. He thought that had he been better educated he might not have turned to crime. 'It's been an interesting one,' he said of his life. 'But maybe I'd have liked it to be different.' At his death Papalia had been seen talking to a white man aged about 35 years and walking with him through the car park of the Family-owned business, Galaxy Vending, on Railway Street. The man suddenly turned and shot him before fleeing in a green pick-up truck.

Two days after his boss's death, Barillaro spoke with rival Pasquale Musitano outside The Gathering Spot, a restaurant on Robert Street in Hamilton. He accused Musitano of being responsible for Papalia's death and, when this was denied, said that if he ever found out that Pasquale or his brother Angelo had been involved there would be swift retribution. Those words signed his death warrant. The old saw, 'twice blessed be he who gets his blow in first', proved correct. On 23 July, 35-year-old Kenneth Murdock and Angelo Musitano drove to Niagara Falls to look for Barillaro's two-tone Corvette. They found it in his driveway at 8 p.m. and, under the pretext that Murdock wanted to buy the car, rang the bell. When Barillaro opened the door Murdock pulled out a .9 mm handgun, said 'This is a message from Pat' and shot him.

Occasionally justice can be both swift and certain, and on 24 November 1998 Murdock – who, as it turned out, had taken out both Papalia and Barillaro – was charged, arraigned, pleaded guilty and sentenced to life imprisonment in one day. Apparently he had not negotiated the price before his hit on Papalia, but later he received $2,000 and a quantity of cocaine.

Murdock, who was already in custody on charges of assault and extortion, saw the light when tapes which indicated that he himself was marked for death were played to him. He thought that prison was safer than the streets. Following his conviction for the murders, along with the machine-gun killing in 1985 of Salvatore Alaimo, also in Hamilton – for which he will be eligible for parole within a decade – he agreed to give evidence for the Crown. Pasquale (Pat) Musitano and his brother Angelo, whose father Dominic and the Family had been feuding with Papalia and others of the Toronto old school for years, were charged with the first-degree murder of Papalia. On 4 February 2000 both Musitanos pleaded guilty to conspiracy and received a ten-year sentence with the opportunity to apply for parole after they had served a third. There was some criticism that the Crown had not pressed the murder charge, but it was pointed out that the only evidence was that of Murdock whose credibility would have been crucial. A plea in the hand is generally regarded as better than an acquittal in the court.[20]

It is not often that there is an equal partnership between husband and wife but the career of Bessie Perri, the so-called Queen of Toronto, ended – and with it to all intents and purposes that of her husband Rocco, the city's leading racketeer – when she was shot to death in her garage at 166 Bay Street South, Toronto, on 13 August 1930. Many commentators believe she was by far the smarter of the two.

On the evening of her killing, she telephoned her maid shortly before 11 p.m. to ask her to make up her room and then drove with Rocco to their luxurious home. Their practice was for Bessie to take the garage key, turn on the lights and then go indoors leaving him to put away their car and lock up.

According to Rocco this is precisely what happened at about 11.35 p.m., except that when Bessie went into the garage she was shot twice by men with shotguns. He panicked and ran for help. A third shot was fired. The police were called immediately and when the area was searched shells designed to cause the maximum possible damage were found.

Her actual husband, Harry Tobin, whom she had left along with their two daughters in 1913, was less than sympathetic when told of her death. 'I can say thank God,' he told the *Toronto Star*. 'She died as she deserved to die.'

---

[20] For an account of the career of Papalia and his feuds with the Musitanos see Peter Edwards and Antonio Nicaso, *Deadly Silence*; Adrian Humphreys, *The Enforcer*; James Morton, *Gangland International*. See also *Toronto News*, 5 February 2000.

Rocco announced that the motive for the killing was robbery. This was not an explanation accepted by everyone, for none of Bessie's expensive jewellery had been touched. There were a number of more attractive theories. First was that the killing had been carried out by underlings in the Perri Gang. Bessie was not simply Rocco's mistress, she was the power behind the organisation and took an active and autocratic interest in day-to-day events. While he was always happy to look after those who went to prison on his behalf, Bessie was made of sterner stuff and the payments to wives and children were not always going through. Another theory was that the killing was over a bundle of drugs for which Bessie was refusing to pay, telling New York State gangsters that they could sue her. Yet again, her killers could have been members of the Rochester organisation. It is also possible that Rocco Perri knew it was likely to take place but was powerless to prevent it.

Perri's fortunes sank, rose and sank after Bessie's death. He worked with another Jewish woman, Annie Newman, who also became his constant companion. He was less fortunate to be interned during the Second World War. On his release in 1943 he began to plan a campaign to regain his territory lost to the Magaddino Family from Buffalo. In the meantime he worked as a doorman at a Bloor Street theatre, hardly a position of strength. Still, somebody must have thought he was worth time and attention. On 23 April 1944 while staying with his cousin, Joe Serge, in Hamilton he complained of a headache and said he was going out for a walk. He was never seen again, nor was his body ever discovered. However, it is possible that he survived. Journalist and writer Antonio Nicaso reported that Perri may have made his way to upstate New York and then to Mexico. He had seen a letter apparently from Perri to a cousin dated 10 June 1949, which said the old mobster was alive and in good health.[21]

Overall the Australian underworld has been just as hard on its bosses, although until recently those who have reached the top in Sydney have generally survived to die of old age, or in prison or

[21] For an account of their careers see James Dubro and Robin Rowland, *King of the Mob*; Peter Edwards and Michel Auger, *The Encyclopedia of Canadian Organized Crime*.

both. Melbourne's gang history dates back to the 1920s, and particularly violent spats centred on the city's fruit and vegetable markets and the unions in the 1960s and 1970s.

Life has been harder for the lieutenants and soldiers. On 22 June 1927 Norman Bruhn, one of the top men of former jockey, armed robber, murderer, knifeman and general no-good, Melbourne-based Leslie 'Squizzy' Taylor, was shot in Sydney.[22] Bruhn had robbed a drug trader who had good connections in the New South Wales underworld. His killer was thought to be John 'Snowy' Cutmore, once Taylor's associate but now a leader of the Safe Prosecution Gang, so called because they only attacked people whom they knew would not prosecute them.

There followed a series of shootings and knifings in what came to be known as the Cocaine War. Then on 26 October 1927 Cutmore was drinking heavily at a bar in St Kilda's which was under the temporary protection of Taylor. He smashed the premises and stripped a woman naked before turning her onto the street – not something which Taylor, even in decline, could allow to go unpunished.

According to one version of the double killing on the afternoon of 27 October, Cutmore was in bed at his home in Fitzroy when Taylor walked in and shot him. Cutmore, who had a pistol under the sheets, returned the fire; he died on the bed and Taylor was taken to hospital where he also died. Although the police accepted that Cutmore and Taylor had shot each other, different versions of the killings have emerged. One is that Cutmore was killed by Sydney criminals; fortuitously Taylor happened to be there and was killed at the same time. Another is that somehow Cutmore shot Taylor first and then was shot by Taylor's companion. If this version is right it was almost certainly set up by Henry Stokes, Taylor's former partner who now, for a time, became the newest undisputed King of the Victoria Underworld. Whichever is correct Mrs Bridget Cutmore, Snowy's widow, who was in the house at the time, was quite unable to help the police.

There is another theory that she or Cutmore's mother, Gladys,

---

[22] For the career of Leslie 'Squizzy' Taylor and his friends of the time see H. Anderson, *Larrikin Crook: The Rise and Fall of Squizzy Taylor*; James Morton, *Gangland International*, Chapter 37.

seeing Taylor shoot Cutmore, took a gun and killed him. A further name in the frame has been that of Leslie 'Scotland Yard' Walkerden, a Melbourne identity who was killed in Richmond in September 1945.[23]

In recent years, however, with the profits to be made from drugs, particularly amphetamines, things have changed radically. One of the problems in the rise of gang violence in Melbourne stems from the high-risk policy adopted by the police in Victoria during the 1990s of manufacturing its own amphetamines in an attempt to break into the city's network of dealers.

Opinion over the cause of the present troubles in the city varies, but everyone agrees that serious troubles they are. Either they stem from the 1999 arrest of John Samuel William Higgs, the country's biggest amphetamine producer, or the murder of Melbourne gang figure Alphonse John Gangitano in Templestone the previous year. Whichever is correct, as a result there has been a long-running turf war as New Boys Carl Williams and Andrew 'Benji' Veniamin have struggled for power against the old Carlton Crew. Since 1998 there have been over thirty gangland killings in Melbourne, of which at least eleven can be linked to the power struggle between the rival bosses. Had he still been alive Chris Flannery, the contract killer who flitted between Melbourne and Sydney, would have been a rich man.

Gangitano was shot dead at his home in 1998. Known as the Robert De Niro of Lygon Street, just above the central business district, he had no visible means of support and in his will gave his occupation as 'Gentleman'. At the time of his death he was awaiting trial on a charge of affray, but he had faced far worse. He was confidently suspected of killing the popular gangland figure, Gregory John Workman. The two went to a wake together on 7 February 1995 and then went on to a party to raise bail for an alleged robber. Gangitano became abusive and he and Workman went outside. Two sisters saw the shooting and made detailed statements that they had seen Gangitano almost literally with a smoking gun in his hand. They went into a form of protective custody – living in a caravan,

---

[23] See Chapter 15.

dining on takeaway food and collecting their clothes in a lay-by. But unfortunately from the viewpoint of the authorities it was not all that protective. They were contacted by Carlton Crew stalwart Jason Moran, who told them that if they gave evidence they and their families would inevitably be killed. They were taken to see a lawyer and made statements withdrawing their evidence, after which they absented themselves from Victoria, spending a year in Europe on a trip paid for by Gangitano. Inevitably the charges were dismissed and Gangitano's lawyer, George Defteros, put in a bill to the police for $69,975.35. At the time it was thought highly probable that East St Kilda criminals would exact revenge, but none came immediately.

Three years later Gangitano had other problems. He had fallen out with the Moran brothers who now controlled a large part of the drug-dealing on Lygon. On 16 January 1998 he was killed, almost certainly by Jason Moran – another who despite limited earning capacity in the outside world, was able to send his children to private schools.[24] Moran, in a link with history, was married to the daughter of Les Kane, a standover man of the 1970s.

Although he denied it, also present at Gangitano's home when he was shot was Graham Allan 'The Munster' Kinniburgh, once a member of the dying breed of safebreakers, who had risen to become a kingpin of the city's crime scene. Kinniburgh, whose career spanned three decades, was one of the relatively few mobsters who have bridged the gap between the underworld and respectability, and was well known for his discreet connections to Melbourne's establishment.[25] When his son married into one of the city's grandest families, the reception was held at the oldest of the Melbourne establishments, the Windsor. In a scene which could have been taken from *The Godfather*, intelligence police snapped not the bride and groom but the guests, so updating their files.

The police believed that Moran was involved in an argument with Gangitano and shot him; Kinniburgh was there, saw what was happening and ran out through a security mesh on the front door,

---

[24] John Silvester, 'Death of a Gangster' in *The Sunday Age*, 18 January 1998.
[25] John Silvester and ors, 'Modest Mobster who kept the Peace' in *The Age*, 14 December 2003.

cutting himself. Later he went upstairs to see what the security video had recorded. On the sound principle that lies should be as close to the truth as possible, he told the police he had indeed been to see Gangitano who was on the telephone and had asked him to leave while he had a meeting with an unnamed man. Kinniburgh went to buy some cigarettes and returned half an hour later only to find his host dead. The coroner had no doubt that both he and Moran were implicated.

Moran posted a touching eulogy in the *Herald-Sun*:

> Words can't express how I feel. There will never be a man such as yourself. Whatever I asked of you was done 110 per cent. I will love you always. Your little mate Jase.

Things could not possibly be left like this. Moran's half-brother, designer drug dealer and standover man Mark, was shot dead on 15 June 2000 as he was getting into his car outside his luxury home in Essendon. Two blasts from a shotgun were followed by one in the head from a revolver. The killing was thought to be over a quarrel with another crime boss whom Mark had shot in the stomach in 1999. On that occasion, the wounded man gallantly made no complaint and still claims he does not know the identity of the shooter. Between the deaths of Gangitano and Mark Moran eight others were killed in Melbourne, though not all of them were necessarily involved in the drugs war. For example Frank Benvenuto, shot on 8 May 2000, may have died as part of a long-running struggle for control of the fruit and vegetable market. It is true, however, that shortly before his death he had quarrelled with the Moran brothers.[26] His killer was probably Dino Dibra, from the New Boys, who himself was shot dead on 14 October that year.

After that things remained relatively quiet for two years although Victor Peirce went down in Port Melbourne. Peirce, the sixth child of the notorious and one-eyed Kate 'Ma' Pettingill, the so-called

---

[26] In 1992 Benvenuto and his late father Liborio were suspected of being behind the killing of their one-time business partner Alfonso Muratano. Alfonso's father Vicenzo had been killed in 1964. See Paul Anderson, *Shotgun City*.

Matriarch who produced a number of violent sons,[27] was thought to have been a member of the Flemington Crew, a team of armed robbers. He had been acquitted following the ambush killing of two constables in Walsh Street, South Yarra, in 1988. On 1 May 2002 he was shot repeatedly with a .45 handgun as he sat in his car in Bay Street. His death also drew a number of notices, including an oblique one from the robber Mark 'Chopper' Read, 'Don't worry, Vic, Kath will keep an eye on things.' It was thought he was killed because he had accepted a contract and failed to deliver.[28]

The Melbourne drug war appears to have escalated following what was intended to be a peace meeting in the La Porcella restaurant at Faraday and Rathdowne Streets in the Little Italy district of fashionable Carlton in late 2002. Present were representatives of the Carlton Crew and the New Boys as well as biker Troy Mercante and Antonious Mokbel, the latter allegedly a major amphetamine dealer. The meeting quickly degenerated into violence. Mokbel upset Nik 'The Russian' Radev and, after his bodyguards had been taken out, was beaten within a few inches of his life. Carl Williams was ordered to take him to a doctor to be patched up, and it was then that Williams changed sides. None of the Carlton Crew had intervened to prevent the beating and he no longer felt safe.[29]

The following year the body count began to mount once more. Sometimes it was personal, more often it was business. The veteran crime reporter John Silvester, who thought there were simply too many people in Melbourne trying to deal in drugs, saw it as a game of musical chairs in which the loser was usually shot.

Arsonist, extortionist and drug dealer Radev died in the afternoon of 15 April 2003, shot after he met with what has been

---

[27] Perhaps the most notorious of the sons was Dennis Bruce Allen, known as Mr Death and known to have killed a number of Melbourne's low life before his own death in 1997 from heart disease worsened by drug abuse. His victims included male prostitute Greg Pasche, stabbed in the head in May 1983, and drug addict Victor Gouroff who disappeared the same year. For an account of the family see Adrian Tame, *The Matriarch*.

[28] Read, whose nickname comes from self-mutilation of his ears, has written a series of highly popular books in which he is the hero of the underworld. He came to prominence when, in an effort to secure the release of his friend Jimmy Loughnan, he kidnapped Judge Martin. He received thirteen years and was later convicted of a biker murder in Tasmania. He was paroled in 1997 and his books have been made into a very successful film.

[29] Adam Shand, 'Burial Ground' in *The Bulletin*, 6 April 2004.

described as 'a group of criminal identities' at the Brighton Baths Café. Two men who were with him ran away and so could not identify his killer, believed to be Benji Veniamin. Nor has the contractor been identified, although the motive was thought to be drugs. Regarded as a violent – even in the circles in which he moved – and dangerous competitor, he was believed to have killed one man and taken his identity until his own naturalisation papers came through. His funeral was not well attended.

Jason Moran lasted for some years longer than his half-brother, until 21 June 2003 when he was shot dead in front of his children in the car park of the Cross Keys hotel in Essendon North. Down with him went Pasquale Barbaro, his bodyguard.[30] Victor 'The Marathon Man' Brincat was accused of both murders, something he denies.

With Moran gone, it was probably only a matter of time before a move was made on Kinniburgh. A few months before his death, his daughter had married the son of a former Attorney-General. The week before he was killed, Kinniburgh held a series of meetings in Carlton restaurants with the cream of the local villains, and also met a detective from Melbourne's criminal investigation branch.[31] He was shot dead in the chest as he left his car outside his home on 13 December 2003. It was thought he managed to get one shot off from his own gun.

Things climaxed early in 2004 when on 23 March, Andrew 'Benji' Veniamin, regarded as dangerously erratic and now the bodyguard of Carl Williams, was shot in the head at lunchtime in a back room of La Porcella. He had gone there for a meeting with another of the city's top men, Dominic 'Mick' Gatto, a member of the Carlton Crew. The heavily tattooed Veniamin, a small man who was said to have lively soft brown eyes and was thought to receive $100,000 a hit, arrived at the restaurant at 2 p.m. in a borrowed silver

---

[30] His death has had an unlikely postscript. Mark and Cheryl McEachran, frustrated by their inability to conceive a child, snatched a three-week-old baby in a shopping centre. Their choice could not have been much more unfortunate. The baby was that of Barbaro's cousin Joe, an alleged drug dealer with links to the upper echelons of the crime scene. When the pair were remanded it was he who was in the public gallery mouthing threats. *Sydney Morning Herald*, 11, 25, 26 August 2004; *The Observer*, 15 August 2004.
[31] *The Sunday Age*, 14 December 2003.

Mercedes which he double-parked. At the time he was disqualified from driving, and in the months before his death had racked up some forty speeding and parking tickets. Gatto, regarded as a great fixer and who required a fee of $5,000 to sit with him, was at his usual table. A former heavyweight professional boxer, the Royal Commission into the Building Industry had described him as a standover man. He preferred 'industrial consultant'. It was said of him that no gangland killing could be regarded as such until he had inserted a flowery death notice in the *Herald-Sun*. His tribute to The Munster is a fair example of his work:

> You were a true Chameleon, you could adapt to any situation, rubbing shoulders with the best of them and being able to talk at any level about any topic. I was so proud to be part of your life. This has left a void in my heart that can't be replaced. I love you 'Pa' and I will never forget you.

Later it would be said that Veniamin was on the verge of giving up his criminal enterprises but was reluctant to do so in case he was thought to be a quitter. Quitter or not, the police had him in their sights over five murders including those of Frank Benvenuto, Dino Dibra, Paul Kallipolitis and Nic Radev.[32]

Veniamin died after what has been described as 'an altercation'. As he waited for the police Gatto apologised to the restaurant owner for the undoubted inconvenience caused by the shooting. Now prices were rising on the street if not in the restaurant, which closed shortly afterwards. It is said the price on Gatto is $400,000.

The word on the street was that Williams would be killed before he arrived at the church to bury his friend. On this occasion, as indeed on so many others, the word was wrong. Over the years there have been a number of attacks on Carl Williams and his demise has been confidently and regularly, if so far erroneously, predicted. Now the deaths and attempted hits came faster. The next victim was not in fact Williams, but Lewis Moran. The decision to kill Jason's father and Mark's stepfather, a man with strong ties to the

---

[32] *Herald-Sun* (Melbourne), 23 November 2004.

Painters and Dockers Union, was said to have been taken at the wake for Veniamin. Lewis Moran had been in the crosshairs if only because he had offered a mere $50,000 for the killing of Williams. It was only thirty hours after Veniamin was buried before Moran was shot in the Brunswick Poker Club on Sydney Road. Two men – one with a handgun, the other armed with a shotgun – came into the main room of the club, shot and injured the man with whom Moran was drinking and, with Moran running in a panicked circle, killed him at close range.

As Raymond Zemour discovered years earlier in Paris, walking one's dogs has often been a dangerous time for the gangster. An attack on the struck-off solicitor and alleged member of the Carlton Crew, Mario Condello, was foiled by the police as he walked his Jack Russell terriers near Brighton cemetery close to his home. Perhaps foolishly he then went into print on the subject of the gang wars and within a matter of weeks, along with his own solicitor George Defteros, was arrested for conspiracy to murder Carl Williams. He was said to have offered $150,000 a head to kill Williams, his father George and a bodyguard; there was to be a bonus of $50,000 on completion.[33] Again Condello went into print, saying that the inquiries he was making into the value of contracts etc. were simply to find out how endangered a species he was himself. Defteros, who adamantly denied any involvement, voluntarily gave up his practising certificate until things were sorted out.[34]

Then on 9 June Carl Williams himself was arrested and charged with conspiracy to murder Jason Moran and Pasquale Barbaro as well as Michael Ronald Marshall – shot outside his South Yarra home on 25 October 2003 – along with existing charges of conspiracy to murder a police detective and drug trafficking. What did the apparently generous man do for a living? He thought himself to be a commissioner; that is, he bought and sold jewellery on

---

[33] This was one of the less remarkable bonuses on offer. In Detroit, Harry Kalasho had two of his rivals, Salem Munthir and Salem Gago, killed by hitman Buck Lavell. The payment was $5,000 each, and a further $10,000 if their heads were deposited on the disputed turf of Seven Mile. Lavell completed the contract but did not deposit the heads. He was convicted but never gave Kalasho up. In his turn Harry Kalasho was killed in the long-running feud.

[34] *Sunday Age* (Melbourne), 8 August 2004.

commission. He was remanded in custody and that summer collected a seven-year sentence, with a minimum of five to be served, for a $450,000 drug-trafficking operation.[35]

Will the Carlton Crew and the New Boys survive these deaths and arrests? John Silvester thinks, 'The survival of the Carlton Crew will depend on the acquittals of some of their senior members.' And as for the New Boys? 'There'll be the New, New Boys.'[36]

[35] *Geelong Advertiser*, 30 October 2004; *The Age*, 30 October 2004. For a series of highly entertaining accounts of the war see the articles by Adam Shand, *The Bulletin*, including 6, 15 April, 22 June 2004.
[36] Conversation with author.

9

When Thieves Fall Out

One of the staple plots of the *film noir* or the crime thriller is the successful robbery after which the thieves fall out amongst themselves or into the arms of another more powerful gang who relieve them of their hard-earned money. Some of the greatest real-life fallouts in the last fifty years may have been a long time in coming, but come they surely did.

The first in time came in the mid-1950s when Corsican gangs clashed over the proceeds of cigarette smuggling from Tangier. Cigarette smuggling was then, as it is now, capable of providing an enormous tax saving and in the 1950s there was a great demand in France for what were known as *Les Blondes*, made with the light-coloured American tobacco. The export of cigarettes from Tangier was then perfectly legal, as was the transfer of the cargo to another vessel provided it was done outside territorial limits. It was the second boat which ran the gauntlet of Customs patrols and had to land its cargo without interception.

Apart from the Customs there was, however, the risk of an attack by pirates, and the Mediterranean at the time was a haven for them. One Corsican team of hijackers based in Marseilles was headed by Antoine Paolini, known as *Planche* or 'The Board', who ran an illegal wholesale tobacco business as a distribution centre from a bar in the Palmier quarter. Paolini had grown up in a Corsican ghetto in

Marseilles and had served a sentence in the Bat d'Afrique. His right-hand man was another Corsican, Dominique Muzziotti. One problem was that neither Muzziotti nor his crews were sailors, and so Paolini put up the proposition of a partnership to an American, Elliott Forrest, hero of the Murmansk Russian convoy run and decorated four times in the Second World War. At the end of September 1952 Forrest was attending a bullfight in Tangier when he was contacted by another American, 'Nylon' Sid Paley, who told him that he had received a coded message that Paolini wanted to see Forrest urgently. This time the job was a big one. The biggest ever load of *Blondes*, twenty-seven tons in all, was to be smuggled on 4 October on a Dutch vessel the *Combinatie*. It was a sufficiently big job that if successful Forrest would be able to retire. Just how many times has one heard that phrase?

Now Forrest, together with Julio Renucci, hired a high-speed motor torpedo boat the *Esmé*, crewed by some unsuspecting British adventurers, and on 3 October left Tangier a little before the *Combinatie*. Shortly before dawn the *Combinatie* was boarded; the Dutch captain was shot and seriously wounded. A grenade was exploded behind the vessel's control panel, and the crew were locked below along with their injured captain. The cargo of contraband cigarettes was now transferred to the *Esmé*. In turn it was then transferred to a boat under the command of Muzziotti which sailed out of Marseilles. Forrest went with them. The crew of the *Combinatie* managed to repair most of the damage and made for the city. Now Forrest fled to Cavaillon in the Luberon district. With an appalling accent there was no chance of his pretending to be a Frenchman and so, enterprisingly, he posed as a deaf-and-dumb American writer putting together a series of articles on smuggling and women.

Shortly afterwards Sid Paley was tried by an American court in Tangier over the affair and received three years imprisonment from the consular judge, Judge Helnick. The other two judges sitting with him wished to return verdicts of not guilty, but the minority prevailed. This led to an automatic appeal and in May 1953 the sentence was changed to a modest fine and probation to be served in America.

This was the signal for a bloody struggle in the spirit of the pre-war French gangsters Spirito and Carbone. It began on the French mainland with Paolini's betrayal of Forrest to the police. The reasoning was simple. With Forrest gone Paolini, apart from handing out a few small percentages, largely had the cargo for himself and his own associates. Unfortunately Paolini was himself arrested at l'Isolella near Ajaccio and while he was serving a two-month sentence his gang split. Some wanted to wait until his release; others wanted to divvi up immediately.

However, Forrest, now in Les Baumettes prison in Marseilles awaiting trial, had other powerful Corsican friends. On 17 February, Paolini man Jean Colonna was shot in Ajaccio, losing both legs to a cartridge which contained a dozen lead balls wired together through their centres.[1] His would-be killers then drove their van across his legs but amazingly he survived. On 12 March Paolini survived an attack in broad daylight outside his bar in the quartier Pannier, when he was shot in the lungs, pancreas and knee. In Corsica his cousin Tristaini was killed. Now their friends fought back.

Reprisal followed reprisal. Paolini's bodyguard Jacques Oliva was killed. In return Julio Renucci was murdered, followed by the death of Jacques Colonna on the Cours Napoléon in Ajaccio. On 18 July Jean Colonna was killed, and on 27 August so also was Paolini's second bodyguard, François Casssegrain. Finally Paolini, now recovered from the first attack, was shot and killed as he attended a funeral at the Saint-Julien cemetery in Marseilles.

Dominique Muzziotti, who was said to be a Gregory Peck lookalike, had survived the slaughter mainly because he was serving time in Les Baumettes for carrying a gun of a greater calibre than that permitted to gangsters. He was released shortly before Christmas 1955 and renounced a life of crime. In future he would carry religious *objets* rather than a gun. They did not protect him for long; on New Year's Eve that year he was machine-gunned as he stood in Mon Bar.

---

[1] Although this was the first recorded case of the technique in the twentieth century, it was a favourite of cannoneers in the Middle Ages. For more on the process and a more detailed account of the war see Derek Goodman, *Villainy Unlimited*, Chapter 8 and Lawrence Wilkinson, *Behind the Face of Crime*, Chapter 9; also Marcel Montarron, 'Les Pirates du "Combinatie"' in *Detective*, 13 February 1956.

It was not until 1956 that Elliott Forrest and fifteen others involved in the *Combinatie* affair went on trial. Originally the authorities intended that there should be thirty-eight defendants, but eight failed to appear and another fifteen were dead. Forrest was convicted in Marseilles and sentenced to three years imprisonment, later increased to five years by the Court of Appeal in Aix. He was also fined a massive three milliard francs, and was then banned from living in France for five years after completing his sentence.[2]

The second of these fallouts followed a highly successful raid; the most famous of Melbourne's many robberies. The so-called Bookie Robbery took place on 21 April 1976 shortly after midday at the Victoria Club at 141 Queen Street. The premises, built in 1880, was where the Victorian bookies would meet to settle up on the first working day after a weekend's racing. Even though security was amazingly informal – three detectives would drop in to see things were all right, and invariably they were – over the years the Club had been looked at by a number of teams of criminals who had decided it was just too difficult. The raid was finally devised by Raymond 'Chuck' Bennett when he was serving a sentence on the Isle of Wight. He along with his great friend Brian O'Callaghan, members of the Kangaroo Gang operating throughout Europe robbing jewellers, were caught following a raid in London. While on remand in Pentonville, O'Callaghan swapped clothes with another prisoner who was being released on bail and, given twenty-eight pence for his bus fare, walked free. Bennett received five years for his part in the robbery. The other prisoner received three for helping O'Callaghan escape.

During a period of home leave in 1995 Bennett had taken just that and returned to Australia to case the Victoria Club premises before flying back to Parkhurst to complete his sentence. Like Bruce Reynolds, the leader of the Great Train Robbery, he had the brains to organise and the charisma to lead a team. He was regarded by former standover man turned writer Mark 'Chopper' Read, himself no slouch, as being not only a top gang tactician but also 'one of

---

[2] *The Times*, 20 December 1952, 5 May 1953, 16 February 1956.

the Australian underworld's foremost bank robbers'.[3] However, just as there have been few, if any, success stories amongst the Great Train Robbers so, over the years, it was thought there was a similar jinx on the participants in the Bookie Robbery.[4]

Bennett, who in his younger days had acted as a minder for Billy 'The Texan' Longley in the Melbourne Painters and Dockers waterfront war, put together a team of nine serious professionals and took them out of the city for a period of training away from their wives and girlfriends and the capital's snares and attractions. Bennett had learned from his time in English prisons, and his team copied the raids of Bertie Smalls and his Wembley gang of bank robbers.[5] His team included Ian Revell Carroll, who became the Quarter-Master Sergeant, and Anthony Paul McNamara.

When Bennett was satisfied the training had gone well and the team was ready, he chose the day. An armed guard was carrying what would be the increased takings into the Club from 116 bookmakers at both the Caulfield and Moonee Valley meetings for the three-day Easter weekend's racing. It was to be a quick in-and-out job. The Club was deserted at the weekend and Bennett took his team of six with three back-ups into the premises for a dress rehearsal.

The money was delivered by armoured car and at midday a man arrived to say he had been called to repair the refrigerator in the second-floor bar. At 12.07 he met with at least five accomplices, wearing balaclavas, dustcoats and overalls, in the stairwell. Armed with machine guns they burst into the settling room, tackled the armed guards and ordered the bookmakers to lie on the floor. Telephones were ripped out, bolt-cutters were used to open up metal cash-boxes filled with over a hundred calico bags containing

[3] Mark Brandon Read, *Chopper* 2, p. 82.
[4] One who was said to have considered and declined the job was James 'Jockey' Smith, a celebrated armed robber of the 1970s. When he was arrested in Sydney as a suspect for the murder of a bookmaker, he attempted to shoot a police officer who saved himself by pushing his thumb between the hammer and the firing pin. Smith was convicted of attempted murder and released in 1992, after which he survived three shootings in two days. For more details of his career see Mark Brandon Read, *Chopper*.
[5] For an account of Bertie Smalls and the Wembley gang whose 1960s activities ended in lengthy prison sentences but curiously no subsequent reprisals, see John Ball and ors, *Cops and Robbers*; James Morton, *Gangland*.

untraceable notes variously said to total between $1.5 million and $15 million. The gang jammed the lift with the empty security boxes and in only eleven minutes the raid was over and the robbers were gone into the traffic in Queen Street.[6] A reward of $70,000 was promptly offered.

The next problem faced by Bennett was the disposal of the money. An earlier successful job had gone wrong when Peter Macari began spending like water from his $500,000 taking from the 'Mr Brown-Quantas' hoax. The Great Train Robbers had been trapped largely because of their inability to hide the large sums of cash they stole. The wiser Bennett had already made arrangements for the laundering, and some money was invested through a Sydney estate agent. Other money went to Manila and some to Canada.

There was, however, also the danger of other gangs taking an interest and the much feared Sydney gang, The Toecutters – named because of their tendencies to amputate the toes of criminals to persuade them to part with their ill-gotten gains – were said to have looked at Bennett. Led by Kevin Gore along with the crooked ex-police officer Fred Krahe, victims of the Toecutters included Frank 'Baldy' Blair whose toes were cut and testicles torched to persuade him to reveal where he had deposited his $90,000 share of the $587,890 from the Mayne Nickless security van in Guildford, Sydney, on 4 March 1970. Blair died from his injuries. It spoke enormously well of the regard in which Bennett was held that the Toecutters decided to leave him alone.[7]

Some of the laundering did not go well. Bennett's mother collapsed

---

[6] *The Age* (Melbourne), 22, 23 April 1976.

[7] The previous record haul in Australia had been the Mayne Nickless robbery on 4 March 1970. The raid had been a simple one. Almost unbelievably the guards regularly parked the van in a shopping centre when they had their lunch. One of the security guards was persuaded to open the door to put out the rubbish at a certain time. The Toecutters also attacked Stephen Nittes who was on the Mayne Nickless raid. He handed over a substantial part of his share. Alan Jones escaped their attention, but both he and Nittes received sixteen years. Gore was later killed by John Regan who also killed another Toecutter, Jake Maloney. Some accounts of the Toecutters claim they were led by an Englishman, Linus or Jimmy 'The Pom' Driscoll or O'Driscoll who was said to have been a friend of the Krays. There does not seem to be any evidence of the existence of such a relationship unless it was very early in their youth. Driscoll was framed for the Maloney murder but was released on appeal and later deported. He was also for a time sought in the 1953 Whiskey Au Go Go nightclub bombing in Brisbane. Krahe died in 1981. Mark Read, *Chopper*; Neddy Smith, *Catch and Kill Your Own*.

on a visit to a Melbourne solicitor, and when the paramedics undressed her they found some $90,000 in cash in her clothes. One theory about solving crime is to follow the money and a close friend of Bennett, Norman Leung Lee, who ran a dim-sum restaurant, was arrested and appeared in court in the autumn charged with the robbery. The evidence against him was circumstantial. In the month after the robbery he had spent $13,000 on extensions to his house and had bought $60,000 of dim-sum equipment. He was also said to have laundered money through his solicitor's trust account. On 19 August he took $60,000 in a plastic bag to his solicitors, saying he wanted to invest it for a friend. But when he was raided Lee remained as staunch as Bennett had expected him to be. The magistrate ruled that there was no evidence to link the money to the robbery and Lee was discharged. He was the only person ever charged in the case, and shortly after his acquittal the squad investigating the robbery was dissolved.

The predatory Toecutters may have decided to leave Bennett alone and the police to abandon their squad but the Kane brothers, Les and Brian, also connected to the Painters and Dockers Union, who led a team of standover men into illegal gambling and casino protection, were his arch-rivals. The Kanes had grown up as children with a mutual dislike of Bennett, who had long believed that they were informers. Earlier they had fought in the Royal Oak Hotel in Richmond when Bennett was fortunate not to lose an ear. Unfortunately Les Kane then made threats against Bennett's family, and it was that which probably sealed his fate. On 17 October 1978 three men went to Les Kane's home in Wantirna, a Melbourne suburb, and after pushing him in the bath they shot him with machine guns. His body was never found; it is regarded as quite possible that he became dim-sum.

Bennett, Francis William Mikkelsen and Laurence Joseph Pendergast were charged with and acquitted of the murder. Mikkelsen and Pendergast went straight into hiding but on 12 November 1979 Bennett, charged with a separate armed robbery, had a court appearance to attend and while he was waiting without handcuffs and with an unarmed guard outside the court, he was shot three times in the chest. He staggered out of the courthouse followed by police and died in St Vincent's Hospital within the hour.[8] It is highly probable that the gunman was Brian Kane, who had refused to accept the 'not guilty' verdict in relation to his brother's death. Another suggestion is that the killer was Chris Flannery, possibly along with a police officer. This was certainly put forward by the press. At the inquest the coroner found that two named officers were not involved. Many years later one of them claimed the killer was indeed Brian Kane.[9]

The day after his death, Bennett's old mate Brian O'Callaghan escaped from a prison van taking him to work at the prison bakery. He then published a tribute in the *Herald-Sun*:

> No words I speak will say how I feel. I loved you Ray like a brother. Memories of you will be mine to keep. Today and Forever. Much loved friend of Brian O'Callaghan.

With O'Callaghan on the loose the press and police predicted immediate trouble and possibly an all-out gang war, but for the time being it did not materialise. There were, however, further reprisals to come, though not at first from the Bennett side. Early in the morning of 15 July 1981 Norman McLeod, Mikkelsen's brother-in-law, was shot three times through the window of his car outside his home in Coolaroo by two men armed with shotguns. The police thought that possibly he was killed in mistake for Mikkelsen. In November 1982 a gunman finally caught up with Brian Kane as he was sitting with a girl in the Quarry Hotel in Brunswick. Now Pendergast came out of hiding, but he also disappeared in August 1985.

Another of the Bookie robbers, Ian Carroll, following in the master's footsteps, became one of the great planners of armed robberies. He would leave nothing to chance, and team members were supplied not only with weapons but also a medical kit in case of injury. He was killed in an argument in his own backyard in a

---

[8] *The Age* (Melbourne), 13 November 1979. Some thirty-five years later Tony Mokbel, accused of importing drugs, was excused attendance at the Melbourne Magistrates' Court until the end of his committal proceedings. It was argued, possibly with some justification, that he felt at risk from his enemies when so publicly exposed. *The Age*, 16 November 2004.

[9] For a full retrospective of the case and the subsequent inquest see 'Payback' in *Sunday Mail* (Brisbane), 14 November 1999.

WANTED

JOHN HERBERT DILLINGER

On June 23, 1934, HOMER S. CUMMINGS, Attorney General of the United States, under the authority vested in him by an Act of Congress approved June 6, 1934, offered a reward of

$10,000.00

for the capture of John Herbert Dillinger or a reward of

$5,000.00

for information leading to the arrest of John Herbert Dillinger.

DESCRIPTION

Age, 32 years; Height, 5 feet 7-1/8 inches; Weight, 153 pounds; Build, medium; Hair, medium chestnut; Eyes, grey; Complexion, medium; Occupation, machinist; Marks and scars, 1/2 inch scar back left hand, scar middle upper lip, brown mole between eyebrows.

All claims to any of the aforesaid rewards and all questions and disputes that may arise as among claimants to the foregoing rewards shall be passed upon by the Attorney General and his decisions shall be final and conclusive. The right is reserved to divide and allocate portions of any of said rewards as between several claimants. No part of the aforesaid rewards shall be paid to any official or employee of the Department of Justice.

If you are in possession of any information concerning the whereabouts of John Herbert Dillinger, communicate immediately by telephone or telegraph collect to the nearest office of the Division of Investigation, United States Department of Justice, the local addresses of which are set forth on the reverse side of this notice.

JOHN EDGAR HOOVER, DIRECTOR,
DIVISION OF INVESTIGATION,
UNITED STATES DEPARTMENT OF JUSTICE,
WASHINGTON, D. C.

June 25, 1934

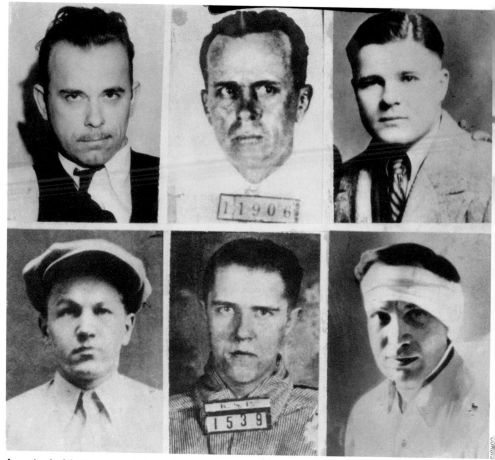

America's Most Wanted: John Dillinger and friends from left to right (top) JD, Arthur Barker, Charles 'Pretty Boy' Floyd (bottom) Homer Van Meter, Alvin Karpis, Baby Face Nelson; plus Lucky Luciano (below)

Al Capone in patriotic mode

The beginning of the end for Big Al

Police frogmen search for the body of anti-drug campaigner Donald Mackay in Griffith, New South Wales

In Melbourne Carl Williams carries the coffin of Andrew 'Benji' Veniamin. In the summer of 2005 Mick Gatto was acquitted of Veniamin's murder

Mick Gatto (top right) carries the coffin of his friend Graeme 'The Munster' Kinninburgh

Eliot Forrest, instigator of the *Combinatie* affair

Antoine Paoloni, 'The Plank'

The Marseilles home of the Paolini gang

Francois Vanverberghe 'Francis the Belgian' lasted over three decades before he was shot in the Club Artois

And then there was only one surviving Zemour

ROLAND ZEMOUR   EDGARD ZEMOUR
1926·1947   1937·1983
WILLIAMS ZEMOUR GILBERT ZEMOUR
1930·1975   1935·1983
RAYMOND ZEMOUR CLAIRETTE ZEMOUR
1904·1975   née ATLANI
                1903·1983

R.Z.

Rangimara Ngarimu, Britain's first female contract killer

METROPOLITAN POLICE

£1,000 REWARD

MURDER

A reward or rewards up to a total of £1,000 will be paid for information leading to the arrest of HARRY MAURICE ROBERTS, b. Wanstead, Essex, on 21-7-36, 5ft. 10in., photo. above, wanted for questioning in connection with the murder of three police officers on the 12th August, 1966, at Braybrook Street, Shepherds Bush.

Information to be given to New Scotland Yard, S.W.1, or at any police station.

The amount of any payment will be in the discretion of the Commissioner of Police for the Metropolis.

J. SIMPSON,
Commissioner of Police.

supposedly safe house in Mount Martha, Mornington Peninsula, on 3 March 1983. Searching the house, the police found what they described as a 'huge number' of weapons including machine guns, along with uniforms from a security firm, some hidden in a false ceiling.[10]

Over the years, those suspected of being on the Victoria Club team or in the three-man backup squad were arrested for other jobs and served long sentences. Anthony McNamara died in Collingwood in 1990; he had become a drug addict and it was suspected that he had been given a 'hot shot' or deliberate overdose. The laundering contact in Manila featured in the Costigan Report on the Painters and Dockers Union and, although wealthy and involved in Rules Football and trotting horses, also became involved in drugs and subsequently received eleven years.

As for Norman Lee, he moved quietly to Singapore but the lure of Victoria proved too much. On 28 July 1992 he and Stephen Bari failed to close the doors as a getaway van accelerated during a robbery at Melbourne airport. Lee was thrown from the van and, armed with a .357, ran after it. An inquest would hear that he appeared to bring up the gun before he was shot by a member of the Police Special Operations Group. A post mortem showed that Lee had a seventy per cent blockage of his left coronary artery, and the chase after the van might well have killed him anyway. It was thought he had returned to Melbourne some time earlier and had been involved in a number of successful robberies.

Just over a year after the Victoria Bookie Robbery, what was then the biggest hold-up in American crime history took place just before dawn on 11 December 1978. Six or seven men – accounts vary – wearing ski masks cleared $5.8 million from the Lufthansa Airlines warehouse at Kennedy International. By the end of the saga the bodies of participants and their unfortunate friends were piled high.

As with most serious robberies there has to have been inside

---

[10] The house had also been used as a safe house for such criminals as the celebrated bank robber and escaper, Russell 'Mad Dog' Cox, and the former South Australian police officer, Colin Creed. Cox was later tried for the Carroll murder and acquitted. He and Creed were identified as part of a gang running through Victoria and New South Wales which had pulled off nine armed robberies netting them in excess of $1.3 million. For an account of Cox's career see Mark Brandon Read, *Chopper*, Chapter 20.

information, and on this occasion the leaker was Louis Werner, a Lufthansa cargo agent who later received sixteen and a half years. The crime itself was planned at what evangelical preachers would call 'a sink of iniquity', Roberts Lounge, owned by James 'Jimmy the Gent' Burke, an Irish-American with Lucchese Family associations. It was situated near the airport and on Leffert's Boulevard, South Ozone Park, conveniently near the Van Wyck Expressway. Burke had obtained his nickname both from his suits and his habit of giving hijacked lorry drivers $50 bills to help them get home. His long-time friend, Henry Hill, who is the pivotal figure in the book and film *Wiseguys*, also feared his temper:

> If there was just the littlest amount of trouble, he'd be all over you in a second. He'd grab a guy's tie and slam his chin into the table before the guy knew he was in a war. If the guy was lucky, Jimmy would let him live . . . Jimmy had a reputation for being wild. He'd whack you. There was no question – Jimmy would plant you just as fast as shake your hand. At dinner he could be the nicest guy in the world, but then he could blow you away for dessert.[11]

His victims included his wife's former boyfriend, whose body was found in pieces in his car on the day of Burke's marriage; a young man who refused to pay his own mother the $5,000 he owed her (Burke paid the $5,000 himself in the morning and killed the man in the evening); informants and potential witnesses against him; a long-time and close friend who betrayed him over a cigarette hijack; and Billy Batts, a man who offended his friend Tommy DeSimone. The list was endless.

Born on 5 July 1931, Burke was brought up in the Manhattan Foundling Home and over the first thirteen years of his life was moved from foster-home to foster-home where he was alternately loved and abused. In 1944 his then foster-father turned to slap him while driving, crashed the car and was killed. His foster-mother blamed Burke and began to mistreat him, but the agency would not move him. He ran away and from there it was a short step into

[11] Nicholas Pileggi, *Wiseguy*, pp. 23–4.

delinquency and the fearsome Mount Loretto, a jail for young offenders on Staten Island. In September 1949 he was caught while passing cheques for Dominick Cerami, but he remained staunch. At the age of 18 he received five years and, sent to Auburn prison, found a welcome from inmates who had heard how he had protected Cerami. From then it was onwards and upwards until by the time he was 25, when he was principally dealing in smuggled cigarettes, he was regarded as a legend; a man known both for his generosity and his ability. He was considered so highly that both the Lucchese and Colombo Families brokered a deal for his services.

By 1970 Burke had moved into hijacking in a big way, operating from Roberts Lounge which then boasted a mixed clientele of thieves and cargo handlers, with undercover detectives observing the other groups. Werner, an habitué of the bar, was recruited by the standard technique of being given credit to gamble far beyond his means and then having the plug pulled on him. In Werner's case he was in debt to a bookie named Martin 'Marty' Krugman who worked out of the bar and who passed on information to Burke. The debts would be wiped out in return for information about the cargo warehouse. Shortly before the robbery Burke had been released from prison after another cargo theft, and it was he who trained the men, putting them through rehearsal after rehearsal. The raid itself took just over an hour. One potentially disastrous mistake was made by Parnell Steven 'Stacks' Edwards, whose duty it was to take the truck used in the raid to Jersey to have it compacted. Instead he left it in Canarsie about a mile and a half from the airport, where it was duly found with ski masks and seemingly foot- and fingerprints. When it came to it, however, the prints were not forensically usable.

Within a matter of weeks, however, people on and associated with the raid began to die or disappear. No great effort was made to hide the murders, and the belief was that Burke was making examples of those he feared might talk. There was also a financial reason: dead people did not require their share of the proceeds. The first to go was Stacks Edwards who was shot by Tommy DeSimone on Burke's orders. His body was found under the covers of his bed at his apartment in Ozone Park; he had been shot six times in the head and chest. The next was Marty Krugman. He had been demanding his share of the proceeds which was due to come to $500,000. The incentive to dispose of him was irresistible, and he was killed on 6 January 1979 at a bar in Rockaway Boulevard.

Tommy DeSimone was killed on 14 January, and three days later it was the turn of Richard Eaton, whose frozen and trussed body was found in a Brooklyn trailer. He had worked as a courier and front-man for Burke. Going through Eaton's pockets, the police came across Burke's name and telephone number. It was thought Eaton had been involved in laundering some of the money.

The only person about whom an effort to hide their identity was made was Theresa Ferrara, a 27-year-old Long Island beautician who had shared a house with DeSimone. She received a telephone call to meet someone in a diner and had gone after telling her niece that she had the chance to make $10,000. She disappeared on 10 February and her dismembered body, which was only identified through X-rays, was not found until 18 May when it was washed ashore near Toms River, New Jersey.

Louis Werner, now under grave suspicion for his part in the robbery, had in fact only met with one member of Burke's team, Joseph 'Joe Buddha' Manri. If Werner was to cut himself any sort of deal with the police he would have to identify Manri, who in turn would have to give up names. The problem for Burke and for Werner was solved in different ways when on 13 April Manri's body, along with that of Robert 'Frenchy' McMahon, was found in a Buick in Schenectady Avenue. Both had been executed with a single bullet in the back of the head. With no cards left to play, Werner pleaded guilty and steadfastly refused to give up any names.

In the end Burke was betrayed by his long-time friend Henry Hill, who was himself facing serious drug charges and who believed that he was the next in line to be killed. Hill, together with his family, went into the Witness Program and gave evidence for the State. Burke was convicted of the murder of Richard Eaton, whom he believed had cheated him in a cocaine deal. When questioned by Burke's lawyer, Hill said that when he had asked about Eaton, The Gent had replied, 'Don't worry about him anymore, I whacked the fucking swindler out.' On 19 February 1985 Burke was sentenced to life imprisonment. Three years earlier he had received a twelve-year sentence for his part in a scam involving point shaving by members of the Boston College basketball team. Hill had already given evidence in that case.

Burke died on 13 April 1996 at the age of 64 while serving his sentence at the Wende Correctional Facility near Buffalo, New York. He had been suffering from stomach cancer.[12] All told, some thirteen others connected in one way or another with the robbery were killed. Paul Vario, reputed to be a *capo* in the Lucchese Family, was said to have been a major beneficiary of the theft. He was never charged, but later received a six-year sentence for extortion at the airport. He died in the Federal prison in Fort Worth.

The largest British robbery, the 1983 Brinks-Mat job, has also produced its share of bodies. While so far they may not have totalled those racked up following the Lufthansa robbery, the cognoscenti believe the toll will still rise. Tony White, who was acquitted, may well have been correct if, as was suggested, he uttered the words about animals getting their hands on the gold. Life could indeed be short, brutal and nasty, and it was a particularly nasty robbery.

On 26 November at 6.40 a.m. the then biggest of the biggest of robberies took place when £26 million in gold was lifted from the Brinks-Mat warehouse on the Heathrow trading estate. Its ramifications would still be running in the twenty-first century. The guards were threatened – one with castration, others had petrol poured over them, another was coshed for not producing keys sufficiently speedily. The gang drove off with 6,400 bars of gold due to be sent to the Middle and Far East. It was clearly an inside job and it was really only a matter of days before the police latched on to Tony Black, the last guard to arrive that morning, who had missed the robbery because he was ten minutes late for work. Black confessed. His sister was living with Brian Robinson, another of the number of villains over the years pleased to be known as 'The Colonel'.[13] Black also identified two more of the team, Tony White and Michael McAvoy.

---

[12] In the film *Wiseguy*, Burke is played by Robert De Niro and Henry Hill by Joe Pesci.
[13] Robinson had been on the William & Glyn's robbery in 1978 and had benefited through the mistakes of the No. 5 Regional Crime Squad. The most famous of the Colonels was Ronnie Kray; another was the South Londoner George Copley.

In December 1984 Robinson and McAvoy received twenty-five years each and White was acquitted. Later there was said to be £50,000 on offer to free McAvoy and Robinson but, if the rumour was true, it came to nothing. Black, who gave evidence for the Crown, was handed a six-year sentence.

There was still the problem for McAvoy of how to protect his interests. A very large amount of property was missing, and in the way of things this could attract a great number of high-quality predators even if they were not as ruthless as the Toecutters. It was essential that he have people whom he could trust to help him on the outside. Two such people were Brian Perry, who ran a minicab agency, and John Lloyd who now lived with Jeannie Savage, the former wife of the celebrated London villain Mickey Ishmael. In turn they recruited Kenneth Noye, who soon came under police surveillance. An officer John Fordham, dressed in a balaclava helmet and combat fatigues, was placed on observation in the grounds of Noye's house. It all went sadly wrong. The officer was stabbed to death and Noye was acquitted when he told the court he had been in fear of this masked man in his grounds. However, he received the maximum of fourteen years after being convicted of handling some of the bullion.

Then, on 19 May 1996, Noye was alleged to have been involved in a road-rage killing. At around 1.15 p.m. Stephen Cameron was stabbed to death in an incident at the Swanley interchange on the M25 while his fiancée watched helplessly. Noye promptly disappeared. Later it was suggested in the underworld that, while the meeting itself may have been accidental, Cameron did in fact know Noye. The L-registration Land Rover Discovery involved in the incident was registered to an Anthony Francis of Bexley, South London, and Anthony Francis was a name Noye had been known to use. Immediately an 'all persons' bulletin went out on him and, like Lord Lucan, he was spotted across the continent, Portugal, the Canaries, Spain of course, Moscow and by the end of the year he was reported to be safe from extradition in Northern Cyprus. This was probably just as well for him because his name cropped up at the Southwark Crown Court where it was alleged he was a principal in a scheme, along with his old friend John 'Little Legs' Lloyd, to break the bank card system in Great Britain. Lloyd received five years after pleading guilty.

Meanwhile, Noye's name was being linked to a number of other deaths over the years. It was not suggested that he had either killed them or instigated their deaths, rather that they had crossed his path. The first was Barbara Harold, who received fatal injuries in a parcel-bomb attack. Keith Cottingham, a friend of Noye, had quarrelled with her and her husband over a tax bill after he had bought their Spanish villa. He believed that he had been cheated and wrote a letter saying that the feud must end with either a peaceful agreement or 'total war'. On 21 May 1984 a parcel bomb was sent to her at her home in Ightham, Kent. Her left hand and a finger from her right were blown off and she received severe stomach wounds; she died in hospital six days later. It was alleged that Cottingham had posted the bomb three days earlier in nearby Bearsted and that evening had caught a ferry on his way back home to Spain. In October 2002 an extradition order was made and he was lodged in Belmarsh prison. Cottingham, who suffered from diabetes, was too ill to stand trial in July 2004 and the case was re-fixed for January 2005. He was found dead in his cell on 29 October. He had always denied sending the bomb, saying, 'I just happened to be in the wrong place at the right time. I never knew her; I never met her, I never wrote to her and I certainly never sent her the bomb.'[14]

The second victim was Alan 'Taffy' Holmes, a thoroughly corrupt former member of the Serious Crime Squad who had worked on Noye's case in the aftermath of Brinks-Mat. On 28 July 1987 Holmes shot himself in the garden of his Croydon home, apparently after being questioned by the Scotland Yard Complaints Division over his relationship with a police officer for whom Noye was alleged to have been an informant. Prior to his death he had gone, gun in hand, looking for the officer whom he believed had betrayed him. It came to nothing; the man, who had received a number of threats, had moved house.[15]

Daniel Morgan cannot really be connected to Noye but he certainly was connected to Holmes. Six months before Holmes'

[14] *The Times*, 1 November 2004.
[15] For a full account of the dealings of Holmes and his associates see Michael Gillard and Laurie Flynn, *Untouchables*, Chapter 7.

death the private detective was killed in the car park of the Golden Lion public house in Sydenham on 10 March 1987. He had been axed to death. It was certainly not a case of robbery because although his Rolex was missing, the £1,000 cash he had on him was not. At the inquest, in the witness box his brother Alistair Morgan named a man he believed was a party to the murder. Detective Superintendent Douglas Campbell said that the day before his death Morgan claimed to have uncovered a story of police corruption and had tried to sell it for £250,000 to a national newspaper. According to a South London officer, Morgan and Holmes were getting ready to blow the whistle before the investigator was killed.[16]

The next was garage owner Nick Whiting, who was kidnapped and then killed in Essex. On 8 June 1990 millionaire Whiting, former British saloon car champion driver, disappeared after a raid on his showroom All Car Equipe in Wrotham, Kent. Along with him went five cars – including a Ford Escort Turbo and an Audi Quattro – worth over £100,000. The cars were all recovered within a matter of days, but of Whiting there was no sign. He had been a long-standing friend of Kenneth Noye.

Two weeks later it was suggested that Whiting had gone on the run with John 'Little Legs' Lloyd, then also wanted in connection with the Brinks-Mat gold robbery and one of those later sued in the civil courts. As an alternative, it was mooted that Whiting had staged his own kidnap. This unkind suggestion was proved totally wrong when, following a tip-off, nearly a month later on 2 July the police dug his body out of a shallow grave on Rainham Marshes in Essex. They believed he had been beaten, bound and gagged, placed in the boot of a car and later frog-marched for some two miles before being shot in the head.

One suggestion was that his killing had been ordered by a major criminal then serving time on the Isle of Wight. It seems to have been a matter of maladministration of funds. The belief was that Whiting had borrowed Brinks-Mat money from the man in order to build houses on a plot of land he had bought, and that somehow the funds had disappeared.

---

[16] *Ibid*, Chapter 6. Evidence given 15 April 1988.

The fourth man to die was another former Scotland Yard officer, Sydney Wink, who had renumbered guns used in Brinks-Mat. In August 1994 he too committed suicide after a visit by police officers. He was also suspected of having the gun used in the shooting of a police officer. The fifth was builder Keith Hedley who was suspected of, but never charged with, laundering Brinks money. He was shot dead on his yacht in Corfu harbour on 26 September 1996 as he chased away gunmen.

All sorts of suggestions were made as to where Noye might be, and indeed in early 1997 it was suggested that the underworld had considered him far too dangerous to be allowed to survive and so, like many of his predecessors, he had been taken out in a damage-limitation exercise.[17] Noye's arrest in Cadiz in September 1988 showed that this was far from the case. He was duly retrieved from Spain and appeared at the Old Bailey where it was suggested he would not get a fair trial because of the notoriety he had acquired both through the Fordham case and after his disappearance. That argument was quickly rejected and much of the evidence against him for killing Stephen Cameron came from a seemingly independent eyewitness, Alan Decabral, who at the time was driving his Rolls-Royce near Swanley. He told the jury that he saw a look on Noye's face after the stabbing which seemed to him as though Noye was saying, 'That sorted him out. You have got yours, mate.' All very compelling stuff. Noye was duly convicted and received life imprisonment.

Alan Decabral turned out to be another who died after crossing Noye's path. He did not long survive the trial and, very quickly, it became clear that he was by no means all he had seemed to be. On 6 October 2000 he was shot twice in the back of the head as he sat in his black Peugeot 205 at lunchtime outside a Halford's store at the Warre Retail Park, Ashford, Kent. He had been waiting for his son, who found him slumped in the front passenger seat. A witness said that Decabral had been calling out, 'Please don't shoot me.' It was reported that he had been receiving death threats.

Now it emerged that Decabral was not just a businessman who traded in vintage cars and motorbikes; he also traded in drugs and

---

[17] *Evening Standard*, 9 January 1997.

was a long-standing associate of the Hells Angels. Drugs and up to sixty guns had been found by police in three separate raids on his home in the previous eighteen months, and he had also been involved in smuggling drink and tobacco. His £350,000 house was unmortgaged and, when he was raided in the months before his death, he was found to have £100,000 in cash in the house. At the time of his death he was banned from one of his local pubs.

It might have been thought that the discrediting, albeit post-humously, of Decabral, the only witness who had suggested vengeance by Noye, would have helped in the appeal. Now Anne Marie Decabral came to say that her former husband was not only a drug dealer but also a consummate liar. The Court of Appeal would have nothing of it. Decabral was only a piece in the jigsaw; there were seventeen other witnesses. Even if his evidence was disregarded, 'the only proper conclusion one can come to is that the jury would come to exactly the same verdict', said the Lord Chief Justice.

As for the Brinks-Mat gold, a great portion of which was still missing, in February 2001 the police started a search of a timber merchant's premises in Hastings. Nothing connected to the robbery was found. So far only some eleven of the gold bars have been re-covered. Later that year Brian Perry, the man entrusted with placing McAvoy's money and for his pains sentenced to nine years for dis-honestly handling part of the proceeds, was shot and killed in Bermondsey on 16 November. Perry, then 63 years old, was running the Blue Car minicab firm in Creedon House. Over the years he had been suspected of not accounting for money deposited with him for safe keeping, and he had declined to help when there was a possi-bility that if some of the missing money was returned there would be a reduction in McAvoy's sentence. Perry also compounded his bad behaviour by appearing on television to comment about McAvoy: 'Once the cell door is closed what's he got to trade?'[18]

At his 1992 trial, when Perry had the ageing but still formidable 'Mad' Frankie Fraser minding him, he received a letter saying that if he believed he was safe because of the long sentences handed out he was signing his own death warrant. While in prison he is thought

---

[18] 'Brinks-Mat "The Greatest Heist"' in *Sunday Mirror*, 23 November 2003.

to have convinced people that he had not misappropriated the money entrusted to him. On his release he built up his cab firm and made a series of intelligent property investments. But, as was said in the killing of another man not connected with the Brinks-Mat case, 'Everyone in the manor knew it was on top except him.'

Perry was killed by a masked gunman as he stepped from his car, the keys still in his hand. 'He had really upset some serious people,' says one London face. One suggestion as to the identity of the killer was that he was the nephew of a member of a well-known and much feared team of London hitmen from the 1960s.

Indeed there were persistent rumours in the underworld that Perry would not be the only victim of the fallout, and it was thought that a number of other people might well be concerned about surviving long enough to collect their pensions. The rumours proved to be true when another well-known and long-standing London face fell two years short of retirement age. George Francis, then 63, was also thought to have looked after some of the money, and accurate book-keeping had not been his long suit either. Francis had led a long and, on the whole, successful criminal career. Over the years he was questioned about a score of murders, robberies, thefts and drug deals, but charges were rare and convictions more so. In 1969 he was believed to have sheltered George Sewell after he had killed the Blackpool police officer Superintendent Gerald Richardson during a jewel theft. In 1980 he was part of a drug-smuggling team whose activities culminated in the murder of Customs officer Peter Bennett, shot in the stomach by 'Silly' Lennie Watkins at the end of a long observation by Customs officers.[19] After a retrial Francis was acquitted at the Old Bailey, but there were stories that witnesses had been bribed. His reputation in the gangland hierarchy was not secure and there were continuing rumours that he was a police informer. Indeed he was generally regarded as unreliable. On one occasion Francis sold a Rolls-Royce to a leading London robber who later discovered that it was only on a lease. On that occasion no action was taken because of Francis's rock-solid South London connections. Not everyone felt that way,

[19] For an account of the investigation see James Morton, *Gangland*.

however, and when in 1985 Francis could be found owning a public house at Hever Castle in Kent a hitman failed in a contract killing. Francis turned at the crucial moment and the bullet struck his shoulder.

Three weeks before his murder Francis told *Mirror* reporter Jeff Edwards:

> I expect to die with my boots on. My old man was a villain and I hope my kids grow up to be villains. I have lived by violence, close to violence all my life and in the end I will die by it. I would rather die quickly by the bullet than slowly in some old people's home that stinks of cabbage water.[20]

He was granted his wish when on 14 May 2003 he was found dead at the steering wheel of his new Rover 75 in Lynton Road, Bermondsey. He had been shot four times in the head as he returned from a late-night drinking session. It was said that four men were seen to leave the scene, driving away in a dark saloon. No charges have yet been brought.

McAvoy has been living a quiet life since his release, and there is no suggestion of his involvement in the deaths of Perry or Francis. However, there are still some more individuals who are looking over their shoulders.

An earlier killing, but one not recognised at the time as having Brinks-Mat links, was that on the evening of 1 March 1994 of Colin Hickman, a 55-year-old solicitor who specialised in civil litigation in Coventry. Hickman was stabbed more than ten times in the head and chest after he opened the front door of his home. The bell had been rung persistently until he answered it. His partner Vera Phillips-Griffiths, a chemistry teacher in Leamington Spa who was speaking on the telephone, ran downstairs as the attacker was raining blows with a stiletto-type knife. The man, heavily bloodstained, ran off into the night.

On 12 March 1995, a 33-year-old business associate Timothy Carlton Caines of Moseley, Birmingham, was charged with Hickman's

---

[20] *Daily Mirror*, 15 May 2003.

murder. The prosecution alleged that the motive had been to prevent the solicitor from blowing the whistle on a series of fraudulent deals. Caines accepted that he had gone to see Hickman, but said their meeting had been interrupted by an intruder. He (Caines) had fled, and his watch and a cap were found nearby. Curiously Ms Phillips-Griffiths said the attacker was white, and Mr Caines was black. He was later jailed for life. Since then he has launched a series of so far unsuccessful appeals and a campaign has been started on his behalf. Then in the summer of 2003 it emerged that Hickman was laundering substantial sums, moving yen and dollars, and that the money had been part of the Brinks-Mat proceeds.[21]

---

[21] *Sunday Mercury* (Birmingham), 27 July 2003.

10

Four Massacres and Several Funerals

The most celebrated of gangland rub-outs – immortalised in so many films, not least of all *Some Like it Hot* – was the St Valentine's Day Massacre of 1929. Seven men from Bugsy Moran's gang, which had been causing Al Capone trouble in Chicago, were slaughtered. It was known that Capone was behind it, but the problem was identifying the actual shooters and proving it. When it came to it no one was ever charged.

As Prohibition ran towards its tenth year, there were many factions in Chicago who formed and re-formed alliances and the main opposition to Capone was then Bugsy Moran. After the death of Vincent Drucci, Moran, the last surviving leader of the Dion O'Banion gang, had formed an alliance with Joey Aiello and now was harrying Capone's lorries. Significantly on 1 July 1928 Frankie Yale, Capone's mentor in New York, was shot to death in that city as he tried out his new automobile; the first man there to die from machine-gun wounds.

On 7 September that year Moran and Aiello shot Capone supporter Tony Lombardo, the president of the Unione Siciliano in Chicago, as he walked with his bodyguards along Dearborn and Madison. On 2 January Aiello killed another Capone supporter, Pasquale Lolordo, who had taken over the lethal position of president of the Unione.

It was this killing, for which again no one was ever charged, which prompted the St Valentine's Day Massacre. It was planned by Capone, who called on the services of 'Machine Gun' Jack McGurn and Frank Nitti while he was well away from the scene in Florida. In turn they hired members of Detroit's notorious Purple Gang, Fred 'Killer' Burke and Fred Goetz. The gunmen were, in all probability, McGurn, Burke, Goetz and Capone's ubiquitous henchmen, John Scalise and Albert Anselmi. The aim was to trap Moran and the remaining members of his entourage.

At about 10.30 a.m. on 14 February 1929 a fake Chicago Police Department car drew up outside Moran's headquarters at the S-M-C Cartage Company, 2122 North Clark Street. Burke and Goetz, dressed as police officers, walked inside and lined up the Gusenberg brothers, John Snyder, James Clark, John May, Albert Weinshank and Dr Rheinhardt H. Schwimmer – who was not a member of the ensemble but who had dropped by for a game of cards – against a wall. The gunmen opened fire, killing all but Frank Gusenberg instantly. Moran survived because he had been late arriving at the office that day; he had seen the police car, and had stopped off at a café until it was over. The look-outs, mistaking Weinshank for Moran, had signalled that he was inside the building. Moran then had himself driven to the haven of a hospital where he remained under guard, blaming Capone for the outrage.[1]

There were no fewer than seventy sub-machine gun cartridges on the floor of the garage. Although Burke, Goetz and McGurn had been seen in the area, there was no other evidence against them nor could any help be expected from the Chicago police who, because of the uniforms, were themselves under suspicion over the murder. The coroner, Dr Herman Bundesen, called a Grand Jury and those citizens decided they needed the help of Calvin Goddard, the new star of American forensic science.

From this would come his dream, the establishment of a national laboratory for scientific criminology. Goddard was given the shells and bullets and he gave his opinion that the killings had been done

---

[1] For a full account of the events leading up to the massacre, see Laurence Bergreen, *Capone*; James Morton, *Gangland International*.

with two .45 calibre Thompson sub-machine guns. One of them had a magazine which held twenty bullets per loading, and the other had a much greater capacity of fifty bullets. He examined all the tommy guns from the Chicago Police Department and then fired the weapons into a waste bin filled with cotton wadding. With the help of the comparison microscope, he was now able to determine that the marks on the bullets from the Police Department did not match those left at the scene of the massacre.

In fact, as is often the case, luck played a considerable part. Today any criminal who is less than a thirty-second cousin to a fool will dispose of weapons used in case they are found and so can be matched. In 1929 there was no need at all for criminals to think, if think they could or did, that ballistics was a sufficiently exact science to link bullets with guns. Indeed, all the previous evidence was that it was not. There was therefore no reason not to use and re-use a perfectly good machine gun until it fell apart in your hands. After all, they were moderately expensive to acquire.

On 15 December 1929 Patrolman Charles Skelly, in the small town of St Joseph, Michigan, was called to an altercation following a minor traffic accident. Fred Burke was refusing to give a farmer $5 for damage he had caused to a bumper. When the officer asked his name, Burke shot him and fled the scene. On 26 May 1930 he was arrested at his father-in-law's farm in Milan, Missouri, where an arsenal of weapons, including two Thompson guns, was found. At first he gave a false name and it is interesting that the *New York Times* reported, long after the system had been discredited and fingerprinting was the norm, 'After Bertillon experts had confronted him with records he admitted his name.'[2]

These guns were now sent to Goddard who again fired test bullets into containers of cotton. He was now convinced that they were the guns used in the St Valentine's Day Massacre, and that one of them had been used in the New York killing of Frankie Yale. This same gun was also matched to the killing of Frank Marlow in Queens Borough, New York, in the summer of 1929.

[2] *New York Times*, 27 March 1931. Before fingerprinting became accepted in the first decade of the twentieth century, Alphonse Bertillon's method of measurements of criminals' ears, noses etc. was the way identification had been made.

Burke escaped the electric chair. Wanted in both Illinois and Michigan, he was sent to the latter where Circuit Judge Charles E. White generously held that he had been intoxicated at the time he shot Skelly and therefore had not been able to premeditate the act which would have turned it into a capital offence. He was sentenced to life imprisonment with hard labour on 27 April 1931 and survived a little under a decade, dying of a heart attack in the State prison in Marquette on 10 July 1940. The leader of the massacre, Jack McGurn, was shot on 15 February 1936 while bowling in Kafora's Bowling and Billiards Parlor at 805 Milwaukee Avenue, Chicago. A comic Valentine card was left by his body.

Detroit's Purple Gang staged two massacres of their own bracketing the St Valentine's Day affair. The first, in 1927, was when local gamblers hired them for the disposal of members of the re-formed Egan's Rats who were muscling in on local interests. There had been a number of kidnappings including that in March 1926 of Meyer 'Fish' Bloomfield, a croupier at the Grand River Athletic Club owned by Charles T. 'Doc' Brady. Clearly the Purples were involved, but on which side is more obscure. There is no doubt, however, that in March the next year Eddie Fletcher and Abe Axler rented a suite at 106 East Alexandrine Avenue and invited Frank Wright[3], Reuben Cohen and Joseph Bloom for what were said to be peace negotiations. They were found machine-gunned to death just outside the doors of the apartment. Fred 'Killer' Burke, then a defecting Rat, was arrested along with Axler and Fletcher. No charges were ever brought.

The second of their massacres, for which they are better remembered, was the Collingwood Massacre which took place on 16 September 1931.[4] The three men who died, Herman 'Hymie' Paul, Joseph 'Nigger Joe' Lebovitz and Joseph 'Izzy' Sutker, were all originally out of Chicago and all members of the Little Jewish Navy, one-time allies and then later rivals of the Purple Gang, who believed

---

[3] Wright was said to have killed Johnny Reid, a friend of Abe Bernstein, on 27 December 1926. He was wanted for a $100,000 diamond robbery in Chicago in May 1926, and it was thought he had been involved in the killing of Adolph E. Fisher, a diamond merchant. He was a known close associate of Eugene 'Red' McLaughlin, murdered in June 1930.
[4] In 1995 there was considerable hostility amongst the Jewish community to an exhibition at Belle Isle's Dossin Great Lakes Museum in Detroit which featured the Purple Gang and their activities, including the Collingwood Massacre.

they were hijacking shipments of alcohol destined for the Windy City.

A local bookmaker, Solomon 'Sollie' Levine, had been invited by Ray Bernstein to take the Jewish Navy members to Apartment 21, 1740 Collingwood Avenue in an apparent effort to sort out the dispute. The Navy had clearly not learned from the prior experience of the dead Rats. Once the men were in the apartment Bernstein said he was going out to see his bookmaker; in reality it was to start the getaway car and give the signal for the killings. The sailors were shot to pieces by Irving Milberg, Harry Keywell (then aged only 18) and Harry Fleischer. Numbers on the guns had already been filed off, and to eradicate fingerprints they dropped their weapons in a pail of green paint left in the kitchen. They took Levine with them as Bernstein drove away almost knocking down a young boy. In a matter of minutes they had made two serious errors. The boy gave evidence against them and, worse, they released Levine after a couple of hours so he was arrested within minutes and became a believable principal prosecution witness. Keywell and Bernstein were arrested on 15 September and Milberg was caught four days later. Of Fleischer there was no sign.

On 17 November 1931 they were found guilty and sentenced to life imprisonment. Judge Donald Van Zile had this to say: 'The crime which you have committed was one of the most sensational that has been committed in Detroit for many years. It was, as has been said, a massacre.'

The newspaper reporters were there to watch them go to prison together. Van Zile had been prepared to send Keywell to a less severe prison than the others, but he opted not to be separated. They duly recorded that the men played pinochle, munched corned-beef sandwiches, and that Bernstein had given the man who brought them a $5 tip. They were also able to record the following tough-guy conversation:

Keywell: I suppose it will be tough at first.
Bernstein: Yeh. Like everything else you have to get settled and organised. It will be new and strange at first, but we'll get organised. We always did.

Keywell: Sure, we will.

Fleischer was later charged but not convicted. By now Levine had disappeared, some said to France with his passage paid by the police.

Not that the Chicago massacre has been the only St Valentine's Day killing in gangland history. One of the benefits of undertaking a criminal enterprise on a particular date, be it a religious festival, that of a parliamentary election or simply a well-known day, is that it is easier to arrange an alibi. The question is always asked by police and prosecutor alike, 'Why do you remember that particular Tuesday above all others?' The answer is, 'Because it was St Valentine's Day.'

In the 1960s and 1970s working alongside, but certainly not in partnership with, the Italians in Montreal was one of the great gangs of brothers, the Dubois. Indeed the Quebec Commission which investigated crime in the city was not entirely sure which was the more powerful. If anything, the brothers with the 'widely dreaded cruelty of their hirelings' were perhaps the more to be feared.

In 1967 the family consisted of Raymond (45), Jean-Guy (43), Normand (41), Claude (39), René (38), Roland (36), Jean-Paul (33) and twins Maurice and Adrien (30). Only Raymond had any claim to being employed – since 1962 he had at least been on the payroll of Entreprises Renald Ltee which controlled supplies to taverns and bars. Meanwhile Claude and Adrien ran independent gangs of several dozen members.

The brothers were brought up in the working-class district of Saint-Henri in south-west Montreal which, at the time, was thought of as almost a village. From the 1950s they worked their way up through burglary, extortion and armed robbery until by the middle 1970s they were active in the importation and distribution of drugs, protection and loan-sharking. One of their earliest exploits had been the victimisation of a Greek restaurateur who, after he refused to pay protection, had a cross carved on his body.

The high watermark in the fortunes of the brothers was 1974 when they won a savage 'war of the West End' defeating the Pierre McSween gang. McSween had been a 'spotter' for the Dubois brothers, pointing out suitable targets for them, but had defected and set up his own enterprise. In the war, which left the Dubois in total control of south-west Montreal, the McSweens were literally almost wiped out.

McSween was not exactly saintlike. Apart from being a former Dubois man until the early 1970s, he had served a sentence for theft of electronic equipment and had escaped with the help of Jean-Guy Dubois. As payment he was expected to take part in a burglary at the Boucherville golf course, but attempts had failed and after his arrest he rather blamed Jean-Guy. While McSween was away his family had been active. His brother Jacques had become involved in a splendid scam involving a sweep on the time when the Montreal Canadians scored their last goal in hockey games. Tickets were sold in book form to waiters at $5.50, and in turn they were sold on at 50c a ticket. The best thing about the lottery, he testified, was that his brother had an arrangement so that the time of the goal could be altered by the official timekeeper. The draw brought in between $15,000 and $18,000 a week.

The real quarrel started when Réal Lepine, a friend of the McSweens, was killed in a bar on Notre Dame Street West because he had refused to deal in drugs sold by Adrien. The killers were a former boxer, Gerald Ratte, who died of a drug overdose within three weeks, and a Dubois strong-arm man, Roger Fontaine.[5]

Then in their own version of a St Valentine's Eve massacre on 13 February 1975, four men were killed and several wounded when three Dubois hitmen opened fire in a McSween watering hole, the dimly lit disco of the South Shore Lapinière Hotel. They timed their attack to coincide with the shooting of blanks by a country and western act.

This brought the total of killings in Montreal in the first six weeks of the year to a staggering fifty-one. It included locking thirteen people in a room of the Gargantua Bar-Saloon on Beaubien East and then setting fire to the building.[6]

[5] Evidence given by McSween to the Quebec Police Commission Inquiry on 4 August 1974.
[6] *Montreal Gazette*, 14,15,16 February 1975.

PART THREE:
INNOCENT AND OTHER
BYSTANDERS

11

Innocent and Other Bystanders

The definition of an innocent bystander may not be quite as clear-cut as at first it seems. Take Mafia girlfriends and wives for a start. Are they truly innocent if they are reaping the benefits of a life of crime? Certainly it is not safe to be one in Naples where there has been a vicious war running throughout 2004 between various Camorra clans. Gelsomina Verde, an attractive 21-year-old, had the misfortune to have an affair with a gangster who had absented himself from the playing field. She was kidnapped as she walked along a road at the edge of the territory of the di Lauro clan currently engaged in the internecine war over the city's drug trade. Tortured in an attempt to discover his whereabouts, she was then shot in the neck and her body put in a car which was set on fire.[1]

In the 1920s visitors to certain bars and cabarets in the Belleville and Pigalle districts of Paris went there knowing they were going to be robbed. It was something to tell their friends on their return. If you are drinking in a known villains' pub, are you not putting yourself at risk for the undoubted *frisson*? Should you move on? 'When Chopper Read was first out and about in Melbourne after his long sentence he

---

[1] *The Independent*, 8 December 2004.

started drinking in the pub where I drink. We were all looking over our shoulders in case there was a drive-by. We still went on drinking there but we were pleased when he stopped,' a librarian told me.[2]

Janet, sometimes Janice, Drake was a particularly unfortunate Mafia girlfriend. The former Miss New Jersey of 1954, who also once shared the Most Beautiful Legs in America title, had the misfortune to be at a dinner with Antonio Carfano, also known as 'Little Augie' Pisano. One version of the events leading to her death is that in the late 1950s Carfano, a one-time gunman for Frankie Yale and Capone before becoming a top lieutenant for Frank Costello, became involved in his boss's war with the malevolent Vito Genovese. When an assassination attempt on Costello failed he tried to rally other Mafia leaders against Genovese. Only the now Miami-based Carfano responded and, for his pains, Genovese ordered his death. On 25 September 1959 Carfano and Miss Drake were at Marino's, a restaurant on Lexington Avenue near the Copacabana nightclub, when, apparently quite by chance, they met Tony Bender who invited them to dine with him. During the meal Carfano took a call from Costello telling him that two other guests, Al Segal and Vincent Mauro, were going to kill him. Saying he had been called away on urgent business and taking Miss Drake with him, he fled. It did neither of them any good. They were found shot dead in his car parked outside 24–50 Ninety-fourth Street, Jackson Heights near La Guardia airport, an hour later. He had a bullet in the neck and another in the temple; she was shot in the neck. It was thought that the killers were hiding in the back of the car and had forced Carfano to drive to a secluded spot. The relationship between Miss Drake and Carfano was never fully explained. The wife of the comedian Alan Drake whose career Carfano furthered, she called the gangster Uncle Gus or Uncle Augie and, charitably, some thought she may have only been what is known as arm-candy.

However, there are other accounts of events which put her in a slightly less favourable light. Carfano was due to give evidence before a Senate Committee over his involvement with the Yonkers' harness racetrack, and the killing may have been over that. The newspapers reported that he and Miss Drake had left the dinner,

[2] Conversation with the author, November 2004.

not in any hurry but to go and watch the Friday-night boxing on television. The killers may not have been Segal and Mauro; two gunmen from Texas, Nick Cassio and Johnny Luke, were seen in town on that Friday. Miss Drake may not have been such an innocent bystander either. Earlier she had been questioned over the death of Anastasia and, perhaps more significantly, in February 1952 over that of Nat Nelson, a playboy from the Garment District who was shot in the mouth and stomach at his apartment at 360 W 55th. The night before he was killed he had been squiring her around the Village nightspots. It may have been the case that she was working with a New York policeman and his team of burglars identifying likely targets. No one was charged with Nelson's killing.[3]

One girl who was definitely not arm-candy and whom the rulers of the underworld ensured was not an innocent bystander was Virginia Hill, renowned for her beauty, personality and ability to administer oral sex, not necessarily in that order. The underworld took pains to ensure she was nowhere near her apartment in Beverly Hills when her lover Bugsy Siegel was shot.

Born in Lipscomb, Alabama, she had been a prostitute at the 1933 World Fair in Chicago before being taken up by Joseph Epstein, who worked for Jake Guzik. Hill was clearly one of the great femmes fatales of her time and Epstein is quoted as saying, 'Once that girl is under your skin, it's like a cancer. It's incurable.' She had then been passed, like the boots in *All Quiet on the Western Front*, from mobster to mobster – Frank Costello, Al Capone's cousins the Fischettis, Frank Nitti, Tony Accardo and latterly Joe Adonis. Siegel called the Flamingo Hotel he was building in Las Vegas after her nickname. She was a bag-lady for the Mob and she took up private work for Siegel, squirrelling funds marked for the hotel to Swiss bank accounts. By the time the year ended the building costs had, one way or another, reached $6 million.

Siegel was now in serious difficulties with the Mob. Accardo, the Fischettis and Murray Humphreys were not pleased, and it required the skill of his old-time friend Meyer Lansky to win him a temporary reprieve when the matter of his death was discussed at a

---

[3] *New York Times*, 10, 17 February 1952, 26, 27, 28, 29, 30 September 1959. Both J. Robert Nash, *World Encyclopedia of Crime* and Carl Sifakis, *The Mafia File* tend to support the Genovese version of events.

conference in Havana at New Year 1946. Any hope of a reprieve ended when, in March 1947, on his opening night, the house suffered a disastrous run of luck. Punters seemingly had only to lay down their chips for them to win.

On the evening of 20 June 1947 he was shot dead as he sat on the sofa at Virginia Hill's home at 810 North Linden Drive, Beverly Hills. She was conveniently away in Europe. Versions of the reason for her absence vary. The more romantic one is that she knew of the contract on him, warned him to leave and when he did not do so fled herself, but she may have been sent on a Mob mission to get her out of the way. Siegel had been out to dinner with a small-time mobster Allen Smiley, Virginia's brother Chick, and another girl. He and Smiley went back to Hill's home. At 10.15 p.m. Siegel was hit with six shots fired through the window, the first of which blew his eye fifteen feet away onto the tile floor. Allen Smiley was unhurt.

Virginia Hill did not attend Siegel's funeral, nor did the Hollywood stars he had cultivated. She remained in Paris supported, it is said, by Joe Epstein. In March 1966 she died of an overdose of pills. She had lain down in the snow near Salzburg. Apparently she had tried to commit suicide on six previous occasions. Some accounts have it that she refunded the stolen money.

Shirley 'Mickey' Finn could never be termed a totally innocent bystander. The very fashionable if by then rather matronly Perth madam, in full evening dress and wearing some $2,000 of jewellery, was found slumped over the wheel of her Dodge Phoenix Sedan – which bore a sticker 'Mafia Staff Car' – near the Royal Perth Golf Club in the early hours of 23 June 1975. She had been shot in the head. There can be no question of robbery. Her jewellery was untouched, as was a diamond she wore – like the pianist Jelly Roll Morton – in her front tooth. She began her career as a sideshow body painter in country fairgrounds before working her way to the top of her profession. Towards the end of her life she had been hosting parties for visiting luminaries such as Elton John. Again there have been a variety of suggestions for her death. At the time there was feuding amongst brothel owners in Perth, and they were also coming under pressure from East Coast mobsters who were seeking to expand. A city of over 800,000 inhabitants was then thought to be large enough to draw professional criminals and Perth was fitting the bill. Perhaps most likely is that some of her girls were relaying pillow talk with the political clients and this was leading to standover and black-mail. Given the diverse reasons offered for her death, it is not surprising that her murderer was never found.[4]

When hitmen get things wrong the results are often fatal. A victim by mistake was the blonde Jane Thurgood-Dove, a Niddrie (Melbourne) housewife chased and shot in front of her children at her home on 6 November 1997, by the very overweight Rebels biker Steven John Moody. In fact the hit was taken out on another blonde woman in the same street, and Moody mistook his target. This second woman was the wife of a man who had been instrumental in sending a former solicitor to prison. On the solicitor's release, the family had tightened security around their home. The children were stopped from playing in the street and the husband always backed the car into the drive; if a strange car was seen, a signal was given and the family locked themselves indoors. In June 2003 the Victoria government offered an unprecedented $1 million reward over the Dove killing. In many ways it was too late. The pot-bellied killer Steven Moody, later identified by a witness, had died of a drug over-dose combined with health problems in September 2001 and the provider of the getaway car, Jamie Reynolds, died in a boating accident in April 2004.[5] This still, of course, left the contractor.

Another earlier mistake happened when a *mafiya* sister-in-law was in the wrong place at the wrong time. On 30 April 1994 Karen Reed was shot dead on the doorstep of her home at 31 Willow Walk on the Barnsbury Farm Estate in Woking, Surrey. It is thought that, in a revenge killing, Mrs Reed was shot by mistake for her sister Alison Ponting, a BBC World Service producer.

The shooting related back to two more contract killings in London in February 1993 when Ruslan Outsiev, the self-styled 'Prime Minister' of Chechnya, and his brother Nazerbeck were shot and killed in their flat at Bickenhall Mansions, Marylebone.[6] Gagic Ter-Ogannisyan and another Armenian, Mkritch Martirossian, were charged.

---

[4] *The West Australian*, 24, 25 June 1975.
[5] *The Age* (Melbourne), 27 July 2004.
[6] See Stephen Handelman, *Comrade Criminal*, p. 259.

The 'Prime Minister' may not have been quite that but he certainly had some political credentials. Ostensibly he was in London to organise the printing of stamps and currency, and was also in the market for missiles – two thousand Stingers. However, Outsiev had not been neglecting his social life during his time in London, spending money like water – £2,000 restaurant bills, £100 tips for waiters and with a string of prostitutes visiting his flat. He was also thought to have become involved in a scam involving raw materials, designed to skim some German businessmen.

It was probably at the beginning of his stay that Ruslan Outsiev hired Gagic as interpreter and high-class gofer. Gagic had been a successful wheeler-dealer in art in the former Soviet Union, where he married Alison Ponting in 1986 in Armenia. They had met two years before when she was reading Russian at Manchester University. In England, still wheeling and dealing if perhaps a little less success-fully, he was a swimming attendant at baths in Wandsworth. Now he negotiated the purchase of the £750,000 Marylebone flat.

Gagic certainly knew of the attempts to buy the Stingers and he reported the negotiations to Martirossian and Ashot Sarkissian. Martirossian had at one time dealt in art with Gagic and was a member of the Armenian KGB; Sarkissian was his superior. Alison Ponting helped Martirossian to obtain a visa to Britain and he stayed at their flat in Chiswick. She also provided him with a reference when he wished to rent a house in Harrow.

Why were Outsiev and his brother killed? Theories vary, ranging from punishment for wasting Chechnyan funds to a throwback to the art business, but the most likely is that Outsiev was invited by the Armenian KGB to desist in his negotiations for the missiles but declined. Initially a hitman from Los Angeles was recruited to deal with the free-spending and thoroughly out-of-hand Outsiev but, rather prosaically, he could not obtain a visa. So on 26 February, with Nazerbeck Outsiev in hospital for a minor operation on his sinuses, Gagic took his brother's German translator on a shopping trip while Outsiev was shot in the head at his flat. Naturally, if unfortunately, the bed on which he was shot was heavily soiled and a new one was ordered along with a fridge-freezer. Into it went Ruslan's body. When deliverymen arrived with the bed they were paid £450 to deliver the fridge-freezer, back in its packing, to the house in Harrow. On the way the carton broke open and a bad smell leaked out. Two days later the men reported the incident to the police. Ruslan's body was in the garage.

Observation was kept on the mansion flat and Gagic and Martirossian were arrested when they arrived with bin-liners, an electric saw and towels. Inside the flat was the body of Nazerbeck Outsiev.

Martirossian, who claimed that in Armenia he had been framed for a murder he had not committed, told the police, 'The murders were planned by the KGB. I had no choice but to obey the KGB. They would have harmed my family.' When Martirossian was searched on his arrest he was found to have snake venom hidden in a bandage. He was to use this if he was caught; he did not. Instead, after a visit by his superior Sarkissian to Belmarsh prison where he was on remand, he hanged himself with a sheet tied to the window of his cell. Meanwhile Alison Ponting was sent snake venom in a jewellery box from Selfridges, addressed to her by an Armenian in Los Angeles. It was intercepted by Customs officers and was said to have contained enough to poison at least 100 people. Gagic Ter-Ogannisyan was sentenced to life imprisonment for murder in October 1993. Soon afterwards Sarkissian was killed in Moscow.

On 15 April 1994 in a routine police check near Woking, the driver of a red Vauxhall Cavalier accelerated away, stopped the car and ran towards Woking Football Club. Inside the car was an SAS-type knife and a Hungarian PA-63 gun together with a silencer. The police provided all the occupants of the estate on which Alison Ponting lived with alarms, and warned them not to open their doors to unexpected callers. However, on 30 April her sister heard a knock on the door, and a voice asked if she had ordered a pizza. Karen Reed opened the door and was shot five times in the head with a .38 revolver. Alison Ponting was on duty that evening working at the BBC. She very closely resembled her sister in age, height and weight, and both wore the same kind of glasses.[7]

---

[7] Jo Durden-Smith, 'Unfinished Business' in *Sunday Telegraph Magazine*, 29 April 1996.

Generally speaking, however, *mafiosi* are regarded as good neighbours who are happy to blend into the district. With some justification they regard themselves, like Kipling's Tommy Atkins, as the saviours of the district:

> I mean we keep our neighbourhoods free of drugs and low-level crimes. It's safe in our neighbourhood because of us! But once we are done they forget all the favours and help we dished out![8]

John Favara found otherwise. He had the misfortune to kill Frank, the 12-year-old son of John Gotti and apple of his eye, who ran from behind a skip in front of his car in the spring of 1980 in the Howard Beach area of Queens. Investigators found that this was a genuine accident – Favara wasn't speeding – but Gotti saw otherwise. Favara should have had the sense to leave the neighbourhood. He received death threats and his car was paint-sprayed with the word 'murderer'. When he went to express his condolences, Gotti's wife Victoria attacked him with a baseball bat. Some months later Favara was kidnapped as he left his job at a furniture factory and was on his way to collect his car parked nearby. He was never seen again. The owner of a nearby diner, Leon Papon, identified Favara from a photograph but, visited by three men, sold his business and moved away. Amongst those suggested as his possible killers were 'Willie Boy' Johnson, himself later shot, and the stone-cold killer Roy DeMeo, later found dead in the boot of his car. There can, of course, be no suggestion of any involvement by Gotti. Like Al Capone at the time of the St Valentine's Day Massacre, he was in Florida when the abduction occurred.[9]

Arthur Henderson was in all probability an innocent bystander albeit an indiscreet one. His death came about after Ronald Ryan, who was serving nine years for shop-breaking, and Peter Walker, serving twelve for armed robbery, took advantage of a warders' Christmas party to escape from Pentridge in Victoria on 19 December 1965. They used knotted bedspreads to scale a wall to a catwalk and there took a warder's Armalite rifle. They then took a visiting Salvation

[8] Letter to author, October 2004.
[9] John H. Davis, *Mafia Dynasty*, pp. 190–92.

Army brigadier hostage, and made for Sydney Road with warders in pursuit. What exactly happened in the next few minutes was long a subject of conjecture. Certainly warder George Henry Hodgson was shot and killed as he tried to grab Walker. Walker and Ryan fled.

They made their way to the then underworld retreat of St Kilda's where, to obtain funds, they held up a bank. On the proceeds they gave a Christmas party where one of the guests, Arthur Henderson, recognised Ryan and mentioned this to Walker whom he had not. A little later Walker suggested that he and Henderson should go to a sly grog shop to buy some more alcohol. The next day Henderson's body was found near a public lavatory; he had been shot in the head.

The pair then went to Sydney where they rented a flat at Coogee. Walker contacted an old girlfriend to set up a double date, but in turn the girls contacted the police. When Ryan and Walker arrived at Sydney's Concord Repatriation General Hospital they were trapped.[10]

The question which divided Australia was whether it was Ryan who had fired the fatal shot or the bullet had come from another warder's gun. All witnesses agreed that only one shot had been fired, and a warder accepted that he had discharged his weapon. In the days when forensic testing does not seem to have overly troubled the courts, the jury found Ryan guilty and a string of appeals was rejected. Since 1955 some thirty-five death sentences had been commuted, and in many circles it was thought Ryan's would have been also. Ryan himself seems to have been more troubled by haemorrhoids than by his impending execution – that at least was the view of the prison psychiatrist.[11] By the time all his appeals had been rejected there was a great deal of public support for him. A crowd of some 3,000 gathered outside the prison in the hours before Ryan's execution.

Walker, convicted of manslaughter and also the manslaughter of Henderson, served nineteen years before being released in 1984. He remained out of the public's eye until in April 2002 he was convicted of cultivating marijuana and was sentenced to a year in

---

[10] *The Age*, 3 February 1967; Jack 'Ace' Ayling, *Nothing But the Truth*. Ayling gives a very personal account of the escape, hunt for the killers and execution of Ryan for whom he had a great deal of sympathy. John Silvester, *Tough*; Mike Richards, *The Hanged Man*.

[11] Letters, Allen Bartholomew to Crown Solicitor and Secretary Law Department, 10 March and 10 December 1966 respectively.

prison and fined. He claimed the six kilos were for his own use and alleviated his asthma.

It is usually young children who are the most innocent of bystanders. At the height of the Gooch-Doddington turf wars in Manchester, one who was seen in that light was Benji Stanley, a 14-year-old shot as he queued to get pies at Alvino's Tattie and Dumplin' shop in January 1993. The killer drove up in a silver Rover and fired through the window, hitting the boy. He then walked into the shop and shot him once more. Unfortunately Stanley was wearing a coloured bandana – red for Gooch, blue for Doddington – and khaki clothing, the uniform of the gangs. Later there were suggestions that Stanley might have had gang connections. Indeed, living where he did it would have been surprising if he had been able to isolate himself.

Nor is it safe to be the child of a *mafioso*, certainly not one who co-operates with the authorities. It was alleged that it was the finger of Giovanni Brusca (known as *u verru* – 'The Pig') on the button which blew up the investigating Judge Falcone in 1992; but his most appalling crime, so it is claimed by a *pentito*, came in November of the same year when he personally tortured and strangled Guiseppe, the 11-year-old son of an informer Santino Di Matteo, before throwing the boy's body into a vat of acid. The child had been snatched by Brusca's men, who told him they were taking him to see his father. Instead he was held captive for eighteen months during which, from time to time, photographs were sent to his father in an effort to persuade him to retract his evidence.

One who was most definitely an innocent victim was five-year-old Dillon Hull, shot along with his stepfather – a small-time drug dealer John Bates and the real object of the hit – by Paul Seddon in Bolton on 7 August 1997.[12] Bates, who survived, had refused to work for the local gang boss Billy Webb who ordered Bates' punishment. Webb was never convicted but, in turn, in May 2001 at the age of 41 he was shot to death in a Wigan flat. At the time he was on bail awaiting trial on charges of conspiracy to supply drugs. In July 2002 four people were charged with his murder.

Overall, Montreal must rate highly as an unsafe place for innocent

---

[12] 'A Life with no Hope' in *Daily Mirror*, 18 November 1998.

bystanders. In October 1974 Richard Blass escaped with four others including Jean-Paul Mercier and Edgar Roussel from a high-security prison. This was not his first escape, but it would be his last. Within the week there was a settling of accounts and Roger Levesque and Raymond Laurin were killed in a North End nightclub. As for the other escapers, Mercier and Robert Frappier were shot a matter of days later following a raid on a bank in the Boulevard Shopping Centre. Mercier died soon afterwards.

It was not until 22 January 1975 that Blass resurfaced in one of the most appalling acts of gangland brutality. First, he killed Rejean Fortin and Pierre Lamarke in the Gargantua Bar-Salon, an upstairs club on Beaubien East. Then he herded eleven potential witnesses into a cramped storeroom, padlocked the door and barred the exit with a heavy jukebox before setting the place alight. No one survived; all were burned to death.

Blass lived for another three days before being trapped by the police in a chalet in the Laurentians. Around 4.30 a.m. they broke into the house and, when he went for his gun, machine-gunned him to death.[13]

Another instance of being in the wrong place at the wrong time arose in Brisbane when the Whiskey Au Go Go club was firebombed at a time when the Sydney underworld was looking for easier pickings. It was thought at the time that Brisbane was safe from organised crime, on the basis that a city had to have a substantial population to support quality criminals. The thinking was wrong and Torinos, a nightclub in the Fortridge Valley area, was bombed. There was extensive damage but no casualties. The police said there was no suggestion of any protection racket. Again they were wrong, and on 8 March 1973 fifteen people died in a fire at the Whiskey Au Go Go club in the same area. Shortly after the main band had finished their stint, two canisters of petrol were rolled onto the carpeted entrance to the club and set alight with a lighted folder of matches.

Immediately afterwards a private detective said he had warned the police of the likelihood of a bombing, though they denied they had ever received such information. The name of Linus Driscoll, 'Jimmy the Pom', was circulated as someone wanted for questioning.

---

[13] *Montreal Gazette*, 2 November 1974, 22, 25, 28 January 1975.

Within a week a Barbara McCulkin and her two daughters disappeared. Shortly after that her husband Billy McCulkin was charged with bombing Torino's, something he denied. The case was dropped when the Director of Public Prosecutions decided there was no prospect of a conviction on the evidence available. Another man, former boxer Ian Hamilton who was alleged to have been the driver, also disappeared. His body was never found, but a Billy Stokes was later convicted of his murder. Meanwhile came the arrest of two serious criminals, John Stuart and Richard Finch.

Stuart had been convicted in November 1965 of shooting John 'Iron Man' Steele in a power struggle in the Sydney underworld. Steele survived the attack which left him with thirty shotgun pellets in his body. Stuart was sentenced to five years and while in Long Bay prison was found what was delicately called 'wandering'. He was thought to have been looking for Steele, who was in the same prison serving twelve months for carrying an unlicensed firearm. Stuart had his own troubles during that jail sentence. In October 1966 he was stabbed in the stomach, and in the following March was stabbed in the back while taking a shower.

In October 1966 Finch had been convicted of wounding with intent to murder following the shooting of John Regan, a colourful Sydney identity. After serving most of a seven-year sentence he had been deported to England. He kept in touch with Stuart, whom he had met in prison, and the allegation was that.Stuart had re-imported Finch to do the bombing while setting himself up with an alibi. Finch had been staying with the McCulkins.

Allegedly both men made confessions, and Finch is said to have named Billy McCulkin as the getaway driver after the Au Go Go fire. The trial was a lengthy affair drawn out by the fact that Stuart took to swallowing twisted paper clips bound with rubber bands. When the bands rotted the clips uncurled and stuck in his intestines. By the time the jury retired he was undergoing his third operation, and was thought to be too ill to attend the hearings. He had already discharged his counsel and the court was regularly reconvened in the hospital.

On 22 October the jury, which had been sequestered for some six weeks, took a bare two hours to find both Stuart and Finch guilty. Neither man accepted his conviction and both staged a series of protests. Stuart sewed his lips together. Finch, denying his confession, claimed to have bitten off a finger to show his indifference to pain, arguing that if he could do such a thing was he likely to show the remorse the police alleged. In fact it was sliced off for him by a fellow prisoner.

On 17 January 1979 Stuart was found dead in his cell; aged 39, he had suffered a heart attack. As is often the case, Finch became the target of romantically inclined females. In 1986 while still in prison he married a woman named Cheryl, who suffered from a debilitating disease. This led to belief in his reformation and a campaign was started for his release after which, since Finch was again deported, the pair moved to England. It was only a few months before his wife returned to Australia. In October 1988 he confessed to the Brisbane-based journalist Dennis Watt, who had campaigned for his release, that he had in fact started the fire. He later retracted this confession, saying he had only made it for the money.[14]

And as drug wars have proliferated worldwide so the number of innocent bystanders has increased. In recent years perhaps the most appalling example has been the slaughter of civilians in the Rock Machine–Hells Angels battle in Montreal. Over the five years from 1995 the war, centred primarily on control of drugs, had brought about the deaths of 153 people along with a further 172 attempts. There were 130 arson attacks and 85 bombings. Unfortunately five per cent of the victims have been innocent bystanders. These included 11-year-old Daniel Desrochers who on 8 August 1995 was killed when a bomb planted in drug dealer Marc Dube's Jeep went off. In the explosion a steel fragment went through his brain, and he died four days later.

Marc Dube was linked to the Angels. The next day a lone gunman went into the shop owned by Renaud Jomphe, described as 'an important member of the Rock Machine', and opened fire, killing a customer and wounding one of the assistants. Jomphe later told *The Globe and Mail* that the killing of Daniel had been by the Hells Angels: 'They made a mistake and they are trying to place the blame on the Rock

[14] *Courier Mail* (Brisbane), 8 March, 23, 24 October 1973, 18 January 1979; *The Sunday Mail* (Brisbane), 8 March 1998, 12 March 2000; Malcolm Brown (ed), *Australian Crime;* Jack Herbert, *The Bagman, The Life and Lies of Jack Herbert.*

Machine. We don't attack and kill children.' His mother refused offers from both sides to pay for the funeral, and one positive outcome was the foundation of the anti-Biker police squad, the Wolverines.

The Angels made another mistake when on 7 January 1997 Guy Lemay was shot when he opened his door to let his dog out. He was taken for a Rock Machine drug dealer who lived in a flat upstairs. In a separate incident Serge Hervieux was shot and killed in a Montreal car-hire office. He looked up when the gunman called 'Serge' and was also killed in mistake for another Rock Machine member.[15]

Nor can there be any blame attached to those who took a flight from O'Hare airport, Chicago to Pittsburgh in 1994. On 8 September they simply had the misfortune to be on the same plane, a Boeing 737–300, as Paul Olson, a former Chicago banker who had rolled over into the Witness Protection Program in 1985. He was flying to give evidence in a cocaine-trafficking case when the plane nose-dived on its approach run. All 132 people on board were killed. It has never been clearly established if this was a hit or, as an inquiry found, an accident caused by a malfunctioning rudder.[16]

Sometimes a number of the elements – innocent bystander, wrong target, disappearance – all come together in one story. Back in London, another completely innocent man was one who attended a Christmas party and was shot by mistake. He was simply one man in a line of those who were dealt with by North London enforcer Gilbert Wynter. It has been alleged but never proved that Wynter, who walked with a limp after being hit by a police car in 1992 and who was an enforcer for a prominent North London family, killed Claude Moseley, the former junior British high-jump champion. Moseley was stabbed to death with a Samurai sword, more or less slicing him in half, over a drugs deal in 1994. Whoever was responsible, it was thought that Moseley had been lax in his accounting methods. A 22-year-old received three months for contempt when he refused to testify against

---

[15] For an account of the war see Yves Lavigne, *Hell's Angels at War*. No one could ever mistake London's Ginger Marks for an innocent bystander, but on 2 January 1965 it appears he also was shot by mistake. The intended victim was a Jimmy Evans who had shot George, the brother of the notorious Freddie Foreman, in a domestic dispute. One version of the story is that he mistook the call of 'Jimmy' for 'Ginger', which did for him. Evans gives a different version in his book, *The Survivor*.

[16] *The Times*, 21 January 1995.

Wynter. The man, who was serving a five-year sentence for armed robbery, had originally made a statement claiming he witnessed the murder which took place in his house while he was on the run from prison. The case against Wynter was dropped.

Wynter also freelanced, running the lucrative doorman trade. In 1998 Paul 'Paddlefoot' Anthony received eighteen years for shooting an innocent stranger in the crowded Emporium nightclub off Regent Street.[17] Two weeks before Christmas 1997, the 43-year-old father-of-two Tony Smith went to the club to join a private party. Anthony, together with another taller man who was never arrested, appeared and shot him three times from a range of six feet. When the first two shots hit Smith in the chest, leaving a hole the size of a fist, he collapsed on the floor and instinctively pretended to be dead. Anthony, however, wanted to make sure and stood over him to fire a third shot. The bullet went through Smith's cheek and out through the palate of his mouth. Amazingly he survived. Another man was also hit; Anthony fled and, when a bouncer set off in pursuit, the second man opened fire again.

The shooting had all the hallmarks of a drug gang execution, but the police were initially baffled. Mr Smith had absolutely no criminal connections and the case was even presented in court as 'motiveless'. In fact Wynter had ordered the hit with a figure of £300 as the price quoted and, perhaps inadvisedly, he chose Anthony, a known drug addict. On the night of the killing Anthony was smoking crack in the Costello Park Hotel in Finsbury Park with a girlfriend. There he tried on the latex gloves he would wear and left with a gun tucked into his waistband, telling her to stay behind.

However, the police believe that Anthony and the 'taller man' deliberately chose to shoot the wrong person when they found out – to their horror – who the real target was intended to be. They dared not shoot this powerful figure for fear of inevitable reprisal. On the other hand, they could not go back to Wynter and his employers having refused to carry out the hit. The only solution was to murder somebody else, and they all but succeeded.

---

[17] Paul Cheston and Justin Davenport, 'The hitman, the innocent victim and a world where life is worth £300' in *Evening Standard*, 27 November 1998.

Wynter, whose mother was said to be a sort of Obeah princess, disappeared a few months later. His former girlfriend, Dee, said he spoke a lot about God but also, backing things each way, used African oils to keep him from harm.

Two years later there was a great deal of speculation over the death of Solly Nahome, a financial adviser for the North London Adams family, and the disappearance of Wynter, their alleged enforcer. As is often the case, a number of conflicting theories were advanced. The most likely is that both Wynter and Solly Nahome, shot to death outside his home in Finchley, were thought to have been double-crossing their employers.[18]

There again, it was believed that Wynter might have killed Nahome and staged his own disappearance. It appears they had been working on a landfill project in a quarry near Oldham as well as being involved in a fraudulent share deal.[19] Ranged against this is the story that Wynter had died because of his vanity. He had been summoned to Islington where a van was waiting for him. It was a rainy day and he was wearing an expensive suit which he did not wish to get wet; holding an umbrella he backed into the van and, by not paying proper attention to detail, to his death. In support of this, it appears that his aunt (who owned five properties in Jamaica) also disappeared about the time Wynter did.[20] Another thought was that he had been killed in a different contract execution ordered by the unnamed man who was the original target of the failed Anthony hit. There was also a suggestion that Wynter was part of the foundations of the Millennium Dome.

In 2003 it was suggested that the police were about to interview an unnamed Mr Big, then in custody, over the deaths of a number of people including Moseley, Wynter and the Greek property millionaire Michael Olymbious, as well as the shooting of Frank Fraser at Turnmills' nightclub in Clerkenwell. It was hoped that he might help in inquiries into the deaths of between thirty and fifty people.[21] If such an interview ever took place, no charges have so far resulted.

[18] John McVicar in *Punch*, 31 July 1999.
[19] *Evening Standard*, 29 November 2000.
[20] *The Guardian*, 19 April 1999.
[21] *Sunday People*, 18 May 2003. Michael Olymbious was shot dead on a South London housing estate in April 1995. He was thought to have had links to the Ukraine, and an alternative version is that he had fallen foul of East European Mafia.

12

Sometimes the Gun Is Mightier than the Pen

With, of course, the exception of South America and the drug trade where everyone, including a Roman Catholic cardinal, has been regarded as fair game, until the 1970s there had been a mere handful of killings of investigative or crusading journalists in the Western world. One of the first was the editor of the *Canton Daily News*, 36-year-old Don J. Mellett who was shot and killed in Canton, Ohio, on 17 July 1926.

Mellett, who was one of seven journalist brothers, had been waging war on vice in Canton for some months and as a consequence was receiving threats. He had been successful in engineering the temporary suspension of the police chief Seranus A. Lengel and was instrumental in the revocation of parole of two of the town's liquor dealers, Harry 'The Greek' Bouklias and Harry Turner. So far that year there had been nine murders in Canton of which only two had been solved.

Of the town it was written:

[Canton] is no less corrupt or vice ridden now than it was several years ago when the Mayor of that time was removed from office by the Governor, and the Mayor's brother whom he had appointed Director of Public Safety was sentenced to a term to be not less than two and not more than ten years in gaol for bootlegging.[1]

Things had reached such a pass with Mellett's continuing attacks on both bootleggers and the police that the week before his death he had hired a suspended policeman George Beresford as a bodyguard. Now he believed the danger was over and gave the officer the night off as he went to a dance at the Molly Stark Club. He and his wife returned home in the early hours, when he was ambushed by a gunman hiding in the garden. Within days a fund of $25,000 had been set up as a reward for capturing the killers. The restored police chief Seranus A. Lengel, unsurprisingly, made no progress with the inquiry and was sacked for his pains. It was not until September that a known hitman Pat McDermott was lured by his brothers to Nanty Glo, Pennsylvania, where he was arrested and charged.

McDermott blamed the hit on the chief prosecution witness Steve Kascholk, saying that on several occasions he himself had warned Mellett of ensuing problems. He also ran an alibi defence to the effect that he had been in a rooming house owned by a Hattie Gearhardt; she supported him, saying he could not possibly have been out of bed murdering Mellett or she would have known. The alibi collapsed when she was shown her earlier Grand Jury testimony to the effect that she had not known where McDermott was on the night of the murder. The closing speeches were on 24 December and McDermott's lawyer clearly knew which way the wind was blowing. He asked for an acquittal but in what is known as a rolled-up plea suggested that if there was a conviction, because it was Christmas and a time of love, the jury should spare McDermott the electric chair – and this they did, convicting him only of second-degree murder. He received life without the possibility of parole. No one had really thought McDermott was innocent and now the interest switched. Was he going to squeal? It depended. 'I'm going to go down and start my stretch if I have to. I'll see what happens to the others before I decide whether I will do any talking.' Meanwhile both the trial judge and the prosecutor received death threats.

[1] *The Times*, 20 July 1926.

When it comes to it, life without parole does not always mean exactly that in America. There is often a little leverage which can be exercised. McDermott did decide to give evidence and throughout the first half of 1927 one by one his co-conspirators turned, pleaded guilty and themselves testified. The new star witness for the prosecution was Louis E. Mezner, who gave evidence against a policeman Floyd Streitenberger. The plot had been hatched at the first hearing of the Civil Service Commission after Lengel had been dismissed for inefficiency. Streitenberger had told him, 'We've got to get this Mellett; he's been making too much trouble for the boss.'

The last to go down was indeed the boss, the former police chief Seranus Lengel. Aged 59 but looking 75, he tottered when – almost a year to the day after the murder – on 16 July 1927 the verdict went against him. 'Before God I didn't do it. I am innocent. There is no justice,' he told the court. He also received life imprisonment. However, things had not improved in Canton. A fortnight later a bomb exploded at 12 St NE, the house of the industrialist William Maxwell. It was thought to have been intended for Judge Hubert C. Pontius, who had been active in the investigation of the murder and who lived at 12 St NW; he had already received a series of threats.[2]

Three years later, the most celebrated of the bootleg killings of a journalist occurred. As a result, for a short time Jake Lingle was posthumously regarded as a star police reporter for the *Chicago Daily Tribune*. The 38-year-old Alfred 'Jake' Lingle was murdered on 9 June 1930. On the face of it the killing was an unusual one, breaking the gangster code of the time that journalists and prosecutors – perhaps on the tramcar principle that there would be another one by in five minutes – should not be touched. Lingle had left the *Tribune* offices saying that he was going to try to get a story about what was left of the Bugsy Moran Gang following the St Valentine's Day Massacre. A short time later he was seen walking down Randolph to catch a train to the Washington Park racetrack. He stopped to buy a racing paper and then headed towards the

[2] *New York Times*, 17, 18, 19 July, 9 September, 11, 12, 14, 24, 25, 26, 28 December 1926, 13 January, 24 February, 1, 8 March, 17 July, 2 August 1927.

underpass at Randolph and Michigan to the station. A well-dressed, fair-haired young man walked behind him and shot Lingle through the head with a bullet from a .38 Colt, engagingly known as a bellygun. Lingle, who was smoking a two-cent cigar at the time and looking at the racing paper, fell with the cigar still in his mouth and holding the paper. A few seconds earlier a man had called out a tip 'Hy Schneider' for him for the third race.[3]

As witnesses came forward the picture became a little clearer. Lingle had known he was in trouble. He had met the corrupt lawyer Louis Piquett in the Loop twenty-four hours earlier and while they were discussing the discovery of Eugene 'Red' McLaughlin's body, which had just surfaced in the river, Lingle had seen a blue sedan stop at the kerb. Apparently he lost the thread of the conversation and hurried into a store. On the day of his death he had met Sergeant Thomas Alcock in the lobby of the Sherman Hotel and told the detective he was being followed.

Witnesses to the killing came forward to say that he had been walking with not only the blond-haired man but also a darker one, and it would seem as though he was being bustled along with a gun held against him. A Patrick Campbell who went to help found his path blocked by a priest who, in a singularly uncharitable way, told him, 'I think someone has been shot. I'm getting out of here.' All in all, it was believed that up to a dozen men were involved in the trap for Lingle. The priest was thought to be the always useful Fred Burke from the Purple Gang.

There was an immediate outcry. Although at the time of his death he was earning $65 a week and had never been credited with a by-line, Lingle was immediately named as a 'first line soldier' in the fight against crime. Rewards of over $55,000 were promptly posted by his paper as well as the *Chicago Evening Post* and William Hearst's *Chicago Herald and Examiner*. Naturally Colonel Robert R. McCormick, the *Tribune's* publisher, was particularly incensed. That evening he held a staff conference and, talking for forty-five minutes, pledged himself to solve the crime. The next day there was an eight-column banner headline *Offer $30,000 for Assassin*, and two days

---

[3] For the record, Hy Schneider finished unplaced.

later an editorial headed *The Challenge* threw down the gauntlet to the Mob:

> The meaning of this murder is plain. It was committed in reprisal and in attempt at intimidation. Mr Lingle was a police reporter and an exceptionally informed one. His personal friendships included the highest police officials and the contacts of his work made him familiar to most of the big and little fellows of gangland. What made him valuable to his newspaper marked him as dangerous to the killers.[4]

That day the headline was *Gangs Raided: Chiefs Flee*, and indeed dozens of gangsters were arrested in a series of swoops by six squads.

But things were not quite the way they seemed, and Lingle was out of the headlines and off the front page by the weekend when *Schmeling wins on a foul* replaced him. For a start, on the day of his death Lingle was wearing a diamond-studded belt given him by Al Capone. An investigation of the finances of this one-time semi-professional baseball player indicated that he was keeping a wife and two children – Buddy aged six and Pansy, a year younger – on an annual salary of $3,380, but that his earnings from somewhere were nearer $60,000. He had a chauffeur-driven Lincoln and he had just bought a $16,000 home at Long Beach on what was considered the Michigan Riviera; he had also taken a suite of rooms at the Stevens, then one of Chicago's toniest hotels. He had explained his apparent wealth by saying it came from a legacy of $50,000 from his father, supplemented by gifts from uncles. The legacy from his father turned out to be one of $500.

Lingle was not good enough for the major leagues and he could not write well enough to have his own by-line, but he certainly could cultivate contacts. It transpired that through his police connections he had the ability to award beer-selling and gambling rights. He had influence in the appointments in the police force and he was into demanding money from brothel-keepers. In two and a half years prior to his death he had deposited $63,900 with the Lake

---

[4]*Chicago Daily Tribune*, 10, 11, 12, 13 June 1930. For accounts of the killing and Lingle's life see Kenneth Allsop, *The Bootleggers*; F.D. Pasley, *Al Capone*.

Shore Trust and Savings Bank. He had also been in an investment partnership with Police Commissioner Bill Russell. Some referred to Lingle as 'the unofficial Chief of Police'. Now his stock slumped and the *Tribune* was reduced to writing articles denouncing other newspaper reporters: 'There are weak men on other newspapers and in other professions, in positions of trust and responsibility greater than that of Alfred Lingle.' This was a snide reference to Julius Rosenheim of the rival *Chicago Daily News* who had been shot to death a few months previously. He, too, had been blackmailing brothel-keepers.

Some months later a small-time gangster, Leo V. Brothers, who was then living at Lake Crest Drive apartments, was unearthed by a former criminal turned Pinkerton detective, Jack Hagan, who had infiltrated the Moran Gang and later Egan's Rats in St Louis to do so. On 21 December Brothers was arrested and charged with Lingle's murder.[5]

He was expensively defended with a battery of five counsel led by the crooked lawyer Louis Piquett, who later represented John Dillinger.[6] The evidence against him was not strong, with half the fourteen identifying witnesses putting him as the killer and the other half not so. Many, including the Chicago Crime Commission, believed that Brothers had been framed. He received fourteen years. 'I can do that standing on my head,' he is said to have announced after the verdict. Brothers was released after eight years. He returned to St Louis, where he was acquitted of a murder charge on which he had been awaiting trial before his arrest, and became a partner in various Mob enterprises such as taxi and loan companies. He died in 1951 without disclosing who had paid him either for the contract or for going to prison.

One idea is that Capone paid for the jury-fixing. If so, what was Brothers doing in the camp of his arch-enemy George Moran? It is also suggested that Moran was displeased with Lingle's political power and his influence over Chief Bill Russell. There was a theory that he had been extorting money over the re-opening of the Sheridan Wave Club, closed following the St Valentine's Day Massacre. Another

---

[5] Little is known of Jack Hagan except that he had once been an associate of the Genna brothers in Chicago. He seems to have cozied up to a Pat Hogan and wheedled the nickname 'Buster' from him. Buster was Leo Bader, alias Leo Brothers.

[6] For an account of Piquett's career see James Morton, *Gangland Lawyers*.

suggestion is that he had been blackmailing a relatively small-time North Side operator, Jack Zuta, and had been scamming money from him under the pretext that he would get back dog-track licences for him. Zuta was briefly questioned over the murder and released.[7]

A more likely version of the killing of Lingle is that he was in a hole. He was a degenerate gambler and, along with Russell, he had lost heavily in the stock market crash. He had borrowed money widely if not wisely, including sums from moneylenders with both Capone and Moran affiliations. His own tax affairs were not exactly squeaky clean, and as a result it was feared he could be squeezed by the IRS to give evidence against Capone. In return he might also collect a finder's fee of ten per cent in the dollar on all money recovered. There is sufficient evidence to show that Capone was prepared to treat tax investigators as his street opponents and not award them the courtesies extended to prosecutors and journalists.[8] Given the number of angles Lingle was playing, it is surprising he lasted as long as he did.

Barely a month later the radio commentator Gerald 'Jerry' Buckley was killed in the lobby of the La Salle and the Detroiter Hotel off Woodward and Adelaide in Detroit.[9] July that year proved to be a particularly hard month for the gangs and the citizenship of Detroit in general. In an eleven-day spree ten gunmen died. Mayor Charles Bowles commented, 'It is just as well to let these gangsters kill each other off, if they are so minded. You have the scientists employ one set of parasites to destroy another. May not that be the plan of

---

[7] Zuta was next seen in Upper Nemahbun, twenty-five miles west of Milwaukee, where he had gone for the summer and where he was shot on 1 August as he played the mechanical piano at the Lake View Hotel. Legend has it that the machine was playing 'Good for you, Bad for Me', a current smash hit, at the crucial moment. The likely reason for Zuta's death is that it was feared he would co-operate with the police. For a time it was suggested that a Frank Foster aka Frank Citro might be involved, and he was certainly questioned. He was formerly a Capone man who defected to O'Banion and Moran. The connection was through a revolver found at the scene of the killing which he had bought from a sporting goods dealer, Peter von Frantzius (d.1968), regarded as one of the more prominent armourers of the Chicago underworld. It was to von Frantzius that the machine gun used to kill Capone's former mentor Frankie Yale was traced. Foster left Chicago before he was questioned. J. Gollomb, *Crimes of the Year*, Chapter 12.

[8] See William Balsamo and George Carpozi jnr, *Crime Incorporated*, p. 238.

[9] The hotel no longer stands. In the 1950s it became a home for the elderly run by Carmelite nuns and was called Carmel Hall. It was never profitable and in the 1980s was taken over as a private nursing home. That venture failed and the hotel stood derelict until on 3 March 1996 it was demolished in under eight seconds with 400 lbs of dynamite.

Providence in these killings among the bandits.' It was not an attitude which appealed to the voters, who two weeks later dismissed him.

On the face of things Buckley himself was something of a crusading journalist. He had grown up in the Irish quarter of Detroit then known as Corktown. Educated locally, he took a degree at the Detroit College of Law. For a time he worked for the Ford Motor Company and then broke into broadcasting, first as a singer and then a commentator. As the Eastside Italians and the Purple Gang grew stronger and more shameless throughout the summer of 1930, so Buckley became more outspoken in his broadcasts and, for his pains, received a string of death threats.

On 22 July 1930 Buckley voiced his support for the recall of Mayor Charles Bowles – then in Kentucky for the horseracing – whom he accused of complicity with the underworld. He was also threatening to name the gangland leaders, not that their names were exactly a secret.

On the evening of the election in which Bowles was ousted from his position, Buckley took a cab from the City Hall to the La Salle Hotel where at 12.15 a.m. he received a telephone call from a woman who was never identified. At 1.30 a.m. he was sitting in the lobby with a hotel resident Jack Klein, a Purple drug dealer. His wife had already received a threatening call saying her husband would not be coming home that night. Three men walked into the hotel and opened fire on Buckley who was reading a newspaper. They rushed out to a getaway car and then a second car screeched to a halt outside the entrance. The woman driver, Lucille Love, a girlfriend of a local mobster Angelo Livecchi – who also lived in the hotel, sharing a room with Leonard 'Black Leo' Cellura and nightclub owner Teddy Pizzino – left the car and ran into the theatre opposite the hotel. Questioned, she said she had heard shots, slammed on the brakes and then run to the theatre for shelter. She was never charged.

Klein and Livecchi were arrested. Klein was released almost at once after he said the incident had happened so fast he 'didn't see a thing'. It was clear that this time the police thought the Eastside elements rather than the Purples had been responsible. The Wayne County prosecutor James Chenor summoned a Grand Jury who promptly indicted Livecchi, Pizzino and a Joe Bommarito, claiming that they had financed the Mayor's campaign and were under his protection. There were no convictions. After a six-week trial the jury deliberated for thirty-five hours before acquitting all the defendants.

Pete Licavoli, who with the collapse of the Purples in the late 1930s would go on to become the head of the Detroit Mafia, left Michigan until the three were acquitted. Another suspected of involvement in the killing was John Mirabella, who had worked with the Licavolis from the time they had sided with the Purples. Prudently, he also absented himself from the city. According to the evidence of former Detroit Police Commissioner George Edwards, the gun used to kill Buckley was later found at the home of 'Cockeyed Joe' Catalanotte. His punishment was exile across the river to Windsor, Ontario, from where he is said to have conducted his Detroit business quite openly.[10]

While his links with organised crime were never as clear-cut as those of Lingle, Buckley was another who may not have had spotless hands. A womaniser and a man about the clubs, he was also thought to have been blackmailing the gangsters, threatening to name them on his show if they did not pay his price. Almost immediately after his killing Frank Chock, a small-time bootlegger, came forward and signed an affidavit saying that Buckley had been the financier of his business, and that he had been using his position on the radio to muscle in. He later swore another affidavit saying he could not read English and had not known to what he was swearing previously.

Another legitimate theory was that Buckley was even more involved with organised crime and had been killed for double-crossing the Eastside Italians. The story goes that he was given $4,000 by Pizzino to arrange for a Canadian lawyer to represent the members in a bootlegging trial in Ontario. However, Canadian exporters paid the lawyer to lose the case and Buckley took the blame.[11]

The award-winning Don Bolles, an investigative reporter for the *Arizona Republic*, has often been cited as the first journalist to be killed by what could be called organised crime. Lingle and Julius Rosenheim were killed because they were participants, as was Buckley. Mellett, who undoubtedly had clean hands, was an editor. Bolles had been investigating Emprise, a Buffalo, New York sports conglomerate which

---

[10] U.S.-Senate, OC and Narcotics Hearings, pp. 428–9. According to Ed Reid a total of 54 weapons was found in the raid. *The Grim Reapers*, pp. 76–7.
[11] See Paul R. Kavieff, *The Purple Gang*, pp. 102–7.

operated greyhound tracks in Arizona and which was linked to organised crime. He was blown up when a bomb exploded in his car on 2 June 1976. He lost both legs and his right arm and died eleven days later. Before he died he told the police, 'John Adamson did it.'

In the December Adamson, a greyhound owner, admitted a murder-for-hire contract implicating Max Dunlap, a wealthy Phoenix builder, and James Robison, another builder from the same city. Adamson claimed that Dunlap had hired him for a fee of $10,000 because Bolles writing had upset Kemper Markey, a 74-year-old rancher and one of the wealthiest men in Arizona. There was some unexplained urgency in the contract: Dunlap wanted Bolles killed before the reporter made a trip to San Diego in the July. Adamson invited Bolles to a hotel in Phoenix and while he was there placed a bomb under his car. It was detonated, he claimed, by Robison using a radio transmitter from a distance of several hundred feet.

Adamson, in return for his evidence against Robison and Dunlap, was allowed to plead to second-degree murder and received twenty years and two months. In 1977 Dunlap and Robison were sentenced to death after a trial based mainly on Adamson's evidence. Both stalwartly maintained their innocence. In February 1980 their convictions were overturned on the ground that the trial judge had not allowed questioning of Adamson about his criminal activities unrelated to the trial. The prosecution announced that it would seek a retrial, but things went awry. Adamson refused to give evidence a second time unless a better deal could be arranged for him. He was retried alone and found guilty. The State then announced that it would push for the death penalty unless Adamson gave evidence. In the meantime, in June 1980 the charges against Dunlap and Robison had been dismissed 'without prejudice'.[12] However, this was not the end of the matter by any means. Adamson was found guilty on 17 October of that year and this time was sentenced to death. Over the next eight years the sentence would be overturned, reinstated and finally overturned on 22 December 1988, a decision upheld by the Supreme Court in June 1990. In the December Dunlap was recharged with Bolles' murder. He and Robison were also charged with conspiracy

[12] Carl Sifakis, *The Encyclopedia of American Crime*, p.84.

to obstruct an investigation into Bolles' death, and Adamson agreed to give evidence if his 1977 plea bargain was reinstated.

It was not perhaps the most promising track on which to race for a conviction. In separate trials Dunlap was found guilty in April 1993 and received life imprisonment without the possibility of parole for twenty-five years. Six months later Robison was acquitted, but two years after that was sentenced to five years for soliciting the murder of Adamson. In 1996 Adamson was released and went into the Witness Protection Program. He died, an alcoholic, on 22 May 2003 in North Carolina where he had been living under a false name.[13]

In March 1992 Manuel de Dios, the editor of the Spanish language newspaper *El Diario-La Prensa*, was executed by a masked gunman in a Queens restaurant. It was the latest in a series of high-profile killings of Hispanic residents in Queens. Another man shot outside his home in Jackson Heights was the anti-drug crusader Pedro Mendez.

Now the attacks on journalists worldwide were occurring more often. The killing of the crusading Irish reporter Veronica Guerin was a telling blow to what was believed to be the immunity of the press. She had received more than one serious warning following her attacks on Dublin's career criminals. In October 1994 shots had been fired at her home. On 30 January 1996, when she answered the door of her house, a man wearing motorcycling gear and a helmet pointed a handgun at her head before lowering the barrel and shooting her in the right thigh.

Veronica Guerin was killed on 26 June 1996 as she drove home from the Nass courthouse where she had just been fined for a speeding offence. She pulled up at the Clondalkin traffic light shortly before 1 p.m. and the rider of a white Kawasaki motorcycle bearing false 1969 Dublin plates shot her through the window. She had been on her mobile telephone to a Garda officer and the call, which was being taped, was interrupted in mid-sentence with a bang as she was shot.

The week before her death she had written about one of Dublin's most notorious drug dealers, labelling Tony Felloni, who had a conviction for living off immoral earnings, as King Scum. Apart from trying to poison his wife he had introduced his daughter to

---

[13] *Arizona Republic* (Phoenix), 9 October 2003.

drugs. He had just been jailed for twenty years but, correctly, it was not thought that he was in any way responsible for Guerin's death.[14]

As the years went by the story of her killing began to unravel and it revolved around the so-called 'Warehouseman', John Gilligan, and his gang of drugs and arms dealers. For years the Gardai believed that he was leader of the so-called Warehouse Gang operating, as all good thieves should, by specialising in identifying a ready market for a particular brand of stolen goods, whether it was animal drugs, videos, video games or children's clothes. The gang, which had operated almost unchecked for ten years, would raid the target factory on a Friday night and by the time the loss was noticed the goods would have been distributed throughout Dublin.

On 7 November 1990 he went to Portaloise prison to begin a four-year sentence for handling stolen goods. It was here that he would recruit the members of his second criminal empire.[15] Genuinely working for better conditions for the prisoners, he also began to plan his transition from warehousebreaker to drug dealer. In Portaloise at the time were Brian Meehan, a getaway driver once used by the so-called 'General' Martin Cahill, and Paul Ward known as Hippo, a man with twenty-five convictions. Both would eventually become tried and trusted members of the Gilligan outfit.

Gilligan was released after serving three years of his sentence on 15 November 1993. At a previous sentence hearing the 38-year-old former seaman was described in court as having no other income than from crime. In 1988 he had been living on social security of £50 a week, from which he was maintaining three ponies at livery in a local riding school. By the time of his conviction in November 1990 he had acquired a house and the Jessbrook stables in Co. Meath, run by his wife Geraldine, buying up every acre on which he could lay his money. During the past three years he had listened to the boasting of men such as Meehan about how much money could be made from drugs, and he was determined to establish his own operation.[16]

---

[14] Paul Reynolds, *King Scum*.
[15] Aspects of Gilligan's career appear in many books on Irish crime but undoubtedly the most thorough is by the investigative journalist John Mooney, *Gangster*.
[16] Meehan had grown up in the Crumlin area and after a series of minor convictions graduated with a six-year sentence imposed in 1989 for robbing Allied Irish Bank premises in Grafton Street.

Now Gilligan turned to John Traynor known as 'The Coach', womaniser, fraudsman, possible blackmailer and certainly retriever of a number of paintings from the Beit collection[17] as well as some 145 files stolen by Cahill from the offices of the Director of Public Prosecutions. Gilligan had known Traynor since his days as a seaman and now The Coach introduced him to Cahill. From then on it was gravy all the way. By the time Veronica Guerin started to investigate him Gilligan was making literally millions of pounds annually, principally from drugs but also from arms smuggling.

It is inconceivable that Gilligan did not understand that the shooting of a prominent Irish journalist in broad daylight would bring down the wrath not only of the police but also of the press on his head. He had threatened her and her son; he had then beaten her up and threatened to rape her son when she had not kowtowed. Instead, she had reported the assault to the police. He now believed, alleged the prosecution at his later trial, that she would go ahead with the prosecution and if, as was almost certain, he was jailed, he would lose control of his empire.

Her death changed his life. Effectively he became a fugitive, moving from place to place and, at the same time, shifting huge sums abroad. One effort to launder money in Holland through a casino failed. Worse, there were defections from within the ranks. At the end of 1998 Gilligan's armourer Charles Bowden, who was himself serving a six-year sentence for drugs and arms dealing, turned informer and gave evidence against Paul Ward who was alleged to have disposed of the gun and the motorcycle used in the attack. On 18 January 1999 Ward was refused leave to appeal against his conviction, for which he received a life sentence.

On 4 October that year Gilligan took a flight from Heathrow to Amsterdam, checking in late with only hand luggage, and he tried to repeat the same procedure two days later. However, he had been noticed on the prior run. This time he was stopped and invited to open his suitcase, which contained £330,000 in various currencies. It was the last time he was free until his trial. During his period in

---

[17] Over the years the Alfred Beit collection of paintings at Russborough House in Co. Wicklow has been the subject of at least three raids by thieves including Rose Dugdale and Martin Cahill. See James Morton, *Gangland Today*.

custody he made spirited efforts in his defence, both legally with challenges to the extradition procedure and illegally with efforts to intimidate the witnesses against him. It was to no effect. He was finally extradited and in December 2000 he went on trial in Dublin for the murder of Veronica Guerin before three judges sitting without a jury at the special criminal court. Opening the case, Peter Charleton for the prosecution told the court: 'He committed this offence through his agents, his agents being members of a gang under his control who all the while acted according to his will.'

Gilligan faced not only the murder charge but also a further fifteen counts of smuggling drugs and firearms between 1994 and 1996. He had, said Charleton, told a Russell Warren to keep the journalist under surveillance after she left court following her speeding case. It was alleged that Brian Meehan had ridden the Kawasaki motorcycle with the gunman as pillion passenger. Meehan had been relegated to driver rather than shooter because of his inability to despatch another gangland leader Martin Foley, known as The Viper, on two occasions. Bowden and two other supergrasses gave evidence against him.

On 15 January 2001 John Gilligan received good and bad news from the court. The good news was that the judges said that the witnesses were so unreliable that they would acquit him of Guerin's murder. The bad news was that he was sentenced to twenty-eight years for running a drug empire.[18]

It was Michel Auger's unremitting attacks on the long-running war between the Hells Angels and the Rock Machine which brought about the shooting of the veteran journalist of *Le Journal de Montréal* on 13 September 2000. Two days before he was attacked he had published a two-page article, *Pagaille chez les Caïds*, in which he surveyed the state of play between the warring parties.[19] In his weekly column Auger made a habit of totalling the gangster deaths and then providing a quarterly update. In the column before his shooting he commented that the senior echelons of both the Hells Angels, which

[18] For something of a revisionist look at the circumstances of Guerin's death see Emily O'Reilly, *Veronica Guerin*.
[19] Translated as 'Chaos Among the Bosses' in *Le Journal de Montréal*, 11 September 2000. Auger was not the first Canadian crime journalist to survive an attack. In 1976 Jean-Claude Charbonneau was shot in the newsroom of *Le Devoir* by a man connected to the Cotroni Family. He later wrote *The Canadian Connection*.

with 100 chapters worldwide was by far Canada's biggest motorcycle gang, and the Canadian Mafia were in disarray.

After Auger left the east-end shopping mall at Place Versailles, where he often met informants, and parked in the lot of his paper, he went to the boot of his car to collect his laptop. It was then that a gunman opened fire, hitting him in the back with five out of six bullets. Before he collapsed Auger managed to dial 911 on his mobile telephone. He underwent two operations and survived. The whole episode had been botched. Not only did the gunman fail to kill Auger but it seems that the radiator hose in the getaway car, an old model Plymouth Acclaim, broke and the vehicle had to be abandoned. In it was a firearm and ammunition.

The would-be killer apparently did not survive. On 18 September the police found a burning car in woods near Saint-Hippolyte. Inside was the body of 26-year-old Yanick Girard, a member of the Rockers Motorcycle Club, a Hells Angels affiliate. He had been due to appear in court the following week on charges of drug trafficking and possession of firearms. Another biker, Sylvain Payant, this time from the Jokers, another affiliate of the Angels, had been shot dead in Saint-Jean-sur-Richlieu four days earlier. There have been suggestions, however, that Girard was not Auger's killer. The police are alleged to know his name, but have not sufficient evidence to bring a charge. On 28 September 2001 Charles Michel Vezina, of St-Hyacinthe, Quebec, an underworld armourer who had supplied the gun used to shoot Auger, received a sentence of nearly five years following a plea bargain.

13

Brief Encounters

For years it was a rule of thumb that – provided they stayed in a strictly professional capacity – lawyers, doctors and accountants were also regarded as safe from attack from disgruntled clients and their friends and relations in criminal cases. Step outside their professional roles and they become fair game.

One of the early recorded victims of Al Capone, armed with his new machine gun, came on 27 April 1926 when Assistant State Attorney William H. McSwiggin was shot to death from a passing car as he left the Pony Inn on West Roosevelt Road, Cicero. Along with him were his former schoolmates, James J. Doherty of the West Side O'Donnells and Tom 'Red' Duffy. McSwiggin had prosecuted Doherty for the murder of ex-boxer Eddie Tancl, but became friendly with him while he was on bail pending his appeal.

It is hardly surprising that there were no lasting witnesses to the killing. Those who initially made statements were unanimous that the machine-gun wielder was Capone, and one theory put about was that he had mistaken McSwiggin for Earl Weiss. This was not tenable. Weiss would not have been out with any of the O'Donnell tribe, of whom he was a sworn enemy. As for the killing, Capone commented, 'Of course I didn't kill him. Why should I? I liked the kid. Only the day before he got killed he was up to my place and when he went home I gave him a bottle of scotch for his old man [a police sergeant].

I paid McSwiggin and I paid him plenty, and I got what I was paying for.' Which successfully blackened the dead Assistant State Attorney's reputation for the foreseeable, and even enduring, future.[1]

There is little doubt that McSwiggin had become far too close to Capone, who referred to him as 'my friend Bill McSwiggin'. The shooting had been part of the war Capone was then conducting against the O'Donnells and Doherty in particular, whom he held responsible for the death of Samoots Amatuna. McSwiggin, who it seems had been out playing cards with Duffy on the night of his death, can possibly just about qualify as an innocent bystander who was simply in the wrong place at the wrong time and, certainly, with the wrong people.

One such Assistant State Prosecutor and later municipal judge, John Sbarbaro, who played both sides, escaped lightly. His garage in Chicago was used to house illegal liquor and he served as the undertaker of choice to the families of dead racketeers such as Dion O'Banion. Sbarbaro lived to tell the tale. The worst that happened to him was that the garage was blown up. He was mystified by this, saying it must have been a revenge for the harsh sentences he had handed down.[2]

Just what happened to Judge Joseph Force Crater of the New York Supreme Court has never been satisfactorily established and probably now it never will be. On 6 August 1930 the 40-year-old judge simply disappeared off the face of the earth. He left Billy Haas' restaurant at 332 W 45th off Broadway, waved goodbye to a friend, caught a taxi and vanished.

Educated at Lafayette and gaining a law degree from Columbia before establishing a successful practice and forging political connections, he rose to the presidency of the Cayuga Democratic Club, a major part of the Tammany Hall connection. In April 1930 he was appointed to the Supreme Court by Roosevelt following the resignation of the magistrate Albert H. Vitali. This in turn followed a proven allegation that Vitali had borrowed $19,000 and change from the mobster Arnold Rothstein, whose killing would dog the administration of Mayor James Walker.

---

[1] For an account of the death of McSwiggin see Laurence Bergreen, *Capone*.
[2] Laurence Bergreen, *Capone*, p. 278; Robert J. Schoenberg, *Mr Capone*, p.196.

Crater's wife, Stella, who had married him after the judge acted for her in the divorce proceedings against her first husband, last saw him on 3 August when he returned to New York from their Augusta, Maine, country home. He had been intending to return six days later, she said, but when nothing was heard from him after ten days she despatched their chauffeur to try to find him. He returned with assurances from the judge's friends that all was well with him, but in fact he had vanished at least four days earlier. No one seems to have done very much until, when the judicial term began on 25 August and there was still no sign of Crater, they organised a search. Even then his disappearance was not reported to the police until 3 September.

As far as could be established, on the day of his disappearance Crater had been in his chambers and had an aide cash two cheques totalling $5,150. Where did he go? What happened to him? And why did he go? Earlier in the evening he had gone to the box office of the Arrow Theatre and asked for a ticket for the show *Dancing Partner*. He was told the performance was sold out but advised to come back for a return. He then dined with lawyer William Klein and a showgirl Sally-Lou Ritz. After dinner he said he was going to see *Dancing Partner* but, in fact, by the time he left Klein and Ritz at 9.15 the curtain had already gone up. Someone did collect the return, but the man at the box office could not remember if it was Crater. This of itself was surprising because the judge was distinctive, if not distinguished-looking. Heavyset, he had a very small head for the size of his body, so resembling a turtle. At the time New York cab drivers were required to keep records of all starting points and destinations. Despite this and rewards of $5,000 from the City and another $2,500 from the *New York World*, no driver came forward.

There were, of course, numerous sightings. He was working as a tout on a Hollywood racecourse; a beggar in Illinois: 'I didn't pull his whiskers, but I'm pretty sure they were false', said a Chicago housewife; an amnesia victim in the Missouri State Insane Asylum. Other sightings showed him to be a gold prospector in California, a tourist in Italy and, perhaps best of all, as late as 1946 the operator of an Arab-only – apart from himself, that is – bingo game in North Africa. There were also numerous confessions, generally by down-and-outs who wanted a whiff of notoriety and the food which for a time would accompany it.

Seven years after he disappeared, Crater was ruled legally dead and his widow remarried. She had been evicted from their apartment at 40 5th Avenue and worked as a secretary. On the pronouncement of his death she received $20,561 insurance monies. The cost of the search was estimated at $300,000. But Crater has lived on in cartoons and jokes, and as recently as 2002 Lawrence Block wrote a Crater joke into his novel *Small Town*.[3] Earlier, one hoaxer suggested the police raid a Montreal hotel where the good judge could be found in room 761. The raid duly took place, to the surprise and annoyance of a honeymoon couple.

In 1954 Henry Krauss, a German butcher, said Crater had used his house in Yonkers. Later he had returned home and found the kitchen full of bloodstains. Unfortunately Krauss died and the investigation did not proceed. Then in 1964 the Dutch psychic Gerard Croiset contacted the authorities to say the body could be found in New York, again in the Yonkers. He predicted that there would be an abandoned road, a small pond and three trees on a roadway to the site, with the body lying two and a half feet beneath the surface. This turned out to be the Krauss house, and there was considerable excitement when the spot, near Sprain Lake as described by Croiset, was found. The excitement was short-lived when the next day, after his men had turned over 15,000 cubic feet of soil, Sheriff John E. Fry told the press, 'There wasn't even a bone some dog might have buried for future reference.'

As to why the judge disappeared, that was seemingly almost as insoluble as the first question. Over a period of months a Grand Jury investigated his disappearance and heard the evidence of hundreds of witnesses, but it produced no solution. For a time there was a flurry of interest when it was announced that a chorine from Atlantic City would give evidence, but nothing came of it. The judge was known to have had a liking for showgirls and had had a long-standing mistress, Constance Braemer Marcus. Perhaps

---

[3] Indeed the fascination for the case continues. In 2005 a new study of the mystery, *The Disappearance of Judge Crater and the New York He Left Behind*, was published.

more importantly he had been a patron of the Broadway speakeasy Club Abbey, also patronised by Legs Diamond and Dutch Schultz. From time to time life could get quite exciting in the club, and it was there that Schultz fought Charles 'Chink' Sherman who shot him in the shoulder. Sherman was stabbed and clubbed with a chair. When Sherman came out of hospital he vowed vengeance, but in fact he ended dead on a county dump heap.

Crater's wife firmly believed his death was linked to corruption in the Cayuga Democratic Club. She was convinced he had been murdered because of 'a sinister something that was connected with politics'.[4] It is certainly possible that the cash the judge withdrew on the day of his disappearance was blackmail money, and that he was killed by people he knew at the Club Abbey. They – if no one else – could easily dispose of a body.

Despite the loyal protestations in his wife's book, Crater almost certainly was involved with at least three women of doubtful reputation. Elaine Dawn, a Ziegfeld girl who had been with him to the club, was one and June Brice, also known as Jean Covell, was another. She disappeared early in the investigation and was in and out of mental hospitals for the rest of her life until she died in 1948. More dangerously he was known to Vivian Gordon, said to have had 'five hundred sugar-daddies', to be an expert blackmailer, adroit at the badger game and a working friend of Abe Rothstein.

Then in 1955 Harry Stein made a confession shortly before he was to die for the killing of Andrew Petrini, a *Readers' Digest* messenger, in a botched $4,000 robbery in New Castle, New York, in 1950.[5] According to him, early in 1929 a man named Joe Lesser was indicted in New York City on first-degree forgery involving some $190,000 real-estate mortgages. At the time Crater was not

---

[4] See *inter alia* the *New York Times*, 5, 12, 17, 18 September, 12 October 1930, 26, 27 June 1964, 24 September 1969. Crater's wife, who died in 1969, wrote a book on the case, *The Empty Robe*.

[5] The robbery was planned by Calman Cooper while serving a sentence in Sing Sing. He recruited Stein, Nathan Wissner and Benjamin Dorfman to execute the robbery, and when Petrini did not respond quickly enough to their orders Wissner shot him. The case was broken when detectives persuaded Dorfman to turn State's evidence. As a reward he received ten to twenty years for manslaughter. Cooper, Stein and Wissner were electrocuted on 9 July 1955. See *White Plains Reporter-Dispatch*, 8, 9, 11 July 1955; *New York Times*, 10 July 1955.

yet a judge and he employed a man, 'Chowderhead' Cohen, as a private investigator. Cohen was acquainted with two men close to Lesser and they approached him to see if something could be done. Cohen enlisted Harry Stein and, through Crater connections, Lesser was guaranteed a walkout for $5,000 which was paid over. In February 1929 he was convicted. Stein knew the gangster Max 'Boo Hoo' Hoff in Philadelphia, and a deal was struck that he would arrange the return of the money from the judge. Through Vivian Gordon, Stein knew Crater's every move. He was kidnapped and, when he laughed at the suggestion that he should repay the $5,000, was shot in the back of the head at 2 p.m. on 13 August 1930. His body was put in acid and when it had dissolved sufficiently the remains were tipped into the Passaic River outside Clifton.[6]

In fact the story is not completely improbable and it harks back again to the 1930s Samuel Seabury inquiry into the payment by New York lawyers for appointments as magistrates and the general conduct of lawyers, police, bail bondsmen and magistrates in the Women's Court – a court specifically used to deal with female vagrants and prostitutes.

On 22 February 1931 Vivian Gordon was found strangled in Van Cortland Park with a rope knotted around her throat. Within four hours of Vivian Gordon's killing, Harold Stein was found in possession of her jewellery and coat. In her diary she had noted she had lent him $1,500, but when questioned Stein maintained he had no idea why she should make any entry about him at all. Earlier he served ten years in Sing Sing for choking a woman and stealing $250 in 1921.

Stein was defended by the great lawyer Samuel Leibowitz. The prosecution relied heavily on a taxi driver, Harry Schitten, who said he had been offered $1,000 to chauffeur a seven-passenger hired Cadillac that night. Vivian Gordon was led to believe her role was to relieve a sucker, Samuel Greenberg, of some $25,000 worth of diamonds. Once she was lured into the car she was taken to Van Cortland Park in the Bronx and strangled. Far from being a sucker,

---

[6] Camilo Weston Leyca in *American Weekly*, 23 September 1956.

the co-conspirator Greenberg was another player in the game. Very surprisingly, both Greenberg and Stein were acquitted.[7]

One of the lawyers who became a player rather than an adviser and died as a result was Samuel Rummel, the long-time representative of – and probably the brains behind – Mickey Cohen who, depending upon one's viewpoint, was either himself the Czar of California of the 1940s or a relatively small-time but thoroughly unpleasant mobster.[8]

On 11 December 1950 Rummel was shot in the back from about ten yards outside his home at 2600 Laurel Canyon Drive, Los Angeles. The weapon used was an unusual 12-gauge double-barrelled sawn-off Remington and was left in the crotch of a tree across the driveway from where the lawyer's body was found. It was traced back to Riley, Kansas, where it had been stolen as long ago as 1913. Although the police rounded up the usual suspects and more, no one was ever charged with the murder.

Rummel had been taking far too close an interest in the Normandie Club in Gardena where he had assumed a forty per cent interest. There had been no professional courtesy in the way he acquired his stake. Another lawyer, Charles W. Cradick, had been forced by Cohen to take $1,000 for the stake which passed to Rummel. He was also involved in the Guarantee Finance Company, in theory a legitimate loan company but in reality a front for a $6 million bookmaking operation. By December 1951 a Grand Jury was making vigorous attempts to investigate pay-offs to law-enforcement officers by the company. Later, it would be estimated that the pay-off totalled a little under a quarter of a million dollars.

On 6 December 1951 a highly secret meeting was held with the foreman of the Grand Jury, four county officials and two process servers who would serve summonses on potential witnesses for a hearing on 12 December. There were immediate leaks of information because the following day Rummel was busying himself calling meetings to determine a course of defence. The potential witnesses scattered.

On 9 December Rummel organised a meeting with Al Guasti, then a captain in the sheriff's office, arranging for him to meet that night

<hr>

[7] *New York Times*, 1, 22 July 1931.
[8] See John Roeburt, *Get Me Giesler*, Chapter III.

with Captain Carl Pearson, then head of the local Vice Squad, and his underling Sergeant Lawrence Schaffer. At Rummel's office Schaffer showed the lawyer confidential files from the sheriff's office dealing with the Guarantee case. It was accepted that apart from the gunman the three police officers were the last to see Rummel alive.

A number of theories for the death were floated, including the suggestions that Rummel was trying to cut a deal or, as the Grand July ruled, that he may have been making threats to 'someone to move over'. According to gangster Jimmy Fratianno, the killers of Rummel were Angelo Polizzi and Carlo Licata. He claimed he had watched them stake out Rummel's home, but gave no explanation for the killing.[9] There was also a suggestion that Rummel had failed to account properly for a war chest provided by the underworld to help unseat the Mayor.[10]

The 42-year-old Gino Gallina, a former District-Attorney turned Mafia defence lawyer, was another who crossed the line and for a few seconds must have regretted the words Grand Jury. Gallina ended his prosecutorial days under something of a cloud. In 1970 a witness in a 1967 murder case claimed that Gallina had pressured him into giving false evidence. He crossed over to defence work and for his pains some time later he was shot seven times in Greenwich Village on 4 November 1977. He had taken a young woman to dinner and was killed as they got out of their car at Carmine Street near Varick. His former colleagues were not surprised: 'He was well known to us as a Mob lawyer. We figured it would only be a matter of time before some disgruntled client would kill him. He had an extensive clientele of organised-crime big shots,' said a member of the District Attorney's office.

Responsibility for the contract on his former lawyer was later claimed by Donald Frankos, who said he was wearing black make-up at the time, along with his friend Joe 'Mad Dog' Sullivan who was disguised as a priest. What was particularly interesting about the killing was that Frankos was in prison at the time and had bribed his way into being given day release. It made for a perfect alibi.

---

[9] Ovid Demaris, *The Last Mafioso*.
[10] *New York Times*, *Los Angeles Times*, 12, 13 December 1950.

After being arrested and named as a co-conspirator in a narcotics case in 1975, Gallina had rolled over to the FBI and had been appearing in front of a Newark Grand Jury giving evidence about – amongst other things – Mafia executions by a special hit squad armed with .22-calibre automatic pistols. He was also giving evidence about how money was being laundered through real-estate deals. As an additional *bonne bouche*, he had, he said, hidden a tape giving details of the burial place of former Teamster leader Jimmy Hoffa. It was never found, and if one accepts the version of Hoffa's death from The Builder then the story is nonsense.[11] It was thought that there had been a leak from the Grand Jury. A spokesman for the FBI denied that Gallina had been wearing a wiretap or that he was working for the Feds.[12]

Of all the police forces over the years some officers in the Sydney, New South Wales, police of the 1970s and early 1980s must rank among the most corrupt. And corrupt police officers always like a bagman to act as the intermediary between themselves and the criminals from whom they are extracting favours, money or both. Brian Alexander was a solicitor's clerk who filled the position admirably.

Born in Sydney in 1939, although he often referred to himself as a solicitor he was not qualified and indeed did not do particularly well at St Anne's Marist Brothers School in Bondi. Initially he worked with Philip N. Roach, a solicitor with a practice dealing with lower-level criminals and the prostitutes of the King's Cross area. During this time he took correspondence courses to qualify either as a solicitor or barrister, but he never completed them. While employed by Roach he became known to – and later became the associate of – not only criminals convicted and not, but also a group of detectives in the New South Wales force.

Alexander worked for Roach for nearly twenty years and then changed firms and joined John Aston, a commercial lawyer who had aspirations for a practice with a quality criminal clientele. This was unusual. Normally a solicitor with a commercial practice would regard anything criminal, with the possible exception of a little high-class fraud, as being beneath him.

---

[11] See Chapter 4.
[12] *New York Times*, 5, 6 November 1977; *Time*, 21 November 1977; Donald Frankos, *Contract Killer*, pp. 325–6.

A major problem for police officers who accept bribes or lean on criminals is that one day, if it suits him or he feels the officer is taking more than his fair share, the criminal may turn. The authorities may well then be prepared to offer him a lesser sentence if he informs on the corrupt officer. A cut-out is therefore an extremely welcome addition to the game. He provides some guarantee of fair treatment to the criminal and some degree of protection to the officer and one of the men with whom Alexander dealt was the notorious Neddy Smith.

Smith, who would later serve a series of life sentences for murder and would be regarded as, if not proved to be, a killing machine, recalled his first meeting with Alexander:

> He was standing there looking like a combined advert for top brand-name fashions, like Simon Ackerman suits, Yves St Laurent shirts and Gucci shoes. He was decked out to impress, and impress he did. But still there was something missing.[13]

Smith had been charged with receiving something, which was not of itself too much of a problem. His difficulty was that he was still on parole for rape.[14] Alexander took some $3,000 from him to obtain bail on the receiving charge, and later came to his aid when Smith fell foul of Roger Caleb Rogerson and the force's Armed Hold-Up Squad when he was charged with shooting with intent to kill and armed robbery.[15] Despite Smith's quite appalling record and the seriousness of the charges, he was given bail and later acquitted of all the counts against him. Alexander later put himself about when Smith was found to have some $39,000 for which he could not account, and which the police said came from drug smuggling. Smith's half-brother had also been arrested, and Alexander sold Smith the statements his brother had allegedly made against him.

Smith then allegedly bought the whole of the evidence against him for $4,000, and was asked for $50,000 for the case to be

---

[13] Neddy Smith, *Catch and Kill Your Own*.

[14] In 1968 Smith and Robert Arthur Chapman received twelve years for raping a young mother after they broke into her home and threatened to drop her baby on its head if she screamed. They also threatened to bomb her house if she reported things to the police.

[15] For an account of crime and the police in New South Wales after the Second World War see James Morton, *Gangland International*.

dropped against his wife who was about to be charged. He paid the money, but the next day conspiracy charges were preferred. He sent for Alexander who refunded $25,000, saying the rest had gone to two police officers.

However, Alexander was involved not only with Smith but also with some seriously heavy players in international drug smuggling, members of the so-called Mr Asia Syndicate led by Terrence John Clark. What later emerged at the Stewart inquiry was that Alexander was a tried and trusted man on Clark's staff with valuable contacts in the Narcotics Bureau.[16] Witnesses told the Commission that if a member of the syndicate was arrested, Alexander would be contacted and would not only provide legal representation but would also report back to Clark on whether they were remaining staunch. On a legitimate income of $32,000, Alexander earned $130,000 in the year before his death.

On 9 June 1978 Douglas and Isabel Wilson were arrested by the Queensland Police in Brisbane. Although they were never charged, they spent some time providing information on tape on the workings of the Clark organisation. Through Alexander, Clark purchased copies of the tapes. On 18 May 1979 their bodies were found in a shallow grave in Danny Street, Rye, Victoria. They had both been shot by James Bazeley, who had also shot the anti-drug campaigner Donald Mackay.

On 25 March 1981 Alexander was arrested and charged with conspiracy with two Federal Narcotic Agents. The allegation was that the three of them had disclosed confidential information to Clark. The case was dismissed at the committal proceedings because the Crown could not prove the source of the leaks beyond doubt. It was, however, the end of Alexander's legal career; he was effectively unemployable and drifted into drink and working in hotels. Now it was learned that he was likely to give evidence and name names, dates, places and amounts. His position was untenable.

On 21 December 1981, shortly after he had been seen drinking with three men in the King's Head Tavern on Park Street, he

---

[16] Mr Justice D.G. Stewart, *Royal Commission of Inquiry into Drug Trafficking*, 1983.

disappeared. Two weeks later his car was found abandoned near The Gap at Watson's Bay, a place known for suicides.

According to Smith, however, Alexander was too much of a coward to commit suicide in that way and he heard a story that he had been driven to the Darling Street wharf in Balmain and, handcuffed behind his back, was thrown from a launch with an old gas stove tied around his body. He was apparently still alive and crying when he went in the water. Smith concludes this moral tale, 'But I had no part in it. That was something I wouldn't wish even on someone like Brian Alexander.'[17]

One of gangland's worst nightmares is to find that one's own lawyer has been working for the police. In 1993 it was made public that Sidney Leithman – lawyer to the cream of the Montreal underworld including Frank Cotroni and Frank Ryan, the head of the West End Gang – was a registered police informer. Cotroni was a controlling part of the Family who ran large portions of Montreal crime from the 1940s until the 1990s, and it was estimated that at one time Ryan employed some 300 people in his drug-dealing empire before he was lured to a room in Nittolo's Garden Motel on St Jacques Street, tied to a chair and shot.

Ultimately Leithman's double game proved fatal for him. From what leaked out, apparently it was in 1985 that he had first given information to the police in a drug investigation into a man who was not his client and was from outside Quebec. The information was good and the man was arrested. Well, perhaps that wasn't so reprehensible. In fact it helped preserve the status quo in the city. From then on Leithman really rather spoiled things as he acted as a coded informant if not a paid one:

> Once you're coded you always stay there. You stay in the system. You don't disappear. You stay there. So, you know, in 1993 I can really honestly tell you that, yeah he was coded at one time.[18]

[17] Neddy Smith, *Catch and Kill Your Own*, p. 115.
[18] Unnamed source quoted in William Marsden, 'Lawyer was informant, RCMP confirm' in *Montreal Gazette*, 13 April 1993.

For a time there was talk of the possibility of upsetting convictions in cases in which Leithman had been involved, but nothing came of it. Montreal lawyer Paul Skolnik wrote to the Solicitor General, Doug Lewis, asking whether Leithman was ever a coded informer and if so had he revealed any information about Vincent Lore – a former client convicted in 1991 of a drugs offence and sentenced to life imprisonment. The Solicitor General replied that Leithman was not a coded informant, but many were not satisfied.[19]

Whether Leithman was actually on the books really makes little difference. He was certainly in bed with the authorities and it is probable that word of his poor behaviour had leaked out sometime earlier, because at 6.48 a.m. on 13 May 1991 he was shot dead at the wheel of his black Saab convertible while at the junction of Jean Talon Street and Rockland Road. He had just left his Mount Royal home when a car cut him off at a traffic light. A man walked from a nearby telephone kiosk and shot him with a .45 gun, once at a distance of ten metres and then three times at close range. A bag of smoked meat was then contemptuously thrown onto his body. An autopsy showed traces of cocaine in his blood. His killer was never found. Nor, officially, was there ever a motive offered for his killing, although it was thought that with a developing cocaine habit the lawyer was becoming a liability. At the time of his death he was being investigated as a co-conspirator in the 1992 case of another of his clients, Alan Ross, charged with drug dealing in Florida. It was also thought that the US Government was considering charging him with obstructing the course of justice. Drug dealers reported that he had been bribing them not to talk to the police. If he had been charged and had himself rolled over, the potential damage would have been enormous.

Leithman's death was linked to that of a senior RCMP officer, Inspector Claude Savoie. In December 1992 Savoie, who was second in command and then head of the Drug Squad between 1988 and his death, shot himself in his office just before he was due to be interviewed by internal affairs investigators regarding his contacts with Leithman. When Leithman was shot he had Savoie's telephone number in his pocket, and before his death Savoie told Montreal

---

[19] *Montreal Gazette*, 5 May 1993.

police that the lawyer had been his informant. It was known that, with no other officers present, Savoie had met with Leithman and Ross in the lawyer's office and at a restaurant on Phillips Square. At the time, Ross was under investigation by the United States Drug Enforcement Administration.

Generally, Montreal has not been that safe a city for its dodgier criminal lawyers. Some eight years earlier Frank Shoofey, who over the years had also acted for many of the city's finest including the Dubois family and Richard Blass, was killed on 15 October 1985 at 11.30 p.m., shot in the hallway of his offices at Cherrier Street. At the time of his death he was locked in a struggle to prevent Frank Cotroni from taking over the interests of the Hilton boxing brothers, and trying to keep the American promoter Don King from co-promoting the contest between Matthew Hilton and Vito Antuofermo. Shoofey, who spent much of his spare time working with inner-city children and trying to get the Liberal nomination in the Saint-Jacques district of the city, was described as . . . 'a shameless publicity hound but also a social benefactor of the highest order'.[20] Curiously, it was in the same hallway that Shoofey's client Pierre Quintal was shot in May 1979 while awaiting trial on a charge of manufacturing narcotics. Although Shoofey and a receptionist were in his office they heard nothing. The year before Shoofey's death, four men were acquitted of that killing.[21]

Lawyers have always been at their most vulnerable when they are – or criminals think they are – about to pull a number of plugs, as François Payette, a lawyer who specialised in commercial cases, discovered. In February 1966 he was found shot in his Thunderbird in north-end Montreal. He had no criminal practice or connections, but his misfortune was that he had arranged to talk with police about a bogus bankruptcy in the building industry. The information was leaked before the meeting could take place. Loose lips cost lives, and the life in this case was that of Payette.

Another wholly innocent solicitor was Melbourne-based Keith Allan, killed because he was too trusting for too long – and also because he was about to whistle-blow. Not the most gifted of men,

[20] Kirk Makin in *The Globe and Mail*, 26 October 1985.
[21] *Montreal Gazette*, 17 October 1985.

he nevertheless made a fair living until he employed Julian Michael Clarke as a law clerk in 1995. Unfortunately Clarke had a taste for casino life and soon some $2.7 million found its way out of the client account. With Allan one step from going to the police, Clarke contacted Costas 'Con' Athanasi, curiously the cousin of Peter Kypri whose family had been at risk from another crooked lawyer.[22] In turn Athanasi recruited Sudo Cavkic whom he knew from playing indoor soccer. Allan's body was never found, although the police discovered his blue Mercedes with a shovel and hoe covered with soil on the back seat. Clarke received a minimum of twenty-five years, Athanasi a year less and Cavkic twenty-three.[23]

One lawyer who may have been killed simply for doing the best for her client is the Hamilton, Canada-based Lynn Gilbank, executed in her own bed at her home on Postans Path on 15 November 1998. At about 5.30 a.m. her husband Fred opened the front door and was shot. The killer then went to the Gilbank bedroom and shot the lawyer. The killing of her husband had simply been because he was in the way.

There was no suggestion that Mrs Gilbank had been involved in any extra-curricular activity, rather that the killing was because she had managed to get a mule into the Witness Protection Program in a high-profile drug-smuggling case. The police believe that while it was a gangland execution it was not ordered by the traditional Italian Mafia – who have long held a significant place in Ontarian crime – nor was it Biker-ordered. One convicted drug smuggler told the local newspaper that he believed the police were wrongly trying to pin the murder on him and his brothers. By the end of 2004 no one had been charged with the murder.[24]

One of the greatest hooks criminals can use to gain control over their lawyers is sex and one of the saddest of such stories, of a lawyer who mixed with the *mafiya* to his fatal cost, is that of New Zealand-born Hong Kong lawyer Gary Alderdice and his lover Natalya Samofalova.

[22] See Chapter 11.
[23] John Silvester, 'The Anatomy of a Suburban Hit' in *The Age* (Melbourne), 31 July 2004.
[24] *Hamilton Spectator*, 16 November 2003. For an account of the ramifications of the case in which two criminals have sued the police see James Morton, *Gangland Today*.

From 1973 the volatile Alderdice had worked as a prosecutor in Hong Kong before resigning and switching to defence work, when he became known as 'Never Plead Guilty Gary'. Within a short time he had became one of Hong Kong's leading criminal lawyers and, on an island where the shores were washed with money, this meant both substantial wealth and a position in society. Along with it also came the collapse of his second marriage to Pippa, the ex-wife of a friend and colleague.

It was then that Alderdice started making trips on the hydrofoil to Macau, then a Portuguese colony, a little under an hour away. While the horse-racing there was not up to the standard of Hong Kong's Happy Valley and Sha Tin, there was legal casino gambling. Macau had been invaded by Russian *mafiya* who were working with the local Triad organisations; it also had a whole army of Russian prostitutes, mainly from the Vladivostock area and euphemistically described as hostesses and dancers, working the hotel circuit. Amongst them was an exceptionally attractive strawberry blonde, Natalya Samofalova. Her contract had been signed in Macau and as protection for themselves, very sensibly, the local Triads had retained her work papers.

For Alderdice it was a question of love at first sight, and it does seem to have been reciprocated. He took up with Samofalova in early April 1994 and the pair stayed first in his hotel room and then in a cottage at the Westin Resort until 9 May. Then came Alderdice's fatal mistake. Genuinely in love with her, he refused to pay her owners for her services. When her papers came up for renewal the local Triads refused to return them to her and she was obliged to leave.

Alderdice returned to Hong Kong and on 23 June flew to Vladivostock where he was met by Samofalova at the airport. It was said that he had taken with him approximately $150,000. The next day Samofalova's mother called at her flat, could get no reply and with the help of a neighbour pried open the steel door. Inside she found both Alderdice and her daughter, who seemed to have been tortured, dead. $20,000 was later found in the ransacked apartment.

The most prevalent rumour was that Alderdice had taken the money to buy his girlfriend's contract, but they had been killed to demonstrate the power of the *mafiya*. In some stories all the money was left untouched. Other versions of the reason for the killing included the KGB, involvement in the smuggling of nuclear weapons and an exotically-named substance, red mercury.

Five years after the killings came a confession from a woman the police would initially identify only as Olga but who was thought to be a heroin-addicted prostitute, Olga Bogdacheuskaia, who had worked with Samofalova. Her version of events was much more prosaic. It had been a simple case of robbery; she and her husband had been persuaded to rob the pair. Alderdice was talking with her and her husband in the kitchen of the apartment when he heard a scream from the living room. He had rushed in and was shot in the eye. Samofalova was tied to a chair and tortured to make her reveal the whereabouts of the money, but according to Bogdacheuskaia only $2,000 was found.

Unfortunately for the police Bogdacheuskaia, dying from her addiction, did just that four days later. Her husband subsequently denied the story and a mystery 'second man', who actually shot Alderdice and who was regarded as a street-level hood rather than a mastermind, was thought to have died in a gangland killing back in 1995.[25] However, it is one of those stories where the suspects are conveniently dead or untouchable. It may be just another instance where fiction is more romantic than the truth, but it still serves as a warning to lawyers who find that their hearts are located around the seventh waistcoat button.

Over the years it was believed that judges were untouchable if only because of the wrath any assault, let alone a fatal one, would produce, and in the main English judges have been free from attack. Indeed worldwide attacks have generally come from the outraged or deranged litigants rather than from organised crime. The worst attack on an English judge occurred on 26 July 1898 when the Manchester County Court judge Edward Parry was shot. He had been trying an action between two bailiffs and, as he was noting his judgment, the loser William Taylor approached the bench and shot him in the face and neck. He was immediately arrested. Parry survived and very

[25] *The Vancouver Sun*, 16 May 2000.

charitably sent a message saying he wished Taylor no ill will. When charged Taylor, a lay preacher with a history of mental instability, replied, 'It must be so, I suppose; it was done by satanic influence.' In the November Taylor was found guilty of attempted murder and the jury recommended leniency. However, the court was not prepared to pass a sentence which might be interpreted as encouragement to other dissatisfied litigants. The 55-year-old Taylor received twenty years penal servitude.[26]

In the early years of the twentieth century one Californian prosecutor survived a courtroom assassination attempt when Francis J. Heney was seriously wounded during an afternoon recess in the trial of Abe Ruef. A small, nondescript man with greying hair shot him while he was talking to court staff. The dubious lawyer Earl Rogers was suspected of complicity, although he was not at the time acting for Ruef. It turned out to be Morris Hass, a man with a conviction many years earlier who now had a wife and family and had held down a job. He had been called for jury service, and in the *voir dire* Heney had ruthlessly exposed Hass's well-hidden past life to the public. Hass lost his job and, as an ex-convict, could not obtain another. As a result he shot Heney and, after he was arrested, hanged himself in his cell.[27]

In Australia judges again seem to have been at risk from the run-of-the-mill litigant. On 23 June 1980 Judge David Opas was shot and killed as he opened the security gate of his home in Wollahra. He had been sitting in the family court and had a daily list of forty or more cases. On 6 March 1984 the home of his replacement Judge Richard Gee was bombed, blowing out the front of the house but leaving the family miraculously unharmed; it was estimated that fifty sticks of dynamite had been used. Four months later Pearl Watson, the wife of Judge Ray Watson, was killed when she opened a suitcase packed with explosives. It was reckoned that of the thousands of cases the Family Court handled annually, some fifteen to twenty per cent of one or other of the parties had mental problems.[28]

Naturally it has not been the same in America. In May 1979 Judge John Wood, 63 years old and known as 'Maximum John'

---

[26] *The Times*, 27, 28 July, 16 November 1898.
[27] See Adele Rogers St Johns, *Final Verdict*, Chapter 36.
[28] *Sydney Morning Herald*, 24 June 1980, 7 March 1984.

because of his tough sentencing in drug cases, became the first Federal judge in America to be killed. Wood, a judge of eight years' standing, was shot in the back with a single dum-dum bullet as he went to get into his car in the parking lot of his apartment block in San Antonio, Texas, on 29 May.[29] He was pronounced dead on arrival at the Northeast Baptist Hospital in the city. Almost immediately the police announced that they were seeking a curly-haired man aged about twenty who had been seen driving a small red car.

However, the killer was not a 20-year-old but Charles V. Harrelson, the son of a prison guard, and father of the actor and star of *Cheers* Woody Harrelson, who on 14 December 1982 was convicted of being the hitman in a $250,000 contract. He received life imprisonment.

Wood was, in fact, the third man whom Harrelson had been charged with killing. Described by historian John H. Davis as a Dallas-based racketeer, in 1968 he had been acquitted of the murder of a carpet salesman but in 1973 was convicted of killing a grain dealer in Texas. For this he received fifteen years and was paroled some eight months before the killing of Wood. By the time he came up for trial on that murder charge, he was already serving sentences totalling forty years for cocaine and weapons offences.[30] Harrelson has been described as a man of charm who at times looked out of place facing a charge of murder, but also as someone without respect for authority. He is quoted as saying:

> The Gestapo is alive and well and highly refined and doing business as usual in Washington D.C. First they pick on the ones that are easy to deal with like me, but before long they'll be herding all you poor bastards into boxcars that don't go anywhere and showers without water.[31]

---

[29] Kirk Wilson, *Investigating Murder*.

[30] John H. Davis comments on allegations that Harrelson was one of three 'tramps' arrested in Dealey Plaza immediately after the assassination of President Kennedy. Jack White, a Fort Worth graphics expert who testified on the identity of the tramps before the House Select Committee on Assassinations in 1978, had concluded without reservation that Harrelson was the youngest tramp. He also points out that when Harrelson was arrested for the Wood murder he had a business card of Russell D. Mathews, another Dallas man who had been a close associate of Jack Ruby in the 1960s and who had documented connections to both Santos Trafficante and Carlos Marcello. *Mafia Kingfish*, p. 470.

[31] Teresa H. Anderson, U.P.I., 14 December 1982.

Certainly he was a man with considerable charm for women. Tape recordings made secretly while he was in prison have him promising three women that he loved and wished to marry them.

The prosecution alleged that Harrelson had killed Wood in a contract bought by El Paso drugs dealer Jimmy Chagra, a one-time rug salesman who by then had an empire stretching from Florida to Las Vegas running marijuana. He was also known as a high-rolling gambler who had once paid off a $900,000 casino debt in cash and had lost a $580,000 game of golf. Chagra had been found guilty on drug-smuggling charges and was due to appear for sentencing before Maximum John.

It would seem that the contract was suggested to Chagra by his El Paso lawyer brother, Joseph, who was then indicted on charges of lying to a Grand Jury investigating the killing of the judge as well as an attempt on the life of US Attorney James Kerr. Known also to be harsh on drug cases, on 21 November 1978 Kerr was shot at, six blocks from where Wood was later killed, as he drove to work. He escaped by ducking down under the dashboard. Joseph Chagra, who had been recorded talking with his brother in the investigation into the BRILAB scam, was given immunity from prosecution and allegedly had discussed the murder.[32]

Chagra's wife Elizabeth was also found guilty in the drugs conspiracy and Harrelson's third wife, Jo Ann, was found guilty of obstructing the course of justice. The prosecution alleged she had bought the murder weapon. Elizabeth Chagra's conviction was overturned and a re-trial set.

Jimmy Chagra, then in his late thirties, was acquitted on the murder charge but received a total of forty-seven years for drug smuggling and impeding the course of justice over the Wood killing. His brother Joseph pleaded guilty to conspiracy to kill the judge and received a ten-year sentence; he was paroled in 1988.

Joseph Chagra then gave evidence against his sister-in-law Elizabeth, saying that although she had no part in the decision to

---

[32] BRILAB (after bribery and labor) was a Justice Department nationwide sting operation begun in 1979 to investigate 'criminally involved labor officials' suspected of being involved in illegal activities in association with leaders of organised crime. One of the targets was the New Orleans alleged racketeer Carlos Marcello.

have Wood killed she had delivered the pay-off of $250,000. She maintained that she thought the money was to pay off some of her husband's gambling debts, and she did not know its destination until Joe Chagra told her. Convicted again after her re-trial, she was sentenced to thirty years in prison. Eligible for parole in 1992, she had not been released when she died of cancer in 1997.

In a case which has rumbled on over the years, Harrelson has always denied his involvement in the killing of Wood, saying that he had simply been trying to con Chagra out of $250,000. The case was reopened in 2000 in Denver where Harrelson was being held. Now he endeavoured to overturn the conviction, alleging that the government had lied and that it was in collusion with his defence lawyer.

Since the Wood case there have been more killings of Federal judges. In 1987 Robert Daronco was shot by Charles Koster, a retired police officer, while he was gardening. The shooting occurred two days after he had dismissed a sexual-harassment suit brought by the daughter of the officer. Koster then killed himself.

In 1989 Judge Robert Vance was killed by a mail-bomb which had been sent to his home in Birmingham, Alabama. Initially it was thought he had been the target of Colombian drug dealers, but this was soon discounted. The same year Maryland Judge J.P. Corderman lost part of his hand when a bomb exploded in his apartment. He too was known for heavy sentencing.

In the Vance case, in which Walter Leroy Moody junior was charged with his murder and that of a Savannah civil-rights lawyer Robert Robinson, judges were quite willing to recuse themselves. In February 1990 the entire US Court of Appeals for the 11th Circuit stood itself down in a civil suit growing out of a Federal investigation of the mail-bomb murders. All three judges in the Middle District of Georgia then withdrew when a separate Federal prosecution accused Moody and his wife of tampering with a witness.

This did not satisfy Moody or his lawyers, who wanted the recusal of all United States judges and magistrates and for the Senate Judiciary Committee to appoint an 'independent judicial officer'.[33]

---

[33] Jane Okrasinski, 'Who tries a colleague's killer' in *Legal Times*, 26 November 1990.

He did not manage it and Moody was convicted on 28 June 1991 in St Paul, Minnesota, on seventy-one Federal counts; he was given seven life terms plus 400 years. The killing of the judge and the civil rights lawyer was part of a vendetta which he had waged against the court system following his release from a sentence imposed in 1972 for possessing bomb-making equipment, coupled with his belief that black people received preferential treatment over whites.

More recently District Judge Mark Luitjen had round-the-clock protection from the Texas Rangers for two months while police investigated a plot to kill him. The threat followed Luitjen's refusal to recommend that a higher court hear an appeal of Robert E. Lee whom he had sentenced in 1997 to twenty-five years for the attempted murder of his wife. In that case the two would-be hitmen were convicted of attempted murder and received 15-25-year terms. The plan had been to make it appear that the murder had taken place during a burglary.

After the case it is alleged that Lee and his friend, a high school teacher Carroll Parker, had tried to raise the money to hire a hitman to kill the judge. The prosecution claimed that the plan came to nothing when the potential hitman turned out to be an undercover officer.

A judge who became involved with the Mob died both denying and regretting it. The beneficiary of his kindness was the fearsome Chicago hitman Harry Aleman. Judge Frank J. Wilson in May 1977, holding a bench trial without a jury, had acquitted the mobster of the 1972 murder of Teamsters Union steward William Logan, estimated to be the 1,015th known Mob killing in and around the city. The next year Aleman was described by Robert D. Rose, of the Justice Department, as a 'man who kills human beings in cold blood'. Over the years Aleman was also suspected of killing both Richard Cain and Anthony J. Reitinger, a freelance bookie who had been shot by two masked men in a Northwest Side Chicago restaurant in 1975. More importantly Aleman, of Mexican descent, was believed to be the Mexican connection to the Mob and was a prime suspect in the murder of Sam Giancana. Unfortunately for both Wilson and Aleman, the Logan case resurfaced twenty years later when it was discovered that a $10,000 bribe had been paid for the acquittal. Protesting that he had been placed in double jeopardy, Aleman was re-tried and convicted. The judge, denying in the teeth of the evidence that he had accepted a bribe, committed suicide at his ranch in Arizona in 1993. Aleman, who is serving 100–300 years, had his parole application rejected in December 2002.[34]

The killings by the Italian Mafia of judges and police officers who were actively working against them have continued. Despite major security, judges have been singularly vulnerable not only to the Kalashnikov-bearing motorcycle pillion passenger but to the bomb. On 23 May 1992 Giovanni Falcone, who had been a major scourge of the Mafia, decided to take a short break with his wife and go home for the weekend to Palermo. They drove in a motorcade to a military airport in Rome and took the flight to Sicily. Someone in the Ministry of Justice betrayed them and, at the turn-off to Capaci, a two-ton bomb exploded in the road. Falcone and three bodyguards died instantly; his wife, Francesca, died five hours later from her injuries. Twenty other bodyguards and civilians were injured. His colleague, Paolo Borsellino, vowed to continue the fight but survived for only a few months. He too was blown up when leaving his mother after a Sunday visit on 19 July that year.[35]

On 29 July 1993 Antonio Gioe was found in his Rome prison cell hanged from the bars by his shoelaces. He was known to have been at Palermo airport when Falcone's plane landed, and was thought to have been the one who passed on the message. In the past year he had become prone to mistakes, and there was speculation that he killed himself to spare his family from the reprisals which were then commonly being wrought.

Drive-by shootings of lawyers have become common in South America, and they are no longer so unusual in Europe. However, it is not always clear who has ordered the execution. On 18 December 1996 Neapolitan lawyer Aniello Arcella was killed as he drove home shortly after midnight. Four killers on two motorcycles overtook his

[34] Robert Cooley, *When Corruption Was King*; Maurice Possey and Rich Kogan, *Two Men, One Murder and the Price of Truth*; Gavin Scott, 'An Evocative Tale of Crime in Chicago' in *Chicago Tribune*, 30 September 2001; *Chicago Tribune*, 28 December 2002; 'A Death Wish' in *Chicago Tribune*, 20 August 2004.
[35] *The Sunday Times*, 31 May 1992; *Time*, 3 June 1996; Paul Lunde, *Organized Crime*; Andrew Stille, *Excellent Cadavers*.

car on either side and opened fire. Arcella had once defended both Luigi Giuliano and Raffaele Stolder, two heads of the Camorra who started as allies and ended as enemies. He had also been suspected of helping organised crime figures, including Stolder, to avoid prosecution rather more than a lawyer should.

As gangs have become less controlled and their members younger, the old rules have been scrapped. For a time it was believed that the young and extremely unpleasant Boston-based Intervale Gang (named after the street from which members operated) killed a prosecutor. Paul R. McLaughlin, a special Assistant Attorney General assigned to prosecute gang crimes, was shot on 25 September 1995 near the railway station in commuterland West Roxbury. It was a killing of which gang members boasted.

But the longer the investigation went on, the more it seemed that the claims were largely just that. In July 1997 a Grand Jury began hearing evidence about McLaughlin's murder, focusing on Jeffrey Bly, a member not of Intervale but of the rival Theodore Street Gang. The day after his death McLaughlin had been due to prosecute Bly on car-jacking charges for which the youth was later given ten to fifteen years. Bly, who was now given life without parole for the murder, had remarked just before he shot McLaughlin, 'He's not my D.A. any more.'

On 5 June 2000 Commonwealth Attorney Fred Capps was shot and killed in his home in Burkesville. Dying, he returned the fire and killed his attacker, a man he was due to prosecute that day. He was the third prosecutor to be killed in the past twenty years. In January 1982, Florida prosecutor Eugene Berry had been shot to death by Bonnie Kelly, whose husband was being prosecuted by him.

In the 12 months ending in 1999 there were just under five hundred threats logged against judges and prosecutors in America. Seventy Federal judges and prosecutors were assigned round-the-clock security which lasted three or more days. In Texas, a judge who sentenced a man who hired a hitman to kill his wife and make it appear a burglary gone wrong, spent two months of 2000 under twenty-four-hour surveillance. The man's girlfriend, a schoolteacher no less, was arrested for trying to drum up the funds to pay another hitman – the two in the first case were now in prison. Fortunately the man she chose was an undercover agent.

Any gang worth its name will have a tame doctor on call to patch up bullet and knife wounds, so saving the police from the necessity of troubling the health services. Perhaps the most famous of gangsters' doctors was Joseph Patrick Moran – no relation to Bugsy, on whose payroll he appeared for a time. Moran had started life well enough, qualifying with honours from Tufts Medical School. Convicted twice of performing illegal abortions, he then worked as the quasi-resident house physician for Al Capone.

One version of his death is that in 1934 Fred Barker and Alvin Karpis paid him $1,000 to change their appearances. Moran was drunk and he botched all his work, leaving the men in extreme pain for weeks. When the bandages came off Karpis was, if possible, even uglier than before, and he had merely burned away the top skin on the men's fingers. Moran was taken by Barker and Karpis to Toledo where he was shot and dumped in a lake. Another theory is that after the Battle of Little Bohemia in April 1934 he refused to treat John 'Red' Hamilton, who later died at a Barker-Karpis hideout in Aurora, Illinois. This, together with his unreliability in drink, caused him to be shot after John Dillinger's death. The third version is that while in drink he was boasting in the Casino Club near Toledo where he was last seen that, 'I have you guys in the palms of my hands.' Later Fred Barker is said to have remarked, 'Doc will do no more operating. The fishes probably have eat him up by now.'

Now techniques have improved. In February 1997, 68-year-old Dr José Castillo was convicted of harbouring a fugitive and obstructing justice. He had been the confidant of Philadelphia drug lord Richie Ramos, whose face he had successfully altered after he disappeared in 1990. He also sliced 50 lbs of fat from his waist and cheeks and turned his fingerprints upside down. Ramos was not found until 1992 when, offered the chance of thirty years instead of life without parole, he agreed to give evidence against Castillo. In court Ramos did what he could for his doctor by failing to recognise him in a courtroom identification where the choices were Castillo, a 39-year-old lawyer and a young woman, but the damage had been done. At least the good doctor lived.

Not so in the case of Dr Jaime Godoy Singh, who had the misfortune to lead the team of surgeons who operated on the Mexican drug baron Amado Carrillo Fuentes in an effort to change his appearance. Fuentes died following a heart attack during a liposuction operation to remove 15 lbs from his stomach on 3 July 1997 at Santa Monica Hospital, Mexico City. Reprisals were not long in coming. In November that year the tortured bodies of Singh and two colleagues were found in oil drums, dumped on the Mexico City–Acapulco highway in Guerrero.

Drug gangs in Colombia are now recruiting children as hitmen and women. Just as there are schools to teach the art of pickpocketing, so there are now murder schools where children first learn on dogs. One boy aged eight, thought to have killed thirty people, was arrested and released as too young to charge. He was shot the same evening.[36]

[36] *Deutsche Press-Agentur*, 17 October 2004.

14

They Were Expendable

Although some have had long and often surprisingly healthy lives, as a profession informers have always been amongst those most at risk. And not only professional informers, as Arnold Schuster, a Broadway garment salesman, discovered to his cost after the capture of the bank robber Willie Sutton. Nicknamed 'Willie the Actor', he was on the FBI's Most Wanted list following prison escapes in 1932 and again in 1947 when he and Frederick J. Tenuto, known as 'The Angel' or 'St John', along with three others, escaped from the Holmesburg penitentiary in Pennsylvania under a hail of gunfire. A master of disguise, Sutton remained at liberty until 18 February 1952.

Sutton was caught because the 24-year-old Schuster had spotted him in a New York subway a month earlier and trailed him until he found a policeman. Unfortunately Schuster did not keep anything resembling a low profile and appeared on television to give interviews during his fifteen minutes of fame. On 9 March he was found shot in both eyes and the groin on the street where he lived. The order for his killing came from Albert Anastasia, who had a consummate dislike of informers.[1] The killer was almost certainly Tenuto,

---

[1] See Carl Sifakis, *The Encyclopedia of American Crime*. Because of public opinion over the killing of Schuster, Sutton received a sixty-year sentence. On his release in 1969 he became a security consultant to a number of banks. He died on 2 November 1980 while living in retirement in Spring Hill, Florida.

himself on the FBI's list after the 1947 prison break. He had already escaped in 1942 and again in 1945. Tenuto was never captured, principally because it is almost certain he was killed shortly afterwards, again on the orders of Anastasia, to eliminate the vital link in the chain of command. It is thought that he was buried in a double-decker coffin. In 1964 he was presumed dead by the FBI and his name removed from the Most Wanted list.

Although grasses in every country have always been at risk, the death rate for them in England has been on the low side. Bertie Smalls, the original British supergrass of the 1970s, claimed that he had never been seriously inconvenienced in his later life although there were underworld reports of a knife attack on him. Maurice O'Mahoney, his successor, survived and a third man from the 1970s, Donald Barrett, who was a supergrass on no fewer than two occasions and an informer on another, still found people willing to work with him.

The survival of these three major players in the underworld can be measured against the fate of the relatively low-level Alan 'Chalky' White who disappeared in February 1989. He had been due to give evidence against a Danny Gardiner with whom, so White said, he had robbed a petrol station in Slough in 1986. The take had been rather under £5,000. White, who had a drug problem, declined a new identity and instead was given a panic button. Most nights he could be found in The Crown public house near his home in Minchington, Gloucestershire, but when he disappeared he was seen walking to an off-licence. His body was found three months later wrapped in tarpaulin at the Cotswold Water Park; he had been stabbed in the heart. The case against Gardiner collapsed. It was through Interpol that Gardiner, who for a time was wrongly thought to have died in Cairo, was traced to Israel. On 4 January 1991 he returned voluntarily, and was later convicted of White's murder.

It was a time for grasses to take care. In 1990 an informer, who had told of a planned contract which resulted in the arrest of the hitman, was killed in Germany. The whole process could not be described as a success. The prosecution declined to reveal his identity at the time of the trial and the case was abandoned. He and his family had been resettled at a cost of around £100,000. A second killing took place in Amsterdam; this time the man had given information about drug traffickers. The third was in Ireland. The withdrawal of the case seems to have tipped off the identity of the informer.

One of the more celebrated names – if only through his son – of a grass who was killed was Edward J. O'Hare, known as Artful Eddie, Al Capone's silent partner in greyhound racing. He tipped off the authorities that the jury in Capone's 1931 income tax case had been tampered with. Revenge, as the Sicilians say, is a dish best eaten cold, and for O'Hare it was a decade in coming. On 8 November 1942 O'Hare was shot to death while driving along Ogden Avenue, Chicago, a bare week before Capone was due for release. Chicago's O'Hare airport is named not after him but his son, an ace fighter-pilot in the Second World War.[2]

Contracts may be a long time in their execution. They may come and go; be suspended, cancelled, bought off, renewed. One man on whom they were regularly issued was the one-time Frank Cotroni chauffeur in Toronto, the former boxer Eddie 'Hurricane' Melo. There is no suggestion that he was a grass, but his death was certainly a long time in coming. As early as November 1989 there was said to be a definite $15,000 contract on him.

That month he and an underworld associate, Frank Roda, were told by the Combined Forces Special Enforcement unit that they had learned there was a contract out for each of them. A former biker, John Avery, who had met Melo in the Don jail in Toronto and liked him, said that back in 1985 he had been rather vaguely offered $10,000 by Danny Cappuccitti to kill Melo, but the contract had lapsed. It had been renewed when Melo had first given what was described as a 'tune-up' to one of Cappuccitti's crew, and then had given Larry Cappuccitti (Danny's younger brother) a public slapping in a College Street pool hall.

Two months earlier Melo, along with Roda, had been involved in the beating of a Toronto car dealer also named Frank. The salesman Frank had been owed money by Roda following a drug deal and, in an effort to get his payment, he had refused to hand over a car to a woman friend of both Melo and Roda. Sweet talking

---

[2] For an account of O'Hare's dealings with Capone see Laurence Bergreen, *Capone*.

had failed to persuade the dealer to release the car, and a beating in a Toronto tile factory was the 'tune-up' referred to.

The figure offered to Avery, which was to include Roda, was now $30,000. Melo's and Roda's bodies were to be wrapped in garbage bags around the neck with the heads covered, and tied tightly so that no blood leaked out. However, Avery was by now a police informer and was wearing a wire. The police took Melo and Roda into protective custody outside Toronto and two wrapped dummies were left in a van parked in the Yorkdale Holiday Inn car park. When Avery met Danny Cappuccitti the following morning to ask for the balance of his money he was asked for a full description of the killings, telling his paymaster how he had kidnapped the pair at gunpoint and then shot them on the floor of a stolen van. Danny Cappuccitti and his brother Vincent pleaded guilty to conspiracy to murder and received eight years six months and three years respectively.

Roda was unhappy over the sentences, which he believed were far too lenient. On 8 July 1991 he and David Gabor Fisher blew themselves up while planting a pipe bomb in a lane near to a Cappuccitti business. Roda lost a hand and Fisher suffered severe wounds to his leg. Both were later imprisoned for this failed enterprise.

It was another ten years before Melo was finally dealt with, shot and killed in a Mississauga parking lot along with his friend Joao (Joe) Pavao on 6 April 2001 by Charles Gagné, another who at the time was on day release from prison.[3] For some while it was thought that Melo's death was just part of the then current Montreal power struggle, but in fact it appears it was a personal matter. Gagné, who took the contract on behalf of a Delio Manuel Pereira, pleaded guilty in September 2003, in a bargain which allowed him the possibility of parole after twelve years. In December 2003 Pereira pleaded guilty to conspiracy to murder. It appears this was a completely new contract.

On the other hand, Leicester's Jason Hill lasted a mere four years. In 1995 he was accused of shooting Eugene Hinds in a field off Gartree Road, Oadby. Despite the evidence of Kevin Finnemore who had been the driver, Hill and another man were acquitted. Finnemore

---

[3] For those interested in Melo's career in and out of the ring see James Morton, *Gangland Today*.

received five years. On 25 December 1999 in turn Hill was shot at the Eden nightclub in Leicester. He had told the police that he thought there was a contract on him, and he was right.[4]

Overall there has not been a high mortality rate amongst British witnesses, at least not a published one. However, one case with a most extraordinary death rate was that of Alan McCandless, charged with the murder on 18 November 1980 of Glaswegian John Docherty, a one-time cat burglar who had worked with Archie Hall, the murdering butler, and who at the time of his death controlled prostitutes in the King's Cross area. By the summer of 1982 five prosecution witnesses had died. Patricia McClellan was shot, and the dismembered body of Pat Malone was found in Epping Forest, that happy dumping ground of the London criminal, while yet another took a heroin overdose. The fourth seems to have died from natural causes, and the fifth drank himself to death. Finally, the case aborted in July 1982 when former bouncer 'Big' James Gibson failed to appear and, despite being under surveillance, they could not find him in time. Shortly before the trial the detective sergeant – described as Gibson's 'minder and mentor' for ten years – went abroad on holiday, leaving him in the care of two other detective sergeants. Gibson simply walked out of his girlfriend's flat in Leicester in the middle of the night, leaving behind his clothes and car. At an earlier trial which collapsed, Gibson told the jury he had been offered £500 to kill Docherty. Two days after the case was finished Gibson telephoned the *Leicester Mercury* to say he was safe and well and would surrender himself in a short while. In another twist Malcolm MacDougall appeared at the Old Bailey accused of making a false confession in the case. Since he was now serving a life sentence for wounding a shopkeeper in a robbery, the charge was left on the file.[5] Five hundred pounds seems to have been a fair price for the contract. That year George Bradshaw, also known as Maxie Piggot, told the Old Bailey that he had been paid the sum of £1,000 to kill the rather higher-profile 'Italian' Tony Zomparelli.

The McCandless case was echoed in the 1992 trial of brothers Tony and Patrick Brindle, charged with the murder of Ahmed

[4] *The Sun*, 27 December 1999; *Leicester Mercury*, 28 October 2000.
[5] *The Times*, 29 July 1982; *Daily Record*, 29, 30, 31 July 1982; *Leicester Mercury*, 31 July 1982.

'Turkish Abbi' Abdullah in the crowded William Hill betting shop in Walworth. One witness committed suicide and two others disappeared. The remainder were permitted to give evidence behind screens and were identified by numbers rather than their names. The brothers were acquitted after Tony Brindle told the jury he had been drinking with friends in The Bell public house about a mile away, and that he did not know Abdullah from Adam.

After their acquittal in the May, their brother David was shot and killed along with a bystander on 3 August in the self-same Bell public house. Two masked men burst in shortly before closing time and screamed, 'This is for Abbi', before firing on Brindle as he tried to scramble over the bar. A man drinking in the bar was also killed.

However, it was not the end of troubles for the Brindle family. In early 1995 the fourth Brindle brother, George, survived being shot from a passing van. Then later that year in the September Tony was ambushed and shot outside his home in Christopher Close, Rotherhithe. The prosecution alleged that it was a hit set up by a George Mitchell – the drug dealer in Dublin known as The Penguin – on behalf of Peter Daly, whose family had been at cross-purposes with the Brindles for some time over a variety of matters, and who had been financing him. The gunman was Dubliner Michael Boyle, who was arrested by the police on the spot. The police had been waiting for some time to foil the attempt on Brindle's life.

Over the years Boyle served a series of long sentences for major crimes before he was finally arrested on 22 February 1994 after the hijacking of a lorry-load of vodka. The Director of Public Prosecutions ultimately decided there was not enough evidence to go to court, but Boyle had made an independent decision. He would talk to the police, and was given the cover name of Pius O'Callaghan.

What the Gardai had in mind was the arrest of Peter Daly's friend whom they considered even more trouble than Boyle. Now Boyle told the police amongst other things about the possibility of a hit on Tony Brindle contracted, he said, by Mitchell. He was advised to have nothing to do with it. Nevertheless, during the summer of 1995 Boyle was making his way between Dublin and London.

Boyle decided to have his shot, so to speak, on 20 September 1995. At 7.30 a.m. he took up a position in a stolen van outside Brindle's

home and waited. At 10.42 Brindle came out and walked to his parked
car. The police had thought Boyle would get out of his van, and that
was when they planned to arrest him. He did no such thing and,
firing from inside, he hit Brindle in the elbow, chest and both thighs.
It was only when Brindle turned and tried to reach the safety of his
house that Boyle leaped from the van and in turn was shot by police
marksmen who hit him five times, also in the elbow and chest.

At his trial in January 1997 Boyle claimed that he had been
'allowed' to shoot Brindle, and that the police knew everything. He
had certainly not intended to kill the man, merely kneecap him.
The blame lay with The Penguin who, he claimed, had threatened
to kill Boyle's girlfriend's young daughter if he did not carry out the
contract. The story did not wholly appeal to the jury. Boyle received
three life sentences for attempted murder and a co-defendant, David
Roads, who had been keeping the guns for him, was sentenced to
ten years imprisonment.

In April 2001 Roads was killed in an alleyway off Cowper Road
in Kingston. At that time he was in Latchmere House, near Richmond,
finishing off his sentence and working on day release. The supposi-
tion was that he had been followed on his way back as he tried to
get there before the 10 o'clock curfew. He was shot twice in the head.
In breach of prison regulations he had a car, which was parked a
little way from the prison, and a mobile telephone on which he had
called his son at 9.51 p.m. His mistake had been always to take the
same route.

Six months later in the October, Tony Brindle's legally aided action
against the Metropolitan Police – claiming they owed a duty of care
and had failed to tell him his life was in danger – was heard in the
High Court. After the attack he had spent a fortnight in hospital. Now
he suffered severe shock, distress, had palpitations, insomnia, and
both the inability to concentrate and difficulty in breathing. He had,
it was claimed, been a labourer earning £200 a week but now was
unable to work. The action failed, with the trial judge commenting that
the shooting 'could not reasonably have been foreseen.' In all seven
people were said to have died as a result of the Brindle-Daly feud.[6]

---

[6] *The Guardian*, 16 October 2001.

Even gangsters who believe in their immortality are at risk. A matter of days before a documentary about Dessie Noonan was due to be aired, the Manchester gangleader was found stabbed to death near his home in Chorlton. In the documentary he boasted that he believed no one would be brave enough to touch him. Asked how many people he had killed, he held up seven fingers and then burst into laughter. In 1992 he had been acquitted of killing a man when witnesses failed to appear at the trial. Shortly before his death he was said to have been involved in a £250,000 drug rip-off with another local firm.[7]

Recently judges have tended to be more severe with witnesses who will not give evidence. When a witness declined to give evidence against Gilbert Wynter, accused of the murder of Claude Moseley, Judge Coombe said:

> It is terrible that a man who can commit this kind of crime can get away with it because another man refuses to do his duty and give evidence. If a murderer gets away with it they are likely to kill again until men have the courage to give evidence.[8]

But there again, some will argue that the judge did not have to live and work in the area. 'You can put me in jail,' said a potential witness to the murder of Alphonse Muratore in Melbourne in August 1992, 'but they can give me the death sentence.'

One who found this to her cost was Vicki Jacob, who in 1998 gave evidence against her former husband Gerald David Preston and another man involved in a double execution in Adelaide. In 1996 Preston accepted a $10,000 contract to kill an Adelaide garage proprietor as a favour to a Melbourne Angel. On 15 August 1996 he shot two men at Lee's Auto Repairs and wounded another. This unsuccessful hitman, in another life a marijuana salesman, not only used a rare and easily identifiable gun but failed to dispose of the weapon. After his trial Jacob changed her name and went to live on the outskirts of Bendigo where on 12 July 1999 she was shot to death as she slept on a fold-down bed in Wood Street, Long

[7] Donal MacIntyre, *Gangster*, Channel 5, 22 March 2005; *Observer*, 20 March 2005.
[8] 17 February 1995.

Gully. Her killing was believed to be on the orders of the Hells Angels.[9] Another, earlier, victim of the bikers was the American Margo Compton who moved to Oregon after she had made a statement to the police regarding the influence of an Angels Chapter in the vice industry. In 1976 she, her twin six-year-old daughters and a nineteen-year-old visitor were shot to death two weeks after she gave evidence.

The early 1990s might be signalled as the time when the contract killing of the grass started to surface. No longer was Spain a safe bolt-hole. Charles Mitchell who gave evidence against the Krays was killed there; and another, John Moriarty, who had survived two shooting attempts in London, did not survive when he was dragged from a bar in Benalmadina and thrown under the wheels of a 32-ton lorry.

A more recent death occurred in late 2001 when the remains of likely Dixie Cup Scott Bradfield were discovered in two suitcases which had been found behind a conference centre in Torremolinos. An attempt had been made to burn them and on 26 October they were discovered when the fire brigade was called to the site. Bradfield's arms and legs were found stuffed into a pink Samsonite case, with his head and torso in another. It appeared he had been badly beaten before being killed.

Bradfield, a friend of the Adams family, disappeared after the shooting of James Gaspa at his home in Islington on 8 May 2000. He had been seen with Gaspa the day before the murder and had vanished almost immediately after. Bradfield was thought to have been working as a barman in the Marbella area and the British police were about to request his extradition.[10] Now there was speculation as to whether he had been killed to prevent him talking if he was returned to Britain. Another theory was that he had been dealing in drugs in Spain and his death was a warning to competitors.

However, grasses who are in the Protected Witness Units, designed to take prisoners who are giving evidence for or assistance to the police in cases of serious crime, are known to staff as Bloggs followed by a number. Their true names and reasons for being in

[9] *R. v. Gillard & Preston* [2000] SASC 454; John Silvester and Andrew Rule, *Leadbelly*, Chapter 7.
[10] *The Times*, 3 December 2001; *The Independent*, 4 December 2001.

the PWU are, in theory, known only to senior management.[11] If they are not careful, however, on their release they may end up dead; very often through their own fault.

James Lawson, or rather Peter McNeil to give him his correct name, was one such case. On 10 February 1998 McNeil, whose informing activities had been of nearly the highest quality, was shot. He had been a key informant in the 1985 trial at the Old Bailey involving a member of the Detroit Mafia. Arrested in Colombia that year for his part in a £20 million cocaine deal, McNeil rolled over, naming David Medin from Detroit who was arrested as he went to Grays, Essex, loaded with 36 kg of the drug. He too became an informant and in 1988 John O'Boye, another American, was sentenced to eighteen years. Two other men received ten apiece and McNeil became James Lawson.

At around 8 p.m. he opened the door of his rented detached four-bedroomed house and was shot; he died 90 minutes later on the operating table of the North Hampshire Hospital in Basingstoke. McNeil had not been hiding his light under a bushel. Over the years he had made a number of enemies from his dealings in expensive cars and drugs. He had also been supplying doormen for clubs in the Midlands. A compulsive womaniser, he had attracted displeasure from the husbands and boyfriends of a number of women. Moreover he had – and this was perhaps worst of all – been unable to keep his mouth shut. He was forever boasting of his role as an informant and of the amount of cash he carried with him.

It was, said the prosecution, a domestic affair. McNeil had been involved not only with Lynn, the girlfriend of car dealer James Clelland, but also another former girlfriend. Clelland had arrived one December at McNeil's house making threats for which he was remanded in custody. The prosecution's case was that while on remand Clelland had passed details of McNeil to two brothers and asked them to sort matters out. There were, of course, many others with a grudge against McNeil, and Clelland was acquitted after a three-week trial.

In England there is now a suggestion that there should be a

[11] Tony Thompson, *Bloggs 19.*

written immunity for supergrasses.[12] The aim is to encourage them
to give evidence against the new breed of Mr Bigs of the underworld. The immediate attraction for the supergrass is the reduction
in a prison sentence. Whether the long-term benefits are as attractive is another matter. It was all very well in the 1970s and 1980s
for the likes of Bertie Smalls to grass up his friends with whom he
had committed bank robberies. They were loosely knit and un-
structured groups. It will be quite another to give evidence against
the so-called Godfathers. The Witness Protection Scheme for the
family will be a necessity and whereas the old-fashioned bank robber
had spent the takings by the end of a Friday night in the Astor
Club, today's major criminal has much more in the way of financial and other resources at his disposal. There has also been a string
of witnesses who have somehow fallen foul of the protection
programme and as a result have been left on their own. It may
prove to be an interesting equation for interested parties.

[12] *Daily Telegraph*, 25 November 2004.

15

The Thin Blue Line

As a rule, police officers both in Britain and abroad have been killed on the streets when a criminal is trying to escape or the officer has intervened in a dispute rather than from contracts being taken out on them. It was only a matter of months after the formation of the Metropolitan Police that on 29 June 1830 PC Joseph Grantham died while trying to break up a fight between two Irishmen, one of whom was said to be beating his wife, in Somers Town in Docklands. He was knocked to the ground and kicked on the temple. Michael Duggan was arrested, but the inquest jury returned the odd verdict that 'the death of the deceased was caused by the extravasation of some fluid on the brain occasioned by over exertion in the discharge of his duty'. And there the matter seems to have ended and as a result, sadly, his death has gone almost wholly unremarked in chronicles of the police.[1]

His death was soon followed by another when on 18 August 1830 John Long became the first officer to be killed by a professional criminal. Long had been a night-watchman before joining the force and while patrolling what is now Gray's Inn Road near Holborn, he was stabbed in the heart by a well-known burglar William Sapwell whom, along with two others, he had stopped for questioning. Another officer,

[1] *The Times*, 30 June, 1 July 1830.

John Newton, chased Sapwell who was caught by a night-watchman. Sapwell's defence was one of mistaken identity. He had, he said, heard the cry, 'Stop, thief!' and had joined in the pursuit. Throughout the case he maintained his name was John Smith and witnesses were called to disprove this claim. One, also curiously called Long, testified that Sapwell had given evidence against him twenty years earlier. Sapwell had arranged for the robbery of his aunt but had turned King's Evidence, and Long and another youth had been condemned to death before being reprieved.[2] Sapwell, who continued to protest his innocence, was hanged at the Old Bailey on 20 September 1830. Long left a widow and five children and a subscription was set up for his family by several newspapers, to one of which the three Bow Street magistrates contributed. And so the killings went on.

In America the first FBI agent to be killed on duty was Edwin C. Shanahan, shot and killed by Martin James Durkin on 11 October 1925 in Chicago. Durkin, a car thief – usually of upper-range models such as Cadillacs and Pierce Arrows – had already shot and wounded three other officers in Chicago as well as a fourth in California, and was known to be armed and dangerous. Having obtained information that Durkin would be bringing a stolen car from New Mexico to a garage in Chicago, Shanahan spent the day at the garage with a back-up team. There was no sign of Durkin and when the other officers left to find reliefs, Shanahan remained behind. It was then that Durkin finally drove in and Shanahan, bravely if foolishly, tried to make a single-handed arrest. Durkin swept up the automatic pistol from the front seat and shot the agent in the chest.

Some weeks later information was given that Durkin and the woman with whom he had been living would be at the home of the woman's relative. When Chicago police officers went to arrest him, one was killed and another wounded in the gun battle after which Durkin again escaped.

He was seen and recognised on 17 January 1926 in Pecos, Texas. For a time it was thought he would head for Mexico, but given his love of comfort and nightlife this was discounted. He was then traced from the Texan village of Alpine to San Antonio, and then to a train

[2] *The Times*, 15 September 1830.

bound for St Louis. At 11 a.m. on 20 January the train was surrounded and boarded just outside the city. Durkin had his guns in his luggage and overcoat, but he was disarmed before he could reach them.

It was not until 1934 that killing a Special Agent of the FBI became a Federal offence, so Durkin was tried in State court. He received thirty-five years for the murder of Shanahan and fifteen years for the car thefts, to be served consecutively. With time off for good behaviour, he was released after twenty-eight years; he was then 53 years old. Shanahan's son became an FBI agent.[3]

One of the most cowardly and deliberate attacks on the police came as part of the war being conducted against Melbourne criminals who retaliated, setting a trap for two young officers. In the period 1987–89 eleven suspects were shot dead by the police.[4] In the most celebrated case on 11 October 1988, Graeme Jensen left a hardware store in Narre Warren, an Eastern Melbourne suburb, and climbed into his Holden Commodore. He was approached by members of the Victoria Police Armed Robbery Squad who told him not to move. Instead he accelerated. Officers opened fire and Jensen was shot in the back of the head. By the time the car crashed into a power pole he was already dead. At the inquest the evidence was that the police saw Jensen pick up a weapon and they shot to protect themselves. A sawn-off bolt-action shotgun was produced which they said had been found in the car, but Jensen's friends and relations would not accept the evidence.

Around 4 a.m. on the day after Jensen's death, a newsagent going to open his shop saw a Holden Commodore parked in Walsh Street in the good residential part of South Yarra. It was empty but the lights were on, the doors open, the windows smashed. He telephoned the police and Constables Steven Tynan and Damian Eyre were sent to investigate. While they were looking at the damage they were attacked. Tynan was shot in the head at almost point-blank range and Eyre, who had an instant's notice of the attack and tried to struggle with the gunman, was shot three times.[5]

---

[3] Athan G. Theoharis (ed.), *The FBI*.
[4] Deaths included Mark Militano on 25 March 1997. His case, along with that of Jensen and Jedd Houghton, is recounted as part of *Police Shootings in Victoria 1987–1989*.
[5] The double killing of police officers was the first since Ned Kelly's gang shot three officers near Mansfield, north-east of Melbourne, in 1878.

The police search which followed was, not unexpectedly, a massive one. The Victoria Government posted a $200,000 reward. With a hundred police drafted to comb the underworld, the crime rate dropped. One of the men whose name came into the frame was Jedd Houghton, a known friend of Jensen. He was traced to Bendigo where he was staying in a caravan park with his girlfriend. A listening device was planted and discovered by Houghton. Listening before he dismantled it, the police realised their cover was blown and moved to arrest him. He was in the caravan park when the police opened fire and was hit with two shotgun blasts. He died instantly, and his friends believed that he had been shot as a reprisal for Walsh Street.

One of them, Gary Abdallah, had been named to the police by an accomplished little thief, the 17-year-old Jason Ryan, a nephew of Dennis Allen, who, after being convicted of a drug-dealing offence, decided co-operation was the best way towards daylight and became an informant. On 22 February, Abdallah went to see the police with his solicitor and was told that it was only rumour against him. Six weeks later on 9 April he was killed when police, not connected with the Walsh Street inquiry, shot him. They said he had threatened them with a firearm. It turned out to be an imitation weapon, and his friends once again refused to accept the police version. Abdallah died after forty days in a coma.

It appeared that Ryan had been trying to deflect interest from himself. The police arrested him, along with Victor George Peirce and Trevor Pettingill, Anthony Leigh Farrell – Ryan's best friend – and Peter David McEvoy, who lodged with Ryan's mother. The police named Houghton as the sixth man involved in the Walsh Street attack.

Ryan, who became a witness for the Crown, gave the following self-exculpatory version of the killing. The other four had stolen a Commodore, left it in Walsh Street and waited for the police to come. He had not wanted to be part of the crime and had stayed behind. When they returned Farrell told Ryan that he was the one who had done the shooting. There was some back-up to the story from Peirce's wife Wendy who went into the Witness Protection Program.

Wendy Peirce gave evidence that on the night of the police murders her husband had left her and the children at a motel, saying,

'Don't worry, I won't be late. I'm going to kill the jacks that knocked Graeme.' The next morning he had told her they were dead.

The prosecution's case at the trial suffered from the loss of Mrs Peirce, who by the time of the trial had walked out of the Witness Protection Program and declined to give evidence. She was eventually convicted of perjury and given a prison sentence. The case now effectively depended on the evidence of Ryan whose story became less and less credible as he was questioned, finally admitting to a string of lies. There were no eyewitnesses, forensic or fingerprints of the men to assist the prosecution. On 26 March, after a retirement of six days, the jury returned a verdict of not guilty on all the men.[6]

Detectives rather than uniformed police are more likely to be the targets of organised criminals. During his investigation into the empire of the Kray Twins, a contract was taken out on the life of Leonard 'Nipper' Read and a hitman was flown in from America. He never got further than Ireland, for he was detained at Shannon airport and sent on his way. Nevertheless Read took long-term precautions: 'Now I started to look under my car before I started and when I went home I made sure I varied my journey.'[7]

There have been a number of attacks when an officer has been dealt with by the criminal in his or her own home for other reasons. The Chicago boss Lawrence Mangano, who for a time ruled the Near Westside, had the home of Captain Luke Garrick of Des Plaines Street police station bombed in 1928. Garrick had been aggravating him by having gambling houses raided. The officer was lucky to escape with his life.

Although no longer on the Tampa Bay police force, Detective Richard Cloud continued to work with various agencies in an attempt to bring down that city's Mob. Regarded as a hard-nosed officer, not altogether popular with some of his less committed colleagues, he was getting close to establishing a case against drug dealers when in March 1976 he was accused of roughing up a suspect in a police parking lot. He declined to take a lie-detector test and was promptly fired. Shortly after his dismissal he answered

---

[6] For a full account of the case see Tom Noble, *Walsh Street*. For a shortened account see also Tom Noble, 'The Walsh Street Shootings' in *Australian Crime*.
[7] Leonard Read, *Nipper Read, The Man Who Nicked the Krays*.

the door on Alva Street in Tampa and was shot in the chest. Five more shots were fired into his stomach and legs before the gunman fled in a green and black Dodge Charger.

The next year a local landlord passed information that a tenant was both causing problems and taking what he believed was an unhealthy interest in the Cloud killing. The tenant was Benjamin Roy Gilford and he was an escapee from the State prison. Questioned, he told officers that an Ellis Haskew had broken him out of prison and brought him into the contract. The information was good. Haskew owned a black and green Charger and he was traced to South Florida where, extraordinarily, he continued to report to his probation officer. In turn he gave up Anthony Antone as a middle man, and also an undisclosed financier. Quite how much was on offer for the contract is not clear, but he claimed Antone was given $10,000 with which to pay the gunmen. The money had come from drug trafficker and bar-owner Victor Acosta who promptly fled the city, smuggled out with the help of a serving police officer, passed to Harlan Blackburn in Orlando and then left to make his way up the East Coast.[8]

That left the three gunmen to stand trial, but before it took place Gilford was found dead in his cell with a sheet looped around his neck and tied to the cell door. Before his death he had made a statement to the police explaining how the killing took place. Now Ellis Haskew became the principal witness for the prosecution, and he told how Acosta was upset with Cloud. Acosta had also tried to organise the car-bombing of a lawyer to whom he owed fees and whom he had discovered also represented Cloud. On 17 December 1976 Antone received the death penalty. Haskew was sentenced to thirty-five years, and two other conspirators received forty and sixty years. This still left Acosta. He was another criminal to undergo extensive plastic surgery, but an attempt to alter his fingerprints failed and in January 1978 he was traced in Brooklyn. Brought back to Tampa and the Hillsborough County jail, he apparently committed suicide. Later a guard admitted smuggling a quantity of sleeping

[8] Blackburn, another known as The Colonel, a leading light in the Dixie Mafia and a close associate of Santo Trafficante jnr, died aged 79 on 21 October 1998. W.T. Brannon, 'How they tracked down the Hit Men Killers of Florida's Top Vice Cop' in *Official Detective Stories*, December 1977; Scott M. Deitche, *Cigar City Mafia*.

pills to Acosta; he had, he said, felt sorry for him. Antone was electrocuted at 7.08 a.m on 26 January 1984. His last words were, 'The
only thing is Forgive them Father, for in their ignorance they know
not what they do. And that's it.' Cloud was posthumously reinstated
in the Tampa force.[9]

On 10 January 1989 Assistant Commissioner of the Federal Police
Colin Winchester became the highest-ranking police officer in
Australia to be killed when at about 9.15 p.m. he was shot in the
back of the head in the driveway of his home in Lawley Street,
Canberra. The killing led to a long and, in the end, unsatisfactory
inquiry in the form of a 125-day inquest in which a variety of alternative solutions was advanced. One line of the inquiry related to the
involvement by the Australian police dealing in the distribution of
drugs in collaboration with the Calabrian Mafia.[10] What was
undoubtedly correct was that Winchester was shot in the back of
the head and in the neck by bullets from a .22 Rutger rifle as he
was about to step from his car. More likely it was the work of a
man who had a personal grudge against the officer.[11]

There are not too many instances of the killing of retired officers, but there are exceptions. One was Lou Lewis, the friend of
Don Hancock. The death of both these retired police officers
followed the shooting of Gypsy Joker biker Billy Grierson. Lewis's
friend Hancock may not have been quite so innocent. Grierson had
been banned from Hancock's hotel after he and other bikers
had been swearing in front of Hancock's daughter. It was claimed
the bikers had been waging a war of terror against him and his
family, and the biker was shot dead at a campfire in the remote
town of Ora Banda on 1 October 2000. Over the next few weeks
Hancock's home was fire-bombed, as was a store he owned, and
the hotel was blown up. Finally on 1 September 2001 a bomb was
placed in Lewis's car, probably while he and Hancock were at
Belmont racetrack in Perth. Remotely detonated, it exploded, killing
both him and Hancock. The police had heard there was a plot to

---

[9] *New York.Times*, 27 January 1984.
[10] R.J. Cahill, *Findings of an inquest into the death of the late Assistant Commissioner Colin Stanley Winchester at Canberra on 10 January 1989.*
[11] Roderick Campbell and ors, *The Winchester Scandal.*

kill him at a Kalgoorlie race meeting and had persuaded Hancock not to go. In October 2003, another Gypsy Joker biker Graeme Slater was acquitted of the double murder.[12]

In their turn the police have been regarded as killers with the setting-up of the so-called Death Squads: rogue officers dedicated to eliminating killers and those they see as other social undesirables with whom the courts are unable or unwilling to deal. Over the years they have flourished in various countries, not least in South America. The foundation of the E.M., the *Esquadrao Motorizado*, in Rio de Janeiro followed the death of one of the city's most popular detectives, Milton de Oliviera, known as Le Cocq after the character created by Emil Gaboriou. Some have suggested that from time to time over the years the squadron's initials stood more properly for *Esquadrao da Morte* or Death Squad.

De Oliviera was killed by a small-time gangster Manuel Moreira, known as Cara de Cavalo (Horseface), in an attempted arrest which went severely wrong on 27 August 1964. He was shot in the chest and the jugular and died that night in hospital. During the search for Moreira the police killed a number of wanted men including Paraibinha, suspected of killing a number of tourists. One detective, Perpetuo de Freitas, was killed in the Favela do Esqueleto by other officers who did not wish him to capture Moreira alive. Finally, on 3 October 1964 the police received information that Moreira was hiding in a cottage in Cabo Frio some fifty miles north of Rio. He was killed in the inevitable shoot-out and his body dumped at Kilometre 23 on the Busios Highway.[13]

In fact the so-called Death Squad was created in the early 1960s when the police began to clean up the city by shooting beggars and dumping their corpses in the Guarda River. Its existence was acknowledged in January 1963 when Olindina Alves Jupiacu, a

---

[12] *Sydney Daily Telegraph*, 1 October 2001; *Weekend Australian*, 28 August 2004. One Gypsy Joker who did go down was Garry John Collie, convicted of the execution of drug dealers John Powers and Leila Hoppo in January 2002. In September 2004 he was sentenced to thirty years for the contract killings. The shooting had been so swift that Leila still had a lit cigarette in her hand when her body was found. *Adelaide Advertiser*, 27 February, 24 August 2004.

[13] For an account of the career of de Oliviera see Bruce Henderson and Sam Summerlin, 'The Legend of Le Cocq' in *The Super Sleuths*.

female beggar who had once been a champion swimmer, escaped by swimming to safety and telling her story. Police officers received sentences totalling 1,000 years.

Then in 1968 the Death Squad was revived, this time with the help of a publicity agent who called himself Red Rose. On 6 May the newspapers received a call that a body could be found in the Bara de Tiuca. Sure enough there was a body, its arms tied behind its back and a nylon rope around its neck. The man had also been shot. Near the corpse was a piece of cardboard with a drawing of a Volkswagen captioned, 'I am a car thief.' After a number of further calls from Red Rose which led to the discovery of more bodies, once again a number of police officers were convicted and sentenced.

In fact the Rio police cannot claim the dubious honour of creating the Death Squad. During the Prohibition wars in Chicago, police officers were often suspected of killing some of the victims. After the St Valentine's Day Massacre an outside force investigated the killings on the basis that, given the killers wore police uniforms, it might indeed have been officers who undertook the work. From then on police and paramilitary Death Squads have flourished throughout the world.

Fortunately it is not often that rogue officers turn armed robbers – at least in Britain – and even rarer that they become police killers. Former Glasgow officer Howard Wilson is an exception. He resigned after being refused promotion and set up a greengrocery store in Allison Street, Govanhill, opposite the police station. If he thought his former officers' custom would be sufficient to keep it going he was soon disabused. In short order the fruit shop failed and, with two other former officers, he took to armed robbery. The first job in 1969 was a success when they held up a bank in Giffnock. Then trouble started when the driver on the raid, Archie McGeachie, declined to drive a second time and disappeared. He is thought to have ended in a mixer processing concrete for Glasgow's Kingston Bridge. There is no suggestion that either Wilson or the others had anything to do with the killing.

The second raid on the Clydesdale Bank in Linwood was also successful and the trio netted £21,000. However, a former colleague Detective Inspector Andrew Hyslop suspected Wilson and saw him and the others carry suitcases and a metal trunk to the basement of the tenement in Allison Street. Along with Detective Constable Angus MacKenzie and Constable Edward Barnett, he went to the flat and cornered Wilson. MacKenzie and Barnett were shot dead and Hyslop was left paralysed after being shot in the neck. Wilson tried to shoot him again, but the gun jammed and he was overpowered. The other former officers took no part, with one named Donaldson leaping out of a window. They were each jailed for twelve years. Wilson received a life sentence. McGeachie was declared dead in 1998.

At first Wilson did not settle well in prison. He was given a further six years for attempting to murder six warders in a foiled break-out at Porterfield jail in Inverness.[14] Later he wrote a praised novel, *Angels of Death*. By the turn of the century, his supporters claimed he was wholly rehabilitated. In May 2002 he went to the High Court in Glasgow to have the 'punishment' term of his sentence reviewed. It was reduced to twenty-seven years and he was released in October that year.[15]

And if a former cop turned police killer is difficult to believe, then the news that two New York officers moonlighted as hitmen for the Mafia is almost unbelievable. In a twenty-seven-page indictment handed down in March 2005 it was alleged that Louis Eppolito and Stephen Caracappa were on a $4,000 retainer providing information for Anthony 'Gaspipe' Casso, the underboss of the Lucchese Family, from 1986. It is also claimed that they provided information which led to hits on three informants. Worse, they are alleged to have carried out a hit on Eddie Lino, a Gambino *capo*, in 1992. It is claimed that for a fee of $65,000 they used their unmarked patrol car to pull Lino over on the Belt Parkway in Brooklyn and shot him. After his retirement Eppolito, who wrote the book *Mafia Cop*, turned to playing gangsters in movies. He had the background. His father Ralph was a Gambino soldier known as 'Fat the Gangster' and his uncle James was known as 'Jimmy the Clam'. Both have denied

---

[14] *Daily Express*, 29 December 1972.
[15] *The Scotsman*, 14 February 2001, 31 October 2002. Joe Beltrami, *The Defender*, Chapter 6. Allison Street was the scene of another tragedy when in March 2004, following a quarrel over drugs, petrol was poured through a letter-box and two people died.

the charges and Caracappa's lawyer claimed, 'The Government is relying on the word of rats.'[16] The case will no doubt run for several years.

Nor are members of the prison service exempt from retribution. Simply being a prison guard can be an unsafe occupation. On 26 June 1997 Diane Lavigne was murdered just because she was wearing her uniform. In an attempt to destabilise the justice system, the Montreal Hells Angel leader Maurice 'Mom' Boucher had ordered the killing. A week earlier, another guard had escaped an attempt when the would-be killers found the pillion passenger was too heavy and they could not get up sufficient speed. Now after she had finished her shift she left the Bordeaux prison in her minivan. Followed and cut off by a motorcyclist, as she braked to avoid a crash she was shot in the arm and lung. On 5 September that year a second guard, Pierre Rondeau, was killed in the prison bus before he began his round to collect prisoners. On 5 May 2002 Boucher was convicted of ordering their murders and was sentenced to life imprisonment.[17]

Prison officials in Canada have not been the only ones under siege. In January 2005 six employees at the Matamaros maximum security jail were killed by hitmen outside the prison.[18]

[16] *The Times*, 12 March 2005; *The Sunday Times*, 13 March 2005.
[17] Julian Sher and William Marsden, *The Road to Hell*.
[18] *The Guardian*, 22 January 2005.

16

Black Widows

The so-called Black Widows seem to fall into two categories: passive and active – those whose men friends suffer unfortunate and early deaths or those who kill. In the first category undoubtedly comes the delectable Nellie Cameron, described as a 'redhead with a ripe figure and provocative china blue eyes'. One of her early lovers was Frank Green who became involved in the Darlinghurst, Sydney, razor wars of the late 1920s. A friend of the British-born madam, Matilda 'Tilly' Devine, Green shot George Gaffney of the rival camp headed by the other great madam of the period, Kate Leigh. Gaffney survived and for his pains was shot and this time killed by Kate's husband, Frank. Green then killed Bernard Dalton and he in turn was shot by Jim Devine with whom he had quarrelled. Finally he was stabbed to death on 26 April 1965 by Beatrice 'Bobby' Haggett with whom he was then living. She was acquitted after tales of his brutality. An autopsy showed there were eight old bullets in his body.

Cameron began life as a prostitute in the Surry Hills and Woolloomooloo districts. Known in the press as 'The Kiss of Death Girl', from time to time she commuted to work in Queensland. Green's long-term rival for her bed was Guido Calletti, with whom she was living when he was shot. A major standover man in Woolloomooloo whose career had begun at the age of nine when he was ruled to be an uncontrollable child, by the time of his death

Calletti had appeared in the courts nearly sixty times in three States. In February 1929 he had been charged with an attempted murder and, after his acquittal, racked up a quick two years for assault with intent to rob. In November 1934 he joined the line of gangsters who thought it worthwhile to draw attention to themselves by bringing libel actions. He was awarded a farthing against the magazine *Truth* and, the story goes, framed the penny stamp he was sent as his winnings. One street fight with Green over Nellie was said to have lasted three-quarters of an hour, ending with honours even and the clothes of both men in tatters.

In August 1939, Calletti, who survived a number of shootings and boasted of his invulnerability, was shot twice in the stomach and killed when he attempted to break up a party in Brougham Street, part of a protection quarrel he was having with the rulers there. Two men were acquitted of his murder. The funeral was spectacular even by gangland standards of the period. Five thousand people were said to have filed past his body as it lay in a Darlinghurst funeral parlour. There were two hundred wreaths at the funeral including one from Cameron who, working out of the area at the time, sent a four-foot-high cross.[1]

In 1942 Cameron returned from Queensland to Sydney, catering for the more lucrative wartime trade. Earlier she had also been the mistress of another standover man Norman Bruhn, the lieutenant of the gang boss Squizzy Taylor, who was shot to death in East Sydney on 22 June 1927. Other lovers who died violently included Ernest Connelly, shot by Calletti in 1929 when walking on Womerah Avenue. He was replaced by Alan Pulley, who in turn was shot by Ned O'Halloran in Wentworth Street, Glebe. He had apparently been trying to stand over Florrie O'Halloran while her husband was on the run.

In March 1952 Cameron herself was shot in the spine at her flat in Darlinghurst. A man was charged but she refused to identify her alleged attacker, claiming she had been shot by a stranger who had emerged from the shadows. The man was discharged and they left

[1] For a highly entertaining account of the Calletti-Green feud over Cameron and the period generally, see David Hickie, *Chow Hayes, Gunman*.

court arm-in-arm. In the operating theatre she was found to have a number of healed bullet wounds.

She gassed herself in November 1953 after apparently being told she was suffering from inoperable cancer generated by the old wounds. She was 41 years old. Earlier she had adopted the seven-year-old daughter of a neighbour and had brought her up conscientiously. After her death it was said of her that she had 'exceptional sex appeal', she had nerve and could be trusted with secrets. 'She was completely loyal to the criminal scale of values.'[2] Which, after all, is not a bad obituary.

It was actually in the arms of 'Pretty' Dulcie Markham – described by Sydney's *Daily Mirror* as having seen 'more violence and death than any other woman in Australia's history' – that Calletti bled to death, two bullets in his stomach, and his head in her lap. In all, eight of her lovers died from either the gun or the knife. A girl with the looks and poise of a model and from a respectable family, she was working the King's Cross area before she was 16. In May 1931 a standover man, Cecil William 'Scotchy' McCormack, wooed the 18-year-old Dulcie away from another youth, Alfred Dillon. With McCormack promptly sentenced to six months for associating with criminals, Dillon reasserted his charm. On the day of his release McCormack reclaimed his property and Dillon stabbed him in the heart. He was sentenced to thirteen years for manslaughter.

The next of her lovers to go was Arthur 'The Egg' Kingsley, shot in a bar in Swanston Street, Melbourne, in December 1937. Then after Calletti was shot she married a mobster, Frank Bowen. In turn he was shot in 1940, the same year that another boyfriend John Charles Abrahams was gunned down outside a gaming house in Melbourne. In January 1945 it was the turn of Donald 'The Duck' Day, shot in an illegal drinking club in Crown Street, Surry Hills. Dulcie was now moving in higher society. The Duck was an associate of the fashionable abortionist Dr Reginald Stuart-Jones, or at least of his wife. Dulcie was now a close friend of the major Sydney crime figures as well as the corrupt but successful police officer Ray Kelly.[3]

[2] *Sun-Herald* (Sydney), 15 November 1953.
[3] For an account of the careers of Stuart-Jones and Ray Kelly see David Hickie, *The Prince and the Premier*.

By the September she was closely associated with another stan-dover man, Leslie Ernest Walkerden known as 'Scotland Yard'. He died when he came out of a Richmond baccarat club he was protecting only to find one of his tyres had been punctured. He was shot by three people, armed with a .32, a .45 and a shotgun, as he began pumping it up.

There followed a time of relative calm until bad luck struck once again in September 1951 when two men burst into her home in St Kilda where she was drinking brandy with some friends. Gavan Walsh was killed and his brother Donald injured. She was hit in the hip and married Leonard 'Redda' Lewis from her hospital bed. Sadly he did not survive long. They returned to Sydney, but on a visit to his mother in April 1952 he opened the door at 1.15 a.m. and was shot six times. In 1955 she survived being thrown off a balcony, probably by a client. On 20 April 1976, then married for a third time and living quietly in Moore Street, Bondi, she went to bed, lit a cigarette and, in turn, the bedding. She died from asphyxiation. During her lifetime, apart from being known as The Black Widow she was also known as The Bad Luck Doll and The One-Way Ticket.

Another of the Kiss of Death girls was the American Evelyn Mittleman, one of whose boyfriends was drowned by the jealous Pittsburgh Phil Strauss. She came from Williamsburg, Brooklyn, and first surfaced as a good-looking blonde when she was about 16 hanging out in dance halls and swimming pools, those training grounds for aspirant mobsters, until she attracted a man named Hy Miller who took her to California. There he was killed in a dance hall in a fight over her. She returned to Brooklyn and began step-ping out with Robert Feurer who for his pains was killed by Jack Goldstein, a racketeer who had an interest in both the wholesale fish market and Mittleman. In turn Goldstein was eventually killed by Strauss. First, however, he was badly beaten with a pool cue and for a time disappeared from the scene. He was killed some four years later in a contract over his business activities. Strauss insisted that he be beaten unconscious and then brought to him to be drowned. Mittleman remained loyal to Strauss and was the last person to visit him in the death cell. After that she disappeared from view.

Yet another woman whose attraction could prove fatal was Mary Margaret Collings, known as 'Kiss of Death Maggie' because six of her husbands perished in Chicago's Prohibition wars. When wagers were made on the likely survival time of the next husband, one reporter is said to have suggested, 'six months was about par for the course'.

Perhaps the most celebrated of the Black Widows of the London underworld in the 1950s was the rather plain-looking one-time prostitute and prostitute's maid Fay Richardson, who captivated – amongst others – the handsome Tommy Smithson, the equally good-looking Selwyn Cooney and the noted Jack Rosa. All failed to survive into middle age.

According to Commander Bert Wickstead she was:

> A blonde lady of many secrets, very preoccupied and very hard . . . She couldn't have been described as a beautiful woman by any stretch of the imagination. When she spoke there was no outward sign of any great wit, warmth, intelligence or charm. Yet she did have the most devastating effect upon the men in her life – so there must have been something special about the lady.[4]

In 1953 Tommy Smithson, generally thought of as a failure if a brave and foolish one, was cut within an inch of his life by Jack Spot and Billy Hill. He survived, and in recognition of his loyalty to the code of silence was given £500 to open a club. It was not a success and he returned to minding small-time Maltese clubs in the East End. He also contracted an unfortunate alliance: he fell in love with Fay Richardson. Originally from Stockport where she had been a mill girl, she was what could be described both as a gangster's moll and a *femme fatale*. She said of the handsome Smithson admiringly: '[He was] a dapper dresser, very fussy about having a clean shirt every day. He was a big gambler. He could have £400 on the nose.'

By June 1956 she was on remand in Holloway prison awaiting trial on forged cheque allegations. Money was needed for her defence. The former police officer turned barrister William Hemming was to be her counsel, and he was not known for accepting legal aid work. Smithson set about raising it with a will. On 13 June 1956 he,

---

[4] Bert Wickstead, *Gangbuster*, p. 26.

together with Walter Downs and Christopher Thomas, went to a café in Berner Street, Stepney, and confronted his one-time employer George Caruana and Philip Ellul, a Maltese who ran a second- or third-division string of prostitutes. Smithson said he wanted more than £50 from Caruana and in the ensuing fight Caruana's fingers were slashed as he protected his face from a flick-knife. Other Maltese in the café were held off at gunpoint by Thomas and an additional £30 was produced. In accordance with standard gangland practice, Ellul was told to start a collection for Fay and was provided with a book to record the contributions.

The damage had been done. On 25 June Smithson was found dying in the gutter outside George Caruana's house in Carlton Vale. He had been shot in the arm and neck. His last words were said to be, 'Good morning, I'm dying.'

Fay Richardson was not allowed out of Holloway for the traditional gangland funeral which included wreaths in the form of dice and, given Smithson's earlier naval career, an anchor. She sent a wreath: 'Till we meet again.' Smithson's death worked well in her favour and she was placed on probation on condition that she returned to Lancashire and did not visit London for three years. She duly headed north with the press in tow, stopping to record a visit to Tommy's grave in St Patrick's Cemetery, Langthorne Road, Leytonstone. Later she married a gaming-club owner Alex Sadler, and next surfaced as manageress of the notorious Pen Club in Spitalfields which was said to have been bought with the proceeds of a robbery at the Parker Pen company. On 7 February 1960 her then lover Selwyn Cooney was shot and killed.

Also injured in the shooting was boxer Billy Ambrose, and Fay Sadler, giving the name of Mrs Patrick Callaghan, was seen leaving the London Hospital where he was detained. Brought in for questioning, she pointed the finger at a Jimmy Nash whose brother had quarrelled with Cooney over who should pay for the damage in a car accident. She then vanished, resurfacing only after the trial in which Nash was acquitted of Cooney's murder.[5]

---

[5] For a full account of the case see Duncan Campbell, *The Underworld*; Bert Wickstead, *Gangbuster*.

On 12 May she allowed herself to be photographed in the Anchor public house in the appropriately named Clink Street. The reason she had not appeared – she disclosed after the reporter Victor Davies had paid a fee for the interview to her minder – was that she had been ill and this had given her the opportunity to rethink her lifestyle:

> I was just being faithful to the code by which I have lived. I am waving goodbye to the drinking clubs, the dog tracks, the mad parties and all the baloney that I thought was the essence of life when I was a kid.

She thought she might go to live somewhere 'ducky' like Cheltenham.[6]

The third of her men who died an untimely death was Jack Rosa, one of a hard family from the Elephant and Castle area, who had been in Broadmoor and who was killed in a car accident. He was a disqualified driver at the time and, game to the last, his final words to the police were said to have been, 'It wasn't me who was driving.'[7]

Although over the years there have been reports of another marriage to a London club owner, as well as sightings in the company of visiting Australians, Richardson/Sadler faded into obscurity.

Just as the men in Fay Richardson's life ended up dead or in prison so did those in the life of Linda Calvey, a classic gangster's moll turned gangster. Was she a contractor, the killer or, as she maintains, simply in the wrong place at the wrong time? According to the prosecution at her trial, when the hitman she had hired to kill her lover proved too wimpish to shoot him properly she took over and did the job herself.

In 1973 Linda Calvey's first husband Mickey received eight years along with his friend Mickey Ishmael for robbing a branch of Marks & Spencers. She had married him in 1970 when he was taken from Wandsworth prison to a local register office. In 1977 he was acquitted of charges of burglary brought on the evidence of supergrass Charles Lowe. Then on Saturday 9 December 1978 Calvey died in a shoot-out when he tried to rob Caters supermarket in Eltham, South-East London. Four men attacked security guards as

[6] Victor Davies, 'Fay Sadler Talks' in *Daily Express*, 13 May 1960.
[7] For more on Jack Rosa and his brother Ray, see Frankie Fraser, *Mad Frank*.

they carried a box containing £10,000. The other three men fled after discharging a shotgun over the heads of the crowd.

On hearing of his death Linda said, 'Mickey has been in trouble before, I know, but he's been trying hard since he came out of prison a year ago.' Some two hundred people attended his funeral at the East London crematorium.

Linda was first dubbed the Black Widow by shouting 'murderer' at the police officer who stood trial for the shooting. There had been some evidence that Calvey had been shot in the back, but the officer explained that this was the way he had been standing rather than that he was shot while fleeing. He was acquitted and given a bravery award.

Shortly after that she became involved with robber Ronnie Cook, going with him on trips abroad including one to Las Vegas when it was said they spent £30,000 in just over a week. He lavished gifts on her – clothes from Harrods, jewellery, money, a car, even £4,000 for cosmetic surgery. However, there was a down side. Cook was obsessively jealous, forbidding Linda to speak to other men, beating her savagely and, according to reports, subjecting her to sadistic sexual practices.

Three years later he was jailed for sixteen years for his part in what was described as one of the 'most spectacular and well-planned robberies in the history of crime'. While that is quite often a phrase used by prosecuting counsel opening the case to a jury, this did have the hallmarks of brilliance. It was Billy Tobin's Dulwich raid when a hijacked mobile crane was rammed into the back of a security vehicle containing almost £1 million.

Calvey promised to wait for him and as a mark of her fidelity had 'True Love Ron Cook' tattooed on her leg. But it seems she could not now give up the lifestyle to which she had grown accustomed. Almost certainly Cook had money salted away and she began to spend it, taking up with one of his friends, Brian Thorogood, whom Cook had arranged to act as a 'minder' for him while he was inside. Thorogood left his wife, bought a house in Harold Wood, Essex, and moved in with her. Later he too was sentenced, receiving eighteen years for a post office robbery. Linda, who it seems supplemented her income by being the armourer for various robbery teams, served three of a five-year term for conspiracy to rob. That was the end of Thorogood, but now Cook was due for release. What was she to do?

Fearful that he would find out about both her infidelity and her dissipation of his money, she planned to kill him, offering a £10,000 contract. Finding no immediate takers, she turned to Daniel Reece (also known as Danny Woods), a convicted rapist whose evidence had assisted the police convict David Lashley, the killer of Australian heiress Janie Shepherd. Quite apart from the money, Reece also was enamoured with Calvey and agreed to do the job.

In theory Ron Cook had a cleaning job outside the prison but, as with so many before and after him, he absented himself and took to having more agreeable days out. According to the prosecution, on 19 January 1990 Linda Calvey collected him from Maidstone prison and drove him to London while Reece, whom she had already collected from another prison, waited outside her flat. Cook brought in the milk and as he stood holding it Reece followed him in and shot him in the elbow. He could not, he later told police, bring himself to kill the man: 'I could not kill him. I shot to his side and he fell backwards into the kitchen. I moved forward and stood over him. I could not kill him. I have never killed anyone.'

But, the prosecution claimed, Linda Calvey had no such qualms. She grabbed the gun from him, ordered Cook to kneel and then shot him in the head. Reece took a train back to the West Country to continue his thirteen-year sentence for rape, buggery and false imprisonment.

At first it seemed as though Calvey had been successful. The police appeared to accept her story that an unknown gunman had burst in and shot Cook while she cowered in a corner. Then it was discovered that Reece had been with her over the weekend and had been her lover. It was curious that he had not been mentioned in her statement. Under questioning Reece cracked first, telling all.

Reece – not notedly popular in prison following the evidence he had given against Lashley – thought twice about squealing again and withdrew his confession in court. Linda Calvey told the jury his story was a fabrication. 'Ron meant everything to me,' she said. His gesture of solidarity did Reece no good; he too received a life sentence for murder. Later he maintained that although he had been the gunman Calvey had not known he was going to kill Cook. Calvey does not seem to have held Reece's temporary defection against him, for they married in prison in 2002. She continues to maintain her innocence.[8]

---

[8] For a fuller account of Linda Calvey, her life and hopes, see Kate Kray and Chester Stern, *Black Widow*.

17

Into the Sunset

There are relatively few records of hitmen successfully retiring to Florida or to the South Coast to live in a bungalow and walk on the pier and listen to the band on a Sunday. Of course, it may be simply because they are not known. Burglars may be able to have their memoirs printed after they have completed their last sentence but, given there is generally no statute of limitations on murder, the same does not apply to hitmen which may be something of a bridle on their tongues. There is some anecdotal evidence that provided they are not betrayed to the police they can indeed retire. One made American thinks it is easy for the retired killer to be relatively safe:

> I know of killers and made guys who walk away and nothing happens. See, people aren't afraid of the bosses. They are afraid of the work horses. It's not the boss. It's who the boss is going to send.[1]

One English hitman who at least died on the South Coast was Alfie Gerard, but he was thought to be in hiding rather than retirement. In August 1981 he was found dead in a flat belonging to a member

---

[1] Letter to author.

of the South East London family, the Callaghans, in Brighton, that town beloved of Max Miller and Graham Greene. An inquest showed he died of cirrhosis of the liver. However, the preferred version, more in keeping with his lifestyle and culinary artistry, is that he choked over a lobster.

Alf Gerard may have managed something approaching retirement, but his son Nicky did not. Regarded as two of the most formidable hitmen of the London scene of their time, they rank in the pantheon with Jimmy Moody and Teddy Machin, neither of whom survived to retirement age.

On 23 May 1973 Machin, thought to have killed half a dozen people in his career as an enforcer, was shot dead while walking near his home in Forest Gate. In January 1971 he had survived one previous attempt when he was shot in the legs and buttocks in his bedroom. This was a serious attempt, for a bullet landed chest-high in the wall. It was said to have been a contract with £500 on offer to the successful killer. Machin fled to the relative sanctuary of Streatham, and in his last years he became increasingly unpleasant: 'Machin was a tapper. You only had to meet him once and he'd be round your door the next morning blagging you for a score or a fifty,' recalls one of his victims.[2]

The long-time associate of the Richardsons, Jimmy Moody, was last seen alive on 1 June 1993 when he was gunned down at the bar of the Royal Hotel, Hackney, where he was known to the staff as Mick. According to reports a man in his early forties dressed in a leather jacket went to the lavatory and, returning a few moments later, fired three rounds from a .38 into Moody's chest. As Moody fell he fired again, this time into his back. The man then walked out and was driven away in a Ford Fiesta XR2. No one has ever been charged.

Before that night the last confirmed sighting of Moody had been thirteen years earlier when he had been locked in his cell in Brixton prison where he was awaiting trial. Known as a hard man, his first conviction in 1967 was for the manslaughter of a young man, merchant navy steward William Day, at a South London party, for which he and his brother Richard were sentenced to six years apiece.

[2] Conversation with author.

It was his last conviction but by no means his last involvement in crime.

During the 1960s he was a member of Charles Richardson's South-East London team and was at Mr Smith's club on 9 March 1966, the night when Dickie Hart was killed in the affray there. It was Moody who drove both Eddie Richardson and Harry Rawlins away from the club in his Jaguar, carrying the badly injured Rawlins into Dulwich Hospital before disappearing into the early morning light. When Moody was charged with the affray the jury could not agree and he was discharged. Then he was charged along with Charles and Eddie Richardson and Frank Fraser in the so-called Torture Trial. Again Moody was acquitted.

In the late 1970s he became an invaluable member of Billy Tobin's so-called Chainsaw Gang – sometimes called the Thursday Gang – which specialised in hijacking (often with considerable violence) security vans in the South-East London area. On one occasion Moody, dressed as a policeman, jumped out of a car in the Blackwall Tunnel and forced a security van to stop. To prevent the alarm being given he took the keys from a number of nearby motorists. The end for Tobin, and in a way Moody, came about when he was arrested at Dulwich in the act of hijacking a security van with a mobile crane.

The ever-resourceful Moody escaped and hid out in a lock-up garage which he furnished with books, food, body-building equipment and a chemical toilet, but he was caught when he visited his son's flat in Brixton. He was charged with a series of robberies totalling £930,000 and sent to Brixton prison to await trial. In the 1980s it was still possible for remand prisoners to have food, wine and beer brought in by friends and relatives. Moody's brother Richard brought, with the Sunday lunches, hacksaw blades, drill bits and other tools.[3]

Moody had noticed that outside his cell was a flat roof and it was to this that he and cell mates Gerard Tuite, a Provisional IRA bomb-maker, and Stanley Thompson, veteran of the Parkhurst prison riot of 1969 and now charged with armed robbery, cut

[3] There is a full account of Moody's life and death in Cal McCrystal's 'The Hit at the Royal Hotel' in *The Independent on Sunday*, 8 August 1993.

through the brickwork. Every morning the rubble was removed in their chamber pots at slopping-out time. On 16 December 1980 they pushed out the loosened brickwork of their cell, stepped on to the roof where a ladder had been left by roofers and were away.

Moody simply vanished. Apart from an unsuccessful raid on a flat in West London where his fingerprints and nothing else was found of him, and an occasional card signed 'Jim', there was no sign at all for the next thirteen years. Where had he been and why was he shot?

According to Frank Fraser it was well known that a hit was coming. He believes it was over the killing of David Brindle:

> In June this year I had a telephone call telling me to go away for a few days. I didn't ask why, because it was a friendly call. So I packed a bag and caught the train from Euston to the North . . . Later that evening I got a call to say Jimmy Moody had been shot. I stayed up North another couple of days and then came back . . . I suppose if someone who knew it was going off had really pleaded for him it might have made some difference, but I doubt it.[4]

At the time of his death Moody had been living in Wadeson Street, a back alley off Mare Street in Hackney. As to why, one theory was that it was a killing done on behalf of a cuckolded husband, for Moody was very much a ladies' man who is said to have required the services of a different woman each evening.[5]

It is likely that Moody was one of the victims in the Brindle–Daly struggle and specifically his death was in revenge for the killing of David Brindle in the Bell public house in Walworth in August 1991. It was suggested that he had beaten David Brindle with a baseball bat and had later shot him before reprisals could be taken. Moody had been working as a barman in the area in a public house owned by the Daly family.

What is certain is that Moody was employed as a contract killer during his years on the run. Now that he is dead his is the most

[4] Frank Fraser, *Mad Frank*, pp. 220–22.
[5] Marilyn Wisbey, *Gangster's Moll*, pp. 26–7. In the book she gives a personal account of their relationship.

convenient name in the frame for a number of unsolved murders, regarded as contract killings, including Gwenda and Peter Dixon who disappeared while on a walking tour of Pembrokeshire in June 1989. Another pair that year – 32-year-old Maxine Arnold and her boyfriend Terry Gooderham – were found shot dead in their black Mercedes in Epping Forest on 22 December 1989. Most likely she was a bystander; he may have been more of a player, which resulted in what was almost certainly a gangland execution. Gooderham had been a stocktaker for a number of clubs and pubs in London and Hertfordshire, and one anonymous friend put it, 'It is nothing to do with his love life or his own business but a lot of money is involved.' The sum suggested is £150,000, euphemistically described as having been redirected. Another of the deaths was that on 24 March 1991 of the 47-year-old antiques and cocaine dealer Peter Raisini who was shot in the garden of his home in Palmers Green, North London, possibly over a failed drug deal or a failure to pay for drugs. Then there was the killing which has been laid on Moody's doorstep of 42-year-old Patricia Parsons, whose body was found in her Volkswagen Cabriolet in Epping Forest. However, attributing all these deaths to Moody may be just another way of clearing up the books.

There is no question but that Alfred Robert Gerard was involved in the death of Frank Mitchell, the so-called Mad Axeman, helped by the Kray Twins to escape from Dartmoor and killed when he became an encumbrance and started to threaten them. Gerard was also part of the team who killed the thief Ginger Marks. Neither of the bodies has been found. There are also a number of others who disappeared at the time, for which the blame is laid on Gerard.

'We were none of us nice, but you wouldn't turn your back on him,' said Kray lieutenant Albert Donaghue, mildly, of Gerard. 'I thought of him as an original member of Murder Incorporated,' said Mickey Bailey, himself a former East End hardman. 'Alfie Gerard was all right. The likes of Gerard wouldn't tolerate things as they do today. They wouldn't tolerate a bully or a car thief. He wasn't very tall but he was a very nasty man. Never pulled his punches. He probably killed dozens of people.'

A former bank robber was less enthusiastic:

> He was a very hard man. Most hateful, frightening man because he was so fucking ugly. He had a horrible disposition. In fact he was the most hateful man God ever put breath into.[6]

Nor was the former club owner Ronnie Diamond any more enthusiastic: 'He had not an ounce of feeling in his body. He could have killed his own son without batting an eyelid.'

On the other hand Marilyn Wisbey, daughter of a Great Train Robber, liked him, thinking that physically he resembled the actor James Cagney but was far bigger.[7] Gerard was regarded as an excellent cook, who at one time owned the Blue Plaice in Southwark Park Road which was highly regarded amongst the cognoscenti for its conger eel and mash with parsley sauce. He also had the City Club in the City Road. Even there his customers were frightened of him. Ronnie Diamond recalls:

> No one would drink in the club. They were terrified. We were up there one day and my friend Tel ordered a steak sandwich. He didn't finish it and Alf was on to him, 'What's wrong?' 'Nothing.' 'So you eat it. You'd better eat it before you go or I'll batter you.' Another time Alf would do a Sunday lunch and someone asked for gravy. Alf was outraged. 'I'll give you fucking gravy. I don't spoil my food with gravy.' The fellow ate it up and flew out.

Of the Mitchell death Freddie Foreman, the former helpmate of the Twins, had this to say:

> Alfie Gerard was with me. He was a good man to have with you to get it done as quick as possible. It was all over in seconds. If you're sitting on a cold winter's night in the back of a van waiting to commit the horrible crime it's not very nice. It's not something you get pleasure out of doing. It's got to be done properly and mercifully and as quickly as possible. As soon as it was over

---

[6] Where there is no separate footnote all quotes are from conversations with the author.
[7] Marilyn Wisbey, *Gangster's Moll*, p. 78.

and done with the better. I know that sounds very clinical and cold blooded. I was Frank Mitchell's final executioner.[8]

It has been suggested that Nicky Gerard's total number of contracts exceeded thirteen. 'Nicky Gerard was the dead spit of his father but he had a much nicer nature. Personally I liked Nicky. Alfie, when he died in Brighton, was not missed by many. He was a hateful bastard,' says a former robber. 'He [Alfie] would lean on anybody who took liberties,' said another acquaintance. 'But he wasn't only a muscle for hire man. He was known and feared throughout the East End.' As for Nicky, 'He was another lunatic. He was an out-and-out bully.'

Known as Snakehips, Nicky Gerard is regularly credited with the killing of André Mizelas, the Mile End-born owner of the André Bernard hairdressing chain. Mizelas is alleged to have reneged on a £100,000 debt due to a South London moneylender. Others believe that it was more of a domestic matter, and that Mizelas had slept in the bed of one husband too many. Whichever is correct, on 9 November 1970 Mizelas was shot twice as he drove his red Triumph TR5 sports car through Hyde Park. Some sources claim Gerard was paid £2,500 for each bullet.[9]

His most celebrated killing was that of Alfredo 'Italian Tony' Zomparelli in the Golden Goose amusement arcade in Old Compton Street on 4 September 1974 on behalf of Ronnie Knight, for which he is said to have received £1,000 for the hit. The discount may have been because of a personal interest; at the time, Gerard was seeing Zomparelli's wife. It arose out of the beating of Knight's younger brother David in a fight with a Johnny Isaacs in a pub at the Angel, Islington.

On 7 May 1970, when David was out of hospital, Ronnie took him round to the Latin Quarter nightclub off Leicester Square to see Isaacs, to whom Ronnie had already given a retaliatory beating. He maintains it was to receive an apology, but the police thought protection was a more apposite word. In the ensuing fight Zomparelli,

---

[8] ITV. *The Krays: Unfinished Business* (Part 1) transmitted 13 January 2000; *The Krays: Inside the Firm* (Part 2) transmitted 17 January 2000.
[9] *Daily Mail*, 10 December 1999.

run-around man for Albert Dimes, and then working as a bouncer for the club, stabbed David Knight twice in the chest. Zomparelli received what was regarded by Knight as a merciful four-year sentence for manslaughter.

After serving his prison sentence Zomparelli ran a bucket-shop travel agency in Frith Street. Much of his leisure time was spent playing the pinball machines in the Golden Goose, not far from the A. & R. Club. It was in the pinball arcade that he was shot in the head and the back by two men wearing dark glasses and moustaches a few months after his release. Appropriately, he was playing a game called Wild Life.

In 1980 Maxie Piggot aka George Bradshaw became the super-grass with most to confess in his generation. On 17 January 1980 he received a life sentence for the murder of Zomparelli, with a ten-year concurrent sentence for all the rest. In his long confession, in which he admitted to over a hundred armed robberies, he also named Nicky Gerard as his co-hitman, indeed as the one who pulled the trigger of a .38 revolver. Gerard had paid him £325 as a lookout, but the shock of hearing gunfire made Bradshaw involuntarily pull the trigger of his own .22. Oh yes?

But by 1980 supergrasses did not always have the ear of the jury. Ten years of practice had taught defence barristers how to over-come the witness's all-consuming repentance and a desire to bare his soul so that justice could at last be done. The public was also becoming a little tired of hearing the evidence of men who had committed the most outrageous crimes and who were serving relatively nominal sentences. They did not like hearing how brave these men had been by telling all, so when they sat on a jury they were rightly sceptical. Ronnie Knight also had the bonus of his then wife, the actress Barbara Windsor, on his side. The jury acquitted both him and Gerard.

Some years later, after a long stay in Spain and his release from a seven-year sentence for handling part of the proceeds in the £7 million Security Express robbery of 1983, Knight admitted he had paid for the contract. Gerard had called him and asked if he had an alibi:

'Ronnie, it's done, are you covered?' I replied, 'Don't worry, I've got so many witnesses there ain't a court big enough to hold them.'[10]

Nicky Gerard did not last all that long after his acquittal, for in June 1982 he was shot dead in South London. Before the Zomparelli trial, in May 1978 he had been gaoled for seven years for an attack on boxer Michael Gluckstead at the Norseman Club in Canning Town. He was found not guilty of the attempted murder of Gluckstead who, widely regarded as a local bully, had been jailed for sex offences; crimes unacceptable to the underworld. Gluckstead had his cheek slit from ear to nose and was shot twice, as well as being hit about the head and stomped. The trial judge Melford Stevenson wanted to give Gerard an opportunity to explain his part, but he declined to do so. While he was in prison Gerard had been sentenced, *in absentia*, by a kangaroo court. His wife Linda had received threats and a wreath with the message: 'Nicky Gerard, Rest in Peace'.[11]

On 27 June 1982, when leaving his daughter's eleventh-birthday party, Gerard was ambushed by gunmen wearing boiler suits and balaclava helmets at the lock-up garage to which he had driven his Oldsmobile. Shots were fired through the windscreen and he was hit in the stomach. He managed to get out of the car and to stagger a hundred yards but his attackers followed him, smashing him so hard on the head with a gun that the stock shattered. He was then beaten unconscious before the gunmen reloaded and shot him. Gerard had not been sufficiently careful. Over the previous few days he had known he was being followed, but he thought they were undercover police.

On 22 November his cousin and 'best friend' Thomas Hole was arrested and charged with his murder. Tried at the Old Bailey in April 1983, he had been picked out on an identification parade by a 'Mr Fisher', the pseudonym given to a protected witness who said he had seen a man with one rubber washing-up glove acting suspiciously. 'But,' he added, 'I am not sure it was the man I had seen that day in June in the car park.' Despite protests that the Crown had more

---

[10] For Knight's version of the case see Ronnie Knight, *Black Knight*.
[11] *East London Advertiser*, 26 May 1978.

evidence which it had not been allowed to produce, on 27 April the trial judge stopped the case at the end of the prosecution evidence. Hole, who left court with his friends, said, 'My head is reeling.'

Possibly Nicky Gerard's killing resurfaced thirty years later when Tommy Hole, now aged 57, was killed in the Beckton Arms, Beckton, on 5 December 1999 along with Joey 'The Crow' Evans, two years younger. They had been watching television on the pub's giant screen. The balaclava-wearing killers waited until 3.20 p.m. when the pub was emptying and then six shots were fired at point-blank range, killing The Crow first and then Hole as he tried to flee. The killers then walked out of the pub and escaped through a subway.

One version of the reason for this killing is that Hole and The Crow had short-changed their colleagues in an £80,000 drug deal. Another is that it relates back to the Gerard killing. Gerard's uncle James had died the month before the shooting of Hole, and it is suggested that Hole had been at the funeral bragging how he had killed Nicky. Not so, said Mrs Hole, he had been at home with her putting up blinds. Since his release from prison he had apparently led a quiet life.[12]

The Great Train Robber Charlie Wilson was certainly one who made it to the Costa del Sol, that haven for European gangsters, only to be shot at his villa overlooking Marbella. Whether he was actually in retirement is a moot point. The Glasgow hitman Stewart 'Specky' Boyd also made it to the Costa del Sol, even though his stay was a short one. It was there in June 2003 that he was killed in a 100 m.p.h. head-on collision near Malaga. His daughter, another girl and a three-year-old child were also killed in the fireball which engulfed the car. In 1996 Boyd had been acquitted of killing the Paisley gangster Mark Rennie, and was the one-time right-hand man to the drug baron John Healy, the associate of 'The Licensee' Tam McGraw whose fortune in 2003 was estimated at £14 million. In the months before his death Boyd had been involved in the security firm wars which have bedevilled Glasgow in recent years.

Spain could be just as dangerous for travelling Irishmen on occasions. On 10 August 2000, Michael McGuinness from

---

[12] *Daily Mail*, 10 December 1999; *The Independent*, 11 December 1999.

Limvady, Co. Derry – or rather his rotting remains – were found in the boot of a Range Rover parked at Malaga airport where the temperature was 35°C. Initially the police thought it might be a booby-trap set by the Basque organisation ETA but it was only McGuinness, his hands cuffed behind his back and his head in a black plastic bag.

Very little information was forthcoming about his death, but he had rented a flat in Puebla Aida just outside Mijas. At 2 o'clock on the previous Monday morning two men were let in through the gate security by him, seemingly to collect money. An argument followed and he was taken away at gunpoint. His girlfriend was unable to give any real description of the men and has since disappeared. One suggestion is that McGuinness had been money-laundering on behalf of a major Dublin criminal and the accounting procedures had gone awry in his favour. His death was the fifth on the Costa in 2000 which could reasonably be attributed to gangland crime. The previous week a Frenchman had been shot and killed in San Pedro. Two other victims were Arabs who were shot at close range as they sat in their vehicles near Marbella.

Over the years the face of Dublin crime has changed, with many major players moving to Spain. It was there in Torrevieja that Liam Judge died of a heart attack in November 2003 at the age of 47. Living with John Gilligan's daughter Tracey, Judge had been running a building business as well as dealing in cocaine. He was said to be drinking a bottle of whiskey at each meal as well as taking drugs.[13]

After the 2003 shooting of Bernard Sugg in Dublin, his brother Stephen and Shane Coates, the boss of the Westies, fled to Spain, living near Alicante where they dealt in cocaine and cannabis. The pair disappeared early in 2004 and at first the authorities thought it was a fake so that they could return to Dublin and settle a few accounts. However, as the days went by and they did not resurface the theory was revised, and it was believed they had been kidnapped and disposed of following a failure to pay for some 200 kilos of cannabis.[14]

Murder has not been confined to the mainland. In November

---

[13] Jim Cusack in *The Sunday Independent*, 21 December 2003.
[14] *Irish Times*, 3 January 2004; *Irish Independent*, 13 February 2004.

1997 Manfred Meisel, the self-styled King of Beer who ran the Bier K:nig Palace in Majorca, was found executed at his home. His eight-year-old son Patrick had been shot twice through the head and the child's nanny, Claudia Liestein, had also been killed. She had been bound with her hands behind her back in Meisel's office where both she and the beer king were shot. It seems she was pushed to the floor and a pillow placed over her head. Unusually the killings, which otherwise had the hallmark of the professional, had been done with small-calibre 6.35 bullets.

Another who made it to the south of Spain, although he was far too young to retire, was Scott Bradfield, a friend of the Adams family from North London, whose chopped-up remains were found packed into two suitcases at a conference centre in Torremolinos. Bradfield, the chief suspect for the shooting of James Gaspa, 22, in Islington in May 2000, had possibly become another Dixie Cup. One theory is that Bradfield, a drugs dealer, was murdered by East European hitmen on the orders of a British drugs baron. He had left the country the day Gaspa was murdered. Spanish detectives believe his body was then left by his killers to be discovered as a warning to other dealers on the Costa del Crime. Another possibility is that he was about to blow a long blast on a high-pitched whistle.[15]

For many, the alternatives to retirement are death at the hands of the state or an enemy, or a long term of imprisonment. A notable example is the Australian Chris Flannery who, back in the 1980s, was said to have charged $50,000 a hit and was a completely loose cannon. His disappearance occupied Sydney's courts on and off for the better part of the 1990s. He was so hated and feared in the underworld that any of six people, including old-time characters such as George Freeman and Lennie McPherson, could have been involved in his killing.[16] If anything is clear about his death it is that he was last seen on 9 May 1985 when, according to his wife

---

[15] *Evening Standard*, 3 December 2001.

[16] The former safebreaker George Freeman regarded himself as a misunderstood racing identity. The *Sydney Morning Herald* regarded him as no lower than No. 3 in the Sydney criminal hierarchy for the twenty years prior to his death in 1988. *Sydney Morning Herald*, 18 September 1994. Lennie McPherson was thought of as the Mr Big of Sydney crime. He collapsed and died in prison after making a telephone call to his wife. For an account of these giants of crime see James Morton, *Gangland International*, Chapter 37.

Kathleen, he told her he was going to visit Freeman at his home at Yowie Bay.

Prominent amongst the conflicting theories is that he was killed by either the underworld or the police – shot by a police officer at Geelong racetrack; lured to Sydney Harbour and killed with a machine gun; shot by police at traffic lights; buried at sea; killed at a hide-out in Connaught; buried in Sydney's western suburbs or killed by a biker and fed through a tree-shredder. But there is a minority Lord Lucan theory that he lived on. What is also absolutely clear is that while the heroin war killings in which he was involved did not cease with Flannery's disappearance, for a time there was a much greater survival rate amongst the combatants.[17]

One rare exception who did survive comfortably was the Detroit hitman from the 1930s John Mirabella, who had handled the killing of Jerry Buckley.[18] He also had the contract for the killing of gambler and beer baron Jack Kennedy and two other men and a woman in Toledo, a city some half an hour from Detroit. Toledo, like many another city of the era, normally provided a safe home for criminals on the understanding that it was not used by them for unsanctioned, unlawful activities. The reason for the deaths had been a bootlegging dispute. Kennedy had refused to listen to his bodyguard, the appropriately named Howard Vice, who warned him that his involvement with a girl known as Miss Tiger Woman would lead to his death. It did.

By now there were warrants out for Mirabella's arrest over both the Buckley and Kennedy killings. This itself put Mirabella at risk, not only from the authorities but also from the Mob. A hitman with too much knowledge who is under threat from the police generally has a short life expectancy. However, Mirabella again disappeared, this time to neighbouring Youngstown, where he remained on the face of things running a grocery business until his death in 1955.

In fact he was supported by payments from 'Cadillac' Charley

---

[17] The tree-shredder story is from Mark Read, *Chopper* 2. See also Mark Khazar, 'Chopper's Whoppers' in *Australian Penthouse*, December 1994. For a fuller review of the Flannery theories see Paul McGeough, 'Flannery Fictions' in *Sydney Morning Herald*, 11 May 1996.

[18] See Chapter 12.

Cavallaro, the Youngstown boss who met him on a weekly, if reluctant, basis. They would embrace and, according to Cavallaro's chauffeur-cum-bodyguard, 'had a helluva reunion as if they hadn't seen each other for years'. Cavallaro would then hand over 'a wad of dough'. On the way home he would complain bitterly about having to give money to 'shortcoats and leeches'. But, apart from his formidable reputation Mirabella must have had some insurance somewhere because he survived, living under the name Paul Magine and in 1945 marrying a local woman, before dying of cirrhosis at the age of 50.[19]

As an alternative there is sometimes the opportunity to build a new life by giving evidence against former colleagues and vanishing into a witness programme. Unfortunately, no longer can the hitman hope to trade up with the authorities and give them higher ranking bodies. The boss may have done it first. In what appears to be an amazing turn around, the so-called last Don Joseph Massino of the Bonanno Family, convicted in late 2004 of conspiracy to murder and facing the death penalty and possible forfeiture proceedings, may have started to trade down. In an indictment unsealed in January 2005 against Vincent Basciano, known as Vinny Gorgeous, Massino was named as having spoken to another senior Mob figure about killing the prosecutor, Greg D. Andres. It would appear that Massino was now co-operating with the authorities.[20]

It is, however, now most likely to be only the really heavy hitter who seems to qualify for this good fortune. Star killer-informers have included the trio from Montreal, Réal Simard, Donald Lavoie and Yves 'Apache' Trudeau.

However, perhaps the most famous of the American converts has been Sammy 'The Bull' Gravano, who murdered nineteen people and then provided the evidence to convict John Gotti senior. He served about five years for his trouble. Old Mafia watchers had seen Gravano give an impressive courtroom display. The former boxer had been with Gotti from around 1977 and, he later admitted, was the driver at the killing of Gotti's former boss Paul Castellano outside

---

[19] Hank Messick, *The Private Lives of Public Enemies.*
[20] *New York Times*, 28 January 2005.

Sparks Steak House at 210 E 46th after which Gotti had taken over the Donship.

Gravano was a fairly rare flower. Formerly a member of the Colombo Family, after a dispute he had been allowed to transfer to the Gambinos. Under Gotti, his rise in his adopted Family had been almost unceasing. He had taken over Castellano's interests in the construction industry and simply had his associates killed – Liborio Milito and Louis DiBono were two examples – if he thought they were being greedy. In 1989 it was estimated that the annual income of this man, born into a poor family from Sicily, was in the region of three-quarters of a million dollars.[21]

The blow fell on 12 December 1990 when Gotti was indicted on five murder conspiracies including the killing of Castellano and Bilotti. Also in the indictment were Frank Locascio and Gravano, as was Thomas Gambino, one of Carlos' sons. There was almost immediately bad news for Gotti. His lawyer, the flamboyant Bruce Cutler, was disqualified by the judge from acting at the trial and replaced by the Miami-based veteran Albert Krieger. Worse, there was a witness who could place Gotti outside the steakhouse shortly before Castellano was shot. That was bad enough, but there was still more to come. Gravano defected. Not only did he face fifty years if convicted after a plea of not guilty but also the confiscation of his property. However, he was the man who could unravel and expand on the hours of tapes taken from the bugs the police had placed in the Gotti hangout, the Ravinelli Club on Mulberry Street in Little Italy. It was cut-a-deal time or, as the French would say, *sauve qui peut*. The prosecution was also expected to call on the defecting Philadelphian mobster, Crazy Phil Leonetti, to tell the jury that Gotti had told him about the Castellano hit.

In the end Leonetti was not called, but Gravano managed quite well enough. As might be expected, it was suggested that he was giving evidence for his own ends, which of course he undoubtedly was. The agreement he had reached was a maximum term of twenty years and a $250,000 fine. To a certain extent his fate was in his own hands. If he did well, Judge Glasser could give him less than

[21] For an account of Gravano's life with the Gambinos see Peter Maas, *Underboss*.

twenty. If he was found to have lied, he could be prosecuted for any of the crimes he had admitted. What he did was catalogue a seemingly endless number of killings – nineteen in all – for such diverse reasons as cheating, failing to show respect, lying, giving evidence to a Grand Jury and so on.

The trial judge must have been enchanted with the result because he sentenced Gravano to a little over five years. Gravano had sung sufficiently well to be released in early 1995, and was also well into the Federal Witness Program. In the spring of 1997, with the help of Peter Maas who had earlier assisted Joe Valachi, Gravano published his memoirs. The book was not wholly well received, particularly by the relatives of his victims who, perhaps understandably, thought some of the revenues should go to them.

Moreover, the face-lifted Gravano lived to tell his tale on television, appearing on such programmes as *PrimeTime Live*. Offers by an Illinois police union of a payment of $500 for spotting The Bull in exile, something which could be interpreted as a bounty, went uncollected.

In April 1997 a former Police Association President, John Flood, suggested that he expected Gravano to commit more crimes. He was not disappointed because, now resident in Arizona, Gravano had proved that there was, after all, life to be had after betraying John Gotti senior. Eight years after his evidence had brought down the Don, Gravano was again arrested, this time together with his wife Debra, his son Gerard and his daughter Karen along with thirty-two others including the alleged white supremacist Michael Papa, said to be the founder of the Devil Dogs.

Gravano had left the Witness Program in 1995 and had been living unmolested under the name of Jimmy Moran in Tempe, Arizona, where he ran the Marathon Swimming Pool Company. He had, said the prosecution in February 2000, also been overseeing an operation which sold between 20,000 and 25,000 Ecstasy tablets a week. Gravano had, said the police, also been acting as tutor to the Devil Dogs and other vendors and collectors. They had adopted a much more positive stance towards their debtors since Gravano became involved.

It was only a matter of time before Gravano junior, Gerard, turned on his father. He wanted a separate trial in the New York case, fearing, 'All the evils that will be visited upon [his] fair-trial rights will result solely from his father's presence in the case.' Immediately after, the government released a thirty-four-page document claiming that Gravano had plotted to murder Gerard's girlfriend because she had boasted of her relationship. There was also an allegation that he had tried to found the Arizona Mafia as a chapter of La Cosa Nostra. Yet another allegation in the document was that he planned to murder Ronald Kuby, the New York lawyer who was bringing civil actions on behalf of the relations of some of the nineteen men whom Gravano admitted murdering. The idea had been to lure Mr Kuby with the prospect of a new case and then kill him. It was something Gravano's New York lawyer, Lynne Stewart, was quick to deny.

A fortnight later it was all over. Both Sammy and Gerard Gravano bowed to the inevitable and agreed to plead guilty in New York, and by doing so limited their liability to fifteen years apiece. Meanwhile reprisals against Gravano had been both put in place and thwarted. On 3 August 2003 the 55-year-old Thomas 'Huck' Carbonaro shrugged after the jury in Brooklyn found him guilty of conspiring to murder Gravano. The jury cleared him on two gun charges.

Prosecutors said Carbonaro and a Mob associate had managed to locate Gravano in 1999 in Arizona. While stalking their target, they allegedly devised two ways to kill him: by blowing him up with a remote-control bomb fashioned from shotgun shells, or by shooting him from long range with a sniper rifle. Gravano was arrested before the alleged hit was carried out. Called as a witness by the defence in the hope of showing that Carbonaro had no motive to kill him, this time he did his best. Giving evidence, he described himself as an expert hitman who would have made a difficult target, and said that he knew Carbonaro 'from a mile away'. He also told the court that at one time he was so close to Carbonaro that their families holidayed together in Florida to 'get away from "the life"' – the everyday grind of being in Cosa Nostra.[22]

A minor league version of Gravano has been Carmine Sessa. He started in a lowly position with the Mafia, shining shoes in social clubs before working his way up to become a *consiglieri* with the Colombo Family. On the way he took part in thirteen murders of

[22] *Birmingham Evening News*, 4 August 2003.

which he pulled the trigger in four. Arrested in 1993, he turned informer and gave evidence in eight Federal trials. He was able to explain away his lifestyle: 'I wound up growing up around a life that was a disease that has destroyed so many families throughout the years including my own.' After his shoeshining experiences, 'From there the crimes started escalating eventually to murder and seemed to never stop. One day you are a friend and the next day somebody said he's got to go for whatever reason, and sometimes you are a part of it or even have to pull the trigger.' And with that it was another month inside and then into the Witness Protection Program.

His public-spiritedness did not appeal to New York lawyer Gerald Shargel, defending in a case in which Sessa had given evidence. He commented that the sentence of 'time served' passed on Sessa sent a 'message that no matter how many people you kill, no matter how vicious the killings, if you sign up with the government, you can win remarkable benefits'. He thought Sessa's case 'particularly egregious' because the former Colombo man had been released on bail in 1997 but was back in prison in March 1999 for beating his wife and possessing two guns.[23]

At least for those in prison the conditions are unlikely to be as bad as at the Petak Island prison midway between St Petersburg and Vologda from which, like the old Alcatraz, escape is impossible. In 2004 hired killer Valery told a visiting journalist, 'There are no lavatories, no proper washing facilities and you spend your whole life in a cell.' Lock-up in a two-man cell is for twenty-two and a half hours a day, and the other ninety minutes is spent in a small exercise cage. Offences are punished severely; the prisoner is locked in a small room with only a metal bucket for fifteen days, with no books. In the day-time the bed must be stowed away and the prisoner can either stand or sit on what amounts to a ledge. Within a matter of years most prisoners have lost all contact with their families. Half have tuberculosis, and those who die are buried in a small graveyard nearby.[24]

Clearly hitmen can survive after their sell-by date and giving

---

[23] *Daily News*, 29 September 2000.
[24] Julian Strauss, 'Waiting for death in Russia's Alcatraz' in *Daily Telegraph*, 10 August 2004.

evidence. One who disappeared into the wilds was Donald Lavoie, the celebrated hitman for the feared Dubois clan who ruled the French-Canadian underworld of Montreal in the 1970s. Lavoie and his brother Carl grew up in orphanages and foster homes in and around Chicoutimi. After serving two years for burglary, he gravitated to Montreal where he worked for the notorious Claude Dubois. His first contract was on Louis Fournier and Robert Beaupré, the owner and manager of the Jan-Lou café, after they refused to pay protection money. However, he was recognised and fled to New York from where a year later he was deported. In October 1972 he was acquitted. By the end of the 1970s Lavoie had killed some twenty-seven people on behalf of the clan. The end came at a wedding on 22 November 1980 at the Quality Inn hotel in Sherbrooke Street when he overheard Dubois and another gang member, Alain Charron, discussing his death.

Resourcefulness is another quality required of the contract killer, and Lavoie escaped a search organised by Charron by sliding down a laundry shute to the basement. The next day he telephoned Dubois to say he would not give up without a fight and joined forces with Jean Tremblay, another ex-Dubois man, to kill Claude. They needed money and, along with Tremblay's brother Paul and a Marc-André Blanchette, decided to rob bank manager Thomas Prucha in what was becoming a standard kidnap and hostage-taking of the period. On 7 December that year Lavoie held Prucha's wife and mother-in-law in their flat while the others took him to the bank. The take was $135,000, but a fortnight later he and Tremblay were arrested in his chalet near Joliette.

Shortly after Christmas he became a supergrass. Tremblay went down on 7 January 1982 when he received twenty years. On 8 December that year Claude Dubois, Claude Dubeau and Yvon Belzil were sentenced to life imprisonment – later reduced to ten years – after Lavoie gave evidence that he had murdered Richard Desormiers and Jaques-André Bourassa on Dubois' orders on 25 June 1973. He went on to give evidence against other Dubois brothers and provided information relating to some eighty other murders. His reward was eight years in the informers' quarters on the fourth floor of the Parthenais prison in Montreal. After his release he was given a new identity and disappeared.

One who disappeared only to resurface was Lavoie's contemporary in Parthenais, Réal Simard, who had been part of the legendary Frank Cotroni's team of Italians. In 1986 he pleaded guilty to three charges of manslaughter and received a lenient sentence in return for giving evidence against members of the Cotroni clan. Released, he disappeared in 1999 after his parole was suspended when he was suspected of using false identification. He went to Mexico but when he published a second book *Trahisons*, foolishly he appeared on television back in Canada to publicise it. He then worked as a security guard at a fashionable school until on 16 October 2004 he was arrested in the St Michel district of the city when he went with his 12-year-old son to see his sister.

And finally, as a none too encouraging near end piece the third inmate of the Parthenais at the time was the Montreal-based contractor, Hells Angel Yves 'The Mad Bumper' Trudeau. His defection into the arms of the law came when, in March 1985, it was announced that the North Chapter of which he was a member was to be closed down. Four members would be relocated and the rest would be retired, a euphemism for killed. Trudeau promptly saw The Light. By any standards his career working not only for the Angels but also for members of the city's Irish Mob, the West End Gang, had been an amazing one. Dark-haired, square-jawed, relatively small at 5'6" and weighing 136 lbs, he was born on 2 April 1946 and was the first Canadian Angel to be used as a Hells Angel killer and member of the elite Filthy Few, the Angels' death arm. Before he sought the protection of the police he had – from September 1970 until July 1985 – murdered forty-three people. Twenty-nine were shot, ten blown up, three beaten to death, one was strangled. Two of the deaths were innocent bystanders; William Weichold was mistaken for an Outlaw biker with whom the Angels were feuding at the time, and was killed on 8 December 1978, while the other, Robert Morin, was blown up when he borrowed a friend's car on 14 March 1981. There were half-innocent bystanders as well. Five days earlier on Mother's Day, 9 March 1981, Lucille Vallières was sitting on her porch when she was shot along with the intended target – another drug dealer, Donat Lemieux. Rachelle Francoeur was another who was simply in the wrong place when the drug dealer Phillip Galipeau was shot and killed in 1984. Yves Lavigne, the fearless chronicler of the Angels, thought Trudeau epitomised:

> the success and failure of Hell's Angels. His fearlessness and ability to take care of business are attributes on which the club's power is based . . . Trudeau himself, the most dedicated and exemplary Angel by original standards . . .[25]

Whether or not he actually knew of the message sent to American headquarters, Trudeau's antennae were on overtime. He avoided a massacre at the club headquarters by checking into a drug rehabilitation centre at Oka, but he knew his life expectancy was short when he was told he had been dishonourable. He was ordered to remove his Angels tattoos and obediently he blacked them out.

Now, with the dissolution of the North Chapter and the fear that with a cocaine habit spiralling out of control Trudeau was becoming unreliable, a contract of $50,000 was put out on him but, cynically, he still had work to do for the Angels. For a start his chopper had been seized, as had $46,000 he had left in the North Chapter clubhouse. The money was gone for ever, but he redeemed his bike by strangling Jean-Marc 'La Grand Geule' Deniger. He put the body in a car and contacted the *Journal de Montréal* to tell them where it might be found. This was in accordance with Hells Angels' policy that a hit had to be verified in the media.

It was the thought of the contract which persuaded Trudeau to become a supergrass. He had been arrested on a charge of theft and was soon to be released when a perspicacious officer, Sgt Marcel Lacoste, showed him the report of an inquest at which the contract had been mentioned. When he pointed out that Trudeau would soon be back on the streets and in danger, the Bumper pleaded guilty to the theft charge and was moved to the fourth floor of the Parthenais prison. Self-justification set in: 'I was a dead man anyways. I had decided to stop doing coke. I thought of my wife and my child.'[26]

---

[25] Yves Lavigne, *Hell's Angels*, p. 278.
[26] Ibid., p. 222.

What was so amazing was that the police had no evidence against Trudeau for any single one of his forty-three killings. All they ended up with was his confession. In return a bargain was struck and the prosecutors were obliged to accept pleas to manslaughter – in other words, that the killings were not intentional.[27] To those not conversant with the courts, this must have been hard to comprehend in the case of André Desjardins, his wife Berthe and his mother Jeanne. Beaten to death by Trudeau as he was in the process of abducting her son and daughter-in-law, Jeanne's body was put in a sleeping bag, fastened to a concrete block and dropped off a dock. André was consigned to a similar grave. But from time to time the authorities must link hands with the most unlikely companions, and Trudeau received a mere seven years for his services. After all, he was able to name ninety-five other murderers – of whom, it must be said, thirty-four were already dead.

Trudeau did extremely well for himself in the plea bargain. A trust fund to pay him $10,000 a year was set up, and while in Parthenais jail he had a private bathroom and colour cable TV. He was allowed $35 a week for cigarettes. He was also taken on a fortnightly visit to see his common-law wife and children for, as Lavigne delicately puts it, 'servicing'. He was released in 1991 and went to live under the name Denis Côté in Valleyfield. Unfortunately it was not the last heard of him. In the spring of 2004, representing himself, he pleaded for a two-year sentence at the Laval courthouse after pleading guilty to six sexual assault charges on an adolescent boy. He was sentenced to the four years recommended by the Crown.[28]

And as a postscript for those who wish to play amateur detective – for at the time of writing the professionals have completely failed to find him – Boston's Whitey Bulger has been in a sort of fugitive retirement for many years. On the FBI's Ten Most Wanted list, he is described as between 5'7" and 5'9", Caucasian, male aged

---

[27] For more detailed accounts of these heroes see Thomas C. Renner and Cecil Kirby, *Mafia Enforcer*; Peter Edwards and Michel Auger, *The Encyclopedia of Canadian Organized Crime*.

[28] *Les Nouvelles sur LCN*, 19 March 2004. For a fuller account of Trudeau's career and victims see Yves Lavigne, *Hell's Angels*. I am very grateful to Yves Lavigne for the help he has given me over the activities of the Hells Angels in Canada for this and other books.

in his seventies. His weight was given at between 150 and 160 lbs, blue eyes, silver white hair, with no scars or tattoos. Just the man to stand out in a crowd of old-age pensioners snowbirding in Miami or Palm Springs. There was also a suggestion that he had gone to Canada where his former colleague, the now imprisoned Stephen Flemmi, had camped out some years previously.

Despite the offer of rewards, by the end of 2004 Bulger was still leading the pursuers a merry dance and has been reported as being sighted in (apart from Canada, and in alphabetical order) Alabama, Florida, Iowa, Ireland, Italy, Louisiana, and even South Boston itself. Regular sightings have also been reported in Southern California, including two at a beauty salon where it was thought that his girlfriend, Catherine Greig, might have had her hair done. At the beginning of the year there was what the FBI described as a definite sighting, but a spokesman declined to say exactly where or when. If by the time of publication it has not been claimed, there is up to $250,000 on offer for information leading to his capture.

Bibliography

Alexander, S., *The Pizza Connection* (1988) New York, Weidenfeld & Nicolson.

Allsop, K., *The Bootleggers and Their Era* (1961) New York, Doubleday.

Anderson, H., *Larrikin Crook: The Rise and Fall of Squizzy Taylor* (1971) Melbourne, Jacaranda Press.

Anderson, P., *Shotgun City* (2004) Prahan, Victoria, Hardie Grant Books.

Auda, G., *Les Belles Années du Milieu* (2002) Paris, ed. Michalon.

Ayling, J., *Nothing but the Truth* (1993) Chippendale, NSW, Ironbark.

Ball, J., Chester, L. and Perrott, L., *Cops and Robbers* (1978) Harmondsworth, Penguin Books.

Barnao, T., *Violent Crimes that Shocked a Nation* (1985) Sydney, QB Books.

Bazal, J., *Le Milieu & Co.* (1990) Paris, Hervé Mourances.

Bean, J.P., *Crime in Sheffield* (1987) Sheffield, Sheffield City Libraries.

——*Over the Wall* (1994) London, Headline.

——*Verbals* (1995) London, Headline.

——(ed.) *The Book of Criminal Quotations* (2003) London, Artnick.

Beltrami, J., *The Defender* (1988) East Kilbride, M. & A. Thomson.

Bergreen, L., *Capone* (1994) London, Macmillan.

Block, A., *East Side – West Side, Organising Crime in New York 1930–1950* (1980) Cardiff, University College, Cardiff Press.

Botton, B., *Shadow of Shame* (1998) South Melbourne, Sun Books.

Brandt, C., '*I Heard You Paint Houses*' (2004) Hanover, New Hampshire, Steerforth Press.

Brashler, W., *The Don: The Life and Death of Sam Giancana* (1977) New York, Harper & Row.

Bresler, F., *Reprieve* (1965) London, George G. Harrap & Co.

Brown, M. (ed.), *Australian Crime* (1993) Sydney, Lansdowne.

Bruno, A., *The Iceman* (1993) London, Robert Hale.

Callaghan, C. and Byron Jones, B., *Heritage of an Outlaw: The Story of Frank Nash* (1979) Hobart, Okla., Schoonmaker Publishers.

Campbell, D., *The Underworld* (1994) London, BBC Books.

Campbell, R., Toohey, B. and Pinwell, W., *The Winchester Scandal* (1992) Milsons Point, NSW, Random House.

Cannon, M., *The Woman as Murderer* (1994) Mornington, Victoria, Today's Australia Publishing Co.

Cartwright, G., *Blood Will Tell* (1989) New York, Harcourt Brace Jovanovich.

Clarkson, W., *Mooney* (2003) London, Blake.

——*Costa Del Crime* (2004) London, Blake.

Cohen, M., *In My Own Words* (1975) New York, Prentice Hall.

Cohen, R., *Tough Jews* (1998) London, Jonathan Cape.

Cooley, R., *When Corruption Was King* (2004) Chicago, Avalon Publishing Group.

Cray, E., *Burden of Proof* (1973) New York, Macmillan.

Cummings, J. and Volkman, E., *Mobster* (1990) London, Futura.

David, J.H., *Mafia Dynasty* (1993) New York, HarperPaperbacks.

Deeley, P., *The Manhunters* (1970) London, Hodder & Stoughton.

Deitche, S.M., *Cigar City Mafia* (2004) New Jersey, Barricade Books.

Demaris, O., *The Last Mafioso* (1981) New York, Times Books.

DeMeo, A. and Ross, M.J., *For the Sins of My Father: The Legacy of a Mafia Life* (2002) New York, Broadway Books.

Desmarais, R., *Le Clan des Dubois* (1976) Montreal, Stanke.

De Vault, C., *Donald Lavoie, tueur à gages* (1984) Montreal, Quebec Livres.

Dewey, T., *Twenty Against the Underworld* (1974) New York, Doubleday.

Dower, A., *Deadline* (1979) Richmond, Vict., Hutchinson.

Dubois, C. and Jodoin, C., *Claude Dubois se raconte* (1976) Quebec, Private.

Dubro, J. and Rowland, R.F., *King of the Mob* (1979) Markham, Ont., Viking.

Edwards, P., *Blood Brothers* (1990) Toronto, McClellan-Bantam.

——and Auger, M., *The Encyclopedia of Canadian Organized Crime* (2004) Toronto, McClelland and Stewart.

——and Nicaso, A., *Deadly Silence* (1993) Toronto, Macmillan.

English, T.J., *The Westies* (1990) New York, G.P. Putnam's Sons.

Evans, J. and Short, M., *The Survivor* (2001) Edinburgh, Mainstream Publishing.

Feral, R., *Hit Man* (1983) Boulder, Colo., Paladin Press.

Forbes, G. and Meehan, P., *Such Bad Company* (1982) Edinburgh, Paul Harris.

Forbes, I., *Squad Man* (1973) London, W.H. Allen.

Fraser, F., *Mad Frank* (1995) London, Warner Books.

——*Mad Frank's Britain* (2003) London, Virgin Books.

Fried, A., *The Rise and Fall of the Jewish Gangster in America* (1980) New York, Columbia University Press.

Furo, J., *Team Killers* (2001) New York, Algora.

Gillard, M. and Flynn, L., *Untouchables* (2004) Edinburgh, Cutting Edge Press.

Hall, A. (ed), *Crimes of Horror* (1976) New York, Crescent Books.

Haller, M., *Life Under Bruno* (1991) Conshocken, Pa., Pennsylvania Crime Commission.

Hammer, R., *Playboy's Illustrated History of Organized Crime* (1975) Chicago, Playboy Press.

Hearn, D., *Legal Executions in New York 1639–1963* (1997) Jefferson, N.C., McFarland & Company Inc.

Henderson, B. and Summerlin, S., *The Supersleuths* (1977) London, Cassell.

Herbert, J. and Gilling, T., *The Bagman: The Life and Lies of Jack Herbert* (2004) Sydney, ABC Books.

Hickie, D., *The Prince and the Premier* (1985) North Ryde, NSW, Angus & Robertson.

——*Chow Hayes, Gunman* (1990) North Ryde, Angus & Robertson.

Higgins, R., *In The Name Of The Law* (1958) London, John Long.

Horn, T., *Life of Tom Horn, Government Scout and Interpreter written by Himself* (1964) Norman, University of Oklahoma Press.

Hurwood, B.J., *Society and the Assassin: A Background Book on Political Murder* (1970) New York, Parents' Magazine Press.

'Joey' and Fisher, D., *Killer* (1987) London, Star.

Jones, F., *Paid to Kill* (1995) London, Headline.

Kavieff, P.R., *The Purple Gang* (2000) New York, Barricade Books.

Kelleher, M.D. and C.L., *Murder Most Rare: The Female Serial Killer* (1998) New York, Dell/Random House.

Kidner, J., *Crimaldi: Contract Killer* (1976) Washington, Acropolis Books.

King, P. and R., *Contract Killers* (1995) London, Batsford.

Knight, R., *Black Knight* (1990) London, Century.

Kray, K. and Stern, C., *The Black Widow* (2002) London, Headline.

Kray, Reg., *Villains We Have Known* (1993) Leeds, N.K. Publications.

Lake, H. and Hoffman, W., *Loud and Clear* (1990) New York, Henry Holt.

Lane, B. and Gregg, W., *The New Encyclopedia of Serial Killers* (1992) London, Headline.

Larue, A., *Les Flics* (1969) Paris, Fayard.

Lavigne, Y., *Hell's Angels* (1987) Toronto, Ballantine.

Léauthier, A., *Mort d'un voyou* (2004) Paris, Éditions Grasset.

Longrigg, C., *Mafia Women* (1997) London, Chatto & Windus.

Lunde, P., *Organized Crime* (2004) London, Dorling Kindersley.

McLagan, G., *Bent Coppers* (2003) London, Weidenfeld & Nicolson.

Main, J., *Murder Australian Style* (1980) Melbourne, Union Books.

Matthews, B., *A Fine and Private Place* (2000) Sydney, Pan Macmillan.

Messick, H., *Syndicate Wife* (1969) London, Robert Hale.

Milmer, E.R., *The Lives and Times of Bonnie & Clyde* (1996) Carbondae, Southern Illinois University Press.

Montarron, M., *Histoire du Milieu* (1969) Paris, Librairie Plon.

Morain, A., *The Underworld of Paris* (1930) London, Jarrolds.

Morton, J., *Gangland* (1993) London, Warner Books.

——*Gangland International* (1999) London, Warner Books.

——*East End Gangland* (2001) London, Warner Books.

——*Gangland Today* (2003) London, Time Warner.

——*Gangland: The Lawyers* (2003) London, Virgin Books.

——*Gangland: The Early Years* (2004) London, Time Warner.

Morton, J. and Parker, G., *Gangland Bosses* (2004) London, Time Warner.

Mustain, G. and Capeci, J., *Murder Machine: A True Story of Murder, Madness and the Mafia* (1992) New York, Penguin Books USA.

Newton, M., *Bad Girls Do It* (1993) New York, Loom Panics Unlimited.

Nicaso, A., *Rocco Perri, the Story of Canada's Most Notorious Bootlegger* (2005) Toronto, John Wiley & Sons.

Noble, T., *Neddy* (1993) Balmain, Kerr Publishing Pty Ltd.

Norris, J., *Henry Lee Lucas* (1993) London, Constable.

O'Reilly, E., *Veronica Guerin* (1998) London, Vintage.

Parker, J., *The Walking Dead* (1995) London, Simon & Schuster.

Pasley, F.D., *Al Capone* (1966) London, Faber & Faber.

Pierrat, J., *Une histoire du Milieu* (2003) Paris, Éditions Denoël.

Pileggi, N., *Wiseguy* (1987) New York, Pocket Books.

Possey, M. and Kogan, R., *Two Men, One Murder and the Price of Truth* (2001) New York, The Berkley Publishing Group.

Rappleye, C. and Ed Becker, E., *All American Mafioso* (1995) New York, Barricade Books.

Read, L., *Nipper Read, The Man Who Nicked the Krays* (2002) London, Time Warner.

Read, M. B., *Chopper* (1991) Smithfield NSW, Floradale Productions.

——*Chopper 2 Hits and Memories* (1992) Smithfield NSW, Floradale Productions.

Reid, E., *The Grim Reapers* (1969) Chicago, Bantam Books.

Renner, T.C. and Kirby, C., *Mafia Enforcer* (1987) London, Corgi Books.

Reynolds, P., *King Scum* (1998) Dublin, Gill & Macmillan.

Richards, M., *The Hanged Man* (2002) Carlton North, Scribe Publications.

Richards, S., *Viv (Graham) Simply the Best* (1998) Gateshead, Mirage Publishing.

Rockaway, R.A., *But – He Was Good To His Mother* (1993) Jerusalem, Geffen.

Roth, A., *Infamous Manhattan* (1996) New York, Citadel Press.

Rule, A., *A Rose for her Grave* (1993) New York, Pocket Books.

Sabljak, M. and Greenberg, M.H., *Most Wanted* (1990) New York, Bonanza Books.

Schoenberg, R.J., *Mr Capone* (1992) London, Robson Books.

Seagrave, K., *Women Serial and Mass Murderers* (1992) London, Macfarland.

Selvaggi, G., *La Mia Tomba e New York* translated as *The Rise of the*

Mafia in New York: from 1896 through World War II, trans. William A. Packer (1948) Indianapolis, Bobbs & Merrill.

Sher, J. and Marsden, W., *The Road of Hell: How the Biker Gangs are Conquering Canada* (2003) Toronto, Alfred A. Knopf.

Silvester, J. and Rule, A., *Tough* (2002) Camberwell, Vict., Floradale Productions and Sly Ink.

——*Leadbelly: Inside Australia's Underworld Wars* (2004) Camberwell, Vict., Floradale Productions and Sly Ink.

Simard, R. and Vastel, M. (trans. D. Homel), *The Nephew* (1987) Scarborough, Ont., Prentice Hall.

——*Trahisons* (2000) Quebec, M. Vastel.

Siringo, C.A., *Two Evil Isms: Pinkertonism and Anarchism* (1915) Chicago, Charles A. Siringo.

Smith, N., *Catch and Kill Your Own* (1995) Sydney, Pan Macmillan.

Stille, A., *Excellent Cadavers, The Mafia and the Death of the First Italian Republic* (1995) London, Cape.

Stockman, R., *The Hangman's Diary* (1993) London, Headline.

Summers, A., *Official and Confidential* (1998) London, Corgi Books.

Swain, J., *Being Informed* (1995) London, Janus.

Teresa, V., *My Life in the Mafia* (1973) Greenwich, Conn., Fawcett Publications.

Theoharis, A. (ed.), *The FBI* (2000) New York, The Oryx Press.

Thompson, Thomas, *Blood and Money* (1976) New York, Dell Publishing.

Thompson, Tony, *Gangland Britain* (1995) London, Hodder & Stoughton.

—— *Gangs* (2004) London, Hodder & Stoughton.

Tofel, Richard J., *The Disappearance of Judge Crater, and the New York He Left Behind* (2005) New York, Ivan R. Dee.

Treherne, J., *The Strange History of Bonnie and Clyde* (1984) London, Jonathan Cape.

Turkus, B. and Feder, S., *Murder Inc* (1952) London, Victor Gollancz.

Whitburn, D., *Penthouse History of Crime in Australia* (1988) Sydney, Horwitz.

Williams, P., *The General* (1995) Dublin, The O'Brien Press.

——*Gangland* (1998) Dublin, The O'Brien Press.

Wilson, D. and Murdoch, M., *Big Shots* (1985) South Melbourne, Sun Books.

Wilson, D. and Robinson, P., *Big Shots II* (1987) South Melbourne, Sun Books.

Wilson, K., *Investigating Murder* (1990) London, Robinson Publishing.

Wilson, P., Trele, D. and Lincoln, R., *The Last Woman Hanged in Australia* (1997) Milsons Point, NSW, Random House.

Winchell, W., *Things That Happened to Me – and Me to Them* (1975) New York, Prentice Hall.

Wright, L., *Razor: a true story of slashers, gangsters, prostitutes and sly grog* (2001) South Melbourne, Macmillan.

Wyden, P., *The Hired Killers* (1965) London, Panther.

Zampa, M., *Tchao Parrain* (1986) Paris, Olivier Orban.

Articles, reports etc.

J.H. Amen, *Report of Kings County Investigation 1938–1942* (1942) New York.

John M. Bland, 'The True Story of the Last Crime and Capture of The "Lewis Gang".'

Fenton Bresler, 'Contract Killers . . . it's murder 90s style' in *Daily Express*, 27 March 1995.

Julian Broadhead, 'Hugh Collins Interview' in *Prison Writing*, No. 11 1977.

R.J. Cahill, *Findings of an inquest into the death of the late Assistant Commissioner Colin Stanley Winchester at Canberra on 10 January 1989.*

Duncan Campbell, 'Number one in the hit parade' in *The Guardian*, 22 August 1998.

Jean-Michel Caradec'h, 'Interview with Gilbert Zemour' in *Paris Match*, 29 April 1983.

Tim Cornwell, 'Killer for Hire' in *The Independent on Sunday*, 5 October 1997.

'Deep Six for Johnny' in *Time*, 23 August 1976.

Jo Durden-Smith, 'Unfinished Business' in *Sunday Telegraph Magazine*, 29 April 1996.

Paul Eddy and Sara Walden, 'Natural Born Killers' in *Sunday Times*

Magazine, 23 November 1997.

Eric Furrier, 'Les nouveaux caïds' in *L'Éxprès*, 16 October 2004.

G.H. Gudjonsson, 'The making of a serial false confessor: the confessions of Henry Lee Lucas' in *The Journal of Forensic Psychiatry*, Volume 10, No. 2, September 1999.

Lorne Gunter, 'New laws won't stop criminals' in *Calgary Herald*, 21 September 2000.

Graham Johnson, 'Investigation: Magnum for Hire' in *Daily Mirror*, 17 October 2004.

Tristram Korten, 'The strange saga of a smooth-talking hit man, jealous secretaries, and a ruined prosecutor' in *Miami New Times*, 26 November 1998.

'Le Milieu' in *Historia*, 1973.

'Les Bas-Fonds de Paris' in *Le Crapouillot*, numéro spéciale, Septembre, 1939.

K. Levi, 'Becoming a hitman: Neutralization in a very deviant career', in *Urban Life*, Vol.10, No.1, pp. 47–83.

Cal McCrystal, 'The hit at the Royal Hotel' in *The Independent on Sunday*, 8 August 1993.

'MAFIYA Organized Crime in Russia', Jane's Intelligence Review Special Report No. 10.

Kirk Makin, 'Murder splits Montreal Legal Community' in *The Globe and Mail*, 26 October 1985.

Marcel Montarron, 'Les Pirates du Combinatie' in *Détective*, 13 février 1956.

Jenny Mouzos and John Venditto, *Contract Killings in Australia* (2003) Canberra, ACT, Australian Institute of Criminology.

'Murder He Wrote' in *GQ*, August 1997.

'Murdering Madams' in *Newsweek*, 2 November 1964.

New Jersey Commission of Investigation, *Organised Crime in Bars, Part II*, June 1995.

'Police Shootings in Victoria 1987–1989', Flemington/Kensington Community Legal Centre, Melbourne.

Yvonne Ridley, 'Charlie Kray in Vengeance Killing From Beyond Grave' in *Express on Sunday*, 25 February 2001.

Royal Commission on the Activities of the Federated Ship Painters and Dockers Union, Canberra, Government Printer, 1984.

L.B. Schlesinger, 'The contract murderer: Patterns, characteristics, and dynamics in *Journal of Forensic Science*, Vol. 46, No.5, p. 1120.

Adam Shand, 'Burial Ground' in *The Bulletin*, 6 April 2004.

——'Piece Talks' in *The Bulletin*, 22 June 2004.

——and Julie-Anne Davies, 'Killing Time' in *The Bulletin*, 15 June 2004.

John Silvester, 'The Anatomy of a Suburban Hit' in *The Age*, 31 August 2004.

Julian Strauss, 'Waiting for death in Russia's Alcatraz' in *The Daily Telegraph*, 10 August 2004.

'The Contract Killer' in *FHM*, March 2000.

'The Hit Man is shooting for arrests' in *The National Law Journal*, 18 October 1993.

'Uncovering FBI Informant Underworld' in *Washington Post*, 16 March 2003.

Richard Whittington-Egan, 'A Pellet for the Preacher' in *New Law Journal*, 23 November 1990.

Bernard Wis and Christophe Buchard, 'Cinq balles pour un Zemour' in *Paris Match*, 29 April 1983.

INDEX